The Fathers of the Church in Christian Theology

The Fathers of the Church in Christian Theology

Michel Fédou, SJ

Translated by Peggy Manning Meyer

Foreword by Brian E. Daley, SJ

The Catholic University of America Press
Washington, D.C.

Originally published as:
Les Pères de l'Église et la théologie chrétienne

The paper used in this publication meets the minimum requirements of American National Standards for Information Science—Permanence of Paper for Printed Library Materials, ANSI Z39.48-1984.
∞

Cataloging-in-Publication Data available from the Library of Congress
ISBN 978-0-8132-3171-6

Each time, in our West, that a Christian renewal has flourished, in the area of thinking as in that of life (and the two areas are always linked), it has flourished under the sign of the Fathers. Every century testifies to this—the history would be too long to retrace—and the law is verified even in ours.

—HENRI DE LUBAC, SJ

We would like to reread a few pages from that intimate journal written by the Church when she was seventeen years old.

—HANS URS VON BALTHASAR, SJ

... the fragment, from our past, that forms our future

—KARL RAHNER, SJ

Contents

Foreword by Brian E. Daley, SJ

The way forward in Christian theology is often seen, paradoxically, as beginning in "a return to the sources." This is not just a sentimental exercise in antiquarianism. It is based on the realization that our faith and our life as a Church are rooted in our collective memory—that it is by reflecting on our history as a people that we discover the presence of our God. This is, after all, the origin of what we call the Bible, those widely varied books where Israel recalls what it believes to be its origin as a people, in the call of Abraham; in the wanderings and adventures of his heirs; the miraculous rescue of his descendants from Egypt; their journey through the desert; their covenant with the God who had called and formed them; their settlement in the land that was Abraham's promised home; their struggles with rival peoples; the warnings and promises of prophets to them; the hope for peace that always stretched ahead.... Within that story of Israel and her God, Christian disciples see their own origin, as followers of a Galilean preacher and wonder-worker of twenty centuries ago—a failed Jewish prophet of the Kingdom of God whose death and astonishing resurrection to life has meant, to those who receive the news in faith, the beginning of a new history, a new confidence in God's presence.

For both Jews and Christians, in other words, believing in God means believing that God is with us, as he has been in the often tragic, often uplifting story of our own past. The confession of faith we make today is simply a new articulation of the message preached to Jews and Gentiles by the disciples of Jesus. And what we call *theology* is really only a thoughtful form of meditation and preaching on that story: intelligent reflection on its meaning and all it implies for how we can truly understand our world and ourselves today. In the context of contemporary science and technology, in the midst of all the challenges to self-understanding and moral choice posed by today's social and political surroundings, what does the story of Israel, the story of Jesus and the Apostles, the story of the Church's faith through the ages, enable us responsibly to say and to do?

This anchoring of our faith, and our ongoing reflection on faith, in a continuing tradition is what gives those early writers from the first seven or eight Christian centuries whom we call "the Fathers of the Church" a unique significance for later theology, whatever our particular Church tradition may be. It was in their reflections, their debates and correspondence, their explanations of puzzling passages in the Bible, that the wider Christian community gradually distinguished the outlines of its own distinctive understanding of the God of Israel, of Jesus' place within God's mysterious life, of the canonical shape and meaning of Scripture, and of the Church's own identity as the community of Jesus' disciples. It was in their developing forms of worship, too, that the main outlines of Christian liturgy and sacramental practice took shape. Clearly, theological reflection on these and a whole range of related topics has continued since late antiquity, as the world around us changes; but the main trajectories of Christian reflection are rooted there, in the formative early centuries of a distinctive Christian identity. To be connected with the original community of disciples and to reshape their self-understanding and practice in an authentic way, modern Christians need to keep returning to those roots.

This is why one of the main influences on the readiness for liturgical, institutional, and theological renewal that came to expression in the Catholic Church at the Second Vatican Council was a new emphasis on the recovery and study of early Christian theology, often called by the French term *ressourcement,* which began in Europe in the 1930s. In searching for a new vision of the role of the Church in modern society, a significant group of young theologians—most of them French and German Dominicans and Jesuits—reached not simply to the arguments and categories used in the Catholic neo-scholastic handbooks of the nineteenth and twentieth centuries, which had largely been intended to counter the rationalist critique of European philosophers and social theorists in the decades before the First Vatican Council, but turned instead to the writers of the Church's first several centuries, who suddenly seemed to present the Christian vision in fresher, less theoretical, less defensive terms. Henri de Lubac, SJ, for instance, published his first great book, *Catholicism*, in 1938, to argue the thesis that the Church's understanding of its faith is not, as Marxists sometimes charged, primarily an attempt to turn individual believers' eyes toward a better world after death, but "is essentially social. It is social in the deepest sense of the word: not merely in its applications in the field of natural institutions, but first and foremost in itself, in the heart of its mystery, in the essence of its dogma."[1] A sense of the Church's relevance for a new political atmosphere, deeply concerned for equality and for the welfare of all of society, needed to be supported by a return to the way early Christians conceived Christian revelation in history, of Christian worship, Christian moral responsibility, Christian institutions. This return to a less abstract, less deductive sense of revealed truth, de Lubac argued, could best be illustrated by rediscovering the way early Christian writers interpreted the Jewish-Christian Bible as a narrative of how God acts in the world.

> Indeed, what we call nowadays the Old and New Testaments is not primarily a book. It is a twofold event, a twofold "covenant," a twofold dispensation which unfolds its development through the ages.... History, just like nature, or to an even greater degree, was a language to them. It was the word of God. Now throughout this history they encountered mystery which was to be fulfilled, to be accomplished historically and socially, though always in a spiritual manner: the mystery of Christ and his Church.[2]

In the writings of early Christian exegetes and thinkers, de Lubac suggests throughout his book, a conception of God's activity in the world can be found that is at once more historically concrete and more socially oriented than standard Catholic theology had been in the modern era—an approach to faith that seemed to him more promising as a response to modern questions than the approach of his older contemporaries or their nineteenth-century forebears.

De Lubac's sense of the importance of early Christian theology for the contemporary Church—of the Fathers' sense of God's working through history, of their commitment to social outreach, of their liturgical and sacramental grounding, their spiritual earnestness—was shared, in a variety of ways, by other young theologians of his day: no-

1. Henri de Lubac, *Catholicism: Christ and the Common Destiny of Man*, trans. Lancelot Shepard and Sr. Elizabeth Englund, OCD (San Francisco: Ignatius Press, 1988), 15.

2. Ibid., 169–70.

tably by Yves Congar, OP, by the Jesuits Jean Daniélou, Otto Semmelroth, Karl Rahner, and Hugo Rahner, and by de Lubac's pupil and lifelong friend Hans Urs von Balthasar. A new series of translations and (eventually) of authoritative critical editions of early Christian texts, significantly called Sources Chrétiennes—now numbering six hundred volumes—was begun in 1943 in Lyons, by Claude Mondésert and a few Jesuit colleagues. At the same time, basic research on the patristic origins of Christian liturgy was being published by Josef Jungmann, SJ, the Belgian, Benedictine Bernard Botte, and others that enabled mid-twentieth-century Catholics to envision a form of liturgy that would be at once simpler and more comprehensible to the faithful, more obviously a form of prayer involving the whole local community. Studying the "sources" of contemporary theology and worship seemed to open undreamt-of possibilities for reform that would both speak to the perceived needs of twentieth-century Catholic life and be given credibility by antiquity. To know more about the distant origins of Christian life, to encounter ancient theological and liturgical texts first-hand, inevitably inspired twentieth-century Catholic thinkers with images of how the Church might develop its thought-structures and worship in the future.

Today, the situation of Catholic thought and pastoral practice is undoubtedly different from what it was in the 1930s and '40s. Young Catholics today, often disappointed by the shallowness of the catechesis and preaching they have experienced, or alienated by what seems a lack of solemnity in so much contemporary liturgy, may yearn for a return to the Church their parents and grandparents grew up in, rather than to a re-created Church of the Fathers. For that very reason, though, it seems all the more important for today's believers to have a clearer sense of the dimensions and the influence of the twentieth-century patristic revival: of what *ressourcement* meant and made possible then, of why it seemed so urgent, and of why a clear understanding of early Christianity is always of crucial importance for the Church's present freedom to act. This new book, by my old friend and fellow-Jesuit Michel Fédou, is a uniquely valuable tool to help us understand that influential revival, with all its implications for today's Catholic thought and practice.

Michel Fédou is himself a Patristics scholar of the highest quality, who has written and taught about the theology and biblical interpretation of the Church Fathers for almost forty years; he also is active in dialogue with east Asian religious traditions, and studies broader questions of Christian theology and spirituality. A native of Lyon—the ancient city of early martyrs and of St. Irenaeus, as well as of many nineteenth-century movements of Catholic reform, and more recently of Sources Chrétiennes—he has made Paris his academic home and is one of the key faculty members at the Jesuit theological institute there, Centre Sèvres. He is uniquely qualified to speak about the indebtedness of modern Catholic life and thought to the mid-twentieth-century patristic revival, and about the relevance of early Christian thought for today and tomorrow.

This book, *The Fathers of the Church in Christian Theology*, has no parallels that I know of in contemporary Catholic theological scholarship. After a first chapter surveying the origin and development of the concept of "Church Fathers" and the influence of early Christian thought on medieval and early modern theology, Fr. Fédou offers—in part 1 of the book—a detailed and perceptive narrative of the *ressourcement* movement and its key thinkers (chaps. 2–3), and of the present situation of patristic scholarship (chap. 4). In chapters 5–7, he considers the broad and continuing implications of early Christian thought for theology and biblical studies today (chap. 5), for the engagement of Christian theology with other branches of human thought and knowledge (chap. 6), and for ecumenical and "contextual" or intercultural theology in our present world. In part 2, Fr. Fédou looks more closely at individual themes in the contemporary Church's continuing reflection, and asks (chaps. 8–14) how knowledge of early Christian writings might be of service to that reflection: to our thought about the Church (chap.8), about the human person (chap. 9), about Christian moral teaching (chap. 10), about God and the person of Christ (chap. 11), about the Church's relations with other branches of Christianity (chap. 12), about our engagement with non-Christian religious traditions (chap. 13), and about our individual spiritual journeys toward God (chap. 14). This not a handbook of Patrology, in other words—not a reference work on who the individual Fathers were, or where we can find their works; it is a book on patristic studies as an intrinsic part of the Church's continuing self-understanding, and on the theological potential in the Church today of encountering early Christianity—as setting some of the major questions, and empowering some of our own possible answers, in our continuing quest for an understanding of faith.

I have found Michel Fédou's *The Fathers of the Church in Christian Theology* both informative and inspiring. It is a remarkable book, and it has helped me to understand better how centrally important it is for thoughtful Christians today to live conscious of the long tradition in which we live, and in which together we seek God. May it do the same for its English readers!

Preface to the English Edition

A few months after the publication of this book in French, Fr. Jean-Yves Grenet, SJ—then the provincial of the Jesuits of France—shared his hope that my book would be translated into English, thus gaining a wider public. I am deeply grateful for his encouragement, and also to Fr. Franck Delorme, SJ, who took the steps necessary for an English version to appear. And of course I owe great thanks to Peggy Meyer, who was given the task of translation.

As the reader will quickly see, this book is not a book on patristic theology as such, even though it speaks constantly about the Fathers of the Church and their writings. Rather, it deals with the place and the role of patristics in contemporary Christian theology. Its main purpose is to show the significance of patristic studies for ongoing Christian reflection, not only in Europe but also in the context of the so-called contextual theologies prevalent in America, in Africa, and in Asia.

I have written this book because I am aware of a paradox in the current situation of patristic and theological studies. On the one hand, it is clear that the reading of the Fathers has been a major source of inspiration for many theologians, leading to a renewal for Christian thought, between 1920 and 1960. On the other hand, today there seems to be some distance between patristic studies and contemporary theological research itself. Of course, generalizations of this kind always admit of exceptions, and it would be possible to cite some theologians who find in the study of the Fathers fertile ground for the elaboration of their theological thought. But there are also many theological writings which, though unquestionably of high quality, make little reference to the patristic tradition—or at least are only interested in it as a historical reminder, without expecting from it any real inspiration for their thought today. The field of patristic studies itself, on the other hand, has undergone an unprecedented development in the last forty years or so. And yet in many cases those who devote themselves to these studies—providing us with excellent editions of texts or monographs animated primarily by philological, sociological, or historical concerns—sometimes risk omitting a reflection on the theological stakes animating patristic texts.

Hence the question that is at the origin of my book: since the study of the Fathers was indeed a source of renewal for Christian theology in the first half of the twentieth century, should we not consider such study potentially very fruitful for today's theology? In other words, should we not consider that, despite the epistemological shifts and cultural changes that have taken place over the last forty years, the reading and study of the Fathers must continue to inspire and enrich the understanding of the faith today? The purpose of this book is precisely to support this view and to offer a theological justification for it.

As this book was written in French, for a French-speaking audience, it will first of all mention patristic works which have been produced in France or more broadly in Europe. Moreover, it will mostly underline the reception of the Fathers by Catholic writers, and chapters 2 and 3 will pay special attention to the "Patristic Revival" of the nineteenth and twentieth centuries in Catholic theology and its influence upon the Second Vatican Council. It is clear that similar reflection on the role of patristic thought could also be offered from the viewpoint of other Christian traditions, rooted in different languages and cultures (for example, it would be possible to present the role of patristic thought for modern Greek Orthodox theology, or the modern reception of the Fathers by Anglicans or other Protestant communities). Though its primary focus is the Catholic Church, this book will address many issues that are also significant for other Churches, and for countries outside of Europe. Therefore I believe that this book, such as it is, will be useful for an English-speaking audience.

In preparing this edition, I have made some changes or additions to the original footnotes. As much as possible, I give references to British or American editions of patristic texts; I do the same, too, for references to some modern authors. Of course, when it is not possible, or when it has seemed to me better to give a direct translation from the texts as they are quoted in the French edition, I will always mention the sources of these quotations (whether in French, Greek, Latin, or any other language). Moreover, in the footnotes and in the bibliography, I have added the titles of publications that were not necessary in the French edition but will be helpful for this English edition.

Once again, I would like to express my deep gratitude to Peggy Meyer for her translation of my book. I would also thank Fr. Brian Daley, SJ, and Fr. Joseph Mueller, SJ, who helped me to find a publishing house in the United States. I am particularly indebted to Fr. Daley, who was my teacher at Weston School of Theology in 1985–86: he not only shared his knowledge, but also his love for the Fathers of the Church and his awareness of their importance for contemporary theology. I am also very grateful to Fr. Philip Endean, SJ, who helped me to check the translation of some quotations for the English edition. My thanks are due, too, to Fr. Joseph Koczera, SJ, and to Fr. Timothy O'Brien, SJ, for their advice on some English language issues. Lastly, I would like to thank John Martino for accepting my book for publication with the Catholic University of America Press.

November 19, 2017

Preface to the French Edition

I have had the opportunity, for more than twenty years, to present lectures on the contribution of the Fathers of the Church to Christian theology, either by treating this subject in the most general form or by tackling it from a more specific point of view (ecclesiology, anthropology, Christology, as well as other subjects). Since some of these lectures resulted in a publication, it became apparent to me that it would be possible to collect them in order to turn the material into a book. Yet, when I undertook this work in 2010, I quickly perceived that I could not just compile an anthology: apart from the fact that I did not intend, more often than not, to repeat those studies already published, I above all realized that I had to supplement them with new studies; even more, it was necessary to give to the collection an overall coherence and, through or beyond the particular themes of the various contributions, to propose to the reader a reflection of fundamental theology on the importance of patristics for the understanding of the faith today.

The present book is the fruit of this work. I am happy to express my gratitude to P. Henri Laux, SJ, president of the Centre Sèvres–Facultés jésuites de Paris, who encouraged me to prepare this book and who accepted it for the Éditions Facultés jésuites de Paris. My gratitude also goes to my colleagues in the Département d'études patristiques of the Centre Sèvres, above all Mlle. Isabelle Bochet, SFX, with whom I share the responsibility for this department. It additionally goes to the numerous students who have taken my courses on patristics: they were the first to hear the reflections developed in this book, and they should know that their questions and reactions have more than once helped me to make progress in my own research.

The writing of this book was undertaken at Lyon, in the offices of the Institut des Sources Chrétiennes. I want to express my appreciation to M. Jean-Dominique Durand, president of the Association des amis de Sources Chrétiennes; to M. Bernard Meunier, director of the Institut; as well as to P. Dominique Gonnet, P. Dominique Bertrand, M. Paul Mattei, and all the members of the staff who work for this institute (without forgetting those who since 2010 have died: P. Joseph Paramelle, P. Bernard de Vregille, and P. Louis Neyrand); the pages that this book devotes to the genesis of Sources Chrétiennes will implicitly express all the admiration that I have for their work that is so persevering and so fruitful in the service of the collection. I equally thank F. Luc Bresard (†), with whom I was able to translate for this collection Origen's *Commentary on the Epistle to the Romans*. I also take this opportunity to express my appreciation to the Institut d'Études Augustiniennes for its publishing of the Bibliothèque augustinienne as well as for its other publications in the field of patristic studies.

My gratitude, more broadly, goes to the numerous patrologists and theologians from whom I have received much throughout the years. In addition to Mlle. Isabelle Bochet already mentioned, I would like to mention Mme. Marie-Odile Boulnois, P. Michel Corbin, P. Brian Daley, M. Gilles Dorival, Mme. Martine Dulaey, M. Alain Le Boulluec, P. Joseph Moingt, Mme. Catherine Schmezer, P. Christoph Theobald, and P. Joseph Wolinski, among so many others that could be mentioned as well. But I would above all like to express my most special appreciation to P. Bernard Sesboüé, for he was the first, during 1979–80, to introduce me to the study of the Fathers, thanks to a seminar on Origen, before later directing my master's thesis and doctoral dissertation. For these patristic studies, moreover, I had been prepared, without my being of aware of it, by several professors at Lyon; I am most especially appreciative of one of them, M. Michel Evieux.

I also want to thank the Jesuit community of Lyon, to which I belonged when I began the writing of this work, and the community of Saint-Ignace of Paris, in the midst of which this writing was continued and completed during 2011–12.

Lastly, the author cannot fail to recall that he was born at Lyon—a city marked by the memory of its martyrs in the amphitheater of the Three Gauls in the year 177, and by Irenaeus's witness to "apostolic preaching." He knows as well that his parents had him baptized in the parish of Saint-Augustin on the hill of the Croix-Rousse. This book on the Fathers is itself meant to be an act of gratitude toward the Fathers—Irenaeus and Augustine, but many others also—as well as an act of gratitude for those who through the centuries have contributed to transmitting their memory to me, beginning with my parents.

June 28, 2012
The Feast of Saint Irenaeus

Abbreviations

CSEL	Corpus Scriptorum Ecclesiasticorum Latinorum (Vienna)
GCS	*Die Griechischen christlichen Schriftsteller der ersten drei Jahrhunderten*. Berlin: Akademie Verlag
PG	Patrologiae Cursus Completus: Series Graeca, ed. J.-P. Migne (Paris)
PL	Patrologiae Cursus Completus: Series Latina, ed. J.-P. Migne (Paris)
SC	Sources Chrétiennes. Paris: Cerf

The Fathers of the Church in Christian Theology

Introduction

Anyone who glances around the rooms of libraries devoted to religions, or more specifically to early Christianity, cannot fail to observe on their shelves imposing collections of patristic texts—whether it be Migne's Patrologia, Corpus Christianorum, Sources Chrétiennes, Bibliothèque augustinienne, or still other collections.... There he discovers many of the other "usuals" on the Fathers of the Church—dictionaries, manuals, monographs on this or that author—and he knows that these books that are available to him themselves represent only an infinitesimal portion of the works published in the field of Christian Antiquity: a great many others are stocked in the libraries' storerooms, awaiting readers who perhaps will come to rouse them from their slumber.... And from there, he can go to many more places: not only the institutes specializing in patristic studies but also monasteries, seminaries, universities, and municipal and national libraries in every country of Europe as well as in countries outside of Europe—even to those continents that are the farthest from the Mediterranean Basin around which the literature of the Fathers developed in former times; all these libraries, from the north to the south and from the west to the east, offer patristic works and studies on this subject.

The dissemination of this literature in its own way attests to the remarkable work that has been accomplished on the writings of early Christianity over many decades. This work has been and continues to be conducted by a great number of researchers concerned with editing these writings according to the most rigorous scientific norms and with studying them by using all the resources of philology, history, sociology, archeology, iconography, and still more disciplines. One can only rejoice at such a development, thanks to which patristic literature has progressively become the subject of a more complete and accurate knowledge—converging, moreover, with the no less remarkable development in the studies on Antiquity in general. With the, perhaps dizzying, realization of how difficult the transmission of the patristic heritage has been from ancient centuries (that so many texts have been lost! And how many others could have been lost without the patient labor of monks who, in the Middle Ages, recopied a great number of manuscripts in order to save these texts from oblivion!), the historian will all the more appreciate, by contrast, the great wealth of a situation that continues to be marked by an increasing number of publications, translations, and all kinds of work relating to early Christianity.

The theologian himself is happy for such a situation. How could it be otherwise, given the importance of the Fathers of the Church that his own discipline has always recognized—to the point that until the twentieth century, patrology appeared, to a large extent at least, to be the exclusive property of theology? Admittedly, patristic studies henceforth developed in many more diverse areas, and in the setting of institutions that often did not have any ecclesial affiliation; but far from being jealous, the theologian rather rejoices that the literature of Christian Antiquity is thus available to numerous researchers who, outside of, as well as within, the Church, share the same concern for editing the writings from early Christianity, translating them, and commenting upon them.

A concern, however, exists for the theologian. Indeed, from a Christian point of view, he considers that patristic writings cannot be studied from only the philological angle or from within the context of ancient history or based on the other disciplines mentioned above but that these writings (or more specifically some among them) must also make a contribution to the understanding of the faith today. He remembers what has been called the "Return to the Fathers" in the first half of the twentieth century: as such, this "return" coincided with the renewal of Christian thinking, and its fecundity has been verified both in the work of some theologians (such as Henri de Lubac and Hans Urs von Balthasar) as well as in the life of the Church as a whole (as the use of certain patristic themes in the documents of the Vatican Council II shows). This then is the question: to what extent does the study of the Fathers continue today—and will it continue tomorrow—to nourish and make fruitful Christian thinking? The question arises from the fact that several decades have passed since the patristic renewal of the twentieth century, and that, in the interval, theology has experienced all sorts of developments that consequently must be taken into account. It also arises from more serious reasons: one could fear that the specific interest of Christian thought in the Fathers of the Church might sometimes be threatened—whether from the exterior (if new forms of scientism denied theology the right to study the writings of Antiquity in view of its own reflection) or from the interior (if theology itself came, by its internal changes and by its awareness of the cultural mutations that characterize our times, to judge henceforth superfluous—indeed harmful—any foundation in the literature of early Christianity). Nevertheless, today, no more than yesterday, *the understanding of the faith can happen only with an active reference to patristic writings.* Saying this does not mean that every theologian must be a specialist in patrology, but that—as in other eras, although in necessarily new ways—*the in-depth reading of the Fathers must for its part contribute to the tasks of theology.*

These last statements themselves point to the subject of the present work. It is not a matter of a manual of patrology, the goal of which would be to gather all sorts of information on the writings of early Christianity. Nor is it a matter of a book that claimed to give the state of patristic research on the whole, of the disciplines to which it appeals, of the methods that it utilizes and the fruits that we gather from its knowledge of Christian Antiquity. This book is limited to the following question (but one that is in our eyes of great importance): *what is the relationship between patristics and theology?* We will recall what it has been in history, and particularly in the twentieth century; we will also mention the difficulties and objections that at times could seem to call into question the fecundity of patristics for contemporary theology, but, above all, we will show what, from our own position, actually justifies the possibility and even the necessity of a "patristic theology"; lastly, we will cover some of the fields in which the reading of the Fathers can to some extent provide specific contributions to Christian thinking.

Before more directly stating the different stages of our route, it is necessary for us to provide two important explanations—one touching upon the vocabulary, the other concerning the demarcation of the "patristic" period. On the first point, one will have noted that we have already used several different expressions: "Fathers of the Church," "patrology," "patristic writings," "literature of early Christianity," "literature of Christian Antiquity." Soon, in the first chapter of the book, we will recount how these various expressions have appeared in history. Without anticipating these explanations, we must for now emphasize that, considered by itself, the expression "literature of early Christianity" refers to a *corpus* clearly more vast than the traditional expression "Fathers of the Church"; moreover, it has a much more neutral meaning than the latter that, on the contrary, has from the outset a theological connotation (for, in strict terms, the recognition of this or that author as a "Father of the Church" presupposes the faith of the Christian community). This consideration itself has here led to favoring the words "Fathers of the Church," given the actual subject of our study—and it is, moreover, the expression that we have chosen for the title of the book. However, we must take into account the change manifested by the use, which today is so widespread, of the expressions "literature of early Christianity" and "literature of Christian Antiquity," All things considered, from the theological point of view itself, it is no longer possible to set up too impenetrable boundaries between some authors recognized in the strictest sense as "Fathers of the Church" and other Christian authors who are not designated as such: the first do not necessarily satisfy on all points the definition that, as we will explain later, has traditionally been given to this expression "Fathers of the Church"; and on the contrary, such a definition can be applied, at least partially, to other Christian authors who in the past were not thus described. The appellation "Fathers of the Church" remains fundamental for us, and we will show how today it must be understood; but, far from considering only the authors to whom it has been applied in the past, we will use it in a broad sense, and we will be interested in all Christian literature from Antiquity—to the extent, at least, that it has stakes for theological thought itself.

The second explanation to be provided concerns the duration of the period called "patristic." Traditionally, one gives it the following limits: for the West, the seventh century (with Isidore of Seville, who died in 636); for the East, the eighth century (with John Damascene, who died in 749). Yet a new question has arisen from the research carried out on the Middle Ages: some specialists, without hesitation, have this latter period begin in the fifth century—more precisely in the year 476, which marks the fall of the Western Roman Empire.[1] Such an option is understandable from the point of view of studies that, in our day, place greater emphasis on the dependence of the Carolingian era upon later Antiquity (by seeing in it "the rise of Western Christendom" or by emphasizing the particular influences of Augustine, Gregory the Great, and Boethius).[2] However, we think it is necessary to maintain the usually recognized periodization and not only because authors such as Gregory the Great in the West or Maximus the Confessor and John Damascene in the East have actually been perceived by later eras as "Fathers of the Church." Thus here, we will refer to the totality of what one usually calls the patristic era: from Clement of Rome and Ignatius of Antioch to the authors of the seventh and eighth centuries. The allusion that we just made to medieval studies also provides the opportunity to make, in passing, an important remark: some of the reflections that we will develop in this book could also be valid, *mutatis mutandis*, for the Middle Ages itself (thus, for example, as to typological exegesis and the importance that we can recognize in it today); in any case, it could be largely profitable to reflect more broadly on the way in which Christian theology refers to the medieval period, with a perspective that is analogous to ours in the present work. We will limit ourselves, however, to the patristic era—by considering it, let us repeat, in its greater duration, and by considering the writings of early Christianity from the point of view of their specific interest for the theology of subsequent eras and, above all, for our own.

The itinerary proposed here will consist of two large stages. The first, titled "From Yesterday to Today. The Contribution of Patristics to Christian Theology," will open with a chapter that, after having recalled the genesis of the expression "Fathers of the Church" and similar expressions, will briefly cover the medieval and modern periods from the perspective of our theme: what place has the reading of the Fathers held, up until the nineteenth century, in the development

1. Thus, Alain de Libera, *La philosophie médiévale* [Mediaeval philosophy] (Paris: PUF, 1993), 1.

2. Cf. Peter Brown, *The Rise of Western Christendom: Triumph and Diversity, A.D. 200–1000*, 2nd ed. (Malden: Blackwell Publishers, 2003).

of theology? Chapters 2 and 3 will present the patristic renewal that marked the twentieth century from the 1930s until the era of Vatican Council II: first of all, we will describe this renewal, the forms that it took, and its effects on the life of the Church, then we will show how the study of the Fathers has more specifically inspired certain theologians during those decades and in the immediate post-conciliar period. Chapter 4 will be about more recent decades: we will show how, since Vatican II, theology has benefitted from studies on early Christianity, and we will also reflect on the reasons that other viewpoints have sometimes distanced theology itself from patristics. These reasons are of a diverse nature: some are due to the difficulties that the exegesis of the Fathers raise regarding "critical exegesis"; others are due to certain problems that are today expressed within the cadre of human sciences, of philosophy, and of European theology; finally, others are due to the expansion of theologies called "contextual," the issues of continents that are quite distant from the regions (especially the Mediterranean) in which patristic literature was formerly developed—and of Europe itself that, moreover, is marked by such changes that theology there is also elaborated in new "contexts," ever more distant from the cultures of Antiquity. But chapters 5, 6 and 7, by successively taking up these three sets of issues, will show that they do not constitute decisive objections regarding the project of a "patristic theology" as such; on the contrary, the difficulties will provide us with the occasion of giving to this project its fundamental justifications: in the situations that are ours today, it remains not only legitimate but also necessary to find in the study of the Fathers inspiration and food for our own theological reflection. These chapters (5, 6, and 7) must be in this sense considered as the central chapters; this is where the essential thesis of the book will be established: today, as yesterday, patristics must contribute to the tasks of theology.

This thesis itself requires verification in the various fields in which the understanding of the faith is practiced. This precisely will be the subject of the second part, titled "Reading the Fathers Today: The Present Tasks of Patristic Theology." We will begin with ecclesiology in chapter 8; we will continue with anthropology and ethics in chapters 9 and 10; chapter 11 will be about Christology and Trinitarian theology. We will then examine patristic literature from the point of view of ecumenism, in chapter 12, and the theology of religions, in chapter 13; lastly, in chapter 14, we will discuss the contribution of the Fathers to spiritual theology. It goes without saying that by themselves each of these subjects could be developed at length: far from claiming to be exhaustive, we want simply to highlight—at least with some topics—the capacity of patristic writings to inspire, nourish, and make fruitful our own thought today. Admittedly, the reader could, if he wishes, begin with the second part that will put him more directly in contact with the thinking of the Fathers, leaving to later the discovery of the justifications for the actual project of patristic theology provided in the first part. Here, nevertheless, the adopted order has an important significance: the fundamental exposés on the "patristics and theology" problem have no other goal, in the end, than to lead to "reading the Fathers today" and to experiencing the fecundity of this reading for theology itself. It is truly to this experience that the book would ultimately like to refer—as our epilogue on "The Future of the Fathers" will say.

Part One

From Yesterday to Today

The Contribution of Patristics to Christian Theology

CHAPTER 1

The Genesis and History of "Patristics"

Before presenting the return to the Fathers in the work of theologians of the twentieth century and reflecting upon the current relationship between patristics and theology, it is, first of all, necessary for us to specify the origin and meaning of the expressions "Fathers of the Church," "patrology" and "patristics": this will be the subject of our first exposition. It will then be important to examine how the reading of the Fathers, from the Middle Ages through the nineteenth century, has already made specific contributions to Christian theology. It is on this basis that in the following chapters we will be able to understand the essential developments of patristic theology over several decades.

"Fathers of the Church," "Patrology," "Patristics"

By recalling the words of Christ in Matthew 23:9 ("And call no man your father on earth, for you have one Father, who is in heaven"), one could be tempted to place the expression "Fathers of the Church" in direct contradiction to the Gospel. But that would be a facile solution that would not account for the paradox with which early Christianity instead confronts us: it is a fact that the words of Christ did not dissuade Christians from applying the name of "Father" to some men. Already in the First Letter to the Corinthians Paul himself wrote: "I do not write this to make you ashamed, but to admonish you as my beloved children. For though you have countless guides in Christ, you do not have many fathers. For I became your father in Christ Jesus through the gospel" (1 Cor 4:14–15). Paul is thus implicitly presenting himself as "father." It is true that at the same time he was excluding the extension of this name ("you do not have many fathers"). But, from the second half of the second century, one finds the title of "father" mentioned to describe a bishop: in the *Martyrdom of Polycarp*, the bishop Polycarp is designated as "the Father of the Christians."[1] And a little later, toward the end of the second century, Clement of Alexandria opens his *Stromata* with a reflection on the relationship of the master to the disciple, and on this occasion, uses the "father-children" vocabulary: "We call our religious instructors fathers. Wisdom is open to all, and loves humankind.... Everyone who is educated in obedience to his educator becomes a son."[2] Other uses appear little by little and are developed in the following centuries: in particular, one gives the title of Father to those who have defined the faith of the Church or its discipline at the time of the councils (in this sense, one speaks of the "Fathers of Nicaea"), as well as to those who withdrew to the desert in order to lead an eremitic life or those who are at the head of a community of monks (the "abba" or the "abbot," who is precisely the "father").

The expression "Fathers of the Church" is thus grafted upon a well-attested use of the word "Father" in the first Christian centuries. However, it assumed a particular meaning that should now be pointed out. Eusebius of Caesarea (d. 339) is, to our knowledge, the first to use this expression; he attacks a certain Marcellus who, he says, "rejects all the Fathers of the Church" (*pantas tous ekklesiastikous Pateras athetei*).[3] In the following decades, Basil of Caesarea writes, "What we teach is in no way the result of our personal thoughts, but what we have learned

1. *Martyrdom of Polycarp*, 12.2, trans. Paul Hartog (Oxford: Oxford Apostolic Fathers, 2013), 257; Other trans.: in *The Apostolic Fathers*, vol. 5, trans. William R. Schoedel (London: Thomas Nelson & Sons, 1967), 67. Here we are basically repeating our contribution, Michel Fédou, "Des Pères de l'Église à l'Église des Pères" [From the Fathers of the Church to the Church of the Fathers], in *L'Église des Pères Initiation à la théologie patristique* [Introduction to patristic theology] (Paris: Médiasèvres, 2007), 6 ff.

2. Clement of Alexandria, *Stromateis*, I, I, 1–2; trans. J. Ferguson, The Fathers of the Church 85 (Washington, D.C.: The Catholic University of America Press, 1991), 23–24; see also Clément d'Alexandrie, *Stromate I*, trans. Marcel Caster, SC 30 (Paris: Cerf, 1951), 44–45. One will note the sapiential inspiration of this passage. On the meaning of the word "father" in the Jewish tradition, see Yves Congar. *La Tradition et les traditions*, vol. 2, *Essai théologique*, new ed. (1963; Paris: Cerf, 2010), 193; translated by Michael Naseby and Thomas Rainborough as *Tradition and Traditions: An Historical and a Theological Essay* (London: Burns & Oates, 1966), 437.

3. Eusebius of Caesarea, *Contra Marcellum*, I.4 [PG 24: 752 B].

from the holy Fathers."[4] Beginning with the second half of the fourth century, the word "Fathers" thus already has the meaning (among others) that subsequent theology will adopt: some Christians who have lived in the past and who enjoy a particular authority.

But during this era, the expression "Fathers of the Church" is still not defined in a precise way. Time was needed to arrive at this definition, and one can note several stages marking the progressive development of the concept. Thus, it is the great Christological controversies of the fifth century that provide the occasion for referring to the authority of the Fathers and, at the same time, contribute to the recognition of this authority. Above all, it is important to recall the work of the monk Vincent of Lérins who, in his *Commonitorium* (434), formulates the criteria of authentic Tradition thus: "Only that is to be held as certain, valid, and beyond doubt, which either all or most of them [the Fathers] have confirmed in one and the same sense—manifestly, frequently, and persistently, as though a council of masters stood in agreement—and which they have accepted, kept, and handed on."[5] Vincent of Lérins explains as well that all the ancient authors do not have the same authority, and that some were even mistaken on this or that point; thus is set down the basis for the subsequent distinction between "Fathers of the Church" and "ecclesiastical writers" (this second expression having a broader meaning than the first). This distinction is clearly formulated in the following decades, as a decree attributed to Pope Gelasius I (but which is, in fact, a matter of a private document, which was undoubtedly written in southern Gaul in the sixth century) shows: this writing mentions, on one hand, "the works of the holy Fathers that are received in the Catholic Church," and on the other, works that, without having the same authority, mer-

4. Basil of Caesarea, *Epistula* 104, 2 [PG 32: 588]. See also Gregory of Nazianzus, *Discours* 33, 15; trans. Paul Gallay, SC 318 (Paris: Cerf, 1985), 191: "what I learned from the holy Fathers." In the Latin world, Jerome writes in 393 his *De viris illustribus*, in which he presents the most important Christian authors since the beginning up until his era; cf. *Les hommes illustres*, trans. D. Viellard, Les Pères dans la foi 100 (Paris: Migne, 2009); *Lives of Illustrious Men*, trans. Ernest Cushing Richardson, The Nicene and Post-Nicene Fathers, 2nd ser., vol. 3 (repr. Edinburgh: T&T Clark, 1996), 359–84.

5. Vincent of Lérins, *The Commonitories*, 28, trans. Rudolph E. Morris, The Fathers of the Church 7 (1949; repr. Washington, D.C.: The Catholic University of America Press, 1970), 321–22; see also *Vincent of Lérins. Tradition et progrès* [Tradition and progress], ed. Adalbert-Gautier Hamman (Paris: Desclée de Brouwer, 1978), 93.

it, however, consideration and esteem—as well as other writings that themselves must be entirely rejected.[6]

Thus the concept of "Fathers of the Church" was developed little by little. But just as the closing of the canon of Scriptures was not the feat of the authors of the "New Testament" but an ecclesial act of subsequent generations, similarly (analogically at least) the complete and precise definition of the expression "Fathers of the Church" could only be truly given beginning with the moment when one was aware of no longer belonging to the era of the Fathers. It would be interesting to show how this definition was consolidated over the course of the Middle Ages; notably, it would be necessary to highlight the importance of Peter Lombard (c. 1100–60), whose *Sentences* collected the opinions of the Fathers and thus provided succeeding centuries with an essential base for theological thought and education.

The development of the concept ultimately resulted in the formulations that one finds in the manuals and dictionaries of the modern era. Here is, for example, the definition formerly proposed by E. Amman: one means by Fathers of the Church "a group of ecclesial personages belonging to the past and whose authority is decisive on matters of doctrine."[7] Four elements—or four "traits"—then allow specifying the definition:

- the orthodoxy of doctrine (not necessarily on all points, but at least on essential points);
- holiness of life;
- the approval of the Church;
- antiquity (the traditional usage being, let us recall, the closing of the patristic era in the middle of the seventh century for the West and in the middle of the eighth century for the East[8]—even with the exception of applying the expression to a later author such as Bernard of Clairvaux, described as "the last of the Fathers" because of the great proximity of his exegesis to patristic exegesis).

6. See PL 59, 157 f.

7. Émile Amman, "Pères de l'Église," in *Dictionnaire de théologie catholique* [Dictionary of Catholic theology] 12, pt. 1 (Paris: Letouzey & Ané, 1933), col. 1192.

8. See the introduction above.

This determination of the concept "Fathers of the Church" assuredly relies upon some criteria already formulated during the patristic era; nevertheless, it is necessary to restate that it is, in its final form, the feat of subsequent eras. Let us clarify, in passing, that this expression itself must be distinguished from the expression "Doctors of the Church"; this latter title, designating Christians who have made an eminent contribution to Christian doctrine, is valid for more than the early period (it has also been conferred upon Teresa of Avila and Thérèse of Lisieux). But the two expressions sometimes overlap. Several "Fathers" have indeed been deemed to be "Doctors" by tradition: this was the case for four Fathers of the Greek Church (Athanasius, Basil, Gregory of Nazianzus, and John Chrysostom) and for four Fathers of the Latin Church (Ambrose, Jerome, Augustine, and Gregory the Great).[9]

Lastly, it is necessary to differentiate some notions that were developed in the modern and contemporary period: "patrology," "patristics," "history of early Christian literature."[10] Today, according to current usage, the word "patristics" designates either a part of Christian theology (one then speaks of patristics as one speaks of biblical theology or fundamental theology) or the literary study of works composed by the writers of early Christianity. Actually, in the second case, it is necessary to speak not of "patristics" but rather of "patrology" or of the "history of early Christian literature."

The difference in these expressions can be clarified by the genesis and evolution of the disciplines at issue. The word "patristics" (*patristica*) originated in the seventeenth century, in Lutheran theology, in order to designate the part of theological education that was to systematize the teaching of the Fathers of the Church. The word "patrology" (*patrologia*), itself, appeared for the first time in the title of a work by

9. Let us also add another clarification of a quite different nature. One sometimes asks why Tradition speaks only of the Fathers of the Church in the masculine—a language that risks appearing exclusive, above all to theologies called "feminist." It is a legitimate question in as much as it reflects a correct awareness of the equality between man and woman; on the other hand, it is necessary, however, to avoid yielding here to a certain anachronism. The question must rather be reformulated in these terms: what in patristic literature, in spite of the predominance of the language "Fathers of the Church," attests to the role held by some Christian women who greatly contributed to the ecclesial life of their time?

10. On this point, see Pierre Hadot, art. "Patristique," in *Encyclopædia Universalis*, vol. 17 (Paris: Encyclopaedia Universalis France, 1996), 638–43.

Johann Gerhard, in 1563. It was to designate the study that was limited to the personality of the Fathers, their life, and their works.

In fact, this study assumed at least two major forms. On one hand, it emerged as the scientific edition of the texts: thus, in the nineteenth century, Abbé Migne edited the *Patrologia graeca* and the *Patrologia latina*. But patrology also appeared as literary history, principally interested in the writers and their works. Of course, it was to pay particular attention to doctrines; moreover, that is why one often has confounded "patrology" and "patristics" (notably at the end of the eighteenth century and in the nineteenth century). But even when patrology treats doctrines, it sees in them, above all, the expression of literary personalities instead of being primarily interested (like traditional patristics) in their specifically theological stakes. It is necessary to add that the field of patrology is extremely large, for it does not tackle only those who are considered as Fathers of the Church in the exact meaning of the term but all Christian writers from Antiquity. Patrology thus leads to a discipline that in our day one calls more broadly the "history of early Christian literature."

It is clear that, given its goal, our study is above all interested in "patristics" in the strict meaning, that is to say, the study of the Fathers in so much as it belongs to theology—even if such a study must necessarily take note of the research done in the cadre of "patrology" or of the "history of early Christian literature." This is precisely why, from this perspective, it is important to cover the period that goes from the Middle Ages to the end of the nineteenth century: how has the reading of the Fathers contributed, during this period, to theological thought?

Reading the Fathers in the Middle Ages

As for the East, the authority of the Fathers had been clearly formulated by the one who is considered to be "the real Father of Byzantine theology":[11] Maximus the Confessor. In the context of the theological controversies that marked the seventh century, he deeply wished to

11. John Meyendorff, *Le Christ dans la théologie byzantine* (1969; repr. Paris: Cerf, 2010), 178; translated as *Christ in Eastern Christian Thought* (Crestwood, N.Y.: St. Vladimir's Seminary Press, 1975), 131; see Jaroslav Pelikan, *The Christian Tradition: A History of the Development of Doctrine*, vol. 2, *The Spirit of Eastern Christendom (600–1700)* (Chicago: University of Chicago Press, 1974), 8.

preserve and defend the doctrine that had been handed down by the Fathers: "to confess with his soul and his mouth" was to affirm "what the Fathers have taught us," and in every theological discussion it was thus necessary to put forward "the voice of the Fathers as proof of the faith of the Church."[12] In fact, in the succeeding centuries, all the Byzantine authors invoke their authority (in order to draw divergent conclusions from them, as one sees in the context of the iconoclast crisis): "Unquestioning loyalty to the fathers was a continuing characteristic of Eastern thought."[13] Admittedly, the source of the truth was to be found in the Old and New Testaments. However, the doctrinal controversies had shown that Scripture itself could be read and understood in ways that sometimes conflicted. It was thus necessary to rely upon the Fathers in order to interpret it correctly. Their authority, in fact, was that of the truth that was expressed through them; one recognized that they had benefitted from special graces, as the qualifiers attached to some among them show: Athanasius was a "God-bearing teacher," Basil was "the great eye of the Church," the sentences of Gregory of Nazianzus were "most divine," Dionysius the Areopagite was "the one who truly spoke of God, the great and holy Dionysius."[14] The writings of the Fathers (at least those who were to be recognized as such—because some authors from past centuries, beginning with Origen, were considered as heretics) thus provided the very criteria of Christian orthodoxy. The Byzantine theologians recognized, it is true, that sometimes these Fathers seemed to contradict one another. But they then attempted to demonstrate that these disagreements were only superficial: what was authoritative, in fact, was not, first of all, the personal opinions of the Fathers, but it was their basic consensus, the one that reflected the thinking of the universal Church. Moreover, the ecumenical councils themselves had defined the essential doctrines of the faith; admittedly, Christians were divided on their subject,[15] but it was in these councils that the Byzantine authors recognized a very great authority—an authority that was due, above all, to the fact that the conciliar doctrine was exactly, in their eyes, the "orthodox" doc-

12. Maximus the Confessor, *Epistula* 12 [PG 91: 465]; and *Epistula* 13 [PG 91: 532].

13. Pelikan, *Spirit of Eastern Christendom*, 9.

14. See the references given by Pelikan, in ibid., 19–20.

15. We will later consider the problems linked to these divisions; see chap. 6, 164–65, and chap. 12, 289–93.

trine. Scripture, the Fathers, the councils: these were the foundation of theology. But for all that, everything was not the subject of knowledge: the Byzantine theologians knew that, according to Dionysius the Areopagite, "the negative declarations concerning the divine subjects are the only true declarations"; if they appealed to philosophical concepts such as those of "substance" (*ousia*) or "hypostasis" (*hypostasis*), they, at the same time, kept in mind that God is infinitely beyond the categories thus used—and this also witnessed to their fidelity to the teaching of the Greek Fathers, so concerned with preserving the transcendence of the Divinity.

Undoubtedly, from the point of view that we hold here, it is necessary to avoid accentuating these differences between the West and the East too much. As Henri de Lubac has shown, medieval Latin exegesis was itself dominated by the legacy of patristic exegesis; and in accordance with it, the search for "the meanings of the Scripture" was structured not only for the explanation of the biblical text but also, through it, for a more profound knowledge of the Christian mystery.[16] Even apart from exegesis, one can say, in general, that the Latin Middle Ages also recognized the authority of the Fathers for the understanding of the faith and that the argumentations of theologians could, as in the Greek world, be based upon the witness of their writings. This is obvious in the case of the High Middle Ages: for the Christian authors of this period, and in particular from the ninth century—a century of a patristic renaissance—the "truth of the Church" was exactly what had been defined by the "Fathers," thus named because they had "begotten us in Christ";[17] the compilation of quotations taken from their writings could, henceforth, be seen as an essential method of theology.

16. Cf. Henri de Lubac, *Exégèse médiévale. Les quatre sens de l'Écriture*, 4 vols. (Paris: Aubier-Montaigne, 1959–64); translated by Mark Sebanc and E. M. Macierowski as *Medieval Exegesis: The Four Senses of Scripture*, 3 vols. (Grand Rapids, Mich.: Eerdmans, 2009); also see the works of Rainer Berndt on the exegesis of the Victorians; or also the article of Gilbert Dahan, "Les Pères dans l'exégèse médiévale de la Bible" [The Fathers in the medieval exegesis of the Bible], *Revue des Sciences Philosophiques et Théologiques* 91 (2007): 109–27; and the proceedings of the conference in Paris, Centre Sèvres (June, 11–14, 2008): *Les réceptions des Pères de l'Église au Moyen Âge. Le devenir de la tradition ecclésiale* [The Receptions of the Fathers of the Church in the Middle Ages. The process of the ecclesial tradition], ed. Rainer Berndt and Michel Fédou (Münster: Aschendorff, 2013).

17. Cf. Jaroslav Pelikan, *The Christian Tradition: A History of the Development of Doctrine*, vol. 3, *The Growth of Medieval Theology (600–1300)* (University of Chicago Press, 1978), 15.

During this era, moreover, one recognized an authority of "Fathers" in some Christian authors of the sixth, seventh, and eighth centuries who, in their day, themselves referred to previous "Fathers" (above all, Augustine): this is how Gregory the Great, Isidore of Seville, and the Venerable Bede came to be cited as authorities in their own right. The importance of patristic writings for theology itself was shown as well in the succeeding centuries, notably in the twelfth century, which was another era of a patristic renaissance. This is testified to by works as varied as those of William of Saint-Thierry, Bernard of Clairvaux, Hugh of Saint-Victor, and Peter Abelard. Above all, one cannot fail to recall here the four books of the *Sentences* composed by Peter Lombard in 1155–57. These books, which collected the opinions of the Fathers and rearranged them according to subject, were going to become an essential reference: "Peter Lombard wrote, without knowing it, *the* manual of theology of the Middle Ages. From the thirteenth century on, the primary task of the theologian would consist only of commenting on the *Sentences*—Roger Bacon will in this sense deplore that 'the Master of the Sentences' had ended by surpassing the Holy Scriptures themselves."[18]

But in the Latin Middle Ages, recourse to the authorities also appeared with other characteristics. First of all, it is necessary to emphasize, in contrast to the Byzantine East, the exceptional importance that was here recognized in Augustine. Admittedly, it often occurs that theologians of the West also refer to other Fathers—not only Latin Fathers such as Ambrose, Leo, or Gregory the Great, but also some Greek Fathers such as Basil, Gregory of Nazianzus, John Chrysostom, Cyril of Alexandria, Dionysius the Areopagite, Maximus the Confessor, or John Damascene (this is verified, for example, through the work of Thomas Aquinas who makes great use of Greek patristics and, among others, the works of Dionysius, whose authority was all the greater since one saw in him the hearer of Paul at the Areopagus in Athens ...). The fact remains that Augustine's authority was considerable, and this was throughout every field of theology—in the Eucharistic controversies as well as in Trinitarian theology, in the thoughts on grace regarding the Church or on the "City of God." The other major characteristic to

18. Libera, *La philosophie médiévale*, 339–40.

be identified is the development of a theology that did not just collect the opinions of the Fathers as such but submitted them to "questions" (*quaestiones*). The beginning of this "scholastic" method was Abélard's *Sic et non* in the twelfth century: the author brought together certain texts from the Bible, the Fathers of the Church, and from the councils, but this collection was not a simple anthology precisely because the passages thus collected were sometimes contradictory; it was thus necessary to weigh the arguments on both sides in a way that enabled reaching a decision. And so a new form of thinking appeared: "reason is not opposed to faith or to revelation, it penetrates the patristic data and submits it to questioning. The reasoning used seizes authority in order to make it a step in its own discursiveness."[19] The books of the *Sentences*, mentioned above, must themselves be understood from this perspective: if they illustrate, on one hand, the importance of patristic writings for theology, they invite, on the other, by the very fact of highlighting the diversity and sometimes the contradictions of the "authorities," a "*disputatio*" that can lead toward the correct solution of the problems raised by these contradictions. Thus, with Scholastic theology, a new way of referring to the Fathers was going to be developed. Moreover, the East itself was not a stranger to such a development: the cultural history of Byzantium knew, in its own way, the opposition between partisans and opponents of the dialectic in theology, and some authors were themselves influenced by Thomism.[20] The emergence of Scholastic theology in the Latin Middle Ages had, in any case, as a corollary, or even as a condition, a new way of referring to the authority of the Fathers—even if the last two centuries of the medieval period also show the permanence of a more traditional attitude regarding the patristic legacy.[21]

19. Ibid., 340.

20. Cf. ibid., 45–46.

21. On the reading of the Fathers during the medieval era, numerous contributions were provided during the conference "Réceptions des Pères et de leurs écrits au Moyen Âge. Le devenir de la tradition ecclésiale" (Centre Sèvres, Paris, June, 11–14, 2008); see Berndt and Fédou, *Les réceptions des Pères de l'Église au Moyen Âge*.

From the Renaissance to the Nineteenth Century

It is not necessary here to stress the intense work of publishing that was carried out in the context of the humanist movement and that, from the end of the fifteenth century and throughout the sixteenth century, is evidenced by the dissemination of numerous patristic writings. It is important, on the other hand, to emphasize the importance of this "Renaissance" for theology itself. This is verified by, for example, the case of Pico della Mirandola, so profoundly influenced by the reading of Origen,[22] and especially by the great humanist Erasmus. He found in the Fathers a major inspiration for his thinking, in particular for his works on the text itself of the Scriptures and on their exegesis but also for his argumentation on the theological problems that were then so highly debated—notably the question of free will, in the context of the controversies with the Lutheran Reformation.[23]

This Reformation clearly distanced itself from these matters by not referring to the Fathers who, from its point of view, did not respect the famous principle of "*sola Scriptura*"; it particularly denounced, along this line, all "allegorical" exegesis that risked creating a barrier to the true meaning of the biblical texts. This, nevertheless, does not mean that it did not recognize an authority in the Fathers, at least in those who appeared to it to be authentic interpreters of the Word of God—above all, Augustine. Thus Luther, in his commentary on the Letter to

22. See Henri de Lubac, *Pic de la Mirandole. Études et discussions* [Pico della Mirandola, studies and Discussions] (Paris: Aubier-Montaigne, 1974).

23. See André Godin, *Érasme lecteur d'Origène* [Erasmus, reader of Origen] (Geneva: Droz, 1982). It is also worth mentioning the position held by Ignatius of Loyola in the *Spiritual Exercises*: "We ought to praise both positive theology and Scholastic theology. For just as it is more characteristic of the positive doctors, such as St. Jerome, St. Augustine, St. Gregory, and the rest to stir up our affections toward loving and serving God our Lord in all things, so it is more characteristic of the Scholastic teachers, such as St. Thomas, St. Bonaventure, the Master of the Sentences, and so on to define and explain for our times the matters necessary for salvation, and also to refute and expose all the errors and fallacies." *Spiritual Exercises*, no. 363, in Ignatius of Loyola, *The Spiritual Exercises and Selected Works*, ed. George E. Ganss, Classics of Western Spirituality (Mahwah, N.J.: Paulist Press, 1991), 212. See Ignace de Loyola, *Écrits* [Writings], ed. Maurice Giuliani (Paris: Desclée de Brouwer, 1991), 250. This attitude here advocated gives great importance to the Fathers of the Church, but, unlike the position held by some humanists, emphasizes at the same time the importance of the "scholastic teachers" who, being "more modern," benefit not only from the "holy positive doctors" but "a profitable use of the councils, canons, and constitutions of our Holy Mother Church. *Spiritual Exercises*, no. 363 (Ganss, 212).

the Romans, repeated the polemic that the bishop of Hippo had developed against Pelagius and his partisans regarding justification and grace. Indeed, Erasmus himself also claimed to follow Augustine in his doctrine of free will; Luther, however, considered that Erasmus's position was a misinterpretation of the Augustinian doctrine that actually maintained salvation "by grace alone" (*sola gratia*). The reformer Melanchthon had a more nuanced position, recognizing that some Fathers (such as Origen) gave more importance to free will. But other reformers contested this position in the name of what appeared to them to be Augustine's thinking and, especially, the teaching of Scripture.

The Council of Trent, for its part, opposed Protestantism with the witness of the Fathers of the Church, not only on the questions of justification and grace but also on the other questions raised by the Reformation (for example, regarding the Eucharist and the "Real Presence" or even regarding the priesthood). According to the council, reference to the patristic consensus had all the more weight since it maintained the existence of truths not formulated in Scripture—the Holy Spirit inspiring the Church in order to guide it in the knowledge of the faith. This conviction was unceasingly reaffirmed and developed by Catholic theologians in the context of the controversies with Protestants, as one sees through the work of Bellarmine. The increasing number of editions and translations of patristic texts themselves favored the recourse to the Fathers in theological argumentation; moreover, inversely, the importance given to the patristic consensus in this argumentation contributed, throughout the modern era, to the vitality of the research on the authors of Christian Antiquity (illustrated by, among others, the scholarly works of Fronton du Duc, Denis Petau, and Maurist editors).

The divergences between Catholics and Protestants are thus even manifested through the ways in which they refer to the writings of the first centuries. But it is necessary to clarify that, on this point, there were as well debates and conflicts within both sides. Even within Protestantism, in addition to the case of Melanchthon already mentioned, one sees Calvin complaining that the opponents of early dogmas were ignorant of the patristic tradition;[24] and if the pastor Jean Dai-

24. See Jaroslav Pelikan, *Christian Tradition: A History of the Development of Doctrine*, vol. 4, *Reformation of the Church and Dogma (1300–1700)* (University of Chicago Press, 1984), 324.

llé, in a 1632 treatise, radically contested the authority of the Fathers of the Church whom the Catholics claimed to follow as the solution to contemporary problems,[25] another pastor, Nicolas Des Gallars, had affirmed several decades earlier that knowledge of the Fathers aided in discerning error from the truth; admittedly, he said, it is necessary before all else to read the Scriptures, and one encounters in the Fathers many ideas that "do not agree with them"; however, he added, "their doctrines and their examples are so important that they cannot be disregarded without the sin of ingratitude or of pride."[26] On the other hand, within the Catholic side, there were also disagreements on the importance that it was necessary to give to patristic argument (in some cases, this argument could give the impression that Tradition was like another Scripture, but other positions were much more nuanced); furthermore, if all agreed to recognize the eminent authority of Augustine, his thinking was understood in ways that were quite varied—and sometimes even with a heterodox meaning, as the case of Jansenius shows.[27]

Whatever the debates and conflicts connected with these divergent interpretations, reference to the patristic writings, in any case, had a major place in theology. As we have said above, the word *patristica* itself appeared in the seventeenth century in Lutheran circles; *theologia patristica* emerged there as a theological discipline, along with *theologia biblica*, *theologia scholastica*, *theologia symbolica*, and *theologia speculativa*. In Catholicism, during this same century, "patristics" also appeared as a theological discipline (as one notably sees

25. Jean Daillé, *Traicté de l'employ des saincts Pères pour le jugement des differends, qui sont aujourd'huy en la Religion* (Geneva: Pierre Aubert, 1632); translated by Thomas Smith as *A Treatise on the Right Use of the Fathers in the Decision of Controversies Existing at This Day in Religion* (London: W. White, 1841); see Mario Turchetti, "Jean Daillé et son *Traicté de l'employ des saincts Pères (1632)*. Aperçu sur les changements des critères d'appréciation des Pères de l'Église entre le XVIe et le XVIIe siècles" [John Daillé and his treaty of the use of the Holy Fathers (1632). Overview of the changes in the criteria for assessing the Church Fathers between the seventeenth and the eighteenth centuries], in *Les Pères de l'Église au XVIIe siècle* [The Fathers of the Church in the seventeenth century], ed. Emmanuel Bury and Bernard Meunier (Paris: IRHT—Cerf, Paris, 1993), 70.

26. Nicolas Des Gallars, in his preface to his edition of *Irénée* (Geneva: Jean Le Preux-and Jean Petit, 1570); cited in Turchetti, "Jean Daillé et son *Traicté*," 85.

27. See Jean-Louis Quantin, *Le catholicisme classique et les Pères de l'Église. Un retour aux sources (1669–1713)* [Classical Catholicism and the Fathers of the Church. A return to the sources] (Paris: Institut d'Études Augustiniennes, 1999).

in Denis Petau): it was a matter of going back prior to the medieval Scholastics and looking into the writings of the Fathers for this or that argument which could be utilized in the controversies with Protestants or Jansenists.

With the era of the Enlightenment, new problems suddenly appeared, and a number of theologians were then led to develop an apologetics of the Christian religion in order to respond to the objections of "atheists." In this same context, they referred to the Fathers of the Church in order to draw heavily upon them for all kinds of arguments in favor of the faith. Furthermore, under the influence of Enlightenment philosophy and the ideas of evolution that were more and more widespread at this time, one was aware that the study of the Fathers could not consist merely of the examination of their theological doctrines but that it was also necessary to put these doctrines in a timeframe that included advances, crises, transformations. In fact, the development of philological and historical sciences greatly enriched the knowledge of early Christianity, and the great editorial enterprises—above all that of Abbé Migne in the nineteenth century[28]—allowed access to a considerable number of patristic texts: this was to profit not only the "history of dogmas" (illustrated at the end of the nineteenth and at the beginning of the twentieth centuries by erudite works such as those of Harnack)[29] but also the thought of the theologians who, in spite of the predominance of Neothomism, found in the writings of the Fathers a major inspiration for their own thought. Two names from the nineteenth century, in particular, illustrate the fecundity of patristic work for theology: Möhler and Newman.

28. See Charles Chauvin, *L'Abbé Migne et ses collaborateurs (1800–1875)* [Abbé Migne and his collaborators] (Paris: Desclée de Brouwer, 2010). Other editions and translations could be also mentioned, as those of the works of John Chrysostom by Abbé Bareille or those of the works of Augustine (appearing in the publications of Vivès in the second half of the nineteenth century).

29. See Adolf von Harnack, *Gundriss der Dogmengeschichte* (Tübingen: J.C.B. Mohr, 1889), translated as *History of Dogma*, 7 vols. (London: Williams and Norgate, 1894–99), and by Eugène Choisy as *Histoire des dogmes* (Paris: Cerf, 1993); *Mission et expansion du christianisme aux trois premiers siècles*, trans. Joseph Hoffmann (Paris: Cerf, 2004), translated by James Moffatt as *The Expansion of Christianity in the First Three Centuries*, 2 vols. (New York: Putnam's Sons, 1904–5).

Johann Adam Möhler and John Henry Newman

The first of these names is connected with what one calls the School of Tübingen, which originated around 1820 and which, freeing itself from Scholastic theology, wanted to restore to the history of Christianity its proper place and to recover in particular the major movement of the patristic tradition. Principally known for his ecclesiological work, Johann Adam Möhler (1796–1838) was, in fact, deeply influenced by his in-depth reading of the Fathers.[30] In his book *L'Unité dans l'Église ou le principe du Catholicisme*, he undertakes to show, by studying the first Christian centuries, that all those who have claimed to follow Christ and have lived in his Spirit have belonged to the same body. In this can be heard the voice of the first Fathers: Clement of Rome, Ignatius of Antioch, Irenaeus, Origen, Cyprian, ... Let us cite some lines from this work as examples:

> According to the teaching of the primitive Church, the true faith, the real Christian experience, is ... conditioned by the presence of the Holy Spirit, this presence having in its turn a connection with the Church....
>
> Clement of Rome preaches this profound truth to the Corinthians.... The author of the magnificent letter to Diognetus, another disciple of the Apostles, himself also presents the movement that is the Church as the source that will make known to us the true essence of Christianity....
>
> No one has penetrated more into the depths of this subject than Saint Ignatius. It is from his entire religious soul that this true disciple, faithful image of the Apostle John, grasps the essence of Christianity and expounds it in his writings....
>
> The Fathers of the Church of this era all, without exception, have spoken, and on very diverse occasions, of this foundation of the unity of the Church, of this divine force that seizes it, engenders life in it and from there leads us to the knowledge of the Christian life.[31]

30. See Johann Adam Möhler, *L'Unité de l'Église ou le principe du Catholicisme d'après l'esprit des Pères des trois premiers siècles de l'Église*, trans. Joseph Hoffmann (Paris: Cerf, 1938); translated by Peter C. Erb as *Unity in the Church or the Principle of Catholicism: Presented in the Spirit of the Church Fathers of the First Three Centuries* (Washington, D.C.: The Catholic University of America Press, 1996). On this theologian, see *L'Église est une. Hommage à Moehler* [The Church is one. Tribute to Moehler], ed. Pierre Chaillet (Paris: Bloud & Gay, 1939); see especially the article by Gustave Bardy, "La voix des Pères" [The voice of the Fathers], in Chaillet, *L'Église est une*, 61–81. See also Michel Deneken, *Johann Adam Möhler* (Paris: Cerf, 2007).

31. Moehler, *L'Unité de l'Église*, sec. 4, 12–14.

The reference to the Fathers, here, is not simply meant to give information about what they thought in their time; above all, the reading of their writings led to perceiving, and even experiencing, the very real pertinence of their views for the Church and for what causes its unity. A patrologist of the twentieth century, Gustave Bardy, gives a very good account of the theologian of Tübingen's objective:

> Moehler does not propose anything other than making the voice of the Fathers of the first three centuries heard. Behind these favored testimonies of the early Church, the author hides himself as much as possible, above all in the first chapters. The more he moves toward his goal, the more he allows himself to follow the natural inclination of his mind and speak in his own name. But at the beginning, it is truly the Fathers who are instructing us, and it is not difficult to fall under the spell of their teaching.
>
> There is no need for them to be presented to us individually, that their dates of birth and arenas of activity be made known to us. For what purpose? As soon as they are presented, we know who they are, old friends that the concerns of the present have hardly made us forget, momentarily absent brothers whom we recover with joy, better than this, Fathers, the ancestors of our faith, the witnesses of our traditions, the first leaders of our Churches.[32]

Möhler was thus not looking for only an historical point of view in the writings of early Christianity. By reading them, by the familiarity that he had acquired with their authors, he was actually led to expound theological theses for his own time. And these theses were of great importance for the future: as Y. Congar and other theologians of the twentieth century have emphasized, Möhler was among those who, in the first half of the nineteenth century, renewed the understanding of the Church and opened the way to the future movement of ecumenism; he also contributed to the deepening of connections between Scripture and Tradition, showing that beginning with the Fathers, one could not oppose nor even juxtapose the two of them, but rather that it was necessary to understand the Tradition as "the Gospel living in the Church."[33]

The other name that we must remember here is that of John Henry Newman (1801–90). The discovery of the Fathers held a place of

32. Bardy, "La voix des Pères," 67–68.

33. Cf. Yves Congar, *La Tradition et les traditions, I. Essai historique*, new ed. (Paris: Cerf, 2010), 247; *Tradition and Traditions*, 194–95.

great importance in his itinerary; he himself tells in his *Apologia pro vita sua* that a proposal was made to him in 1830 to write a history of the main councils: "I accepted it," he writes, "and at once set to work on the Council of Nicaea"; but he adds, "It was to launch myself on an ocean with currents innumerable, and I was drifted back first to the ante-Nicaea history, and then to the Church of Alexandria";[34] his work was going to appear in 1834 under the title *The Arians of the Fourth Century*. In his *Apologia*, he goes back over what were his first explorations of patristic literature:

> I do not know when I first learnt to consider that Antiquity was the true exponent of the doctrines of Christianity and the basis of the Church of England; but I take it for granted that the works of Bishop Bull, which at this time I read, were my chief introduction to this principle. The course of reading, which I pursued in the composition of my volume, was directly adapted to develop it in my mind. What principally attracted me in the ante-Nicene period was the great Church of Alexandria, the historical center of teaching in those times. Of Rome for some centuries comparatively little is known. The battle of Arianism was first fought in Alexandria; Athanasius, the champion of the truth, was bishop of Alexandria; and in his writings he refers to the great religious names of an earlier date, to Origen, Dionysius, and others, who were the glory of its see, or of its school. The broad philosophy of Clement and Origen carried me away; the philosophy, not the theological doctrine; and I have drawn out some features of it in my volume, with the zeal and freshness, but with the partiality, of a neophyte. Some portions of their teaching, magnificent in themselves, came like music to my inward ear, as if the response to ideas, which, with little external to encourage them, I had cherished so long.[35]

Newman then summarizes the main points of these ideas, based on "the mystical or sacramental principle": the exterior world is only the manifestation of realities that surpass it; nature is a "parable," and Scripture an "allegory"; there has been "a directly divine dispensation granted to the Jews," but there has also been, in a certain sense, a "dispensation in favor of the Gentiles," and the Greek poets and sages were in one sense "prophets"; the outward context of the ancient world hid, all the while suggesting it, the "Living Truth" that was going to shine brightly with the coming of Christ; thus there had been

34. John Henry Newman, *Apologia pro Vita Sua* (London: Penguin Books, 1994), 43.
35. Ibid.

a progression up until this central moment in history, but still more time would be necessary so that one could acquire a deep knowledge of the mysteries:

> The process of change had been slow; it had been done not rashly, but by rule and measure, "at sundry times and in divers manners," first one disclosure and then another, till the whole evangelical doctrine was brought into full manifestation. And thus room was made for the anticipation of further and deeper disclosures, of truths still under the veil of the letter, and in their season to be revealed. The visible world still remains without its divine interpretation; Holy Church in her sacraments and her hierarchical appointments, will remain, even to the end of the world, after all but a symbol of those heavenly facts which fill eternity. Her mysteries are but the expressions in human language of truths to which the human mind is unequal.[36]

"The anticipation of further and deeper disclosures of truths still under the veil of the letter": one sees here how the exploration of patristic literature inspired Newman in his thought on the "development of dogma" that he would explain as such in his famous essay of 1845.[37] In 1843, in any case, the work *The Arians of the Fourth Century* was a notable example of this doctrine: this work, indeed, was not just a historical study of the Trinitarian doctrine of the ante-Nicaea Fathers and the response of the Council of Nicaea to Arianism; or more precisely, the patristic inquiry showed that, even if the identity of the Son of God had been revealed by Scripture, it had been diversely interpreted, and that the ecclesial tradition thus had a major role in the formulation of the authentic faith. Afterwards, Newman continued to study the Fathers, first as a member of the Anglican Church, then within the Catholic Church to which he was converted in 1845.

As in the case of Möhler, although in a totally different context, his in-depth reading of patristic literature was thus decisive for his own thinking. Other theologians of the nineteenth century could be named as well, such as Matthias Joseph Scheeben (1835–88), who also had a very good knowledge of the Fathers and whose dogmatic synthesis bears witness to this inspiration. But the two examples present-

36. Ibid., 44 (the words in quotation marks refer to Heb 1:1).

37. Newman, *An Essay on the Development of Christian Doctrine*, 6th ed. (Notre Dame, Ind.: University of Notre Dame, 1989). Newman's attachment to the Fathers is manifested, moreover, in his work *Historical Sketches* (London: Longmans, Green, and Co., 1906–9).

ed here are particularly significant, and one notes, in any case, that theologians of the twentieth century such as de Lubac and Congar often referred to them.

Thus it is that in the Middle Ages and throughout the modern era the reading of the Fathers has as such contributed to the development of theological thought—in the most diverse ways, according to the concerns of each era and each author. Admittedly, as we have said, the study of patristic literature gave rise as well to much work that pursued other goals—in particular, in the second half of the nineteenth century, to philological and historical research that before all else tried to obtain a more accurate knowledge of the early texts (but even this was to be very profitable for theologians themselves). Above all, the exemplary cases of Möhler and Newman must not be a cause for forgetting that the teaching of theology was primarily influenced, in the modern era, by Thomistic or rather "Neothomistic" Scholasticism; it is precisely in this context that, in the first half of the twentieth century, a powerful movement of patristic renewal was going to arise.

CHAPTER 2

The Patristic Renewal from the 1930s to the 1960s

Its Contribution to the Life of the Church

The twentieth century was characterized by a powerful movement of a "return to the Fathers." This movement is associated with some well-known names such as those of Henri de Lubac, Jean Daniélou, and other theologians of the same era; in fact, as we will show in the next chapter, the works of these theologians have been, at least to some extent, shaped by a lively contact with the literature of the Fathers. But the patristic renewal of the twentieth century is a much larger phenomenon that must be placed within the history of theology and ecclesial life in the first half of that century. The aim of this chapter is first to explain what in fact authorizes speaking of a return to the Fathers from the 1930s to the 1960s. We will then show how this "return" took shape in, among other things, the genesis and initial stages of the collection Sources Chrétiennes. We will also show how it was more widely manifested during the 1940s and 1950s before finally specifying the contribution of the patristic renewal to the conciliar work of Vatican II.

"Return to the Fathers": The Meaning of This Expression

Upon closer reflection, the meaning of the expression "return to the Fathers" is not as simple as one might believe at first glance. One could initially object that patristic works indeed already held an important place at the end of the nineteenth and the beginning of the twentieth century. This was confirmed by the publication of texts as well as the birth of several collections.[1] Some historical studies also came into being, benefitting from major scientific approaches (without lacking, moreover, specifically theological presuppositions or options, as one sees in the work of Adolf von Harnack). In any case, patrology could not be isolated from the problems brought on by the modernist crisis; it necessarily tackled the question of the relationship between dogma and the Gospel and other questions that were the subject of important debates at the end of the nineteenth and the beginning of the twentieth century. And it is significant that the journal *Recherches de Science Religieuse*, founded in 1910 by Léonce de Grandmaison, very early on had included some reviews on Christian origins.[2]

Above all, the return to the Fathers of which we are going to speak must not lead to forgetting the publication, prior to the 1930s, of some great works on patristic doctrines. This was the case with the work of Théodore de Régnon: *Études de théologie positive sur la Sainte Trinité*. It is worthwhile to reread some lines from the foreword that opens the first volume (published in 1892): the author confesses that he took his documents from the works of Petau and then clarifies:

> The praise of this illustrious scholar no longer needs to be made. It is said over and over again that he had deeply honored patristic theology. Undoubtedly, Scholasticism greatly took into account the Fathers of the Church, above all to find in them the traditional affirmation of dogmatic truths. Undoubtedly, once again, the Masters of the School, coming after the Fathers, profited from the teachings that the Church continued to propagate in the following ages. Lastly, undoubtedly, Scholasticism took advantage of the Aristotelian instrument.... Under all these connections, the great Scholastic School, guided by Saint Thomas, is the glorious witness to this intellectual vitality that causes the Church to progress from light to light. But, perhaps, these successes themselves have contributed to maintaining the science in a single groove, demarcated by the Latin Doctors of the thirteenth century. Perhaps, the habit of having recourse

1. Thus the collection Textes et documents pour l'étude historique du christianisme [Texts and documents for the historical study of Christianity], directed by Hippolyte Hemmer and Paul Lejay (Paris: Picard).

2. In 1921 Jules Lebreton undertook the regular publication of these reviews on the history of Christian origins.

only to these masters has caused losing sight of the richness and the majesty of patristic teachings.[3]

Another example that can be given is that of Jules Lebreton in his *Histoire du dogme de la Trinité des origines au concile de Nicée.* After an initial volume devoted to the New Testament, the author then tackles the first Fathers who contributed to the deepening of the Trinitarian mystery; here, let us also repeat some lines from the introduction:

In this study of the collective faith of the Church of the second and third century, the believer finds great joy: he recognizes the faith that animates him even today, and he delves into this living, inexhaustible source. And the historian finds in it a great light: the early Fathers, whose writings will be the principal subject of our study, have been initiated into this faith, have recited and taught this symbol, have sung these hymns and said these prayers....

Let us add that the Christian is not isolated in his belief: it is from the Church that he has received it, it is in the name of the Church that he transmits it, and each day, it is in the Church, in communion with his brothers, that he lives this faith....

These considerations must be unceasingly present in the mind of the historian; undoubtedly they are not sufficient to explain everything: this truly miraculous preservation of the Christian faith reveals a cause more divine than the profound effort of the Christian soul or the social life of the Church.[4]

One feels, reading these lines, the fervor of a theologian for whom contact with the Fathers was light for understanding and food for faith. And it is also around these same years that Émile Mersch elaborated his historical theology studies on "the mystical body of Christ"; he wrote in the first volume:

The Fathers are authorities in the Church, authentic witnesses of the faith. In order to be instructed on the dogma as God proposes it, it is necessary to listen closely to them.

Clearly ... we are not claiming to restate all that they said.... Nor are we claiming to retrace, in its historical order, the development of Christian instruction in comparison with this truth.... But we do want before everything else to

3. Théodore de Régnon, *Études de théologie positive sur la Sainte Trinité, Première série, exposé du dogme* [Studies of positive theology on the Holy Trinity, first series, presentation of the dogma] (Paris: Victor Retaux, 1892), vii–viii.

4. Jules Lebreton, *Histoire du dogme de la Trinité des origines au concile de Nicée*, vol. 2, *de saint Clément à saint Irénée* [History of the dogma of the Trinity from the origins to the Council of Nicaea], 3rd ed. (Paris: Beauchesne, 1928), xi–xiii.

gather, close to those that God established as his faithful stewards, the quantity of wheat, the amount always more full.[5]

Thus it is necessary not to be mistaken about the meaning of the expression "return to the Fathers." Those who were its principal architects undervalued neither the quality of some of the works that for several decades the historians of Antiquity had carried out nor, above all, the best fruits of "positive theology" as illustrated by the studies of de Régnon, Lebreton, and Mersch. But this only makes the question more pressing: what authorizes speaking of a "return to the Fathers" in the first half of the twentieth century?

The expression must first be understood as a function of a certain state of theology as it was currently being taught or as it was expressed in some works on Christian dogmas. Faced with this theology that was then dominated by Thomism or rather by Neothomism, an entire generation felt the necessity of returning not only to the text itself of Saint Thomas but also to the more ancient sources of the Christian Tradition and thus first to the writings of the Fathers—who themselves returned to Holy Scripture. This was not a simple matter of method; above all, what was at stake was attaining, by this means, a more accurate and deeper understanding of the Christian mystery. In particular, for a generation strongly influenced by the philosophy of Maurice Blondel, as well as the works of Pierre Rousselot, who had shed new light on the thought of Thomas Aquinas, it appeared essential to recover, by going back prior to neo-scholasticism, a vision of the world and of human destiny that was at the same time more faithful to the main Tradition of the Church and, even more, to respond to the fundamental questions of the modern era. One would thus learn to overcome the dualism between the nature of man (understood as "pure nature" ordered only to "natural" ends) and the supernatural (that came "to be added" to human nature from the outside in order to allow it to reach God). One would rediscover with Irenaeus, Gregory of Nyssa, and Augustine a much more unitive vision of the hu-

5. Émile Mersch, *Le corps mystique du Christ. Études de théologie historique* [The Mystical Body of Christ. Studies of historical theology] (Louvain: Museum Lessianum, 1933), 1:225–26; translated by John R. Kelly as Émile Mersch, *The Whole Christ: The Historical Development of the Doctrine of the Mystical Body in Scripture and Tradition* (London: Dennis Dobson LTD, 1938).

man being, called from the beginning to know God and to love Him. Abandoning the often formal and abstract character of the Neothomistic speculations, one would obtain from the Fathers their attention to history, in its various phases, and to the decisive meaning of what had happened with Christ. One would also recognize, far from modern individualism, the vast dimensions of the Christian mystery and its "catholicity." Such convictions become more and more prominent during the years that followed the First World War, notably in the milieu of the formation of the Society of Jesus at Jersey, Hastings, and Lyon-Fourvière—as one sees by the letters then exchanged between Henri de Lubac, Gaston Fessard, Robert Hamel, Yves de Montcheuil, and others.[6]

The movement of thought that was thus born, in reaction against Neothomism, had two important corollaries. On the one hand, it undermined the rigid division that was often established between the various fields of theology, and it placed into question an unwarranted separation between "positive theology" and "dogmatic theology." This latter point must be particularly emphasized: one was convinced that the study of the Fathers must not only provide information of an historical nature on patristic writings, on their authors and on their various opinions, but that it must also as such make a contribution to the thought of the present time. De Lubac's work *Catholicisme*, the appearance of which in 1938 had a great impact, is from this point of view very characteristic: not only is it not presented as a commentary of theses (in the manner that one found in the manuals of Scholastic theology), but neither is it presented as a history of doctrines relating to "Catholicism." In reality, from one end to the other, its chapters interweave patristic expositions and thoughts on the fundamental questions that are the subject of the book.

On the other hand, the architects of the patristic renewal were persuaded that the "return to the sources" was not only vital for theology but that, to a larger extent, it must also nourish the faith of the Christian people. Thus they were concerned with making the writings of the Fathers better known, which meant that these writings could be much more accessible in modern languages. The work *Catholicisme*

6. See Georges Chantraine, *Henri de Lubac*, vol. 2, *Les années de formation (1919–1929)* [Henri de Lubac, vol. 2, The years of training (1919–1929)] (Paris: Cerf, 2009).

is, here again, very significant: it ends with some excerpts that, for the most part, are taken from patristic works; these pages thus allow the readers to have direct contact with writings of the Fathers and to experience for themselves their spiritual significance. From this perspective, the patristic texts are not simply considered as "subjects" for study (and here one can see the shift that has occurred compared with a purely scientific approach to these texts—an approach that theologians such as de Lubac indeed recognize as very useful but that according to them is not sufficient to nourish the understanding of the faith). No longer are patristic texts reserved for circles of specialists in a position to have access to the sources, rather they are put at the disposal of all those who really wish to make progress toward a more profound knowledge of the Christian Tradition and of finding in it inspiration for their thought as well as for their life.

These are the principal reasons that authorize speaking of a "return to the Fathers" in the first half of the twentieth century.[7] But since the renewal involved the exigency of making the writings of the Fathers better known, it is now worthwhile to focus on the genesis of the enterprise that responded so well to this exigency: the collection Sources Chrétiennes.

The Genesis of the Collection Sources Chrétiennes

The collection Sources Chrétiennes was initiated to publish the writings of the Greek Fathers (even if it were very rapidly going to be expanded to Latin and Eastern authors), and the first volume—the *Vie de Moïse* by Gregory of Nyssa—appeared in 1942. The beginning of this collection was in fact the final culmination of the intensive reflections and discussions that occurred throughout the 1930s. At the instigation of Fr. Victor Fontoynont (prefect of studies at the Scholasticate of Lyon-Fourvière and the enterprise's true initiator), several Jesuits had at-

7. For a more complete presentation on what the patristic renewal represented in this period, see Étienne Fouilloux, in *Une Église en quête de liberté: La pensée catholique française entre modernisme et Vatican II. 1914–1962* [A Church in search of freedom: French Catholic thought between Modernism and Vatican II. 1914–1962] (Paris: Desclée de Brouwer, 1998), 182–87.

tempted to specify the objective, the program, and the practical modalities of the future collection: first and foremost, Henri de Lubac and Jean Daniélou, who were its first directors, but also Claude Mondésert, who at the start would be the secretary of the Sources Chrétiennes before later assuming full responsibility. A passage from Fontoynont, which can be dated from 1937, justified the plan of the collection thus: first, he said, the Greek Fathers provide the example of "remarkable minds wanting to conquer for their faith an entire pagan world"; these Fathers, he added, can henceforth be factors in a "renewal of thought ... and of Christian thought faced with the 'new world.'" Then Fontoynont said that making the Greek Fathers known in the West was a way of contributing to the "union of the Churches." Highlighting the patristic texts was also to permit a "reorganization" of theological disciplines. Moreover, it could contribute to the reform of spiritual life, in the sense of a "piety no longer only moral but nourished by dogmas, by religious truths," for the Fathers unite "in a lively and profound way theology, exegesis, and spirituality." Lastly, the project would help to remedy this lack of spirituality that existed in France.[8]

Judging by this passage from Fontoynont, one clearly sees that the future collection Sources Chrétiennes did not have the sole goal of making patristic texts known in French translation but that, in this very way, it was to contribute to a true renewal. The project was very revealing of the movement of thought that we have described above: the willingness to take a step back from a theology that, up to then, was above all dominated by Neothomist Scholasticism; the concern for recovering, prior to Scholasticism, a direct and fecund contact with the patristic sources, which was to rebound upon the very organization of theological disciplines. The passage from Fontoynont, moreover, highlighted three major areas in which this return to the sources had the opportunity of being fruitful: that of then-current Christian thought, which, by rediscovering the effort of the Fathers of the Church to respond to the questions of their times, could find

8. According to Étienne Fouilloux, *La collection "Sources Chrétiennes." Éditer les Pères de l'Église au XXe siècle* [The Sources Chrétiennes Collection. Publishing the Fathers in the twentieth century] (Paris: Cerf, 1995), 67. (A new revised and enlarged edition was published in 2011). See also our study, Michel Fédou, "Sources Chrétiennes. Patristique et renaissance de la théologie" [Christian Sources. Patristics and the rebirth of theology], *Gregorianum* 92 (2011): 787 ff.

in that effort inspiration for its own renewal faced with the questions of its times; that of ecumenism, which would benefit from a better knowledge of Greek patristics in the West. And lastly, that of spirituality, which in the Fathers, moreover, had not been disassociated from exegesis and theology: it was, of course, a matter not of abandoning dogmatics but of uprooting it from its sterile isolation, of recovering the biblical foundation of Christian doctrine, of nourishing the spiritual life of Christians by giving them greater access to patristic sources.

The stakes of this return to the Fathers was specified some years later by Daniélou in a famous article in the journal *Études*, published in 1946 under the title "Les orientations présentes de la pensée religieuse" [Current directions of religious thought]. In this article, which was to be perceived as a manifesto of the so-called "new theology," the author points out that, since the thirteenth century, a division between exegesis and theology had little by little been instituted and that today it was essential to give again to the Bible "its central function in Christian thought." He then put forward the method of the Fathers of the Church, thanks to which the Old Testament became "a living food for souls." Admittedly, he added, such a rehabilitation "actually comes up against the suspicions of some who uphold scientific exegesis and who, rightly gratified to have won out against a reactionary exegesis and to have restored science to its rightful place in the study of Scripture, fear that this return to the Fathers marks a reversal or a facileness." But he responded that these suspicions were groundless, for it was not a matter of calling into question the results of contemporary exegetical science; it was simply necessary to recover "an interpretation that restores to the Old Testament its prophetic and typological character that is a great part of its interest for us." Daniélou then emphasized the "remarkable renewal of patristic theology," due to the very fact that "the work of the Fathers is in great part a vast commentary on Holy Scripture that, from Hippolytus of Rome to Bernard of Clairvaux, constitutes the proper domain of Christian thought."[9] He assuredly recognized that such a renewal had precedents, such as the collection of patristic texts directed by Hemmer and

9. Jean Daniélou, "Les orientations présentes de la pensée religieuse" [Current directions of religious thought], *Études* 79, no. 249 (1946): 7–10.

Lejay;[10] this did not diminish the difference between the new collection of the Sources Chrétiennes and the preceding collection:

For the latter, it was a question above all of publishing historical documents, witnesses to the faith of the ancients. The new one thinks that there is more to ask of the Fathers. They are not only real witnesses of a state of things past; they are even today's best food for men because we find in them precisely some categories that are those that contemporary thought and Scholastic theology had lost.[11]

And here Daniélou gave two major examples: first, the notion of history that is "foreign to Thomism" whereas it is fundamental to patristics; second, the perspective of a salvation that, in the Greek Fathers, is envisioned less on the individual level than on the collective level.[12]

The return to the Fathers in the 1930s and 1940s was thus, in the spirit of its pioneers, to contribute directly to the renewal of Christian thought. This is, moreover, confirmed, paradoxically, by the intensity of some of the criticisms sparked by this movement. Thus, Marie-Michel Labourdette responds in the *Revue thomiste* to the article of Daniélou: all the while praising numerous qualities of the collection Sources Chrétiennes, he questions the spirit that underlies this collection and denounces it as an attempt to subvert Scholasticism. Daniélou responds to the attacks, but, above all, it is de Lubac who affirms that the return to the Fathers is not being made to the detriment of Saint Thomas.[13]

As one knows, the controversy was going to become venomous toward the end of the 1940s. However, it would focus more on the doctrinal questions linked to de Lubac's book *Surnaturel*. Admittedly, the adversaries of the "new theology" would still suspect it of wanting, under the pretext of a "return to the Fathers," to free itself unduly from Thomism, or even from Saint Thomas himself. As to the collection it-

10. Cf. note 1 above.

11. Daniélou, "Les orientations présentes," 10.

12. Ibid., 10–11.

13. See the anonymous "La théologie et ses sources. Réponse" that was published in *Recherches de Science Religieuse* (1946): 385–401 (de Lubac was, according to Fouilloux, "the principal writer": see *La collection "Sources Chrétiennes,"* 121); see also Henri de Lubac, *Mémoire sur l'occasion de mes écrits*, 2nd ed. (Namur: Culture et vérité, 1989), 271; repr. *Œuvres complètes du Cardinal de Lubac*, vol. 33 (Paris: Cerf, 2006), 271; translated by Anne Elizabeth Englund as *At the Service of the Church: Henri de Lubac Reflects on the Circumstances that Occasioned His Writings* (San Francisco: Ignatius Press, 1993).

self, the fact remains that it was largely successful—all the more so since Mondésert, who beginning in 1951 had become the principal responsible for this collection, actively worked for "disseminating to the public at large a very reassuring image of the Sources Chrétiennes."[14] In any case, on January 6, 1952, *L'Osservatore romano* published a review favorable to the collection; and on March 4 of the same year, Mondésert wrote in the newspaper *La Croix*: "Thus the days really seem to be over in which one believed it necessary to be suspicious of an enterprise that, while totally submitting to legitimate scientific requirements, never hid its intention of fidelity to the Church, its dogmas, its tradition, and its magisterium."[15] From then on, the difficulty was of a completely different nature: it was a matter of escaping the financial bankruptcy that threatened the collection and against which Mondésert was, moreover, going to work energetically in the following years.[16] The enterprise of Sources Chrétiennes was, in any case, recognized, and all the more so, because, as one will soon clarify, it benefitted from a "scientific shift" that allowed it to find a greater audience in the academic world.[17] Along with other collections such as that of the Bibliothèque augustinienne (inaugurated in 1933) and the publications of theologians such as de Lubac and Daniélou, it contributed for its part to the dissemination of patristic literature, its fecundity for Christian thought and for the life of the Church being increasingly recognized.

From the 1950s to Vatican Council II

It is not possible to mention all the fruits of the patristic renewal around the middle of the twentieth century and in the years that immediately preceded Vatican Council II. Rather than making an inventory of them that would unavoidably be incomplete, it is, above all, important to convey accurately some phenomena that characterize this period.

14. Fouilloux, *La collection "Sources Chrétiennes,"* 167.

15. Cited in ibid., 169.

16. See ibid., 171–82.

17. This "shift," in addition to the financial advantages that were linked to it, was also a means of escaping from the doctrinal suspicions that were mentioned above; on this point, see ibid., 182.

Let us first recall the impact of some discoveries from the period following the Second World War: on one hand, those of Qumran and Nag Hammadi, which led to considering in a new way later Judaism as well as Gnostic writings (and thus also, indirectly, the patristic texts of the second and third centuries); on the other, the discoveries of new writings emanating from the Fathers themselves in fragmentary form, such as the treatise of Origen on Easter, the excerpts from his *Commentary on the Epistle to the Romans*, or even the works of Didymus the Blind. All these discoveries were important, first of all, for research, but some of them had much larger repercussions (in particular the discovery of the Dead Sea manuscripts, for which there was a feeling that it could enrich our knowledge of Judaism and, up to a point, Christian origins).

The second phenomenon to point out is that patristic studies, which in a country such as France was most often conducted by clerics or in the context of ecclesiastical institutions, were established in the academic world itself. We have already referred to the collection Sources Chrétiennes: even though its primary goal was to put the works of the Fathers within the reach of an educated public, it attempted more and more, under the impetus of Mondésert, to honor a second objective that was to serve the "scientific" research of historians, exegetes, philosophers and theologians. Indeed, the contribution of academics became more important, the criteria of scientizing was more clearly specified (as for the establishment of critical apparatus and indices), and the reviews of some volumes show that this evolution of the collection was completely perceived and appreciated by specialists in early Christianity.[18] It is important to emphasize on this subject, in the specific context of France, the major influence of Henri-Irénée Marrou: this academic (well-known for, among others, his work *Saint Augustin et la fin de la culture antique* [Saint Augustine and the end of ancient culture] as well as for his edition of *À Diognète* in Sources Chrétiennes) is the one who introduced the teaching of patristics at the Sorbonne and who launched the collection Patristica sorbonensia. With him, the study of the Fathers became a recognized discipline among other academic disciplines, and this recognition was

18. See ibid., 182–89.

in his eyes essential for the correct understanding of the relationship between Christianity and culture.[19]

Another phenomenon characterized this period: the growing internationalization of patristic studies. Our previous expositions have certainly placed the emphasis on the essential contribution of French historians and theologians, but the renewal was perceptible as well in countries other than France—such as Germany, with Hugo Rahner, and also with his brother Karl (as one will see in the next chapter), or even with Aloys Grillmeier (who, at the beginning of the 1950s, edited volumes that were to mark the fifteen hundredth anniversary of the Council of Chalcedon). Other countries could be mentioned as well: Switzerland, Italy, Spain, England, the United States, Canada, etc.[20] The fact that patrologists of various countries were able to meet more frequently thanks to university colloquies, in particular those that, beginning in 1951, met every four years at Oxford,[21] is further evidence of this internationalization.

It is necessary to emphasize above all that, well beyond universities, the patristic renewal influenced a number of Christians in the 1950s and, in this way, contributed to preparing the *aggiornamento* of Vatican II. Admittedly, one still did not see many fruits in the life of the Church (even if occasionally some important research was done, for example in the context of the liturgical movement at the Abbey of Maria Laach). The fact remains that the publications of texts, as well as the works of de Lubac, Daniélou, Congar, Bouyer, and others, found a public audience much larger than that of only historians and theologians. One must also emphasize the role of men such as Francois Varillon and Pierre Ganne: without being patrologists by trade, they were influenced by the rediscovery of "Christian sources" and thus allowed their listeners to benefit from it thanks to the numerous conferences, sermons, and retreats (in particular, for Varillon, in the con-

19. On this point, see Marie-Josèphe Rondeau, "Jean Daniélou, Henri-Irénée Marrou et le renouveau des études patristiques" [Jean Daniélou, Henri-Irénée Marrou and the renewal of patristic Studies], in *Les Pères de l'Église au XXe siècle: Histoire–Littérature–Théologie,* "L'aventure des Sources chrétiennes" [The Fathers of the Church in the twentieth century: History–literature–theology. "The adventure of the Sources Chrétiennes"] (Paris: Cerf, 1997), 351–78 (more particularly, 361 ff.).

20. Think, for example, of Hans Urs von Balthasar, George Leonard Prestige, Johannes Quasten, Henry Chadwick, and Antonio Orbe; many other names also could have been cited.

21. See Rondeau, "Jean Daniélou, Henri-Irénée Marrou," 352–53.

text of his talks to the Association Catholique de la Jeunesse Française [ACJF]). In various ways, the public was little by little becoming aware of the patristic renewal. It was not only considered important for the internal life of the Church, it also favored ecumenical discussions between Christians of various confessions. Moreover, it helped to recover the meaning of the mission, or to understand it more correctly. This is witnessed to by the discussions of the Circle of Saint John the Baptist (under the inspiration of Daniélou), and especially in the itinerary of some Christians who were intent upon implementing, in other countries, the best ideas to which the Fathers testify—such as Jules Monchanin, who went to India to found an *ashram* and thus to establish a significant presence of Christianity in this land, just like the Fathers had formerly done among the "Nations" of their times.[22] Let us add that interest in the Fathers also had success, more broadly, in the world of "culture," in particular in literature. Thus Paul Claudel admired patristic exegesis for the richness of its Christian symbolism. The importance of the patristic renewal was even perceived outside of Christianity, as shown by the testimony of the historian of religions Mircea Eliade, who was grateful to theologians such as de Lubac and Daniélou for having drawn attention to the importance of "images" and "symbols" in primitive Christianity.

Therefore, even if it is true that nothing could have predicted the convocation of Vatican Council II by Pope John XXIII, and whatever were the eventful moments of this council (because, in the first place, the project of an *aggiornamento* was in serious jeopardy), one understands that, in the end, it had truly benefited from the "return to the sources" previously mentioned. It is, of course, due to the influence of theologians such as Congar, Daniélou, and de Lubac, who so deeply appreciated the heritage of the Fathers. But it really is more widely due to the fact that, through the publications of these theologians as well as through the other expressions of the patristic renewal in the preceding years, many had become aware of the fecundity of this renewal and that some of its fruits were already perceptible in the very life of the Church.

22. See Henri de Lubac, *Images de l'abbé Monchanin* [Images of Father Monchanin] (Paris: Aubier-Montaigne, 1967).

The Influence of the Patristic Renewal on Vatican Council II

The influence of the Fathers on Vatican Council II is firstly manifested by some citations and references in the documents themselves. The name of Augustine is, by far, the most frequently mentioned; after him come the names of Ignatius of Antioch, Irenaeus, Tertullian, Origen, Cyprian, Ambrose, Jerome, and John Chrysostom; some other authors are mentioned as well, but more rarely (such as Clement of Rome, Justin, Hippolytus, Athanasius, Eusebius of Caesarea, Hilary, Basil, Gregory of Nazianzus, Cyril of Jerusalem, Leo the Great, John Damascene), or even once (thus Clement of Alexandria, Didymus, Epiphanes, and Gregory of Nyssa).[23] However, these references do not suffice to indicate, as is necessary, what was the real influence of patristic literature on Vatican II. To appreciate this better, it is important rather to note what the council itself has written on the subject of the Fathers, and, especially, to discuss some themes through which their legacy is manifested in a special way (and in some cases, without referring to ancient authors).

On the first point, it is the constitution *Dei Verbum* that must serve as a point of departure to the inquiry. This constitution indeed lays out the context in which the reference to the Fathers of the Church takes its true meaning; it is made more precise in its chapter 2, devoted to "Handing on Divine Revelation"; there is clarified the correct articulation between Scripture and Tradition, which, "flowing from the same divine well-spring, both of them merge, in a sense, and move toward the same goal."[24] In fact, the constitution explains that "the apostolic preaching, which is expressed in a special way in the inspired books, was to be preserved in a continuous line of succession until the end of time"; and, it adds, "the sayings of the Church Fathers are a witness to the life-giving presence of this tradition, showing how its riches are poured out in the practice and life of the believing and praying Church."[25] These affirmations are subsequently echoed in the

23. Of course, our list is not exhaustive; one can refer to the section "Pères, docteurs, théologiens" in the index of sources published in *Vatican II. L'intégrale*, rev. bilingual ed. (Paris: Bayard, 2002), 820–21.

24. Vatican Council II, *Dei Verbum*, November 18, 1965, no. 9.

25. Ibid., no. 8.

recommendations in chapter 6 on "Sacred Scripture in the Life of the Church." After having emphasized the importance of Scripture for the Church, the council adds these words: "Taught by the Holy Spirit, the spouse of the incarnate Word, which is the Church, strives to reach an increasingly more profound understanding of the Sacred Scriptures, in order to nourish its children with God's words. For this reason also it duly encourages the study of the Fathers, both Eastern and Western, and of the sacred liturgies."[26] There is thus a close connection between the study of the Fathers and the deep understanding of Holy Scripture, and one understands why *Dei Verbum* has been led by its very subject to emphasize this important point.

Elsewhere, the council mentions other aspects and advantages of referring to the Fathers in the life of the Church, according to whatever is the primary concern of the particular document. Thus, the Constitution on the Sacred Liturgy asks that in the future "there is to be a better selection of readings from the works of the Fathers, Doctors, and ecclesiastical writers."[27] In the Decree on the Ministry and Life of Priests, it is said that the science of sacred ministry, drawn first from the reading of and the meditating on Scripture, "is also fruitfully nourished by the study of the Fathers and Doctors of the Church and other traditional classics."[28] The Decree on Priestly Training declares that one will show seminarians "what the Fathers of the Church (both East and West) have contributed to the faithful transmission and explanation of the revealed truths."[29] Lastly, the Decree on Ecumenism recalls in these words the richness of the spiritual traditions of the Christian East:

> From the glorious times of the holy Fathers, that monastic spirituality flourished in the East which later flowed over into the Western world, and there provided a source from which Latin monastic life took its rise and has often drawn fresh vigor ever since. Therefore, it is earnestly recommended that Catholics avail themselves more often of the spiritual riches of the Eastern Fathers which lift up all that is human to the contemplation of divine mysteries.[30]

26. Ibid., no. 23.
27. Vatican Council II, *Sacrosanctum concilium*, December 4, 1963, no. 92.
28. Vatican Council II, *Presbyterorum ordinis*, December 7, 1965, no. 19.
29. Vatican Council II, *Optatam totius*, October 28, 1965, no. 16.
30. Vatican Council II, *Unitatis redintegratio*, November 21, 1964, no. 15.

The decree adds that since the beginnings the Churches of the East have followed "their own disciplines, sanctioned by the holy Fathers, by synods, and even by ecumenical councils," and such a diversity is not at all an obstacle to the unity of the Church;[31] this is valid as well, it says, for the "authentic theological traditions" that are nourished by "the living tradition of the apostles and by the works of the Fathers and spiritual writers of the East," thus being directed toward "a right ordering of life, indeed, toward a full contemplation of Christian truth."[32]

Knowledge of Holy Scripture, liturgy, spirituality, ecumenism: these were, let us recall, several of the major issues of the patristic renewal during the 1930s and 1940s; and, in a significant way, these are the same issues that appear throughout the conciliar texts here noted. A final point remains to be mentioned and, undoubtedly, the most important. Even independent of references to this or that ancient author or to texts that explicitly rely upon the Fathers of the Church and that exhort referring to them, the influence of patristics is, above all, manifested, in depth, in the very theology of Vatican Council II.

De Lubac has shown this in a very clear way regarding the constitution *Lumen gentium*. If it is true, he writes, that the doctrine of this constitution deeply changes the positions maintained by the dominant theology of the modern era, it is in fact "to allow us to recover or to uphold with more assurance the positions authentically based in tradition."[33] Four themes allow a more precise verification of this assertion. First, *Lumen gentium* speaks of the Church as "mystery," presents it as being at the same time visible and invisible, and points out its subordination in relation to Christ "the light of the nations." Second, *Lumen gentium* chose to highlight the notion of "the people of God." Third, the constitution really grants a place to the "eschatological perspective"; more precisely, whereas the Church had little by little centered eschatology on the fate of the deceased, the council

31. Ibid., no. 16.

32. Ibid., no. 17.

33. Henri de Lubac, "La constitution 'Lumen gentium' et les Pères de l'Église" [The constitution "Lumen gentium" and the Fathers of the Church], in *Paradoxe et mystère de l'Église* (Paris: Aubier-Montaigne, 1967), 60; repr. *Œuvres complètes du Cardinal de Lubac*, vol. 9 (Paris: Cerf, 2010), 59–119; translated by James R. Dunne as Henri de Lubac, *The Church: Paradox and Mystery* (Shannon, Ireland: Ecclesia Press, 1969).

moved to the foreground "a more collective and dynamic concept of the Church" by recalling its march toward human unity in Christ as well as the fulfillment of the universe in God. Last, it is in the constitution *Lumen gentium* that the passage on the Virgin Mary is included; it presented her as the figure of the Church and pointed out her spiritual maternity, not without emphasizing that Mary is herself entirely subordinate to Christ, the sole Mediator and Savior. Admittedly, de Lubac does not hold that, for all this, the text of *Lumen gentium* is reflecting patristic thought on all points. He recalls in particular that, when the Fathers spoke of the Church as the people of God, they were often doing so in reference to the people of the Old Testament, by emphasizing at the same time its value as "prefiguration" and the transformation that had taken place with the newness of the Church; and yet this constitution hardly dwells on this latter doctrine, and "in this passage from one testament to the other, from one people to another, it actually seems to suggest continuity rather than transformation."[34] Nevertheless, the four themes raised by de Lubac attest to the influence, in varying degrees, of the patristic renewal on the ecclesiological doctrine of Vatican II.

Other major themes of the council themselves also testify to this influence. This is verified, above all, within the constitution *Dei Verbum*: this constitution does not only mention, as we have seen, the importance of the Fathers in the life of the Church, it is directly inspired by them in its way of understanding the relationship between Scripture and Tradition, or even in its exposition on inspiration and the interpretation of holy books (it especially records, on these questions, the contributions of Irenaeus and Augustine). The patristic influence is manifested as well in the constitution *Sacrosanctum concilium*. It reminds us, for example, that liturgical actions are not private actions but celebrations of the Church, which is, in the words of Cyprian, "the sacrament of unity;"[35] it repeats the teaching of Augustine on the presence of Christ in the "sacraments": "when anybody baptizes it is really Christ himself who baptizes;"[36] it emphasizes the active participation of the faithful at the Eucharist in such a way that they might be led,

34. Ibid., 80.

35. Vatican Council II, *Sacrosanctum concilium*, no. 26.

36. Ibid., no. 7.

as once again said by Augustine, to the perfection of unity with God and each other.[37] In a more general way, the very importance that the council gives to liturgical and sacramental life (as well as to the catechesis that prepares for it) is like a fruit of the patristic renewal that, in the prior decades, allowed a better understanding of this essential dimension of Christian existence. As for the constitution *Gaudium et spes*, it highlights the vocation of the human being created "in the image of God"—an essential theme of patristic literature—it cites the famous opening of the *Confessions* of Saint Augustine: "Thou hast made us for Thee, and our heart is unquiet till it finds its rest in Thee;"[38] as was done by Irenaeus and many other Fathers, it repeats in its turn the Pauline doctrine of Christ who, as the "new Adam," fully manifests man to himself and reveals to him the ultimate meaning of his very high calling.[39]

Other themes could also be mentioned; thus, in the decree *Ad gentes*, the idea according to which the missionary activity of the Church is based on the very design of God—for God wants the whole human race to form "one People of God," constitute "one Body of Christ" and be built up into "one Temple of the Holy Spirit"—a long footnote recalls precisely that this vision was formerly that of Irenaeus, Hippolytus, Origen, Augustine, and Cyril of Alexandria.[40] It is above all important to draw attention to two themes that (although rejected since then by fundamentalist movements) benefit from the support found in the tradition of the Fathers. First of all, that of religious liberty. Not that the council disregards the intolerance of which Christianity has shown itself to be capable "through the vicissitudes of human history": there have been "patterns of behavior that were not in keeping with the spirit of the Gospel and were even opposed to it."[41] Nevertheless, the declaration *Dignitatis humanae* affirms with clarity: "One of the key truths in Catholic teaching, a truth that is contained in the word of God and is constantly preached by the Fathers, is that human

37. Ibid., no. 48.

38. Augustine, *Confessions*, I, 1, trans. Vernon J. Bourke, The Fathers of the Church 21 (Washington, D.C.: The Catholic University of America Press, 1953), 4; cf. Vatican Council II, *Gaudium et spes*, December 7, 1965, no. 21.

39. Cf. Vatican Council II, *Gaudium et spes*, no. 22.

40. Cf. Vatican Council II, *Ad gentes*, December 7, 1965, no. 7, and note 45.

41. Vatican Council II, *Dignitatis humanae*, December 7, 1965, no. 12.

beings should respond to the word of God freely"; and several patristic references are used in notes to support this affirmation, the consequence of which is that "in religious matters every form of human coercion should be excluded."[42]

The other theme is that of values present even outside of the Church, of those who "without any fault of theirs, have not yet arrived at an explicit knowledge of God, and who, not without grace, strive to lead a good life."[43] *Lumen gentium* refers to these persons by using the famous statement of Eusebius of Caesarea: "Whatever of good or truth is found amongst them is considered by the Church to be a preparation for the Gospel and given by him who enlightens all men and women that they may at length have life."[44] The same view is developed in the Declaration on the Relation of the Church to Non-Christian Religions: "The Catholic Church rejects nothing of what is true and holy in these religions. It has a high regard for the manner of life and conduct, the precepts and doctrines which, although differing in many ways from its own teaching, nevertheless often reflect a ray of that truth which enlightens all men and women."[45] Moreover, the council explicitly repeats the theme of the "seeds of the Word" or the "seeds of the Truth" that had formerly been introduced by the apologist Justin. Thus in *Ad gentes*: those who are to bear witness to Christ should be familiar with the national and religious traditions of the groups of people in which they will live and "uncover with gladness and respect those seeds of the word which lie hidden among them;"[46] and the same document writes a little later that the Holy Spirit "calls all women and men to Christ ... by the seed of the word and the preaching of the gospel."[47] The Church, of course, has the mission of announcing this Gospel and of working for the transformation of those who have the need of being converted; nevertheless, as *Lumen gentium* says, "The effect of its activity is that whatever good is found sown in people's hearts and minds, or in the rites and customs of peoples, is not only saved from destruction, but is purified, raised

42. Ibid., no. 10, and note 8.

43. Vatican Council II, *Lumen gentium*, November 21, 1964, no. 16.

44. Ibid.

45. Vatican Council II, *Nostra aetate*, October 28, 1965, no. 2.

46. Vatican Council II *Ad gentes*, no. 11.

47. Ibid., no. 15.

up, and perfected for the glory of God, the confusion of the devil, and the happiness of humanity."[48]

Our review is clearly not exhaustive, and it would be possible to show, on other points, the influence of the patristic renewal on Vatican Council II. Admittedly, one also finds in the conciliar texts numerous references to Thomas Aquinas, to the Council of Trent, as well as to some encyclicals from the modern era. Furthermore, Vatican Council II relies upon the Fathers in a necessarily partial way, as a function of its primary concerns and the themes that it intends to develop in its various documents. Nevertheless, it reveals, in an exemplary way, the ecclesial fecundity of the patristic renewal that so deeply characterized the preceding decades. In this same way, can it not be hoped that, even tomorrow, the reading of the Fathers will, for its part, be able to contribute to necessary renewals in the life of the Church?

48. Vatican Council II, *Lumen gentium*, no. 17.

CHAPTER 3

The Patristic Renewal from the 1930s to the 1960s

Its Fecundity for Christian Theology

We have attempted, in the preceding chapter, to present the principal characteristics of the patristic renewal of the twentieth century before emphasizing its rich fecundity for the life of the Church at the time of Vatican II. With this background, it is now possible to show how, beginning in the 1930s, the return to the Fathers influenced the specific work of some theologians. From this point of view, the writings of Orthodox Christians (such as Georges Florovsky or Vladimir Lossky)[1] or Protestants (such as Marc Lods),[2] among others, could be examined. However, we will limit ourselves to Catholic authors who, by their study of the Fathers, made exceptional contributions to Christian thinking in the decades that preceded Vatican Council II, and who themselves produced, before this council and in the succeeding years, major theological works.

We will first of all choose to focus on three French theologians,

1. During the first conference of Orthodox theology that was held in Athens in 1936, Georges Florovsky announced the necessity of "returning to the Fathers," and his appeal received a significant response in the following decades; for a presentation on this patristic revival in Orthodoxy, see Pantelis Kalaïtzidis, "Du 'Retour aux Pères' à la nécessité d'une théologie orthodoxe moderne" [From "return to Fathers" to the need for a modern Orthodox theology], *Istina* 56 (2011): 227–51. Vladimir Lossky was, with Georges Florovsky, the great theologian of the "neo-patristic" movement; see especially his book *Essai sur la théologie mystique de l'Église d'Orient* (Paris: Aubier-Montaigne, 1944; new ed., Paris: Cerf, 2005); translated by members of the Fellowship of St. Alban and St. Sergius as *The Mystical Theology of the Eastern Church* (Cambridge: James Clarke, 1973; Crestwood, N.Y.: SVS Press, 1997).

2. See Marc Lods, *Protestantisme et tradition de l'Église* [Protestantism and Church tradition], ed. J.-N. Pérès and J.-D. Dubois (Paris: Cerf, 1988).

whose writings quite especially illustrate the contribution of patristics to the theology of the twentieth century: Henri de Lubac, Jean Daniélou, and Yves Congar. We will then mention two German-speaking theologians: Karl Rahner and Hans Urs von Balthasar. Other choices assuredly could have been made, as our references in the preceding chapter to Yves de Montcheuil, Hugo Rahner, Aloys Grillmeier, Louis Bouyer, and Henri-Irénée Marrou suggest. But our purpose is not to be completely exhaustive; rather it is to make known, through some major examples, how the in-depth reading of the Fathers during these decades was a source of profound inspiration for Christian theology.

Henri de Lubac and "Our Fathers in the Faith"

If it is natural to begin with Henri de Lubac (1896–1991), it is not because other theologians had not already produced, sometime before him, works profoundly influenced by the thinking of the Fathers (such as Théodore de Régnon and Jules Lebreton on Trinitarian theology or Émile Mersch on the doctrine of the mystical body).[3] It is because his first work, *Catholicisme. Les aspects sociaux du dogme*, published in 1938, incontestably marks a decisive date in the theology of the twentieth century. And this is not only by virtue of his fundamental thesis (of the "social," that is to say, universal or, more precisely, "catholic," dimension of Christianity, at the same time as this religion's profoundly "historical" dimension) but also by virtue of his very method and, in particular, by the way in which he refers to the Fathers of the Church. The theologian explains himself in the book's introduction:

> This is not intended as a technical work. If the quotations are numerous—even at the risk of tiring the reader—it is because I wanted to present the subject as impersonally as possible, drawing especially on the treasures, so little utilized, in the patristic writings. This is not to overlook in a frenzy of archaism the precisions and developments in theology which have been made since their time, nor do I take over in their entirety all the ideas they offer us: I seek only to understand them, and listen to what they have to tell us, since they are our Fathers in the faith and since they received from their Church of their time the means to nourish the Church of our times as well.[4]

3. See chap. 2, pp. 31–32.

4. Henri de Lubac, *Catholicism. A Study of Dogma in Relation to the Corporate Destiny of Mankind* (London: Burns, Oates & Washbourne, 1949), xiii.

The entire book is in fact nourished by the thinking of the Fathers, from whom the author makes scores of citations in the body of the text as well as in the notes. He even concludes, as said above, with the translation of some excerpts: at a time when French translations were not very numerous, de Lubac perceived the exigency of making some quite remarkable pages of ancient authors directly known. The book is, in any case, a witness to a new method in theology. The exposition does not consist in commenting on theses of Thomas Aquinas (or even, as was commonly done, on theses taken from modern commentators on Saint Thomas); it is nourished rather from the Christian tradition in its entirety—without excluding, of course, the contribution of Saint Thomas, but by going back prior to him to the testimony of the Fathers and, with them, to the Bible itself. The patristic texts are not "utilized" as a mere reservoir of citations that come to the support of affirmations previously attained, but they serve as texts/sources, with the capacity to enlighten and nourish the understanding of the faith. The theologian's writing, in its own way, illustrates this new status that is recognized in the Fathers. His text not only cites entire sentences from the Fathers, but often he inserts into the interior of his own sentences short expressions that are borrowed from them as well. Such an intertwining—or such a "weave"—demonstrates how the thought of de Lubac takes shape from the tradition that inspires him. Admittedly, as he said in the text cited above, it is not a matter of forgetting the new developments made since the era of the Fathers, and one could not take up all their ideas; the fact remains that the patristic texts have value as sources "since they are our Fathers in the faith, and since they received from their Church of their time the means to nourish the Church of our times as well."

And yet it is not only *Catholicisme* that is influenced by the tradition of the Fathers: many other works of de Lubac bear witness to this same inspiration, and this in the most diverse domains. First of all, it is necessary to mention, with a special emphasis, the book *Histoire et Esprit. L'intelligence de l'Écriture d'après Origène*,[5] not only because this

5. Henri de Lubac, *Histoire et Esprit. L'intelligence de l'Écriture d'après Origène* (Paris: Aubier-Montaigne, 1950); re-published in the *Œuvres complètes du Cardinal de Lubac*, vol. 16 (Paris: Cerf, 2002); translated by Anne Englund Nash as *History and Spirit: The Understanding of Scripture according to Origen* (San Francisco: Ignatius Press, 2007).

book is directly devoted to a Father of the Church but also because the study of this Father (prepared for by several previous publications) leads to a fundamental reflection on the actual significance of patristic exegesis. All the while recognizing the necessary contributions of critical exegesis, the theologian emphasizes the permanent value of "the spiritual understanding" to which the Fathers wanted to introduce believers. This "spiritual understanding" leads to discovering in the texts of the Old Testament the "types" of what is revealed in the New Testament, and this is precisely possible only through conversion to Christ who, fulfilling the ancient Scriptures, opened to us access to their profound meaning. From there, de Lubac explores the lengthy posterity of the Origenian doctrine on the meaning of Scripture during the subsequent patristic era and throughout the Middle Ages: the four volumes of *Exégèse mediévale*,[6] impressive in its historic erudition, are at the same time a major contribution to thought on the exegesis of the Bible, on its "spiritual understanding" and on the relationship between the two Testaments.

Another area of thought attests to the influence of the Fathers on de Lubac—and it is by no means the least, for it was regarding this that the theologian faced severe accusations to the point of his being, in 1950, prohibited from teaching—it is a matter of questions relating to the "supernatural." In the work published under this title in 1946, de Lubac criticized the Neothomistic movements that envisioned a so-called "pure nature" (created only for a "natural" end) and the gift of divine grace, considered as a later gift, in some way "added to" creation. Against this position, he argued that nature, having itself been created, had for its vocation to know God and to love Him—and, moreover, contrary to what one would reproach him for, that the gratuitousness of the supernatural gift must not be undermined, for in no way was it by some necessity that the "natural desire for God" dwelled within man, but it was because God had freely put such a desire in him. Yet this thesis was fundamentally in line with Saint Augustine and his thought on the relationship of man to God (going back prior to the derivatives which Augustinianism had produced over time, and notably in the modern era with Jansenius). De Lubac would later

6. De Lubac, *Exégèse médiévale*.

restate it in his work *Le mystère du Surnaturel*: the work of Saint Augustine brings to us "one of the most profound expressions"[7] of the relationship between man and God, a relationship completely "paradoxical" since man was created by God, and, as a created being, he is from the beginning filled with the "natural desire for God." It is significant that the preface of *Le mystère du Surnatural* closes with the first words of the *Confessions*, *"Fecisti nos ad Te, Deus"*[8] and that the theologian had published that same year another book titled *Augustinisme et théologie moderne*.

The patristic inspiration is equally manifest in a third series of writings that, in the spirit of *Catholicisme*, is principally devoted to ecclesiological and sacramental questions. Admittedly, the book *Corpus mysticum* treats, as the subtitle says, "the Eucharist and the Church in the Middle Ages"; but the author highlights what, in the most profound expositions of the medieval era, arises from the main Tradition on the "body of Christ" as it was expressed at the time of the Fathers. As for the book *Méditation sur l'Église*,[9] it is from one end to the other steeped in patristic references—whether it be to present the reunion of humanity in one body of believers coming from Israel and the nations, to reflect upon the relationship between the ecclesial institution and the mystery to which it has a vocation to refer, to deepen the link between the sacraments and the Church, or to deal with even more subjects. In this book there appears, among others, a beautiful exposition on the paradox according to which the Fathers of the Church, so far from us because of the cultural distance, become no less "our contemporaries":

> How far they are from us, for example, in spite of some cultural elements that have been transmitted from them to us, these Alexandrians of the third century, or these Africans from the fifth! From us to them, what disorientation! ... But over the course of a page, a Name jumps out. Such a light, it dissipates the

7. De Lubac, *Le Mystère du Surnaturel* (Paris: Aubier-Montaigne, 1965), 38; repr. *Œuvres complètes du Cardinal Henri de Lubac*, vol. 12 (Paris: Cerf, 2000), 38; translated by Rosemary Sheed as *The Mystery of the Supernatural* (London: G. Chapmans, 1967).

8. De Lubac, *Le Mystère du Surnaturel*, 17. For Henri de Lubac, moreover, such a perspective was also very much that of the Greek Fathers.

9. Henri de Lubac, *Méditation sur l'Église*, 3rd rev. ed. (Paris: Aubier-Montaigne, 1954); repr. *Œuvres complètes du Cardinal Henri de Lubac*, vol. 8 (Paris: Cerf, 2003); translated by Michael Mason as *The Splendor of the Church* (London: Sheed and Ward, 1956), 32–33.

surrounding mist. Thousands of details are ordered around him, are hierarchized to him. Soon everything draws on his clarity. Everything takes on life. It is no longer only the historian in us who understands and is moved. Nuances of emotions become perceptible, at the highest degrees their delicacy, that cover ours perfectly. In their love of Jesus, an Origen, an Augustine are truly our contemporaries. They are our fathers. They are our brothers.[10]

A last example illustrates the influence of the Fathers on the work of de Lubac: that of his thought on the relationship of Christianity with other religions. Concerning Judaism, it is necessary, above all, to keep in mind the way in which the theologian knew how to argue for, in the very name of patristic thinking on the relationship of the two Testaments, an attitude of esteem and respect vis-à-vis Israel (and this during the same years when Nazi anti-Semitism raged).[11] But it is above all to Buddhism that de Lubac devoted important works; and it is characteristic that some of his studies propose comparisons between this or that Buddhist doctrine and doctrines developed by the Fathers (regarding "charity," the "cosmic tree" and "various appearances of Christ and the Buddha").[12] It is true that in each case these comparisons above all bring to light the profound differences between the two religions, whatever might be some apparent rapprochements. However, this lucidity of the theologian on doctrinal differences does not prevent him from admitting that there might exist—not only in Buddhism but in every religion, or more precisely in every human

10. De Lubac, *Méditation sur l'Église*, 45. Let us also recall that, several years after Vatican Council II, de Lubac was to publish a book titled *Paradoxe et mystère de l'Église* and that a chapter of this book was "The Constitution 'Lumen gentium' and the Fathers of the Church" (59–119); it would show the agreement of this constitution with the main patristic thought (see chap. 2, pp. 45–46).

11. See de Lubac, "Le fondement théologique des missions" (1941) [The Theological Foundation of Missions], reprinted in *Théologie dans l'histoire*, vol. 2, *Questions disputées et résistance au nazisme* (Paris: Desclée de Brouwer, 1990), 159–219, esp. 199 ff.; Translated by Ann Englund Nash as *Theology in History* (San Francisco: Ignatius Press, 1996). Here, one could admittedly recall that, from another point of view, patristic literature has transmitted to us at times some kinds of violent anti-Judaism, as one sees in the homilies *Against the Jews* of John Chrysostom. On the assessment of such anti-Judaism, see below chap. 13, pp. 318–19. In any case, it would be anachronistic to reproach de Lubac for barely tackling this aspect, for it is only in recent decades that we have become more attentive to the violence of some writings *"adversus Judaeos."*

12. See de Lubac, *Aspects du bouddhisme* (Paris: Seuil, 1951); repr. *Œuvres complètes du Cardinal de Lubac*, vol. 21 (Paris: Cerf, 2012), 13–164; translated by George Lamb as *Aspects of Buddhism* (London: Sheed and Ward, 1953).

being that had not had contact with Christian Revelation—"seeds of the truth" that express in their own way the universal desire for God and that, once disengaged from the errors that accompany them, such "seeds" merit being recognized by the Church and contribute to the richness of its "catholicity." Yet this is a theme that the Fathers had developed, just like the theme of "evangelical preparation," or even the idea according to which the men of the nations had in some way been able "to prophesy," even if in a very partial or even veiled way, some mysteries of Christian Revelation. Moreover, de Lubac expounded the entirety of his views on the subject in a study titled "Les religions humaines d'après les Pères."[13]

Independent of the four fields presented here, it would be necessary to add that, in other works bearing upon the most diverse questions (such as *Le drame de l'humanisme athée, Pic de la Mirandole, La pensée religieuse du Père Teilhard de Chardin*, etc.), de Lubac here and there appeals to patristic references—sometimes in order to show the foundation of this or that idea in the main Tradition of the Church, sometimes in order to correct or complete an idea in the light of the Tradition. But the examples that we have considered are especially revealing. It is not enough to speak of a simple influence of the Fathers on the work of de Lubac; it is necessary rather to say that this work (even if it is also nourished by medieval authors, as well as modern authors such as Pascal, Newman, Blondel, and Rousselot—without speaking of Scripture itself) is thoroughly permeated with the patristic tradition and, to a large extent, shaped by it.

This is not, let us emphasize, simply a personal choice; for rather, this choice reflects the conviction according to which patristics, today as yesterday, must as such contribute to the renewal of theology. De Lubac had actually learned this from history as he brings out in this affirmation: "Each time, in our West, that a Christian renewal has flourished, in the area of thought as in that of life, (and the two areas are always linked), it has flourished under the sign of the Fathers. Every century testifies to this—the history would be too long to retrace—and the law is verified even in ours."[14] The recurrence of

13. In de Lubac, *Paradoxe et mystère de l'Église*, 120–67 (see chap. 13, pp. 309–13); *The Church: Paradox and Mystery*, 68–95.

14. Henri de Lubac, preface to F. Quéré-Jaulmes and A. Hamman, *Les Chemins vers Dieu*

the phenomenon is not accidental; it is truly one that is a matter of a "law." In an anonymous article in *Recherches de Science Religieuse* of 1946 (but of which one has every reason to think that it had de Lubac as its principal author), one reads precisely these lines:

> Is it not a law of the mind that it truly progresses, that it deepens its knowledge only by a rhythm that periodically defers back to the origins of its thought and not by an indefinite reflection or by a straight progression always going from consequence to consequence? A law that is also valid, that is valid perhaps above all, for theological reflection.... Thus the more one exalts Saint Thomas, the less one needs to fear that a direct recourse to the sources he himself used will distort his meaning. Quite the contrary: to do this is the prerequisite for understanding him better, for fathoming him better, for better discerning in him these promised "potentialities" for "marvelous developments."[15]

All things considered, added de Lubac, in no way have the riches of Holy Scripture "been so integrated into the definitions of faith and the current teaching of the Church" that we as a matter of course ought not to study the Holy Books. Admittedly, he continued, "the Fathers do not have the same authority, it is clear," they are "secondary sources, derivative, not at all sufficient"; and yet "they play no less of an important role; they have not only played one in the past but they also continue to play one in the present. Sources, not in a restricted sense by which one means literary history, but sources always gushing forth."[16]

From Christian Origins to Gregory of Nyssa: The Patristic Work of Jean Daniélou

It is natural to discuss, right after de Lubac, his confrere Jean Daniélou (1905–74): together they founded, let us recall, the collection Sources Chrétiennes; and for a long time their names appeared on the masthead of the volumes of this collection. The two men were certainly very different, not only in their personalities and their temperaments

---

[The Paths to God] (Paris: Centurion, 1967), cited in *Mémoire sur l'occasion de mes écrits*, 318; see de Lubac, *At the Service of the Church*.

15. [De Lubac], "La théologie et ses sources. Réponse," 395. This is the article mentioned above (chap. 2, note 13), the one that responded to an article of Fr. Labourdette in the *Revue thomiste*.

16. Ibid.

but above all—and this is what is important here—in the type of interest that they brought to patristic literature and in the way in which they referred to it. Both wrote a book on Origen, and yet a comparison is extremely significant. In addition to the differences that are due to each one's subject (Daniélou offers a synthesis on the life and work of Origen, whereas de Lubac concentrates on his interpretation of Scripture), other differences easily become apparent to the reader. Thus, Daniélou places more emphasis on Origen's thinking being rooted in the milieus of Judaism (and notably in the heritage of Philo), as well as the Alexandrian's debt to Greek culture; or even more, he readily focuses on the actual organization of the Christian community as one can reconstitute it based on some Origenian texts, on the institution of the catechumenate, on the way in which the "mysteries" of the Church were celebrated at that time, etc. Some differences are, however, notable, particularly concerning the usage of the words "allegory" and "typology."[17] And yet, the two men were animated by the same admiration for the Fathers of the Church and by the conviction that an in-depth reading of them was essential for the theological and spiritual renewal of their time.

It is difficult to summarize Daniélou's centers of interest in the field of patrology, as they were numerous and multiform; this diversity, which was expressed in, among other things, his "Bulletin des origines chrétiennes" for the journal *Recherches de Science Religieuse*, was the fruit of a great intellectual curiosity as well as a rich reserve of relationships with patrologists and theologians. It is, nevertheless, possible to identify some major axes of study undertaken by Daniélou on early Christianity and to recognize their significance for his own theology.

One of these axes is formed by the ensemble of his works on Gregory of Nyssa, above all his book *Platonisme et théologie mystique*[18]—that was preceded, a few years before, by the publication of a major work of the famous Cappadocian, the *Vie de Moïse* (the first volume in the

17. See chap. 5, pp. 118–20. Cf. Jean Daniélou, *Origène* (Paris: La Table ronde, 1948; Paris: Cerf, 2012); translated by Walter Mitchell as *Origen* (London: Sheed and Ward, 1955).

18. Jean Daniélou, *Platonisme et théologie mystique: Essai sur la doctrine spirituelle de saint Grégoire de Nysse* [Platonism and Mystical Theology: Essay on the Spiritual Doctrine of Gregory of Nyssa], 2nd ed. (1944; Paris: Aubier-Montaigne, 1954).

collection Sources Chrétiennes). Here the erudition is allied to a great capacity for synthesis. The book is, in fact, set out in three parts that themselves suggest the mystical itinerary according to Gregory: the light (purification), the cloud (contemplation), the darkness (love). Admittedly, one has reproached the author for here having posited distinctions that are too rigid or acritical. But be that as it may, in spite of this criticism, is not the theologian's genius to have known how to identify, thanks to his study of Gregory (even if it were at the price of an excessive systematization), the Christian transposition of the itinerary to which Neoplatonic philosophy invited one? Above all, the book's organization actually highlighted the paradox of a progression that is presented as a passage from light to darkness—the latter being more precisely qualified by audacious images, those of the luminous darkness and of the sober drunkenness (inherited from Philo), those of vigilant sleep and immobile movement (from Gregory himself). In this way, Daniélou took into account the thought developed by the Cappadocian, but, by his own research, he also made a larger contribution to the "mystical theology" of Christianity.[19]

A second axis concerns the works on the use of "typology" during the era of the Fathers. The word indeed evokes the debate to which we have alluded above and that concerns the interpretation of ancient Scriptures: Daniélou sees in this term the most accurate expression of what gives Christian exegesis its originality (persons or episodes from the Old Testament being recognized, in the light of the New, as "types" or "figures" of Christ, of the Christian existence, of the Church, etc.), whereas de Lubac places more emphasis on the traditional importance of the word "allegory." But "typology" plays also, or even most of all, a fundamental role in the catechumenate, in the celebration of Baptism and, more largely, in the liturgical life of the ancient Church. Daniélou is particularly sensitive to this aspect, as his article "Le sym-

19. The third part of the work allowed, among other things, taking a position on the problem raised by Nygren in *Eros et agapè*, by showing that, for Gregory, the two notions of *erôs* and *agapè* were not incompatible—in the sense, at least, in which *erôs* designates the irresistible attraction that carries away toward God a soul henceforth purified (that also translates the concept of *epektasis*, for which Daniélou shows the importance in Gregory's thought). See Bernard Pottier, "Le Grégoire de Nysse de Jean Daniélou: Réflexions autour de 'platonisme et théologie mystique'" [The Gregory of Nyssa of Jean Daniélou: Reflections on "platonism and mystical theology"], in *Actualité de Jean Daniélou* [Current relevance of Jean Daniélou], ed. Jacques Fontaine (Paris: Cerf, 2006), 79–96.

bolisme des rites baptismaux" shows in the first issue of the journal *Dieu vivant*, his book *Sacramentum futuri. Études sur les origines de la typologie biblique*, or even his book *Bible et liturgie. La théologie biblique des sacrements et des fêtes d'après les Pères de l'Église*.[20] All his erudition is put to work for a conviction that is both theological and pastoral: the intimate link between the typological interpretation of ancient Scriptures and the practice of the ecclesial life (as one eminently sees in the case of Baptism that uses the symbolism of the crossing of the Red Sea in order to speak of its new meaning in light of the death and resurrection of Christ). It is necessary to add that patristic "typology" is not only important for exegesis and for the understanding of the sacramental liturgy; rather, if it has such an importance, it is because for Daniélou it implies a complete vision of the history of salvation from the preparations of the Old Testament to the fulfillment of the eschatological promises, by passing through the central event of Christ in whom the mysteries are themselves actualized in the sacraments of the Church.[21]

These works on typology often refer to the Jewish or "Judeo-Christian" exegeses of the ancient Scriptures and by doing so reveal another major axis of research undertaken by Daniélou: this is especially shown, in 1958, by the famous work *Théologie du judéo-christianisme*.[22]

20. Jean Daniélou, "Le symbolisme des rites baptismaux" [Symbolism of baptismal rites]: *Dieu vivant* 1 (1945): 15–43; *Sacramentum futuri*: *Études sur les origines de la typologie biblique* [Sacramentum futuri: Studies on the origins of biblical typology] (Paris: Beauchesne, 1950); *Bible et liturgie. La théologie biblique des sacrements et des fêtes d'après les Pères de l'Église*, 2nd ed. (1967; Paris: Cerf, 1982); translated as *The Bible and the Liturgy* (London: Darton, Longman and Todd, 1960).

21. On this point, see Marie-Josèphe Rondeau, "Jean Daniélou théologien" [Jean Daniélou, theologian], in Fontaine, *Actualité de Jean Daniélou*, 141–42.

22. Daniélou, *Théologie du judéo-christianisme: Histoire des doctrines chrétiennes avant Nicée*, vol. 1 (Paris: Desclée, 1958); translated by John A. Baker as *The Theology of Jewish Christianity: A History of Early Christian Doctrine before the Council of Nicaea* (London: Darton, Longman and Todd, 1964). A second edition was published in 1992 (Paris: Desclée-Cerf), with a text established by Marie-Odile Boulnois from the Italian edition of 1974, reviewed and corrected by Joseph Paramelle and Marie-Josèphe Rondeau, a preface by Marie-Josèphe Rondeau, and an updated bibliography. Let us also point out that in 1957 Daniélou had published a book titled *Les manuscrits de la mer Morte et les origines du christianisme* (Paris: Orante); translated by Salvator Attanasio as *The Dead Sea Scrolls and Primitive Christianity* (Baltimore, Md.: Helicon Press, 1958). Daniélou was additionally interested in the Judaism of Greek culture and in 1958 published a book on Philo of Alexandria, *Philon of Alexandrie* (Paris: Fayard, 1958); translated by J. G. Colbert as *Philo of Alexandria* (Eugene, Ore.: Cascade Books, 2014).

Collecting a great deal of information from texts that often were little known, the book successively treats sources of "Judeo-Christianity," its "intellectual milieu," its "doctrines" and its "institutions"; in the third part, notably, it reconstructed the great themes of this "Judeo-Christianity," from the Trinity up to eschatology while passing through Christology and ecclesiology (without forgetting angelology, to which the author, moreover, devoted a book in 1952).[23] The synthesis was so considerable that the concept of "Judeo-Christianity" here had a very great extension: it designated not just the situation of Jews who recognized Jesus as a prophet or Messiah or those Christians attached to the observance of the Jewish Law; it more widely characterized "a form of Christian thought that does not involve a link with the Jewish community but that is expressed in the cadres borrowed from Judaism."[24] On this point, admittedly, one has since argued that "Judeo-Christianity" had to be defined in a more precise way.[25] The fact remains that, through its rich expositions, the book drew attention to a very remarkable form of encounter between the Christian message and the Jewish or Semitic culture (with its accompanying images and symbols). Let us add that this research, from its immediate interest in the understanding of ancient Christianity, was able to lead to taking a new look at the traditions with Jewish origins. It indirectly contributed to transforming the vision that the Church had of its relationship with Israel and, from this point of view, prepared in its own way the turning point of Vatican II.

The *Théologie du judéo-christianisme* was only the first volume of a trilogy, which was also to include a book titled *Message évangélique et culture hellénistique aux IIe and IIIe siècles*, and another book (published posthumously) on *Les origines du christianisme latin*.[26] The presence

23. Daniélou, *Les Anges et leur mission* (Paris: Chevetogne, 1952); translated by David Heimann as *The Angels and Their Mission according to the Fathers and the Church* (Westminster, Md.: Christian Classics Inc., 1982).

24. Daniélou, *Théologie du judéo-christianisme*, 37.

25. Cf. Simon Claude Mimouni, *Le Judéo-christianisme ancien. Essais historiques* [Ancient Jewish Christianity] (Paris: Cerf, 1998), 70.

26. Daniélou, *Message évangélique et culture hellénistique aux IIe et IIIe siècles* (Paris: Desclée, 1961); translated by John A. Baker as *Gospel Message and Hellenistic Culture* (London: Darton, Longman and Todd, 1973); *Les origines du christianisme latin* (Paris: Cerf, 1978); translated by David Smith and John Austin Baker as *The Origins of Latin Christianity* (London: Darton, Longman and Todd, 1977). These are volumes 2 and 3 of the *Histoire des*

of the word "culture" in one of these titles precisely reveals a fourth axis of the research conducted by Daniélou (and which actually was already implicit, in fact, in the work on Judeo-Christianity): the interest in Christianity's encounter with the cultures of the world. Just as in the first volume of the trilogy Daniélou was focused on the encounter of primitive Christianity with the Jewish traditions, in the second volume he is interested in the way in which the Christian authors from the second and third centuries presented the Gospel message to the Greek world. He explains "what they rejected from antique culture and what they kept," or even the use that they made of philosophical reasoning in order to present the faith in a more profound way.[27] Lastly, in the third volume he studies "the encounter between the Christian message and the Latin world," and he characterizes this volume as the culmination of a work that is, in its entirety, a "history of the cultural expressions of original Christianity."[28] And yet patristic inquiries, as such, nourished the broader fundamental reflection that Daniélou undertook on "Christianity and Cultures," as well as on "Christianity and non-Christian religions"[29]—questions that, as one knows, had an increasing importance at the time of Vatican Council II and in the following decades.

The study of the Fathers has thus held a very important place in the theological work of Daniélou. Let us recall that, in the 1940s, he was fully committed to a renewal of the theological method and that, according to him, the return to the patristic sources had to be one of the essential elements of this renewal.[30] Marie-Josèphe Rondeau has even written that he was "the purest representative" of this trend—whereas, in relation to the Fathers, de Lubac maintained more "the

---

doctrines chrétiennes avant Nicée [A history of early Christian doctrine before the Council of Nicaea].

27. Daniélou, *Message évangélique et culture hellénistique*, 2. Joseph Wolinski studied a particularly important theme of this work in "Jean Daniélou et la théologie du Logos avant Nicée (325)," in Fontaine, *Actualité de Jean Daniélou*, 57–78.

28. Daniélou, *Les origines du christianisme latin*, 7.

29. See Xavier Tilliette, "Jean Daniélou et la culture" [Jean Daniélou and culture], in Fontaine, *Actualité de Jean Daniélou*, 99–103; Michel Meslin, "Jean Daniélou et les religions non chrétiennes" [Jean Daniélou and non-Christian religions], in Fontaine, *Actualité de Jean Daniélou*, 155–64; Antoine Guggenheim, "La théologie de l'accomplissement" (The theology of fulfillment], in Fontaine, *Actualité de Jean Daniélou*, 165–87.

30. Cf. his article "Les orientations présentes," 5–21.

distance of the heir who knows that he belongs to another age" and more widely referred to the Christian tradition in its entirety (thus including that of the main current of Scholasticism).[31] De Lubac himself remarked in the review of a book written by his confrere, *Le Signe du Temple ou de la Présence de Dieu*: "Father Daniélou does not just cite the Fathers of the Church, he repeats one of their favorite themes, he enters into their method, and he, so to speak, espouses their rhythm. Better than with dissertations, the proof is thus given that the thought of the first centuries is still alive [...]"[32] And as for this, also regarding Daniélou, Rondeau writes:

> These Fathers, separated from us by a large chronological and cultural fissure, he tried to know what they truly want to say and if what they say has some pertinence for us. This first of all means an effort of detachment of self in order to understand the other. Daniélou has a marvelous art of very simply allowing the Fathers to speak, of listening without prejudice to what they have to say and to what must not be drowned out by the indiscrete noise of our voices, our questions, our culture .... This attentive listening was a profound disposition in him. It allowed him to understand and to make understood, in the Fathers, things that no one had yet noticed. But at the same time, if being objective was fundamental to his scientific work, he did not read them as an archeologist. The Fathers, he believed, were not only the venerable witnesses of a bygone past, they were also "the most appropriate nourishment for people today, because it is from them that we can retrieve some categories that are precisely those of contemporary thought, and that Scholastic theology had lost."[33]

Yves Congar and the Tradition of the Fathers

The third theologian that we are now going to consider, Yves Congar (1904–95), undoubtedly has not written as much on the theology of the Fathers as the previous two. His work, in any case, does not include studies devoted to a particular author (Origen or Gregory of Nyssa) that are equivalent to those of de Lubac and Daniélou, and one finds in it only a limited number of thematic studies on this or that as-

31. Rondeau, "Jean Daniélou théologien," 138–39.

32. Review reproduced in Henri de Lubac, *Mémoire sur l'occasion de mes écrits*, 1992, 46; see *At the Service of the Church*, 47n5.

33. Rondeau, "Jean Daniélou théologien," 140–41; the final citation is borrowed from the article in *Études*, Daniélou, "Les orientations présentes," 7.

pect of patristic literature. Congar is known more for his erudite works on medieval ecclesiology, and, above all, for his contributions, so important to contemporary thought, on the Church, the sacraments and the ministries as well as the theology of the Holy Spirit—all these subjects being tackled by him from a resolutely ecumenical perspective.

Nevertheless, the influence of the Fathers on him, in the various fields just enumerated, was considerable. Thus for ecclesiology: Congar wrote, among others, a detailed study on the theme of the "*Ecclesia ab Abel,*" showing that for the Fathers, the Church was not limited to the community of Christians living since the coming of Christ but that its dimensions extended more broadly to the entirety of holy history.[34] He also cleared up the origins of the famous expression "Outside of the Church no salvation," explaining that originally this expression—which first appeared in Origen and in Cyprian—did not concern relations with non-Christians and thus could not be utilized as a weapon against the Jews or other believers (contrary to the usage that has prevailed up until the twentieth century). Lastly, it is necessary to recall the significant title of his work *L'Église de Saint Augustin à l'époque moderne* [*The Church from Saint Augustine to the modern era*]: Congar knew the ecclesiological doctrine of the bishop of Hippo very well, and he showed both its extensions and transformations through the succeeding centuries. One could similarly verify the importance that the Fathers had for his pneumatological thought: every section of his massive work *Je crois à l'Esprit Saint* [*I Believe in the Holy Spirit*] is precisely devoted to this patristic heritage, from which the theologian gathers the principal fruits in order to bring about, on this basis, a better understanding of the third "Person" of the Trinity. Lastly, many times the "return to the Fathers" allows Congar to develop an argument that would be favorable to a rapprochement with "separated Christians" in order to show that ecclesial communion does not exclude legitimate diversity at the heart of the Church, or to dispel some misunderstandings regarding the "Filioque," or to help, by the historical inquiry itself, to overcome the divergences between the East and the West on this delicate question.

It would be possible to take up each of these themes by them-

34. Yves Congar, "*Ecclesia ab Abel*" [Ecclesia from Abel], in *Abhandlungen über Theologie und Kirche. Festgabe für K. Adam*, ed. Marcel Reding (Düsseldorf: Patmos, 1952), 79–108.

selves. But rather than devoting ourselves to this task, we would like to emphasize that Congar's in-depth reading of the Fathers notably allowed him to deepen one of his favorite themes, that of "Tradition" in the Church, and to clarify how he understood the specific place of the Fathers among the "monuments" of this Tradition.

Congar recognized first of all that "it was indeed the vocation and historic role of the Fathers to give Christianity its shape and expression within the Greco-Latin world of the Roman Empire."[35] But, he adds, this definition does not suffice since there were also Fathers outside of this Greco-Roman culture, and thus one could describe as "Fathers" more recent authors such as Raban Maur and Bernard of Clairvaux.[36] It is thus necessary to acquire a "deeper" understanding of the expression "Fathers." Congar, noting its usages in ancient Christianity, comes to the conclusion that "The name 'Fathers' has been given to *those who have contributed a decisive element to the Church's life*, either in its faith, its discipline, or its general attitude."[37] Congar consequently clarifies our situation in relation to these "Fathers": "In some sense they can be said to have 'fathered' us. That which makes us what we are has its origin beyond us and existed before us; it is a heritage. Such, without any doubt, was the idea the Middle Age had of it."[38] Congar adds that, if the Fathers have thus contributed to the life of the Church, "it is because they were 'inspired,' raised up, enlightened, guided, and strengthened by the Holy Spirit"; so it is good to call them "holy Fathers":

> Indeed, when one reflects on the part played by St. Athanasius or St. Hilary on behalf of faith in the Trinity, by St. Basil in establishing belief in the divine person of the Holy Spirit, by St. Jerome in giving the Latins a better Bible text, by St. Augustine in the doctrine on grace, by St. Cyril and St. Leo on Incarnation, together with the councils which correspond to these stages in doctrinal development, and after them so many other saints and councils, one realizes only too well how none but men and assemblies of men raised up by God and sustained by his Spirit were able to wield such a decisive influence upon the life of the people of God. In the sequence and the total effect of such tasks of clarification, we may discern a real continuation, one that is nevertheless en-

35. Yves Congar, *Essai théologique*, 192; *Tradition and Traditions*, 436.
36. Congar, *Essai théologique*, 193; *Traditions and Traditions*, 436–37.
37. Congar, *Essai théologique*, 194; *Tradition and Traditions*, 438.
38. Congar, *Essai théologique*, 194; *Tradition and Traditions*, 438.

tirely secondary and subordinate, of the part played at the level of the original foundation by Scripture.[39]

One will have noticed Congar's twofold emphasis: he highlights the contribution of the Fathers to the life of the Church as well as what makes such a contribution possible—"the inspiration" itself. This inspiration is certainly secondary compared with that of Scripture, but it is no less real: the "Fathers" are "Fathers" to the extent that the Holy Spirit has dwelled within them. This dual emphasis is highly revealing of the profound interest that Congar brought to ecclesiology, then to pneumatology; it thus does not suffice to say that the Fathers (and medieval authors) helped him to deepen these fields of theology, but it is necessary to add that attention to the life of the Church and reflection on the Spirit conversely helped him to specify the importance of the Fathers in the heart of the Tradition.

This does not mean, however, that he intended to propose an idealized image of the Fathers, whose tradition is in reality "a very human thing": "it is not an epiphany of glory, but a work of God in frail human vessels, a work whose luminosity of outline is apparent only to the eye of faith, which, though it takes into account the contributions of reason, must have overcome numerous objections and difficulties."[40] Congar here recalls that the Fathers were for a large part "conditioned by the culture of their times" and emphasizes in particular the insufficiencies of their exegesis that, besides its excessive tendency to allegorize, "lacks the historical perspective, philological resources, and knowledge of literary contexts, sources, and analogues which we possess today." Thus, it is not a matter of advocating the return to a "naïve" approach to the Scriptures, so as to bypass the exigencies of scientific reason—and Congar then issues this statement that is so revealing of all his thought: "Time has marched on, and no age has been without its special contribution to learning. Our own is certainly not worse off in this respect than its predecessors."[41] Congar here agrees with his friend Dom Clément Lialine, for whom it was necessary to distinguish what was "perennial" in the Fathers and what, also in them, had only a value relative to a precise moment of history

39. Congar, *Essai théologique*, 195; *Tradition and Traditions*, 439–40.
40. Congar, *Essai théologique*, 195–96; *Tradition and Traditions*, 440.
41. Congar, *Essai théologique*, 196; *Tradition and Traditions*, 440.

("It seemed to him that an overprivileged position was being given to one period, although the Holy Spirit has continued to inspire men in succeeding centuries, and continues to do so in our own time").[42] He similarly agrees with the Orthodox theologian Georges Florovsky and his reaction against the idea according to which the Holy Spirit would have only spoken in "the Church of the Fathers" or in "the Church of the seven ecumenical councils" (as if the Orthodox Church could only repeat the inspired texts of the Fathers and the early councils).[43] He additionally recalls that the Western tradition developed, up until the seventeenth century, the idea of an "*Ecclesia universalis*" embracing the Church "from Abel, the first just man, until the last of the elect."[44] He finally comes to this vigorous diagnosis:

> It might, indeed, happen that a systematic preference for the Fathers could derive from a questionable anti-intellectualism. It might also derive, in present-day Catholicism, from a lack of confidence in one's own powers seeking the support of the greater vitality of less sophisticated centuries. Finally, this sort of thing could proceed from an essentially historicizing, documentary, static, and academic theory of Tradition, going together with insufficient esteem for the living Church....
>
> In this case, there would be a risk of gravely wounding the Church's missionary character, that is, the mission (and the corresponding grace) which it has received to make the Gospel coextensive with, and present to, the whole of human history. What the Fathers achieved in proclaiming and explaining the Gospel according to the *logos* of ancient civilization must be done today, too, and will be necessary again tomorrow for other cultural periods. In this respect, the Fathers had a role which was historically conditioned and defined and which must not be allowed to render sterile or impossible other analogous historical roles, but should on the contrary inspire and stimulate them. In order the better to fulfil these roles, the Church at all times and in every century remains as full of vigor and promise as it was in the fourth and fifth centuries.[45]

42. Congar, *Essai théologique*, 196; *Tradition and Traditions*, 441.

43. Congar, *Essai théologique*, 196–98; *Tradition and Traditions*, 441–42. Concerning this statement it is worthwhile to cite a few lines of a contemporary Orthodox theologian, P. Kalaïtzidis: "Is it perhaps not time for us to realize that fidelity to the patristic tradition, the 'We, following the holy Fathers,' does not simply mean the continuation, the updating, or the reinterpretation of this tradition, but—in conformity with the precedents created by the advances made by primitive Christianity and the Fathers—the transcendence of patristic thinking where and when there is need of it?" "Du 'Retour aux Pères,'" 250.

44. Congar, *Essai théologique*, 198; *Tradition and Traditions*, 442 (and see the study "*Ecclesia ab Abel*," cited above in note 34).

45. Congar, *Essai théologique*, 199; *Tradition and Traditions*, 443–44. The deviation

A fundamental conviction of Congar is here being manifested, and it will never be abandoned by him—not even when, in the days following Vatican II, some movements would reproach the Church for being too open to the present world and pleaded for a return to tradition. He will think until the end that this tradition could not be stopped at a certain stage and that it is incumbent upon Christians always and forever to look for new ways of transmitting the Gospel in contemporary cultures. This deeply held idea reflected his vision of the Fathers, the in-depth reading of whom must not turn the Church inward upon its past but rather contribute to its mission to the different eras of history.

The fact remains that the time of the Fathers "is possessed of something quite specific and privileged."[46] This is confirmed in several domains: that of faith, for the Fathers have had an historical role to specify "the fundamentals of belief, the Trinitarian and Christological dogmas": that of the liturgy, for which they have fixed the essential forms; that of the canonical discipline, for which they have posited the bases as well; and even still, those of exegesis and spirituality. In all these domains, writes Congar, the Fathers "had a decisive influence on the Church's life." Admittedly, they were themselves the "sons" of this Church; they have received so much from her and lived in her communion. Nevertheless, they were her fathers "because they all, to some degree, begot, nourished, trained, and instructed this Church;" and this was done less by their personal genius than by reason of a grace and a mission received at a specific moment in history:[47] "This definite historical phase belonged to the Church's youth; it was the period not of birth, nor of the very first years, but the time when there first come to light the themes and images, convictions and deep reactions, first orientations and experiences, and rejections, too, which define the bases of a character, and will continue to have an influence throughout the rest of life."[48] There thus was a time of the Fathers, distinct from that which was going to represent the Scholastic theology

mentioned at the end of the first paragraph is not, for Y. Congar, a simple scholarly hypothesis: "Such was, as we have seen, the case with the Jansenists and sometimes the Gallicans, as also with the historians (Döllinger, for example) who supported the Old Catholic schism," Congar, *Essai théologique*, 199; *Tradition and Traditions*, 443.

46. Congar, *Essai théologique*, 199; *Tradition and Traditions*, 444.

47. Congar, *Essai théologique*, 199–201; *Tradition and Traditions*, 444–46.

48. Congar, *Essai théologique*, 201–2; *Tradition and Traditions*, 446.

of the Middle Ages—a theology that would deepen some subjects, but put into effect "arguments, analyses, and a dialectical method" which would fatally distance it from the center; yet patristic writings bring us closer to this center, by the very fact that the Fathers are closest to the "Christian fundamentals" and that their theology "centers on what is essential."[49] And Congar concludes by bringing out the conditions of spiritual "paternity," acknowledged in this way: it does not suffice to mention here the "eminent doctrine" of the Fathers and their "holiness of life"; it is necessary above all to specify that they were "pastors" trying to "build up God's Church," that for them the Christian mystery was not a simple "subject of research" but first of all a "reality" in which they lived and celebrated, that their theology implemented, beyond the resources of the human *logos*, the spiritual resources of a knowledge first of all linked to their life "in Christ" and "through the grace of the Holy Spirit," and that lastly their thinking honored the totality and the unity of the faith—expounding and illustrating "the inner direction of Revelation, and of the saving economy which comes from God through Christ to the Church as the sacrament of the new order of salvation."[50]

After de Lubac, Daniélou, and Congar, let us now turn to two other theologians of the same generation who, in the German-speaking world, were in various ways influenced by an in-depth reading of the Fathers: Karl Rahner first of all, and then, above all, Hans Urs von Balthasar.

In the German-Speaking Sphere: Karl Rahner and Hans Urs von Balthasar, Readers of the Fathers

Karl Rahner

It may be surprising that we are focusing on Karl Rahner (1904–84) rather than his brother Hugo (1900–1968). Indeed, it is Hugo who especially studied patristics: he taught this discipline, and he devoted himself to important works, such as his book *Mythes grecs et mystère chrétien* [Greek myths and christian mystery] or even his book *L'Église*

49. Congar, *Essai théologique*, 202–3; *Tradition and Traditions*, 447.
50. Congar, *Essai théologique*, 203–5; *Tradition and Traditions*, 448–50.

et l'État dans le christianisme primitif [The Church and State in early Christianity].[51] If we here favor Karl Rahner, it is because it is possible to verify, through some of his themes, the fecundity of patristics for the disciplines to which this theologian is most directly connected: fundamental and dogmatic theology.

Furthermore, his writings on early Christianity are in fact more numerous than one might believe: besides studies on Origen (of which we will soon speak), Rahner undertook an important work on the history of penance in the early Church;[52] he also made numerous inquiries into the theme of the "heart of Jesus" in the patristic tradition;[53] what is more, he translated into the German language a work of Marcel Viller on the spirituality of the first Christian centuries.[54] These studies, which were among the earliest in Rahner's work, influenced his thinking: as shown by, among other things, his later writings on the sacrament of penance (and also on the sacraments in general), or even by his writings on the spirituality of the heart of Jesus. It is additionally necessary to mention the importance that the reading of Augustine had for him: Rahner's theology of grace (one of the major fields of his work) is clearly indebted to it.

We will limit ourselves here to Rahner's studies on Origen.[55] First

51. Hugo Rahner, *Mythes grecs et mystère chrétien*, trans. Henri Voirin (Paris: Payot, 1954); translated by Brian Battershaw as *Greek Myth and Christian Mystery* (New York: Harper and Row, 1963); *L'Église et l'État dans le christianisme primitif*, trans. G. Georges Zinck (Paris: Cerf, 1964; repr. 2010); translated by Leo Donald Davis, SJ, as *Church and the State in Early Christianity* (San Francisco: Ignatius Press, 1992).

52. See the studies collected in *Schriften zur Theologie*, vol. 11, *Frühe Bußgeschichten in Einzeluntersuchungen* (Zurich: Benzinger Verlag, 1973); translated by Lionel Swain as *Theological Investigations*, vol. 15, *Penance in the Early Church* (London: Darton, Longman & Todd, 1983).

53. Rahner completed in 1936 a thesis titled *E latere Christi: L'origine de l'Église comme seconde Ève surgie du côté du Christ, deuxième Adam* [E latere Christi: The origin of the Church as second Eve emerged from the side of Christ, the second Adam]; this thesis, which was not published at the time, was published posthumously in Karl Rahner, *Sämtliche Werke*, vol. 3, *Theologie der Kirchenväter* [Complete works, vol. 3, Theology of the Fathers of the Church] (Zürich: Benzinger, 1999), 1–84.

54. Cf. Maurice Viller, *La spiritualité des premiers siècles chrétiens* [The spirituality of the early Christian centuries] (Paris: Bloud et Gay, 1930); Maurice Viller and Karl Rahner, *Aszese und Mystik in der Väterzeit* [Ascesis and mysticism in the era of the Fathers] (Freiburg im Breisgau: Herder, 1939); republished in vol. 3 of *Sämtliche Werke* (Zürich: Benzinger, 1999), 123–390.

55. See our study Michel Fédou, "Patristique et théologie" [Patristics and theology], in *Penser la foi. Recherches en théologie aujourd'hui, Mélanges offerts à Joseph Moingt*, ed. Joseph

of all, there is an article on the doctrine of spiritual meanings:[56] the theologian expounds the meaning of this doctrine in the work of the Alexandrian by showing how it fits into the whole of Origenian thought; he sees in it Origen's "psychological notion of 'theology,' which he treats as the highest degree of the spiritual life," and adds that the spiritual meanings can be for Origen "the organs of mystical knowledge."[57] This article is itself revealing of the attention that Rahner brings to the question of the knowledge of God, which is engaged precisely through the question of spiritual meanings and more widely the mystical experience—themes that the theologian will take up and develop in his later work.

Then comes a brief article titled "'Cœur de Jésus' chez Origène?"[58] In it, Rahner treats a passage of the Alexandrian that was probably speaking of the "*hégémonikon*" (at least one can deduce this on the basis of the Latin expression used by the translator Rufinus: "*principale cordis*"). He considers that, even if this passage did not use the expression "heart of Jesus," it, nevertheless, reflected "some patristic ideas that in some way correspond to those that underlie our modern devotion to the heart of Jesus."[59] Through this inquiry on Origen, the article is already demonstrating the close attention that Rahner pays to such a spirituality—that, as one has said above, will later be the subject of several publications.

It is above all necessary to focus on the great study that in 1950 appeared in a French version in three editions of *Recherches de Sci-*

Doré and Christoph Theobald (Paris: Cerf—Assas Editions, 1993), 487–95 (on Rahner, see 488–92); also see "Karl Rahner et Hans Urs von Balthasar lecteurs et interprètes des Pères" [Karl Rahner and Hans Urs von Balthasar, readers and interpreters of the Fathers], in *Balthasar, Rahner. Deux pensées en contraste* [Balthasar, Rahner. Two thoughts in contrast], ed. Henri-Jérôme Gagey and Vincent Holzer (Paris: Bayard, 2005), 141–59 (on Rahner as reader of Origen, see 148–56).

56. Karl Rahner, "Le début d'une doctrine des cinq sens spirituels chez Origène" [The beginning of a doctrine of the five spiritual senses by Origen], *Revue d'Ascétique et de Mystique* 13 (1932): 113–45; repr. *Schriften zur Theologie* vol. 12, Theologie aus Erfahrung des Geistes [Zürich : Benziger, 1975]), 111–36; translated by David Morland as Karl Rahner, "The 'Spiritual Senses' according to Origen," in *Theological Investigations*, vol. 16, *Experience of the Spirit: Source of Theology* (London: Darton, Longman & Todd, 1979), 81–103.

57. Rahner, "Le début d'une doctrine," 134 and 136; "The 'Spiritual Senses,'" 96 and 97.

58. Rahner, "'Cœur de Jésus' chez Origène?" ["Heart of Jesus" by Origen?], *Revue d'Ascétique et de Mystique* 15 (1934): 171–74.

59. Ibid., 173.

ence Religieuse: "La doctrine d'Origène sur la pénitence."[60] This study, which is quite lengthy, does not deal only with the particular theme that the title announces: through this theme, the study brings to light major aspects of Origen's thought, and in this way, it gives Rahner the occasion to expound several theses that he will develop as such in subsequent writings. In fact, the theologian does not come to his subject right away; emphasizing that Origen was "the first, in the Church, to attempt a systematic organization of the facts of Revelation," he explains that, first of all, it is important to recall some "fundamental presuppositions" of Origen's theology and method;[61] this itself is characteristic of the concern that Rahner will always have of not considering this or that doctrine in isolation but of grasping it in its relationship to what he here calls "the complete topic of theology."[62] What is, in the case of Origen, this "complete topic of theology"? Rahner qualifies it with the category of "*mystèrion*," following Balthasar who, in the same journal, had published a major study on Origen;[63] he adopts this theologian's analyses on the Origenian understanding of the real, of the connection of the image to the truth, of the sacramental structure of the Church, and of the relationship that must exist between the acts realized by this Church and the interior dispositions of believers.

Rahner's study then intends to verify how this vision of Origen is applied to the specific case of the remission of sins. A first part concerns "Personal Penance": Rahner deals with sins committed after Baptism and explains how these sins can be, according to the Alexandrian, effaced before God thanks to the "fire of penance." A second part deals with "Ecclesiastical Penance": Rahner here shows that sins as such affect the Church and then treats some "salvific acts of the Church on the sinner"; in this latter context, he presents the original meaning of excommunication, then the role of the communion of saints, and lastly the reintegration among the members of the vis-

60. Rahner, "La doctrine d'Origène sur la pénitence" [Origen's doctrine of penance], *Recherches de Science Religieuse* 37 (1950): 47–97, 252–86, and 422–56; see K. Rahner, *Frühe Bußgeschichten in Einzeluntersuchungen*, translated by Lionel Swain as "The Penitential Teaching of Origen," in Rahner, *Theological Investigations*, vol. 15, 246–328. The following quotations will be directly translated from the French text in *Recherches de Science Religieuse*.

61. Rahner, "La doctrine d'Origène sur la penitence," 47 and 48.

62. Ibid., 50.

63. This study, titled "le *mystèrion* d'Origène" [The *Mystèrion* of Origen], was published in 1936–37; see note 74.

ible Church; such are indeed, for Origen, the three "salvific acts" of the Church vis-à-vis the one who has sinned. This is not the place to emphasize the great pertinence of such an exposition regarding the Alexandrian's own thought; the important point is that, through this exposition, Rahner here affirms some central convictions of his later theology.

This is first of all borne out regarding the relationship between man and God. Rahner defends Origen against the suspicion of semi-Pelagianism and against the reproach according to which he would have conceived of an extrinsic "synergism" between grace and human freedom. Here, in reality, grace is not only "the divine adjuvant of a moral humanism," but man is rather "called to participate in the life of the *Logos* in the possession of the Holy Spirit in order to rise to the Father." Admittedly, says Rahner, Origen does not affirm in all clarity the "supernatural" character of this possession of the Spirit; however, he does not misunderstand it, but rather in considering "the concrete being in the order of the real, he, for this reason, is not concerned with differentiating this order as 'supernatural' in comparison to another hypothetical order that would be 'purely natural.'"[64] The words that the German theologian puts in quotation marks are very revealing: Rahner finds in Origen a thinker who, in his own way, has already rejected the dualism between "supernatural" and "pure nature"—this dualism that in contrast was maintained by Neothomistic theology and that de Lubac had just fought against in his 1946 book *Surnatural*. Even more, in his same study on Origen, he clarifies his own way of overcoming the deadlock of Neo-scholastic theory: "In the end contemporary theology, itself, must also recognize in the real man an 'existential' who on one hand is supernatural and yet on the other belongs to the ontological and permanent determination of his real being."[65] This language, which unceasingly appears in the writings of Rahner, is also repeated here in a passage on the interior experience of penance:

> [Grace] is specified by the particular situation of the sinner. It is the experiential reality which is awakened in the depths of his being, an experience of

64. Rahner, "La doctrine d'Origène sur la pénitence," 79.
65. Ibid., 80.

> this burning contradiction which ... freedom itself with its creativity could not dissolve. For there is a burning contradiction between one's own decision, on the one hand, and, on the other, what one's existential reality inescapably is: something ontologically real and supernatural, grounded in God's own self, something specifying without resistance one's *Dasein*. There, at the root of one's being, burns the Fire of God, and God's voice always makes itself heard from the tomb of the sin.[66]

The significance of the study on Origen, from the point of view that we here hold, is also confirmed by another question of great importance: the mode of the efficacy of the sacrament, here interpreted through the category of symbol. Rahner observes that the Alexandrian considers every exterior procedure of penance "as manifesting what happens as much on the interior level of the Church as deep within the heart of the man who is converted."[67] Yet since, in the case of Baptism, Origen designates the exterior rite as a "*symbolon*" or "*typos*" of what happens in the interior, must one not apply these same notions to the other sacraments? Rahner precisely gets through this step when he reflects upon the relationship between the exterior aspect and the interior aspect in the process of penance:

> It is the notion of *typos* or *symbolon* that best allows us to conceive this relationship of reciprocal dependence, without devaluing it either by reducing the *symbolon* to an incidental aspect—one that is fundamentally irrelevant—of an interior event that subsists in itself, or, alternatively, by exaggerating it, as if it were the efficient cause of what happens within, to the extent that we can no longer think of it as at the same time an expression, consequence, and manifestation of this interior event.[68]

Rahner thus takes a position against a unilateral interpretation of sacramental efficacy. If, conforming to the thought of Origen, the exterior rite is understood as "symbol" (thus as a "manifestation" of what happens in the depths of the heart), then it does not suffice to say that this sacramental sign is an efficient cause of grace, but it is necessary to affirm that it is itself, even in its exteriority, a manifestation of grace;

66. Ibid., 84–85. The doctrine of Origen, adds Rahner, offers for the first time "a great theology of *attritio*." For another English translation, compare "The Penitential Teaching of Origen," 270.

67. Rahner, "La doctrine d'Origène sur la pénitence," 447.

68. Ibid., 448 (we transliterate the words written in Greek characters); compare "The Penitential Teaching of Origen," 322.

more precisely, the *typos* "is the reality in which grace expresses itself in such a way that, by expressing it, it first of all realizes itself, so that they each depend upon the other"; the interior aspect and the exterior aspect must thus be understood as being in a reciprocal cause and effect relationship:

> The sacramental image is not, as a current way of looking at the matter would have it, "an image because it has an effect," or alternatively "an image alongside the effect," but rather "efficacious *as* an image," "efficacious *because* it is an image." Grace is produced and becomes present as itself by embodying itself in its symbol, indeed because of the symbol.... Thus the symbol of the sacrament is a cause in and through its being the image of the effect.[69]

Here again, the study of the Alexandrian has itself led to the formulation of a theme that was going to be central in Rahner's later writings on the sacraments: what is at stake is the understanding of sacramental efficacy in a sense that it takes into account the dimension of "sign" or of "symbol," since this is as well constitutive of the sacrament.[70]

Thus, even though patristic works have a much more limited place in the works of Rahner than in those of de Lubac, Daniélou, or Balthasar, they have for their part contributed to the formulation of his theological thinking. The German theologian, moreover, later had the occasion to pay homage to the contribution of patrologists whose research played such a role in the development of future theology:

> What renders historical inquiry so moving in works such as those of M. de la Taille or H. de Lubac? It is the art of reading historical texts in a way that they do not become only ballots of voting for or against our actual (long-held) positions, but that they say to us something about the question itself, something about what *we* up to the present have not yet reflected upon or only insufficiently. This does not mean that one practices historical theology in order to confirm his private and new opinions by citations chosen from the Fathers and from theologians (this misfortune also happens naturally), but that one associates with an ancient thinker, in the end not simply to know his opinion but to

69. Rahner, "La doctrine d'Origène sur la pénitence," 449; compare "The Penitential Teaching of Origen," 323.

70. The significance of the reflection on the "*symbolon*" does not only concern the field of sacramental theology; see K. Rahner, "Pour la théologie du symbole," in *Écrits théologiques*, vol. 9 (Paris: Desclée de Brouwer, 1968), 9–47; translated by Kevin Smyth as "The Theology of the Symbol," in *Theological Investigations*, vol. 4, *More Recent Writings* (Baltimore: Helicon Press), 221–52.

learn something of the question itself. Because historical theology is too often merely a connection and too rarely a *syntheologein*, one most often only learns from it the fragment from the past that, otherwise, is already present in the theology of today, but not the fragment, from our past, that forms our future. It is thus not surprising that the considerable work of historical theology (and it is always necessary to praise its positive result) has only in a small way become a force capable of overcoming the deficiencies, previously noted, of scholarly books.[71]

To learn from historical theology "the fragment, from our past, that forms our future": how better to say that for Rahner, as for other theologians of his generation, patristics ought to make a contribution to future theology?

Hans Urs von Balthasar

We will end this journey with one of the theologians of the twentieth century whose work was the most directly shaped by the reading of the Fathers: the Swiss theologian Hans Urs von Balthasar (1905–88).[72]

In a study that is devoted to Balthasar, de Lubac repeats the impression of a French visitor that had made his acquaintance: "It seemed to me that I was walking with a Father of the Church who would be lost among the Swiss and who would have, among his ancestors, both the Magi and William Tell."[73] The statement, which humorously suggests the rich personality of the Swiss theologian and his immense culture, speaks for itself as to how his work was influenced by an in-depth reading of patristic literature. His formation had allowed him to acquire a great familiarity with the Fathers, first thanks to his meetings with Erich Przywara at Munich (very important for his

71. Rahner, "Essai d'une esquisse de dogmatique," in *Écrits théologiques* (Paris: Desclée de Brouwer, vol. 4, 1966), 20 (we transcribe the word *syntheologein*, written in the original in Greek characters); translated by Cornelius Ernst as "The Prospects for Dogmatic Theology," in *Theological Investigations*, vol. 1, *God, Christ, Mary and Grace* (Baltimore: Helicon Press, 1961), 9–10.

72. On Balthasar and the Fathers, see Elio Guerriero, *Hans Urs von Balthasar*, trans. Frances Georges-Catroux (Paris: Desclée, 1993), 43–80.

73. Henri de Lubac, in "Hommage à Hans Urs von Balthasar" [Tribute to Hans Urs von Balthasar]. In *Œuvres complètes du Cardinal de Lubac*, vol. 9, *Paradoxe et mystère de l'Eglise* suivi de *L'Eglise dans la crise actuelle* (Paris, Cerf, 2010), 366. See also H. de Lubac, "Un témoin du Christ dans l'Église: Hans Urs von Balthasar" [A Witness of Christ in the Church: Hans Urs von Balthasar], in *Paradoxe et mystère de l'Église*; republished in *Œuvres complètes du Cardinal de Lubac*, vol. 9, 180–212 (notably 200–202).

discovery of Augustine), then during his studies of theology at Lyon-Fourvière (at that time he knew de Lubac and devoted himself to numerous patristic lectures).

Shortly thereafter he wrote monographs on three Greek Fathers: "Le *mystèrion* d'Origène," followed by an anthology of Origenian texts under the title *Esprit et feu; Présence et pensée. Essai sur la philosophie religieuse de Grégoire de Nysse* (to which must be added an abridged edition of Gregory's homilies on the *Canticle of Canticles*); and *Liturgie cosmique. Maxime le Confesseur.*[74] Later, in the second volume of *Herrlichkeit*, he wrote monographs on three other Fathers: Irenaeus, Augustine, and Dionysius.[75] He analyzed as well, in his book *Das Ganze im Fragment*, the last books of the *Confessions* of Augustine.[76] But independent of these studies on this or that author, many of Balthasar's other works are permeated with references to patristic literature that is incontestably a major source of his thinking. It is the era of the Fathers itself that, as such, is the subject of theological interpretation. Thus, in *L'Amour seul est digne de foi* [*Love Alone, the Way of Revelation*], Balthasar explains that in the early centuries the *logos* is identified with the *cosmos*, and that Christianity is then presented as the fulfilment of visions themselves fragmentary:

> The ancient image of the world and its divine soul, whether it be contemplated from a manner more Platonic or more Aristotelian or more Stoic or more Plo-

74. H. Urs von Balthasar, "Le *mystèrion* d'Origène," *Recherches de Science Religieuse* 26 (1936): 513–62, and *Recherches de Science Religieuse* 27 (1937), 38–64 (republished under the title *Parole et mystère chez Origène* [Word and mystery by Origen] (Paris: Cerf, 1957); *Origenes: Geist und Feuer.* Ein Aufbau aus seinen Schriften. Salzburg: Otto Müller, 1938), translated by Robert J. Daly as *Origen: Spirit and Fire, An Anthology of His Writings* (Washington, D.C.: The Catholic University of America Press, 1984); *Présence et Pensée. Essai sur la philosophie religieuse de Grégoire de Nysse* (Paris: Beauchesne, 1942), translated by Mark Sebanc as *Presence and Thought: An Essay on the Religious Philosophy of Gregory of Nyssa* (San Francisco: Ignatius Press, 1988); *Der versiegelte Quell: Auslegung des Hohen Liedes, in Kürzung übertragen und eingeleitet* [The sealed source: Interpretation of the Song of Songs, shortened and introduced] (Zurich: Otto Müller, 1939); *Liturgie cosmique, Maxime le Confesseur* (Paris: Aubier, 1947), translated by Brian E. Daley *as Cosmic Liturgy: The Universe According to Maximus the Confessor* (San Francisco: Ignatius Press, 2003).

75. *La Gloire et la Croix: Les aspects esthétiques de la Révélation II: Styles, 1, D'Irénée à Dante*, trans. from German (Aubier-Montaigne, Paris, 1968), 27–192; see *The Glory of the Lord: A Theological Aesthetics*, vol. 2, *Studies in Theological Style: Clerical Styles*, trans. Andrew Louth, Francis McDonagh, and Brian McNeil (Edinburgh: T & T Clark, 1984), 31–210.

76. The work, published in 1963, has been translated into French under the title *De l'intégration: Aspects d'une théologie de l'Histoire* [On integration: Aspects of a theology of history], trans. from German (Paris: Desclée de Brouwer, 1970).

tinist, contained in any case an image of God; it was the image of a sacral world in which, from the formal point of view, only the central point was lacking. When this came to present itself, the cosmic powers of love appeared in abundance fulfilled in the divine love.[77]

This concept, which continues throughout the Middle Ages, is according to Balthasar weakened in the modern era, under the effect of what he calls an "anthropological reduction"; but there is consequently a place for the third way, and it must be looked for in love—not the love limited to man but the infinite love of God who has Himself appeared to humanity and who became the new "logic," capable of giving a cohesion to the different doctrines and of establishing the structure of theology. The consideration brought to ancient theology thus takes place within a global vision of history, the same that is set out at length in the volumes of the great trilogy: *La Gloire et la Croix* [*The Glory of the Lord*], *La Dramatique divine* [*Theo-Drama*], *La Théologique* [*Theo-Logic*].

Taking only into account here the monographs on the Fathers, let us pay particular attention to the foreword of the book *Présence et pensée* [Presence and thought]. Balthasar indeed explains, at this point, the raison d'être of his studies on Origen, Gregory of Nyssa, and Maximus the Confessor. He does not intend "to present what in them appeared more able to influence or be of interest to modern theology" but rather "to penetrate the very vital source of their mind, this fundamental and secret intuition, which directs every expression of their thinking and that reveals to us one of those major possible attitudes that theology has adopted in a unique and concrete situation":

We would like to reread a few pages of that intimate journal written by the Church when she was seventeen years old. This we do from the same distance of age but also with the same respectful admiration for the person we were once. It would be a want of taste to desire, when we are forty, to bring laboriously to a conclusion one of those blazing fragments we had carelessly left undone when we were twenty. Youthful fire is not meant to warm up those who are old. We shall not collect the living and sacred documents of our life (and the history of the Church is our life) as a person would collect stamps

77. *L'Amour seul est digne de foi*, trans. from German (Parole et Silence, Saint-Maur, 1999), 13; see *Love Alone, the Way of Revelation: A Theological Perspective*, trans. Alexander Dru (London: Burns & Oates, 1968).

or butterflies. That would be to demonstrate that we are already dead. Let us read history, our history, as a living account of what we once were, with the double-edge consciousness that all of this has gone forever and that, in spite of everything, that period of youth and every moment of our lives remain mysteriously present at the wellsprings of our soul in a kind of delectable eternity.[78]

Balthasar, like the other theologians previously referred to, is thus very aware of the distance that separates him from the patristic era and of the illusion that would claim to repeat or reproduce such a "moment" of Christian thinking forever past. He, like they, feels no less a mysterious presence of this past; and his diverse monographs show the extent to which he was influenced by it in the very elaboration of his theology.

Thus, his study on Origen highlights the central theme of the "Mystery" of which the Word is the manifestation and shows how this Word gives himself in the Incarnation, in Scripture, and in the sacraments; consequently, the Savior's existence is the symbol of a much wider life of Christ, that of his mystical body. Scripture has not only a literal meaning but a spiritual meaning; and the Church has a sacramental structure that is manifested notably in an exigency of holiness. These are some of the themes that Balthasar develops for themselves in his own theology. He also assuredly recognized that a certain danger marks Origen's vision: a tendency "to skim over the symbols, to lift the last veils, to surpass even the *Logos* in order 'to see' the abyss of the Father, to know instead of living, to overestimate finally the sign of the Word all the while underestimating that of Love." But precisely, even in the formulation of such a reserve, Balthasar expresses a conviction that is dear to him and that he will develop in his later work. In fact, he adds, the tendency that he reveals in his author "is unceasingly denied by what was most profound in him," for "Origen knows that true knowing is love."[79]

Another example is provided to us by the study of Maximus the Confessor. The work *Liturgie cosmique,* indeed, does not just expound—in, moreover, a magisterial manner—the very profound and

78. Balthasar, *Présence et pensée,* xiii–xiv; *Presence and Thought,* 13.

79. Cf. the epilogue of *Parole et mystère chez Origène,* 113–16. See our study "Karl Rahner et Hans Urs von Balthasar lecteurs et interprètes des Pères," 141–59 (on Balthasar reader of Origen, see 143–48).

complex thinking of this Greek Father; at the same time, it reflects, on more than one point, Balthasar's own theological thinking. Thus for the understanding of the relationship of man to God, Maximus speaks of "participation" by emphasizing that there is no confusion between the human and the divine: it is in no way by negation of the world, but in the world and through it, that man must praise God and be united to him. Yet Balthasar finds in this a foundation for a doctrine of the "analogy of being" that is able to reject both the anthropocentrism of transcendental philosophy and the opposing concept of Karl Barth. Thus also for Christocentrism, Balthasar's reading of Maximus is dependent upon his interpretation of Christ, and more precisely by the way in which Christ overcame the abyss between God and man without there being, for all that, the absorption of humanity into the divine. Yet the later work of the theologian will precisely always emphasize the centrality of Christ. Lastly, one reads in *Liturgie cosmique* some phrases that directly announce *Love alone, the way of revelation*—this one, for example, "Christ loved us more than himself, preferring the obscurity of the Incarnation to his life in the celestial light. The Incarnation thus became the measure and the law of all love in this world, and it is on this love that ours must be modeled."[80]

The contribution of patristics to Balthasar's theology can also be illustrated by the opening of his book *Das Ganze im Fragment*. Here the last books of the *Confessions* allow him to expound the Augustinian understanding of temporality: whereas God is eternal and immutable, creation belongs to time and is subject to change; the human being, having the experience of no coincidence between the past, the present, and the future, feels a dispersal or even a *distensio*, linked to his condition as creature and aggravated by sin; however, if he is exiled

80. Balthasar, *Liturgie cosmique*, 209. In his new edition of the work, in 1961, Balthasar additionally inserted other excerpts from Maximus treating the three days—crucifixion, placement in the tomb (descent into Hell), and resurrection. One knows the importance of the thought undertaken by the theologian on this subject, in Balthasar, *Mysterium Paschale: The Mystery of Easter* (London: T & T Clark, 1990), also in *Theo-Drama: Theological Dramatic Theory*, 5 vols (San Francisco: Ignatius Press, 1988–98). For a more complete presentation, see our study "Liturgie cosmique: Lecture de Maxime le Confesseur par Hans Urs von Balthasar" [Cosmic liturgy: A reading of Maximus the Confessor by Hans Urs von Balthasar], in *Avec les Pères de l'Église, penser l'homme devant Dieu, 1. L'homme image de Dieu* [With the Fathers of the Church, thinking the man before God, I. Man, image of God] (Paris: Médiasèvres, 2001), 141–54.

on this earth, he also aspires to the "city of God"; the creature must chose the love that, responding to the premier love of God, allows him to escape the existential alienation of time in order to enter into the time of the heavenly Jerusalem: "The one who definitively loves is raised above time, for what must come is nothing other than what is and what has been."[81] Balthasar observes that the idea of a resolution of time by a return to the origin is not new; but, he says, what is particular to Augustine, is the idea that it is love that precisely allows overcoming the dispersal or the *distensio*. Yet it is onto this analysis of the *Confessions* that he grafts his own theology of history: the events of time are washed in the blood of the last Adam; "The supra-temporal place that is Christ's is not found only 'above' time, 'before,' and 'after it;' it is superior to it in such a manner that it embraces it simultaneously;"[82] and Christ is himself a concrete man, immersed in time and history, who came into the world at the moment when sin had attained its extreme point: "The extreme diastasis—between the sinful time and its receding toward its end, and the totally pure eternity—becomes the place where the most intimate union between the Father and the Son is present and lives."[83] It is from this possibility opened by the love overflowing between the Father and the Son, in the Spirit, that has been born time, creation, and also the fall of the creature—but the time of creation and even of the fall itself becomes, by Christ, the place of self-manifestation of eternal life. Jesus is the today of God, his present "is more than an abstract presence of eternity in time, it is also eternity realized beginning in time; the eternity founded, by the love of election, at the heart of ephemeral time that goes toward death."[84]

Lastly, it is necessary to consider patristics' contribution to the "theological esthetic" in the second volume of *La Gloire et la Croix*. The studies devoted here to Irenaeus, Augustine, and Dionysius are inserted into a part titled *Styles*: it is a matter of presenting a list of authors who, in the history of Christianity, have been moved by "glory" to the point that their works themselves give witness. Thus Irenaeus: in response to the "gnosis, the name of which is liar," he considers

81. Balthasar, *De l'intégration*, 28.
82. Ibid., 47.
83. Ibid., 51.
84. Ibid., 52.

that theology "begins by seeing what is;"[85] he "describes that beautiful surface that is, as such, the true revelation of hidden depths."[86] Since human nature was integrated into the order willed by God, "it also has measure and beauty, and through it, all the cosmos."[87] Balthasar then focuses on Irenaeus's understanding of "the temporal art of God;"[88] he highlights the central concept of "glory," understood as the mutual glorification of God and man: "The man, who preserves within himself the art of God and makes himself malleable to this art, glorifies the artist, and the artist is glorified in his work."[89] The musical images ("rhythm," "melody," "symphony") to which Irenaeus so readily has recourse here find their most profound meaning. Above all, the major themes of his work—such as the unity of the two Testaments and the doctrine of "recapitulation"—appear here in the full light of a theology entirely delighted by the beauty of the mystery as it is offered to the believer. Balthasar is here a very good reader of Irenaeus, but precisely, by his own reading, he remarkably illustrates the "theological esthetic" for which he posited the fundamentals in the first volume of *La Gloire et la Croix*.

It would be possible to focus on his presentations on Augustine and on Dionysius in the same volume, or to be interested in some passages from *La Dramatique divine*, *La Théologique*, or many other works that, on some particular points, here and there, appeal to the witness of the Fathers. It is not only Balthasar's culture in the field of patristics that is impressive; even more is his way of integrating this culture into the entirety of his thinking, and by being all the more connected to it, since the living reference to the Tradition of early Christianity itself makes known what is its great value for him: the ecclesial anchoring of Christian theology.

Our route will have shown the extent to which the theologians presented here have been influenced by an in-depth reading of the Fathers of the Church. Their works are, assuredly, very diverse; they each have a particular and original style. And this is very revealing

85. Balthasar, *La Gloire et la Croix*, II/1, 40; this quotation and the following ones are translated from the French edition; for another English trans., see *Studies in Theological Style*.

86. Balthasar, *La Gloire et la Croix*, II/1, 49.

87. Ibid., 63.

88. Ibid.

89. Ibid., 67.

of what a personal contact with patristic writings produced for this generation: not the pure and simple repetition of what had been said by the ancient authors, but the elaboration of a thinking that, by its familiarity with these authors and by the inspiration that it received from them, contributed as such to the renewal of theology over the course of the twentieth century.

CHAPTER 4

From Vatican II to Our Day

We have seen to what extent the patristic renewal of the twentieth century influenced the generation of theologians discussed in the preceding chapter. It is now important to turn to more recent decades and reflect upon current developments.

An observation is called for at the outset: whether in the matter of prayer (with the presence of patristic texts in the Office of Readings), or more generally of the liturgy as it was instituted following Vatican II, or of catechesis and initiation into the sacraments, or still other dimensions of Christian life (engagement in the world, relationships with other Churches, attention to the values which other human traditions are able to provide), we are, in many respects, the recipients of the fruits of the return to the Fathers that took place over the course of the twentieth century; to tell the truth, in many cases, we no longer even realize that the essential components of ecclesial life owe much to this renewal, as we are now so accustomed to them. But here our purpose is not to focus on what in the life of the Church is consequently marked by the influence of the renewed contact with the Fathers. Rather we will concentrate on what is the central question of our research: since Vatican II, to what extent does the reading of patristic writings remain fecund for Christian thought? How is this fecundity manifested? What, on the contrary, can impede the contribution of patristics to theology?

In order to respond to these questions, it is first of all necessary for us to recognize that, in a general way, the study of the Fathers has not ceased to grow since the era of Vatican Council II. We will thus begin by taking note of this phenomenon or by, at least, indicating some of its particularly significant aspects. It is only then that we will come to the questions formulated above: we will recognize how, since Vatican II, theology has actually benefitted from the patristic legacy; we will then attempt to identify the reasons for which other points of view have, on the contrary, tried to distance themselves from the writings of the Fathers. This last point will take us to the threshold of the chapters that follow, in which it will be a matter of showing what today is, in spite of the difficulties mentioned, the basis for the necessity of a patristic theology.

Publications and Translations

Several collections allow assessing the remarkable growth experienced by publications and translations of patristic texts over the last fifty years. For the French-speaking world, it is, first of all, the case of the collection Sources Chrétiennes, the genesis of which we have retraced above, and that, under the successive direction of Claude Mondésert, Dominique Bertrand, Jean-Noël Guinot, and Bernard Meunier, has expanded with so many publications during these decades—so much so that in 2006 it had already celebrated the publication of its five hundredth volume.[1] The collection of the Bibliothèque augustinienne has, for its part, continued publishing the works of Augustine. To this is added the publication of numerous translations in the collections Lettres chrétiennes and Les Pères dans la foi (under the impetus of Adalbert-Gautier Hamman), as well as in the collection Spiritualité orientale.[2] Many translations of patristic texts have also appeared in English, German, Italian, Spanish, and other languages.[3]

1. This celebration resulted in several colloquies, of which the papers have been published: *Les Pères de l'Église aux sources de l'Europe*, ed. Dominique Gonnet and Michel Stavrou [The Fathers of the Church at the source of Europe] (Paris: Cerf, 2014). Previously, in 1993 the fiftieth anniversary of the collection had already resulted in several works: see the volume Sources Chrétiennes, *Les Pères de l'Église au XX*[e] *siècle*. Also see Fouilloux, *La collection "Sources chrétiennes"*; *Lire les Pères de l'Église dans la collection Sources Chrétiennes* [Reading the Fathers of the Church in the Sources Chrétiennes collection], new revised and enlarged ed., ed. Claude Mondésert and Jean-Claude Guinot (Paris: Cerf, 2010).

2. The collection Lettres chrétiennes was in fact begun before the council (in 1957). The series Les Pères dans la foi [Fathers in faith] (Paris: Desclée de Brouwer) is today the responsibility of the Association Jean-Paul Migne.

3. See, for example, in the United States, the collections The Fathers of the Church (Washington, D.C.: The Catholic University of America Press, 1962–); and Ancient Christian Writers (Mahwah, N.J.: Paulist Press, 1946–); in England, Oxford Early Christian Texts

In addition to Sources Chrétiennes and Bibliothèque augustinienne (which themselves give, on the page facing the translation, the Greek or Latin text of each work), it is necessary to point out the growth of several scientific collections that had been created at the end of the nineteenth century or in the first decades of the twentieth, and that as a whole are little by little replacing the famous Patrologies of Migne: thus the collection Die Griechischen christlichen Schriftsteller der ersten drei Jahrhunderte (known under the appellation Corpus de Berlin, which publishes the texts of the Greek Fathers), and the collection Corpus Scriptorum Ecclesiasticorum Latinorum (or Corpus de Vienne, which publishes the texts of the Latin Fathers); the Corpus Christianorum, which includes both a *series graeca* and a *series latina*, as well as a *continuatio mediaevalis*; or even, in the field of Syriac, Coptic, Armenian, Ethiopian and Arabic literature, the Patrologia orientalis and the Corpus Scriptorum Christianorum Orientalium.[4]

These latter collections merit particular attention. Of course, like the other collections previously mentioned, the Patrologia orientalis and the Corpus scriptorum christianorum orientalium had been launched well before the period with which we are here concerned. But as they continue to expand, they give access to many texts that were most often unknown to us (even though many of the texts of Greek and Latin authors had already been published in the modern era—although imperfectly). Our knowledge of patristic literature finds itself greatly enlarged, which is valuable for historical research as well as for theological thought. Undoubtedly, one clearly continues to favor the Greek and Latin texts, moreover, not only because they are better known, but also because their influence was predominant in the subsequent eras. The

---

(Oxford : Oxford University Press, 1971–2009); in Spain, Biblioteca de autores cristianos (Madrid: Biblioteca de autores cristianos, 1943–); in Italy, Collana di testi patristici (Rome: Città Nuova 1959–); in Germany, Fontes christiani (Freiburg im Breisgau: Herder, 1988–). It is important to emphasize that patrologists consequently benefit from the publication and translation of the "Bible d'Alexandrie" (Paris: Cerf, 1986–), undertaken at the initiative of Marguerite Harl, and from valuable tools of the trade such as the *Biblia patristica* (Paris: CNRS, 1975–2000) and "Biblindex." What is more, beginning in 1961, the works of Philo of Alexandria have been published and translated in the publications of Cerf, under the direction of Roger Arnaldez, Jean Pouilloux, and Claude Mondésert: *Œuvres de Philon d'Alexandrie* [Writings of Philo of Alexandria] (Greek text and French trans.) (Paris: Cerf, 1961–).

4. This list is clearly not exhaustive; other collections could have been mentioned, for example, that of the Vetus latina.

same is not true for Eastern literature, considering the expansion of Islam in the countries of the Near and Middle East. The fact remains that this literature, apart from its specific interest for the Eastern Churches, must be more widely taken into account in studies on early Christianity—including, let us repeat, from the perspective of theological thought. Let us add, moreover, that often the texts written in Syriac or in other Eastern languages are in fact translations from the Greek originals that we otherwise would not have known (or only partially).

However, if there is a broadening of our understanding in the field of early Christianity, it is not simply because we have access to a greater number of Eastern texts (or Eastern translations of Greek originals). In the field of Greek and Latin patrology, important discoveries have been made in recent decades. Let us mention, for example, the thirty letters that have been brought to light by Johannes Divjak, of which twenty-five are ascribed to Augustine; the twenty-six sermons also by Augustine that have been found by François Dolbeau in a manuscript from the library of Mayence[5] or even more recently the twenty-nine homilies on the Psalms that were discovered by Marina Molin Pradel in Munich and that Lorenzo Perrone has confirmed as being homilies of Origen. On the other hand, contemporary research is increasingly interested in not only some texts of Christian authors who are not necessarily "Fathers of the Church" in the strict meaning of the expression but also in other writings that in some way belong to patristic literature in its broadest scope—some that completely reflect "orthodox" Christian thinking, others that deviate from the ecclesial faith on this or that point, others that are located completely on the margin of "orthodox" thinking or that develop doctrines entirely opposed to those of the Fathers of the Church. This great diversity is shown by, among others, the writings called "apocryphal," which are progressively being published in a specific series of Corpus Christianorum.[6]

5. Cf. *Sancti Aurelii Augustini opera, epistulae ex duobus codicibus nuper in lucem prolatae*, ed. Johannes Divjak, CSEL 88 (Vienna: Tempsky, 1981); Augustin d'Hippone, *Vingt-six sermons au peuple d'Afrique* [Twenty-six sermons to the people of Africa], ed. François Dolbeau (Paris: Institut d'Études Augustiniennes, 1996). Other examples of contemporary discoveries are given by Angelo di Berardino, "Orientations actuelles des recherches patristiques" [Current directions of patristic research], in Sources Chrétiennes, *Les Pères de l'Église au XXe siècle*, 386–89.

6. See Corpus Christianorum, Series Apocryphorum; see also the translations assembled

Critical editions and translations have, for several decades, increased, benefitting from all the resources that textual criticism, philology, and the different methods of historical analysis offer. If one takes into account as well the new research on ancient Judaism, on Greco-Latin literature, and on Gnostic and Manichean writings,[7] we find ourselves in the presence of considerable materials that allow a more precise knowledge of the very great complexity of later Antiquity. All this work is of great value and will undoubtedly continue to bear much fruit in the future. But one can also perceive the question that the theologian asks himself: must he only welcome the results of the research that, perennially, contribute to a better knowledge of Christian literature? Must he not also expect this research, by some of its contributions, to nourish and make fecund his own theological thought—and if yes, under what conditions, so that his approach may be both legitimate in the eyes of patristic science and credible with regard to theology?

Later we will return to this essential question, but first it is necessary for us to see how, during recent decades, theologians have been able to refer to patristic literature in their own work.

The Contribution to the History of Dogmas and Christian Theology

This contribution is first of all apparent through numerous monographs on the Fathers of the Church; it is also seen by the renewal in the history of dogmas and the publication of some works that, in the fields of fundamental and dogmatic theology, have been strongly influenced by patristic literature.

The first point is easily verified. Besides the many articles and pa-

---

in *Écrits apocryphes chrétiens* [Christian apocryphal writings], 2 vols., ed. François Bovon and Pierre Geoltrain (Paris: Gallimard, Bibliothèque de la Pléiade, 1997 and 2005); as well as in the collection "Apocryphes" of Brepols.

7. Cf. Berardino, "Orientations actuelles des recherches patristiques," 389 ff.; see in particular *Écrits gnostiques. La bibliothèque de Nag Hammadi* [Gnostic writings. The library of Nag Hammadi], ed. Jean-Pierre Mahé and Paul-Hubert Poirier, Bibliothèque de la Pléiade (Paris: Gallimard, 2007); see also Michel Tardieu and Jean-Daniel Dubois, *Introduction à la littérature gnostique* [Introduction to Gnostic literature] (Paris: Cerf—CNRS, 1986]; Michel Tardieu, *Le manichéisme* [Manicheism] (Paris: PUF, 1981).

pers that have been produced thanks to patristic colloquies,[8] some books have made a better understanding of the thinking of this or that Father possible. Thus for the earliest Christian literature and particularly for the writings of Irenaeus, studied so carefully by Antonio Orbe.[9] Thus for Tertullian, whose Trinitarian theology is the subject of a major publication by Joseph Moingt.[10] Thus for Origen, to whom Henri Crouzel has devoted several fundamental works.[11] Thus for Athanasius, the Cappadocians, Cyril of Alexandria, Theodoret of Cyrus, and Maximus the Confessor; thus also, from the West, for Hilary, Jerome, Augustine, and Gregory the Great.[12] Several collections, in the French language, especially show the importance given to these monographs: the collection Théologie historique; the collection of the Études augustiniennes; the collection Jésus et Jésus Christ, which has also published works on Irenaeus, Tertullian, Origen, and Augustine; and the collection Spiritualité orientale as well. These monographs are, most often, interested in only a particular aspect of the thinking developed by this or that author; but we mention them here because, all the while taking into account the research that has been conducted from the literary and historical point of view, they above all strive to clarify the author's thought on various questions of the faith; these works, in this sense, come well within the discipline that has given its name to one of the collections mentioned above: historical theology. It could be possible to say more about any number of thematic studies, which are not about a specific author but that, regarding a particular

8. Above all, the international colloquy of patristic studies that is held every four years at Oxford, and that, each time, has resulted in several volumes of the collection Studia Patristica; and also the specific colloquies on Origen (also every four years), and the colloquies on other Fathers or on themes relating to patristic literature (such as the colloquies organized each year by the Augustinianum in Rome).

9. See Antonio Orbe, *Introduction à la théologie des IIe et IIIe siècles* [Introduction to the theology of second and third centuries], trans. from the Spanish, 2 vols. (Paris: Cerf, 2012).

10. See Joseph Moingt, *Théologie trinitaire de Tertullian* [Trinitarian theology of Tertullian], 4 vols. (Paris: Aubier-Montaigne, 1966–69).

11. See, among others, Henri Crouzel, *Origène et la "connaissance mystique"* [Origen and "mystical knowledge"] (Paris: Museum Lessianum, 1961); *Origène* [Origen] (Paris: Lethielleux, 1985).

12. Any number of patrologists could have been mentioned here; thus, taking into account the French-speaking world, Monique Alexandre, Isabelle Bochet, Michel Corbin, Henri Crouzel, Claude Dagens, Gilles Dorival, Martine Dulaey, Georges-Matthieu de Durand, Yves-Marie Duval, Charles Kannengiesser, Jean-Noël Guinot, Marguerite Harl, Alain Le Boulluec, Goulven Madec, Bernard Sesboüé, Joseph Wolinski, and many others.

subject, examine several authors, or are even interested in the whole of patristic literature.

The contribution of patristics since Vatican II is confirmed in the field of the history of dogmas, and more widely in the history of theologies. Here are several collections from this field that show a similar influence: the series Mysterium salutis, at least in some of its chapters;[13] also the collection Cogitatio fidei and the collection Jésus et Jésus Christ,[14] in some of their volumes; or even, in a more specific way, the Histoire des Conciles directed by Gervais Dumeige.[15]

The work of several theologians especially illustrates the way in which the renewal in patristic studies has thus contributed to the history of dogmas, and a very special place must here be reserved for Aloys Grillmeier. Admittedly, it was prior to the council that this German theologian undertook fundamental works on the history of Christological dogma; in particular, he had directed, with Heinrich Bacht, the publication of three volumes occasioned by the fifteen hundreth anniversary of the Council of Chalcedon.[16] But in the 1960s he began to publish his famous series of volumes *Le Christ dans la tradition chrétienne*, which was to cover the entirety of the patristic period (even if he was not able to go beyond the sixth century).[17]

13. See *Mysterium salutis. Dogmatique de l'histoire du salut*, ed. R. Ringenbach, translated into French, 15 vols (Paris: Cerf, 1969–75).

14. See in particular Bernard Sesboüé, *Jésus-Christ dans la tradition de l'Église. Pour une actualisation de la christologie de Chalcédoine* [Jesus Christ in the tradition of the Church. Toward an update of Chalcedon], rev. ed. (Paris: Desclée, 2000).

15. The volumes have appeared in the publications of the Orante (Paris); for the patristic era there are four: Iñigo Ortiz de Urbina, *Nicée et Constantinople* [Nicaea and Constantinople] (Paris: Orante, 1963); Pierre-Thomas Camelot, *Ephèse et Chalcédoine* [Ephesus and Chalcedon] (Paris: Orante, 1962); Francis Xavier Murphy and Polycarp Sherwood, *Constantinople II et Constantinople III* (Paris: Orante, 1974); Gervais Dumeige, *Nicée II* [Nicaea II] (Paris: Orante, 1978). See also Jacques Liébaert, *L'Incarnation. I. Des origines au Concile de Chalcédoine* [The Incarnation. I. From the origins to the Council of Chalcedon] (Paris: Cerf, 1966); Bernard Sesboüé and Joseph Wolinski, in *Histoire des dogmes*, vol. 1, *Le Dieu du salut* [History of dogmas, vol. 1, The God of salvation], ed. Bernard Sesboüé (Paris: Desclée, 1994); Jaroslav Pelikan, *The Christian Tradition: A History of the Development of Doctrine*, vol. 1, *The Emergence of the Catholic Tradition, 100–600* (Chicago: University of Chicago Press, 1971); Pelikan, *The Spirit of Eastern Christendom*; Joseph Moingt, *L'homme qui venait de Dieu* [The Man who came from God] (Paris: Cerf, 1993), 81 ff.

16. See *Das Konzil von Chalkedon, Geschichte und Gegenwart* [The Council of Chalcedon. History and Current Relevance], 3 vols., ed. Aloys Grillmeier and Heinrich Bacht (Würzburg: Echter Verlag, 1951–54).

17. Cf. Aloys Grillmeier, *Le Christ dans la tradition chrétienne. De l'âge apostolique à*

These volumes, of an exceptional erudition, gather the fruits of many contemporary studies on ancient texts (not only from texts that had already been studied but from much less known writings, including texts from Coptic and Ethiopian literature).

Grillmeier attempts above all, by this very way, to specify the meaning of early Christology—or rather early Christologies—by not being limited to the formulations of the councils but by retracing step-by-step the thinking of the authors and the debates that often divided them. His history of Christological dogma is, inseparably, an interpretation of Christologies, notably marked by a clear distinction between two concurrent schemas: that of the *Logos—sarx* Christology, which was dear to the Alexandrians; that of the *Logos—anthropos* Christology, which was favored by the Antiochenes. In the eyes of Grillmeier, the first of these schemas risked, by its emphasis on the *Logos* made flesh, favoring a doctrine that would not entirely respect the substance of humanity assumed by the Word of God (as one already sees in Apollinaris), but the second schema risked, on the contrary, not adequately respecting the unity of God and the man Jesus Christ. This rigorous reading of the history of dogma led Grillmeier to rehabilitate, up to a certain point, the thinking of Nestorius, even if he recognized as well the reasons for which Cyril of Alexandria and after him the Council of Chalcedon had to oppose it. Additionally, Grillmeier brings the greatest interest to the later Christological controversies, illuminating the fundamental stakes of these controversies and in this way inferring, at least implicitly, their very real significance for Christological thought.

The in-depth reading of patristic literature has as well influenced, in another way, the works of several French-speaking theologians. At the beginning of his work *L'homme qui venait de Dieu* (published in 1993), Joseph Moingt recalls that, more than thirty years before, he

---

Chalcédoine (451), trans. from German (Paris: Cerf, 1973); 2nd ed. revised by Th. Hainthaler (Paris: Cerf, 2003); translated by John Bowden as *Christ in Christian Tradition*, vol. 1, *From the Apostolic Age to Chalcedon (451)* (London: Mowbrays, 1975). See also Aloys Grillmeier, *Le Christ dans la tradition chrétienne*, vol 2/1, *Le concile de Chalcédoine (451). Réception et opposition (451–513)* [The Council of Chalcedon (451). Reception and contradiction] (Paris: Cerf, 1990); vol. 2/2, *L'Église de Constantinople au VIe siècle* [The Church in Constantinople in the sixth century] (Paris: Cerf, 1993); vol. 2/4, *L'Église d'Alexandrie, la Nubie et l'Éthiopie après 451* [The Church of Alexandria with Nubia and Ethiopia after 451] (Paris, Cerf, 1996). Also see *Mit Ihm und in Ihm. Christologische Forschungen und Perspektiven* [With him and in him. Christological research and perspectives] (Freiburg: Herder, 1975).

had begun to teach the "course on the Word Incarnate" and that this course notably presented "the Tradition of the Church." He refers to the work that he had at that time completed in these terms:

> Thus having studied not only in minute detail but also zealously the acts of the "Christological" councils, but even more, all the texts of the Fathers of the Church and ecclesiastical writers, Greek and Latin, who had developed the doctrine, fought the "heretics," participated at these councils, explained their definitions, from the second to the seventh centuries, and also the Scholastic authors who, from Boethius to Thomas Aquinas and beyond, added to these definitions conceptual explanations, philosophical developments, and reconstructed the subject matter of the dogma in a theoretical and systematic way, I designed my course in the form (inspired by Hegel!) of a "logic of the history" of dogma itself to obtain an understanding of the faith for today.[18]

Of course, Moingt did not produce a book based on this teaching; as he himself explains in the work just cited, he discovered toward the end of the 1960s that the writing of history implied a "distancing" from the Tradition; for this reason it was necessary to follow closely the evolution of culture in the field of philosophy and above all the human sciences, in addition to being more interested in Protestant theology, and that, in any case, "the aim of theology could no longer be simply to comment on or to justify the teaching of the Church" but, more fundamentally, "to give an account of the faith of Christ faced with the critical rationality of our time."[19] The fact remains that the work formerly carried out by Moingt on the Fathers of the Church is still very perceptible in the work *L'homme qui venait de Dieu*, as it is in the volumes of the work that followed, *Dieu qui vient à l'homme*—even if the conciliar tradition is here interpreted according to a new problem, the one developed by the theologian throughout these works in order to attempt to make the faith "thinkable" and "credible" in the context of modernity.

As for the work of Bernard Sesboüé, it also is very illustrative of the fecundity of patristic work for Christian theology. In addition to his monographs on Irenaeus of Lyon and Basil of Caesarea, his books always show the influence of a direct contact with the Fathers, sources of inspiration in many of the fields of his theological thought. Thus

18. Moingt, *L'homme qui venait de Dieu*, 7–8.
19. Ibid., 8–9.

for Christology: Sesboüé does not just retrace the history of the early councils but shows how an appropriate hermeneutic allows updating its message for our time.[20] Thus for soteriology: a vigorous reflection on the mediation of Christ allows him from this point of view to reread the history of the first and second millennia, to assess the various ways in which Tradition has understood salvation, and finally to come to a theological proposal that is both faithful to the narrative of the Scriptures and credible for our times.[21] Thus also for ecclesiology, in particular for the theology of ministries and for the questions opened by ecumenical dialogue—the reading of the Fathers being especially fecund for the discovery of some consensus with Protestants and the Orthodox, due to the very fact that patristic literature takes us back to a period prior to the divisions of the Middle Ages and of the sixteenth century.[22] It is additionally important to draw attention to *Histoire des dogmes,* for which Sesboüé provided the direction and for which he himself wrote a great number of chapters.[23] Since the time of Joseph Tixeront (whose *Histoire des dogmes,* in three volumes, was published between 1905 and 1911), French theology had not known an analogous publication.[24] The work, quite new in its concept, is divided into four volumes centered around the theme of salvation: *Le Dieu du salut, L'Homme et son salut, Les Signes du salut, La Parole du salut.* Yet patris-

20. See Bernard Sesboüé, "Le procès contemporain de Chalcédoine: bilan et perspectives" [The contemporary trial of Chalcedon. Assessment and outlook], *Recherches de Science Religieuse* 65 (1977): 45–80; reprinted in Sesboüé, *Les "trente glorieuses" de la christologie (1968–2000)* [The "glorious thirty" of Christology] (Brussels: Lessius, 2012), 21–51.

21. See Sesboüé, *Jésus-Christ l'unique Médiateur,* vol. 1, *Problématique et relecture doctrinale* [Jesus Christ the Unique Mediator. I: Problematic and Doctrinal Review] (Paris: Desclée, 1988; re-pub. 2003); vol. 2 *Les récits du salut* [The Stories of salvation] (Paris: Desclée, 1991).

22. See Sesboüé, *Pour une théologie œcuménique: Église et sacrements, Eucharistie et ministères. La Vierge Marie* [Toward an ecumenical theology: Church and sacraments, Eucharist and ministries. The Virgin Mary] (Paris: Cerf, 1990).

23. *Histoire des dogmes* [History of dogmas], ed. B. Sesboüé, 4 vols., *Le Dieu du salut; L'Homme et son salut; Les Signes du salut; La Parole du salut* [The God of salvation; Man and his salvation; The signs of salvation; The Word of salvation] (Paris: Desclée, 1994–96).

24. Except for, at least, the voluminous *Histoire des dogmes* of the modernist J. Turmel, 6 vols. (Paris: Rieder, 1931–36), but it was influenced by the presupposition of an insurmountable conflict between the historical development of dogmas and the abstract concept of a theology according to which all the formulas and institutions of the Church came from the Christian origins. Furthermore, the *Handbuch der Dogmengeschichte* [Textbook on the history of dogmas] under the direction of Michael Schmaus, Aloys Grillmeier, Leo Scheffczyk, and Michael Seybold (Freiburg: Herder, 1971–87); this *Handbuch* had only been partially translated, in the publications of Cerf, between 1966 and 1978.

tics is used well in each volume, quite especially in the first volume (that treats Trinitarian theology, Christology and soteriology, and that principally covers the period from the first to the eighth century), and to a lesser degree in the second volume (regarding Christian anthropology, original sin, justification, and grace—themes that occasion, among other things, important expositions on Augustine).

In the same years in which this *Histoire des dogmes* was published, there appeared the French translation of another work which, in the English-speaking world, also demonstrated the fecundity of patristic studies: *La Tradition chrétienne* of Jaroslav Pelikan. This history of doctrines is divided into five volumes, the first three of which refer to—entirely or partially—the patristic era.[25] The author, a professor at Yale University and who was for a long time a Lutheran before joining the Orthodox Church, presents his project in this way: to write the history of "Christian doctrine," that is "what the Church of Jesus Christ believes, teaches, and confesses on the basis of the Word of God."[26] An important clarification then is given:

> The form which Christian doctrine, so defined, has taken in history is tradition. Like the term "doctrine," the word "tradition" refers simultaneously to the process of communication and to its content.... But we shall be dealing not so much with the formal as with the material issue of tradition, that is, with the changes and with the continuities of various Christian doctrines as they shaped history and were shaped by it.[27]

Pelikan is concerned with avoiding two opposing pitfalls: that of "Tradition without history," which had the effect of homogenizing all the stages of the development into a single truth, itself defined in a static manner; and that of "history without Tradition," which had the effect of relativizing the development of the Christian Tradition, without there being a place for a discernment between "authentic belief" and "cancerous aberration." In reality, "the history of Christian doctrine is the most effective means available of exposing the artificial theories of continuity that have often assumed normative status in the churches, and at the same time it is an avenue into the authentic continuity of Christian believing, teaching, and confessing. Tradition is the living

25. Pelikan, *The Christian Tradition*, 5 vols.
26. Pelikan, *Emergence of the Catholic Tradition*, 1.
27. Ibid., 7.

faith of the dead; traditionalism is the dead faith of the living."[28] In the end, the author means equally to affirm "the variety of Christian teachings within history" and "their possible unity within tradition": "The theological presupposition of this history ... is the variety of theologies and the unity of the gospel—the unity as well as the variety, and the unity within the variety."[29] Such is the design that directs the work in its entirety. The first volume, being completely about the patristic era, presents the common basis of the two great traditions that afterwards were going to be differentiated between the East and the West. The next volume, devoted to Eastern Christianity, heavily stresses the continuity with the first centuries; its first chapter highlights that the Fathers' authority is always invoked in the East. Such a continuity, however, does not exclude new contributions, as chapters 2 and 3 show, which present the contribution of the East to Christology (in the context of the debates of the seventh century on the energies and wills of Christ), then its contribution to theological thought on the image understood as "icon" (with notably the contribution of John Damascene). As for volume 3, it is principally devoted to the Latin Middle Ages (up until 1300) but also a part of the end of the patristic era, and thus includes, among other things, expositions on the heritage of the Augustinian synthesis.[30]

Lastly, in 1997, there appeared the French translation of *Histoire des théologies chrétiennes* written by the Spanish Benedictine Evangelista Vilanova, a monk of the abbey of Montserrat and a professor on the Faculty of Theology of Catalonia.[31] The title clearly indicates what differentiates it from the two previously mentioned works: here the emphasis is placed on the development of theologies, of course connected to the history of dogmas (which the work treats as well), but, nevertheless, distinct from it. The work consists of three volumes; the first one, encompassing the period "from the beginnings to the fifteenth century," contains numerous pages on the patristic period. The author notably shows the importance of the confrontation with

28. Ibid., 9.

29. Ibid., 9–10.

30. Volumes 4 and 5 are titled respectively *Reformation of Church and Dogma, 1300–1700*; and *Christian Doctrine and Modern Culture since 1700*.

31. Evangelista Vilanova, *Histoire des théologies chrétiennes* [History of Christian theologies], 3 vols, trans. from the Spanish (Paris: Cerf, 1997).

"the world of gnosis," then devotes an entire chapter to what he calls "the development of a scientific method" (the work of apologists; that of Origen; the new developments of theology following the Constantine revolution), two chapters are specifically devoted to Trinitarian dogma and Christological dogma, and another chapter presents Latin patristic theology from Tertullian to Leo the Great. Lastly, the next part in this first volume, titled "Byzantine Theology," opens with expositions on the theology of the seventh century and on the iconoclast crisis of the eighth century. This patristic route (like the chapters relating to the subsequent periods) wants to respond to the objective that the author proposed in his introduction: "We would like to show, throughout this *Histoire des théologies chrétiennes*, the point to which the convergence of subjects and disciplines, still insufficiently used, reveals itself to be necessary as much to secular history as to the history of Christian thinking."[32] A little later the author added:

> It would be necessary to write a history of theology by following the dynamic of the Incarnation of the Gospel in various generations, and in solidarity with the numerous human projects that have animated societies; and to do this in the very name of the understanding of the Word of God, the proper place of which is in the midst of the world and its changes. We will thus avoid the twofold epistemological dualism that so often causes theology, as well as the unity of Christian life, to fail: materialism and spiritualism on one hand, opposed in their burdensome competition; secular reality and the domain of the sacred on the other, the antagonism of which dismantles the articulation of nature and grace.[33]

The mention of these few works[34] suffices to show how patristic studies have contributed not only to a better knowledge of this or that Father of the Church but also to a profound renewal in the history of Christian doctrines. Yet here it is important to emphasize an essential point: the works to which we have referred do not just bring to light the thinking of ancient authors—rather, they do it only by means

32. Vilanova, *Histoire des théologies chrétiennes*, vol. 1, *Des origines au XVe siècle* [From the origins to the Fifteenth Century], xxiii.

33. Ibid., xxiii–xxiv.

34. Other contributions could also be noted, as for example the *Histoire de la théologie* [History of Theology], ed. Jean-Yves Lacoste (Paris: Seuil, 2009); see the section by Patrick Descourtieux, "Théologie patristique et byzantine" [Patristic and Byzantine theology], 51–152.

of interpretations that each time involve (explicitly or not) theological options. One easily perceives this for "the history of dogmas" and "the history of theologies": the works of Grillmeier, Sesboüé, Pelikan, and Vilanova presuppose diverse understandings of what the Christian tradition is, of the relationship between dogma and history, of the manner in which continuity and innovation is articulated in the development of doctrines, or even of the stakes that are connected to this or that debate from the past (as, for example, in Grillmeier, the assessment of the Christological schemas *Logos/sarx* and *Logos/anthropos*—an assessment that is not without connections to the contemporary debates around Christologies "from above" and "from below"). From this point of view, "the history of dogmas" and "the history of theologies" must be understood as belonging to theology itself.

But the same remark could be made regarding some of the monographs to which we referred at the beginning of this section; not always, undoubtedly, to the same degree: the main aim of some studies can be to provide information on this or that author, without involving or even presupposing any of the theological options of patrology itself. In many cases, however, the studies devoted to this or that Father of the Church (or to some themes of patristic literature) lead the author to theological considerations that, in his eyes, have a real significance for contemporary theology—even if, most often, this significance is itself not set out. Several works that we have mentioned here, in any case, show the manner in which a patristic work can explicitly deal with an aim of fundamental or dogmatic theology. This is the case, as we have seen, in the work of Moingt, *L'homme qui venait de Dieu* (even if, in this instance, the goal of the Christological statements leads the author to a work of "deconstruction," a prelude to a new foundation of Christology based on the Gospel narrative). This is also the case in the work of Sesboüé, *Jésus-Christ dans la tradition de l'Église*, the author's aim being to offer a Christological proposal that can actualize the Christology of Chalcedon for our time; it is also the case in his work *Jésus-Christ l'unique Médiateur*, in which historical development is structured around the project of a soteriology that is both faithful to the Tradition and currently credible. It is the same for the patristic writings of Michel Corbin, not only for his monographs on the texts of Basil or Gregory of Nyssa but also for his thematic works such as *La Trinité ou l'excès de Dieu*.[35] These writings are filled with the conviction that the thinking of the Fathers of the Church—of those, in any case, who at least respect the witness of the Scriptures—meets us today because being prior to subsequent systematizations they allow us to reach the very source of the Word of God and the extraordinary revelation that it brings.

The rich harvest that we have just recounted must not, however, lead to an illusion. Despite the considerable boom in patristic studies, despite their decisive contribution to the history of Christian doctrines, and even if the work of some theologians is, as one has seen, profoundly influenced by an in-depth reading of the Fathers, it is also necessary to recognize that, from other points of view, the distance between patristics and fundamental or dogmatic theology has been widened. This distance emerges when we compare our era with that of de Lubac, Daniélou, Congar, and Balthasar: while they found in the study of the Fathers a preferred way of theological renewal, the interest of others, in our day, is primarily (or even exclusively) historical or literary. One sometimes even radically calls into question the ability of patristic literature to spark or to enrich a theological reflection for our time. It would be futile to underestimate these recent developments and to imply that the study of the Fathers could today inspire Christian thinking in a quasi-direct manner (similar traditionalism would, moreover, not be in accordance with the spirit that marked the return to the Fathers in the theology of the twentieth century). It is important rather to identify the reasons that explain the distance referred to above—such an identification is a condition of being able to overcome the difficulties at issue and to show, in the following chapters, how patristics must still be fruitful for Christian theology. These reasons apply, on one hand, to some of the questions that have been raised in the context of human sciences and philosophy; above all, they apply, as we will soon explain, to some questions that directly relate to exegesis and theology.

35. See Michel Corbin, *La Trinité ou l'Excès de Dieu* [The Trinity or the excess of God] (Paris: Cerf, 1997).

Patristics Questioned by Human Sciences and Philosophy

The present difficulties are first connected to some questions that for several decades have emerged in the framework of the human sciences. These questions can first be delimited through a very significant case: the distance that Michel de Certeau (a great historian of mysticism as well as an anthropologist and cofounder of the Lacanian school) progressively took toward the view of history developed by his elder de Lubac. Certeau had been deeply influenced by him, whom he had known well at Lyon-Fourvière, and had found in him "his primary sources of inspiration."[36] He himself had written for the *Mélanges* presented to de Lubac and, on the occasion of this publication, had devoted an article to his confrere. He welcomed the renewal that de Lubac appeared to him to incarnate; he saw in him a pioneer, a mind always solicitous of fundamental questions, a theologian inclined toward a great spirituality.[37] However, their directions were going to diverge little by little, and notably on the understanding of history—and thus, among other things, on the way of referring to the Fathers of the Church. Whereas de Lubac placed more emphasis on the basic continuity that in his eyes characterized the great river of Tradition, Certeau was more aware of the discontinuities and what he called the "innovating rupture."[38] The first even came to denounce in the second "a model of neo-Joachimism," a reference to Joachim de Flore, who, formerly, conceived the age of the Spirit as a new age (after that of the Father and of the Son). At least Joachim considered that the Spirit would reveal some of the mysteries hidden in the letter of the New Testament to the understanding, clearly maintaining a form of continuity. Yet Certeau, in the eyes of de Lubac, envisaged rather a "surpassing," a "departure," a "progressive distancing"—not that Christianity was not, undoubtedly, in relationship with the event that had instituted it, but

36. François Dosse, *Michel de Certeau: Le marcheur blessé* [The wounded walker] (Paris: La Découverte, 2002), 51.

37. Cf. Michel de Certeau, "Un maître: le père Henri de Lubac" [A Master: Father Henri de Lubac], *Ecclesia*, no. 187 (1964): 83–90.

38. Cf. Michel de Certeau, "La rupture instauratrice, ou le christianisme dans la culture contemporaine" [The innovative rupture or Christianity in contemporary culture], *Esprit* (June 1971): 1177–1214.

that for Certeau the truth is displayed by it "in the mode of disappearing in the differences that it makes possible;" in some way "the relationship to the 'origins' is an increasing absence."[39] It is not possible to expound all the details of these last statements, which would need to be connected with Certeau's views on the writing of history and on the hermeneutics that it implies. De Lubac's reaction is in any case revealing: the practice of historical science, as interpreted by Certeau, appeared to him as a threat to an authentic concept of history, which, of course, did not exclude in his eyes actual variations, indeed even discontinuities, but that, nevertheless, had to be grasped in its fundamental unity by the light of the Christian mystery.

Independent of this conflict that was based on different ways of conceiving the relationship to the past, one must recognize that the considerable boom in human sciences during recent decades has, on one hand, modified the status of patristics and that this has created a new situation, which is often delicate, if not difficult, for theology itself. On the other, one could not overemphasize the remarkable way in which this boom has profited patrology: the critical editions and the works devoted to them are a major indicator of this. But it also complicates the task of theologians: their work can be recognized in the world of research only by taking into account the works conducted in the fields of history, anthropology, and other sciences to which patrology must appeal as well. The situation, of course, is not entirely new, but it has been generalized and radicalized.

Let us go further: the theologian must not only know as much as is possible about the works undertaken within the framework of the human sciences on this author or that theme of the patristic era, he must also, in some cases, attempt to make credible the very aim of his study. For this aim sometimes runs the risk of being suspect: does not the theological preoccupation, one asks, lead to unduly compelling the study of the texts? Is it not at the same time detrimental to the "scientific" objectivity of a work that must only explain these texts for themselves, profiting from the resources of various disciplines? Of course, such questions presuppose a form of scientism and are, from

39. Ibid., 1203; see Henri de Lubac, *La postérité spirituelle de Joachim de Flore II: De Saint Simon à nos jours* [The spiritual posterity of Joachim of Flore II: From Saint Simon to the present day] (Paris: Lethielleux, 1981), 447–49.

this point of view, less neutral than it would first appear. They show, at the least, that the theological orientation of a work on the Fathers of itself is not necessarily accepted in the world of research, even if it is obviously called for from within the Christian community. Hence the demand that theologians be sufficiently informed of the results achieved by human sciences—theologians having, for their part, to justify not staying with these results but also questioning the patristic texts with the aim of a specifically theological reflection.

Other difficulties arise from questions in which patristic literature is the subject from the philosophical point of view. One of these questionings is connected to the reproach against the "Hellenization" of Christianity—according to the perspective formerly developed by Harnack. As understood by him in its broadest generality, this indictment consists above all in denouncing the negative effects of an adaptation to the language of the Greek world—an adaptation that would have caused a deformation of the Gospel message, indeed a rupture with regard to it. But what is called into question by this denunciation is more precisely the language inherited from philosophy: Christianity would have introduced from the Greek (or Greco-Latin) culture words, concepts, and schemas of thinking that, although facilitating, on one hand, its penetration into the ancient world, would have by the same token formed a barrier regarding the Judeo-Christian Revelation. Actually, the process denounced here was already at work, up to a certain point, in the Greek translation of the Old Testament, for example when the Septuagint, in Exodus 3:14, translated the divine Name by the formula "I will be who I will be" (*egô eimi ho ôn*), or even more so in the work of the Jewish exegete Philo of Alexandria. But it is the Christian apologists who, in their concern to respond to the objections of philosophers, would have "Hellenized" then "Latinized" Christian language at the risk of betraying the original meaning. It is also seen in the word "*Logos*" (already used in the prologue of John, of course, but first with the meaning of "Word") having been extensively used beginning with Justin, Clement of Alexandria, and Origen, in a manner that was not only in keeping with its meaning in the Johannine prologue but that little by little integrated its various harmonics from Greek philosophy—notably its meaning of "reason." Thus again, some Fathers were going to devote themselves to metaphysical developments on the being of God, in a way that—one might object—no longer respected the original meaning of the divine Name revealed to Moses. More widely, major concepts of ancient philosophy were going to be called upon by Christian thinking, like the concept of "essence" (*ousia*) or the concept of "substance" (*hypostasis*), even if it received a new meaning (as was exactly the case with *hypostasis*, which in Trinitarian theology would ultimately acquire the meaning of "subsistence"). The conciliar definitions themselves would integrate such concepts—as with the famous "consubstantial" (*homoousios*) from the Council of Nicaea. And the more the Greek and Latin Fathers debated with the Neoplatonists and other schools of thought of the era, the more their own thought risked being contaminated by the conceptualizations foreign to the Judeo-Christian Revelation.

This suspicion, stated here in the most general form, often takes arguments from the philosophy of Heidegger. For him, as one knows, the history of thought has been influenced by the forgetting of Being, from the fact that it favored the knowledge of being and adopted this point of view; the word "being" may still be heard in the pre-Socratics, but its forgetting led to a situation in which philosophy risks yielding before science, indeed, being reduced by it. The history of thinking, read in the light of the fundamental ontology that *Sein und Zeit* develops, thus casts a critical light on metaphysics that is therefore achieved and thus its end must be recognized. Such an end opens onto a new perspective, that of the man who frees himself from the imprisonment in the "ontic" and yields to the truth (*aletheia*)—that is to say to the "not-veiled," to the unveiling of Being. Yet to the extent that this Heideggerian philosophy is accepted, it contributes to fueling a critical distance regarding the conceptualizations of the patristic era: they would participate in the "metaphysical" age and in the "onto-theological" language that signifies the forgetting of Being, and this is what one would notably have to denounce through the interpretation of the divine Name as designating a "Being" among beings, the first among them. It would actually be necessary to take a step back, or retreat, in order to be led again—going back prior to these patristic conceptualizations, beyond even Platonic or Aristotelian philosophy—to the truth of Being or, in the present case, to the truth that is given through the original biblical Revelation.

The questions raised in the framework of human sciences and philosophy, without any doubt, contribute to explaining the real difficulties of theology's relationship with patristic literature. But it is now necessary to come to other questions that theology itself directly raises.

Patristics and Theology: The Present Difficulties

We will principally discern three reasons that explain the present difficulties: one concerns the status of patristic exegesis; another is due to the changes that mark some fields of theology; a third is linked to the consideration of new contexts for Christian thinking, outside of Europe but within as well.

The Status of Patristic Exegesis

Questions relating to the exegesis made by the Fathers have, of course, been the subject of numerous debates since the time of de Lubac and Daniélou. Independent of particular subjects that were then treated in the context of patristic studies—for example, the usage of the words "typology" and "allegory" or even the differences between Alexandrian and Antiochene exegesis—what was at stake in the return to the Fathers for the theologians of this generation was acquiring a more correct understanding of the Scriptures. It was, of course, not a matter of questioning the contributions of the critical sciences but of enrolling in the school of the Fathers in order to understand the biblical texts, beyond their literal meaning, in their spiritual significance as such. This was valid above all else for the writings of the Old Testament: the Fathers precisely learned to discover their "figurative" or "prophetic" meaning in the light of the Revelation transmitted by Christ. The rediscovery of the Fathers, in the same way, ought to contribute to a more profound understanding of the relationship between the two Testaments. Daniélou had summarized these stakes in an article that we have already mentioned above:

> The effort that is asked of us is to rediscover, but in relation to the achievements of contemporary science, an interpretation that restores to the Old Testament its prophetic or figurative character that makes up a great part of its interest for us. This question of figurative exegesis, which is one of the most vital of current exegesis, will undoubtedly be the occasion, during the com-

ing years, of courteous and fruitful confrontations between scientific exegetes and theologian exegetes whose contribution is also necessary. It is necessary to await from these confrontations the elaboration of a new theology of prophesy, that is to say of the relationship of the Old to the New Testament, a notion that is called to play a very important role in the theology of tomorrow.[40]

Whatever the debates about the "spiritual meaning" of the Scriptures in the 1940s and 1950s were, it is a fact that the patristic renewal largely contributed to providing a new access to the source of the Word of God, also advised by Vatican Council II. One not only sees the increase in scholarly studies on the Holy Scriptures, but, much more widely, a number of Christians began to read the scriptural texts and to attempt, with others, to plumb the depths of the meaning: the development of these Bible groups is, without any doubt, one of the most remarkable phenomena in the life of the Church in recent decades.

But consequently, one becomes aware of the question: if Christians have more access to the Bible itself, has not the study of the Fathers therefore produced the fruits that one was awaiting, and so why would it still be necessary to be interested in the Father's own interpretation of Scriptures? From this point of view at least, it is in some ways the very success of the patristic renewal that would seem to have consequently created an obstacle to patristic exegesis. What is more is that their exegesis appeared to have several limitations: on one hand, the Greek Fathers of the first centuries only follow the translation of the Septuagint and (with exceptions, as in the case of Origen) do not refer to the Hebrew version of the Old Testament; on the other, ignorant of the subsequent achievements of critical exegesis, patristic exegesis often risks being misleading on the meaning of this word or that verse; lastly and above all, the priority that it gives to the spiritual importance of the biblical writings seems to contradict the need for an exegetical science that is as respectful as possible of the text itself and that does not try to say more than it does.

This is the first challenge that patristic theology confronts today. So it will be necessary to face up to this set of objections and to show why, in our situation, the exegesis of the Fathers remains essential for Christian knowledge of Scriptures.

40. Daniélou, "Les orientations présentes de la pensée religieuse," 9; see chap. 2, pp. 37–38.

Changes in Some Fields of Theology

To the question touching upon the interpretation of the Bible is added other questions that concern several specific fields of theology.

The questions are about, among other things, the patristic formulations of Christological and Trinitarian dogma: today one is very aware of the distance that exists, in numerous cases, between these formulations and the original statements of the faith (such as one discovers them in the New Testament, and most especially in the Gospels, the Acts of the Apostles, and the letters of Paul); consequently, one asks, is it not necessary to return to the doctrines elaborated prior to the fourth and fifth centuries in order to recover a language closer to Revelation?

It is also necessary to clarify the difficulty to which we are here alluding. Of itself, indeed, the concern to rediscover the language of the New Testament is fully legitimate; what is more, the works that, in this sense, have been undertaken for several decades have already borne important fruits. It is very worthwhile to recall, for example, the detailed study of Rahner on the meanings of the word *Theos* in the New Testament; such a study precisely does not intend to question the statements of the councils on Trinitarian dogma, it rather wants to interpret them correctly, and this thanks to their own confrontation with the original language of the faith.[41] In the same way, when Rahner reflected upon the heritage of Chalcedon, he in no way contested the position that this council had taken in the context of the Nestorian crisis but rather reacted against the erroneous readings that did not give enough importance to the true humanity of Jesus as it appears in the Gospels.[42] More recently, Moingt has emphasized the distance between the conciliar statements of the patristic era (to the extent that they speak of the Incarnation) and the Gospel narrative (that tells what happened with Jesus of Nazareth): it is this narrative

41. Cf. Karl Rahner, "Dieu dans le Nouveau Testament. La signification du mot 'Theos'" [God in New Testament. The Meaning of the Word "Theos"], trans. from German, *Écrits théologiques*, vol. 1 (Paris: Desclée de Brouwer, 1959), 11–111, translated by Cornelius Ernst as "Theos in the New Testament," in Rahner, *Theological Investigations*, 1:79–148.

42. Cf. Karl Rahner, "Problèmes actuels de christologie," in *Écrits théologiques*, 1:113–81, translated by Cornelius Ernst as "Current Problems in Christology," in Rahner, *Theological Investigations*, 1:149–213.

that must henceforth serve as the point of departure for Christology, for a "deconstruction" of the language inherited from the councils.[43] But Moingt's proposal is correct in making the Gospel narratives "a believing reading, in conformity with the faith of the Church."[44] And he announces that, if Christology must henceforth take as fundamental the Pascal event (and not the dogma of the Incarnation), "it is on this basis that the divine filiation of 'this man' dead and resurrected must be established, provided that one then establishes, always being guided by the narratives and the Gospel announcements, the eternity of the gift that God gave to men of his Son and that one verifies thus the concept of incarnation."[45] In other words, the distance taken from the conciliar statements on Christ does not prohibit retaining their goal; even more, according to the intention of the author, it must allow rediscovering this goal, fully honoring the faith of the Church in the divine filiation of Jesus, and, when the time comes, of doing justice to the doctrine of the Incarnation.

The difficulty to which we alluded above is of another kind. It is connected to a perception that, as such, is barely formulated by professional theologians but that, in contrast, is considerably widespread in the public: the statements of the ancient councils, by their very goal, would have totally misrepresented the meaning of the Gospel Revelation, in particular, the affirmation of the divine filiation of Jesus would not have a basis in the synoptic Gospels. It would have only been introduced by the Gospel of John at a relatively late date and above all, would have been imposed by the will of the emperors thanks to the ecumenical councils of the fourth and fifth centuries.[46] One sees how such affirmations change the perception of patristic

43. Cf. Moingt, *L'homme qui venait de Dieu*, 223.

44. Ibid., 281.

45. Ibid.

46. This is notably the thesis of Frédéric Lenoir in his book *Comment Jesus est devenu Dieu* [How Jesus has become God] (Paris: Fayard, 2010). Without a doubt, this book must be placed in the cultural context of our time, particularly aware of the humanity of Christ and of the fact that his true identity cannot be known at the outset. It testifies, moreover, to a real attachment to Jesus, presented as "an unclassifiable man" (ibid., 34). However, it comes up against some objections from the point of view of the traditional faith in the divinity of Jesus. On this point, see Bernard Sesboüé, *Christ, Seigneur et Fils de Dieu. Libre réponse à Frédéric Lenoir* [Christ, Lord and Son of God. Free answer to Frédéric Lenoir] (Paris: Lethielleux, Groupe DDB, 2010).

literature, at the least, of those writings that produced the doctrinal developments on the subject of Christ. This literature would have "added" to the testimony of the Synoptics the affirmation of the divine filiation of Jesus; and, under duress from the imperial power, it would have been written into the conciliar statements. Of course, we must later respond to this last objection, for what is at stake is not only an historical issue but also touches upon the very understanding of the faith. In fact, as we will say later, one cannot associate the doctrinal work of the ecumenical councils so closely to the will of the emperors, nor can one, on this point, oppose the conciliar formulations and the testimony of the Scriptures. But for the moment, it suffices to have drawn attention to the difficulty thus raised. Such a difficulty, let us repeat, today finds quite a widespread consensus; and, from this fact, itself contributes to discrediting the patristic doctrines regarding theologies that would be more immediately faithful to the New Testament and in particular to the synoptic Gospels.

But other difficulties come to the fore, in very diverse domains; we will just briefly enumerate them here, reserving the right to return to them later in this book. One of them concerns the "anti-Judaism" for which it has become common to reproach patristic literature. Of course, one agrees with distinguishing "anti-Judaism" from "anti-Semitism," responsible for so many of the atrocities of subsequent eras and notably the twentieth century. But, one asks, has not the vehemence of many patristic writings against the Jews contributed to what followed? Another difficulty concerns the relationship of the Church with those who were considered as "heretics": one denounces the severity of the charges held against them and, even more, the punishments that were sometimes inflicted upon them. Also regarding "pagans": not only were the debates with them marked by harsh polemics, but beginning with the time at which Christianity became the official religion of the empire, those in power did not retreat from violent acts against the cultic places inherited from the Greco-Roman world. One does not ignore, of course, that it is necessary to take into account the literary genre of the controversies in Antiquity, and, moreover, that Christians themselves could be threatened or attacked at certain periods (even after the Constantinian revolution, as witnessed to by the political decisions of the emperor Julian). But this does not suffice to justify the ancient practices, and therefore one risks thinking that patristic literature can no longer be of any help for the present tasks of ecumenism and the theology of religions. Other difficulties could still be mentioned: the emphasis of some patristic texts on the inferiority of woman; some changes that have characterized the theology of ministries and that are in our day discussed (for example, the recourse to a "sacred" language in order to take into account the ministry exercised by priests); more widely, the decisions that have engaged the Church on new ways in the areas of practices, discipline, and internal organization—decisions that could be as such founded but that, in some cases, are reevaluated in the framework of contemporary ecclesiology. Our purpose, here, is not now to take up each of these questions. It is only to highlight the reasons that, at least apparently, make them obstacles to the project of a patristic theology—but we will hope to show later that, for all that, they do not constitute insurmountable objections.

New Contexts for Christian Thinking

The current difficulties are in the end connected to a major phenomenon—and a very happy one per se—that marks the evolution of theology for several decades: the concern to take into account the diversity of the contexts in which Christian thinking must be elaborated.

It is necessary first of all to say a word about the Latin-American liberation movements that appeared beginning in the 1960s. The theologians who have thought from this perspective have emphasized that their thought, even if it had been informed by European theology and its sources in the Tradition, was not purely "deduced" from it but it was rooted in an original situation: it had to be a theology "beginning" with Latin America, more precisely beginning with the "context" of populations that were victims of injustice and were aspiring to their "liberation." The ideal that these attempts embodied, and, above all, the hope in which they were carried out have also influenced other Christian communities in completely different contexts, and it is thus that one saw, in the same decades, other forms of "liberation theology" being developed: "black American" theologies in the United States, "feminist" theologies on the same continent, theologies of liberation in sub-Saharan Africa and in South Africa. Asia, in its turn, has come to develop such theologies in its own context—even if it means specifying that its liberation theology presents some completely original traits from the fact of its being grounded in a situation that is not only marked by poverty but by the heritage of the great religious traditions of the Asian continent. All these theologies can of course appeal, here and there, to patristic references. But they rest upon the conviction that the Christian communities of the countries concerned do not simply have to "apply" to their respective situations themes or ways of thinking that came from European theology and from the Tradition that it brings. Sometimes they are even led to evaluate the writings of the Fathers in a critical manner (feminist theologies, showing how the tradition was often marked by the predominance of "patriarchal" language—contrary to what was reflective of the relationships of Jesus with the women of his time).

Moreover, the research carried out in Africa and in Asia from the perspective of "inculturation" has also implied a distancing from languages too exclusively dependent upon the "Mediterranean" world. The question is assuredly complex, for this last preoccupation has, at the same time, converged with political and ecclesial problems (that have been posited, as well, in the Latin-American continent): on one hand, one has recalled the violence that was exerted in the past in the framework of colonization, whatever were its benefits. On the other, one has been aware of the support that the Church itself had given, although indirectly, to the expansion of European politics and to the sometimes unjustifiable behaviors toward local populations (this does not place in question the grandeur of the missionary adventure nor, above all, the witness of Christians who dared to denounce vigorously the attitude of some colonizers). But the will to create a distance from the "Mediterranean" or "European" world, even if it has been reinforced by the memory of the political and ecclesial past, also had its raison d'être in a theological consideration. In line with what Vatican II had said on the particular Church and on the necessity of taking into account the values "disseminated" among the nations, some African and Asian theologians relied upon the heritage of their respective traditions in order to invent original languages—for example, beginning with a reflection on the "titles" that could be given to Jesus of Nazareth in the context of sub-Saharan Africa or beginning with images and notions strongly rooted in the cultures of India and the Far East. This can only have contributed to an enrichment of theology. But the question is inevitably asked: to the extent that theologians in search of "inculturation" develop new languages in their own contexts, what from the Christian literature that was created around the Mediterranean Basin in the first centuries of our era is it necessary for them to pass on? Would it not suffice, for African and Asian theologies, to begin exclusively with local or regional contexts, to read the Scriptures in these contexts and thus to find significant languages for Christian communities of this or that country, forgetting what the first expression of Christian theology had been during the age of patristic literature?

In fact, the language of "inculturation" itself is the object of some suspicion in Asia, to the extent that it gives the impression of concealing a kind of ecclesial strategy that calls for the Church to be established in this or that place by integrating only "cultural" values into the Asiatic continent, to the detriment of the religious dimension with which it is intimately connected. Whatever the criticism formulated here, it has the merit of drawing attention to a major given that, at first glance, seems as well to weaken patristic theology: the importance of the great Asian religions such as Hinduism and Buddhism, which for the most part were entirely ignored by the Fathers of the Church or that at the least are only the subject of a very distant and very imprecise knowledge (even if some Nestorian missionaries reached as far as China). Islam itself appeared in the seventh century, and it is thus necessary to await the latter part of the patristic era to find, with John Damascene, the trace of the first debates between Christians and Muslims. If one adds that, conversely, the religions coming from the Greco-Roman world have long since disappeared, it can be tempting to think that—except perhaps in what concerns the relationship of Christianity with Judaism—the writings of the Fathers can no longer be of great help for a contemporary reflection in the field of the theology of religions.

One thus sees how the development of "contextual" theologies—which is in itself, let us repeat, a fundamental achievement of the last decades—seems to raise some specific difficulties regarding the traditional task of patristic theology. But it is necessary to add that in some ways the questions thus raised flow back on Europe itself. On one hand, indeed, the entrance into the age of "globalization" contributes to relativizing the "Mediterranean" world and thus also, as a consequence, the Christian literature that has been elaborated in it. On the other, because of the expansion of Islam, and in no small measure, oriental religions, European Christianity finds itself confronted with beliefs and practices that, as we have recalled, were hardly known during the era of the Fathers. Lastly—and one cannot overly emphasize this point of extreme importance—the technical and cultural changes in modern Europe are so extensive that its own past is becoming more foreign: this is valid, in a general way, for the centuries of Greek and Latin Antiquity but also, in a more specific way, for the first centuries of Christianity's history. There is a direct effect on the world of education, to the extent that the Greek and Latin languages are taught less and less—a change for which one must truly assess the impact: not only the risk that European culture is becoming more and more distant from one of its essential sources but equally, from the point of view that is here ours, the risk that Christian communities are increasingly misunderstanding the heritage of the first Christian theologies. Of course, such a situation does not prohibit there being, in various forms, a real presence of Christianity in European cultures. This is so in art, in some institutions, and more fundamentally in the values and ideas that, even in a "laicized" form, bear the imprint of the Christian heritage. The survival of such a heritage is not, however, sufficient for guaranteeing the experience of a living relationship with those who are our Fathers in the faith—sometimes it can even serve as a pretext. European Christianity is as such confronted with the exigency that a short time ago was (and continues to be) necessary for the communities of Latin America, Africa, and Asia: to take into account its specific context and, in this same context, to read the Scriptures in order to present the faith in a meaningful way. But how will European Christianity be able to do this without exploring and living in the tradition that it brings and thus, above all here, the tradition of early Christianity that has contributed so much to shaping the face of Europe?

We have, in this chapter, first of all noted the considerable development of patristic studies since Vatican II. We have also shown the contribution that they have made to the history of dogma, and the fruits that they have produced in some theologians. But we have also analyzed the reasons for the difficulties that, from other points of view, seem today to characterize the relationship between patristics and Christian theology. These reasons, as we have seen, are sometimes very radical, but we would like to show that they are not decisive. It would, of course, be illusory to circumvent them: rather, it is necessary to confront them straight on and, as much as is possible, to take them into account in our own reflection. But it is not necessary to renounce, because of them, what must remain today as yesterday the ambition of patristic theology. The aim of the three chapters that follow will be precisely to establish the legitimacy and the necessity of such a theology. They will do it by taking up the various difficulties that we have examined and by showing in what way it will be possible to overcome them. We will begin with the questions relating to exegesis; we will then reflect upon what must be, despite the objections referred to above, the contribution of patristic studies to Christian thought; we will lastly show how to treat correctly the questions raised by "contextual" theologies and, more widely, how to envision the study of the Fathers in our age of globalization.

CHAPTER 5

The Stakes of Patristic Exegesis

A first set of difficulties that patristic theology must overcome today concerns, as we have seen, the interpretation of Holy Scripture. We will, first of all, show that these difficulties are in part connected to misunderstandings. Once these have been dispelled, it will be possible to uncover the true meaning of the exegesis of the Fathers. In order to do this, we will examine one of them, Origen, taking into consideration his fundamental thought on the spiritual understanding of the holy books. We will then show how the Fathers' homilies and biblical commentaries today remain, under some conditions, very valuable for the Christian interpretation of the Scriptures: although we must directly study the scriptural texts and henceforth integrate the achievements of critical exegesis, the importance of patristic exegesis, which we will attempt to specify, is no less permanent.

Some Misunderstandings to Be Dispelled

Of course, it is initially necessary to recognize that the rehabilitation of patristic exegesis over the course of the twentieth century had a paradoxical aspect. In fact, for several decades, the development of philology and historical sciences had led to a distancing away from traditional exegeses that, too often, were not concerned enough with the literal meaning. In 1943, the encyclical of Pius XII *Divino afflante Spiritu* advocated recourse to critical methods for the study of the Bible and, all the while affirming that exegetes must expound not only the literal meaning but also the spiritual meaning of texts, asked that they "scrupulously refrain from proposing as the genuine meaning of Sacred Scripture other figurative senses."[1] One additionally recalls the suspicion formulated in 1950 by the encyclical *Humani generis* against the teachers of the "new exegesis":

> according their fictitious opinions, the literal sense of Holy Scripture and its explanation, carefully worked out under the Church's vigilance by so many great exegetes, should yield now to a new exegesis, which they are pleased to call symbolic or spiritual. By means of this new exegesis, the Old Testament, which today in the Church is a sealed book, would finally be thrown open to all the faithful. By this method, they say, all difficulties vanish, difficulties which hinder only those who adhere to the literal meaning of the Scriptures.[2]

However, in spite of the allusion to "spiritual" exegesis, these lines clearly do not intend to denounce the interpretation of Scripture that had been developed by the Fathers, but the attitude of those who, during the contemporary era, risked circumventing the literal meaning of the Scriptures. The encyclical *Divino afflante Spiritu* had, moreover, expressly emphasized the continuing real importance of patristic exegesis:

> the Catholic exegete will find invaluable help in an assiduous study of those works, in which the Holy Fathers, the Doctors of the Church, and the renowned interpreters of past ages have explained the Sacred Books. For, although sometimes less instructed in profane learning and in the knowledge of languages than the Scripture scholars of our time, nevertheless by reason of the office assigned to them by God in the Church, they are distinguished by a certain subtle insight into heavenly things and by a marvelous keenness of intellect, which enables them to penetrate to the very innermost meaning of the divine word and to bring to light all that can help to elucidate the teaching of Christ and to promote holiness of life.[3]

These reminders help to dispel a misunderstanding that hung over and continues to hang over patristic exegesis. Of course, it is not a matter of denying that in many cases the Christian authors of Antiquity were wrong about the literal meaning of the texts; and it is important, in any case, to emphasize that the recourse to their exegesis must not be an excuse for circumventing this literal meaning that henceforth is better known thanks to the methods of critical exegesis.

1. Pius XII, encyclical letter *Divino afflante Spiritu* (1943), no. 27.
2. Pius XII, encyclical letter *Humani Generis* (1950), no. 23.
3. Pius XII, *Divino afflante Spiritu*, no. 28.

But this does not authorize disqualifying patristic exegesis entirely or denying it any pertinence for our times. All things considered, the Fathers were more attentive to the letter of the biblical texts than one might believe. Origen, for example, recognized that the first meaning of the Scriptures (the literal or "corporal" meaning) at times proved to be incoherent or improbable; and he said this not just about some passages of the Old Testament (such as the story of creation in Gn 2) but even regarding a Gospel story such as that of the temptations in the desert:

> the devil is said to have placed Jesus on "a very high mountain" to show Him from there "all the kingdoms of the world and the glory of them" (Mt 4:8). How could it possibly happen according to the letter either that the devil led Jesus to a very high mountain or that to his fleshly eyes he "showed," as though they were below and next to that one mountain, "all the kingdoms of the world," that is, the kingdoms of the Persians, the Scythians, the Indians, and how their kings are glorified by men? Moreover, whoever reads with special care will find a great many other passages like this in the Gospels. In this way he will notice that into these accounts that seem to have been described according to the letter there have been sown in and woven together things that the narrative meaning will not admit.[4]

These lines are all the more remarkable in that Origen was later to be accused of being too versed in allegorism, to the detriment of paying sufficient attention to the letter of the Scriptures! This is the same Origen, who, moreover, undertook the "critical" work of the *Hexaples*, arranging in six parallel columns the Hebrew text of the Old Testament, the translation of the Septuagint, and the other Greek versions of the Bible. After him, some of the Fathers were particularly concerned with respecting the actual text of the Scriptures and of understanding it correctly: thus Jerome, who wanted to find the "*veritas hebraica*" and himself produced a new Latin translation of the Old Testament; thus also the exegetes called "Antiochenes," who were often critics of the Alexandrian exegesis that they judged to be too inclined to allegory

4. Origen, *On First Principles*, IV, 3, 1, trans. Rowan A. Greer, The Classics of Western Spirituality 10 (Mahwah, N.J.: Paulist Press, 1979), 189–90; another translation: Origen, *On First Principles*, trans. G. W. Butterworth (New York: Harper & Row, 1966), 289–90. See also *Commentary on the Gospel according to John, Books 1–10*, Book X, 18–20, trans. Ronald E. Heine, Fathers of the Church 80 (Washington, D.C.: The Catholic University of America Press, 1989), 259–60.

and endeavored to restore with more exactitude the first meaning of the biblical texts. Of course, it is necessary not to overstate these tendencies, for the Fathers did not make use of all the philological and historical resources that today benefit critical exegesis, and the fact is that they were above all preoccupied with searching the Scriptures for the revelation of hidden mysteries, beyond what the letter of biblical texts alone said. At least their goal was to respect this letter, and the examples given also show that they already knew how to propose, if need be, thoughts coming from a specifically "critical" work.

It ought to be clear, in any case, that the rehabilitation of patristic exegesis in the twentieth century does not itself imply calling into question philological and historical sciences. Henri de Lubac has clearly defended this point: "The spiritual interpretation must not interfere in an indiscreet or premature manner with the historical work. It especially must not be taken as history, even religious history, or be substituted for history."[5]

The rediscovery of patristic exegesis has, nonetheless, brought to the fore the spiritual interpretation of the Scriptures, and we will soon have to specify the significance of this emphasis. But it is necessary for us first to dispel another misunderstanding: that which would consist of identifying the spiritual exegesis of the Fathers with any form of allegorism.

Truly, we are here in the presence of a very old debate.[6] We have already alluded to the criticisms against Origen by those who, during the patristic era, reproached him for giving too much importance to allegory. A comparison of the biblical commentaries of this "Alexandrian" and those of the "Antiochene" Theodore of Mopsuestia indeed

5. Henri de Lubac, "Sens spirituel" [Spiritual sense], *Recherches de Science Religieuse* 36 (1949): 563. H. de Lubac had also written in 1947: "the praise of a Greek Father is not directed against the Latins; a work on patristics is not directed against Scholasticism; a study on the spiritual meaning of Scripture *does not imply disfavor with scientific exegesis*, etc. Nothing is more contrary to me than such oppositions. In a more general way, there are not any 'ulterior motives' in my writings" (cited in Fouilloux, *La collection "Sources chrétiennes,"* 121–22; emphasis is ours). On the history and importance of critical exegesis, see the works of Pierre Gibert, in particular his book *L'invention critique de la Bible. XVe–XVIIIe siècle* [The critical invention of the Bible] (Paris: Gallimard, 2010).

6. For what follows, see our article Michel Fédou, "Les débats sur le 'sens spirituel' dans les *Recherches de Science Religieuse* (années 1940–1950) [Debates on the "spiritual sense" in the "Recherches de Science Religieuse" (years 1940–1950)], *Recherches de Science Religieuse* 99 (2011): 195–205.

allows, as formerly shown by Jacques Guillet, identifying some differences: thus Theodore was interested in David as prophet, as the one who had seen in advance the history to come; what, on the contrary, interested Origen was not David, but it was rather to know who David was—and in this instance, he saw in him and through him Jesus himself.[7] More widely, Guillet recognized in these two exegeses two different orientations:

> from the typism of the Old Testament, Antioch retained the prophetic aspect, Alexandria the symbolic aspect and the spiritual content. For Antioch, the dominant fact of biblical history, the miracle that permanently attests to the continuity of divine history and that directly prepares for the coming of Christ, is prophetism. Alexandria, without ignoring the prophetic texts, does not find them to be sufficient for nourishing Christian thought and the spiritual life. It is necessary for it to find the presence of the Lord in each page.[8]

Of course, added Guillet, "symbolism and prophetism ... are not mutually exclusive"; however, he wrote "the points of view are different enough to lead to two exegeses in ways that are poles apart, to the point that sometimes results in believing them to be actually opposed to each other."[9] But undoubtedly it is not necessary to exaggerate the conflict between the exegeses of Antioch and those of Alexandria. Guillet himself recognized that these exegeses have common traits: not only respect for the text, attention to the precise meaning of the words, concern for finding the coherence of the passage commented upon but also the preoccupation of looking for a meaning more profound than the immediate meaning. Even more clearly, de Lubac affirms that, even if Alexandria's trend gave such importance to "*allegoria*" while that of Antioch preferred speaking of "*theôria*,"[10] these two words "do not refer to two totally antagonistic concepts" and, in

7. Jacques Guillet, "Les exégèses d'Alexandrie et d'Antioche. Conflit ou malentendu?" [The exegeses of Alexandria and Antioch. Conflict or misunderstanding?], *Recherches de Science Religieuse* 34 (1947): 267–68.

8. Ibid., 274.

9. Ibid.

10. Cf. Diodorus of Tarsus: "Not only does divine Scripture not destroy the prior foundation of history, but, moreover, it sees through history, with theory, other similar events, but without destroying the actual history" (*Prologue au Psaume 118*; cited in Henri de Lubac, "'Typologie' et 'allégorisme'" ["Typology" and "allegorism"], *Recherches de Science Religieuse* 34 (1947): 202.

fact, "can pass for synonyms."[11] Whatever were, in any case, their differences, the Antiochenes did not question the search for a meaning that was not limited to the single letter of the Scriptures—that is, in the broadest meaning of this word, a "spiritual" meaning.

The problem, nevertheless, remains: did not the quest for this "spiritual" meaning, most especially in the Alexandrians, lead to developing numerous allegories that today appear to us quite arbitrary and that, regarding critical exegesis, create an obstacle to the correct understanding of scriptural texts? In order to try to understand this clearly, it is, first of all, useful to recall some of the discussions that took place among patrologists over the course of the twentieth century. In 1946, Jean Daniélou published an article titled: "Traversée de la mer Rouge et baptême aux premiers siècles."[12] In it he notably wrote: "What is particular to the Alexandrians, is not typology, but allegorism;"[13] for "typology" that consists, for example, in recognizing Isaac as a "type" or "figure" of Christ or the crossing of the Red Sea as a "figure" of Baptism is completely traditional since the time of the New Testament and the first Fathers: far from being particular to the Alexandrians, it is itself specifically Christian. On the contrary, according to Daniélou, allegorism is a legacy from Philo, and the Christian exegesis of Alexandria has the particularity of being abundantly influenced by it. Daniélou added that for us today typology maintains all its value, whereas allegorism is a reality from a culture that today is obsolete.

However, de Lubac, in an article published the following year, objected that such a distinction between "typology" and "allegorism" was "neither scriptural nor truly traditional."[14] He indeed recalled that Paul himself had lent weight to the word "allegory" in the vocabulary of Christian exegesis (with the famous passage of Gal 4:22–31 on Hagar and Sarah); of course, the word *typos*, from which "typology" is derived, is also Pauline, but this word "type" only designated the first of the two terms that are connected (let us think, for example, of Adam

11. De Lubac, "'Typologie' et 'allégorisme,'" 203.

12. Jean Daniélou, "Traversée de la mer Rouge et baptême aux premiers siècles" [Crossing the Red Sea and Baptism in the first centuries], *Recherches de Science Religieuse* 33 (1946): 402–30.

13. Ibid., 416.

14. De Lubac, "'Typologie' et 'allégorisme,'" 180–81.

as a "type" or "figure" of Christ, in Rom 5:14) whereas allegory signified the "living link" of one term to the other: "Far from the two vocables generally being opposed to each other, one must thus say that allegorical interpretation, in its traditional understanding, consists in discerning the types or figures that, in Israel, announced Christ,—in all Israel, Christ in the totality of his mystery. It established the relationship of the figure to the truth, of the letter to the spirit, of the old to the new."[15] De Lubac was, for all that, not denying Origen's debt to Philo's allegorism. Above all, he was fully aware of the reasons that subsequently would contribute to depreciating the word "allegory" in Christian exegesis:

> Allegory: it is the word that is going to be used for the transposition of Ovid or Virgil according to the antique mode or for the *Roman de la rose*.... More and more, in modern times, the Christian sense of the term will be lost. Today it also almost guarantees evoking a lack of realism, which is in opposition to the faith, that is joined to a contempt for historical science, which is shocking for our minds.[16]

De Lubac also willingly accepted the word "typology" that would be used more frequently in his time;[17] at least he clarified that, even if Origen is dependent upon Philo's exegesis, the spiritual meaning that he established based on the biblical text is however "very different ... from the tropological or moral meaning that he indeed in large part did owe to Philo."[18] Finally, he summarized the difference of his position from that of his confrere thus: "The Rev. Fr. Daniélou is ... more sensitive to the contamination in Origen of typological exegesis by Philo's allegorism. I confess to be above all sensitive to the fact that Origen's allegorism is above all 'typological.'"[19]

This difference does not prohibit the two patrologists from agreeing on this fundamental point: what directly characterizes Christian exegesis is that it identifies, through persons or events from the Old

15. Ibid., 185.

16. Ibid., 218.

17. Ibid., 209.

18. Ibid., 219.

19. Ibid., 219–21. The article formulates a second remark: where Daniélou considers the Alexandrians to seem to be pressed to bypass the catechumenal typology in order to get to the allegorical interpretations, de Lubac fears that he is here the victim of a prejudice against Origen's esotericism (221).

Testament, figures of Christ and the Church (recognizing that this itself is possible only in the light of the New Testament Revelation). If it is true that Daniélou emphasized most particularly the influence of Philo's allegorism (as well as the influence of the allegorism practiced by the grammarians and philosophers of the Hellenistic world), they were both in agreement in recognizing that Christian exegesis, in what was specific to it, is of a totally different order: whether one designates it as "typology" (Daniélou) or one highlights its traditional appellation of "allegory" (de Lubac), it, in any case, is the product of faith in Christ and, in this light, rereads the texts of the Old Testament in order to discover, under the veil of the letter, the revelation of the mysteries that have been revealed by the coming of the Word of God and the Easter event.

De Lubac was once again going to stress this uniqueness of Christian exegesis, twelve years later, by vigorously opposing some historians who were attempting to "place all Christian allegory, by its origin and nature, in an essential relationship with the doctrines of intellectual paganism that allegorized its myths, at the same time with Philo's exegesis."[20] The attack was carried out, above all, against J. Pepin, who in the preceding year had published his work *Mythe et allégorie*.[21] De Lubac here recalled the Pauline foundation of Christian allegory. Without denying the participation of Christians from the past in the culture of their time, he highlighted that the principle of their allegorical exegesis was totally different from that of the grammarians and philosophers of Antiquity:

> Is the novelty of Christianity still today so recent that historians—even if they in no way adhere to the Christian faith—cannot yet sense something of it? Has Christian allegory had so little time and so little opportunity to explain itself ... that people still completely misunderstand its nature? ... It goes from history to history—although not a single history nor on the threshold outside of history. It connects singular facts with another uncommon fact ... so that everything reaches its climax with a great Event that, in its singularity is completely unique, brings all its spiritual fecundity. Thus its end is at the same time

20. Henri de Lubac, "À propos de l'allégorie chrétienne" [About the Christian allegory], *Recherches de Science Religieuse* 47 (1959): 5.

21. Jean Pépin, *Mythe et allégorie: Les origines grecques et les contestations judéo-chrétiennes* [Myth and allegory: The Greek origins and the Jewish-Christian protests] (Paris: Aubier: 1958).

"historical," "mystical," and "heavenly." It is the Christ Event, both unique and universal; it is the Christian Mystery in all its dimensions.... Thus, whereas philosophical allegorization of myths is more and more a phenomenon of stultification, the Christian allegorization of Scripture appears linked, in history, to the triumphant feeling of the Christian innovation.[22]

Such debates must help to overcome the second misunderstanding that we mentioned above. On one hand, it is not a matter of denying that the exegesis of the Fathers, and in particular the Alexandrians, had been subjected to the influence of Philo as well as the Greek grammarians and philosophers; what this reveals rather is the debt of these Fathers to Hellenistic Judaism as well as their concern for profiting from methods of interpretation already developed in the Hellenistic and Greco-Roman world (and in fact, as we will clarify later, the very "arbitrariness" of many allegories itself contributes to the richness of the patristic reading—provided it is recognized as such and that it itself serves the understanding of the faith). On the other, the presence of this allegorism must not prohibit recognizing the profound meaning of the exegesis practiced by the Fathers as this exegesis is essentially structured upon the "Christ Event"—this "Event" that projects its light on the texts of Scripture and that reveals totally new resonances.

Thus considered in its essential intention (and thus independent of some of the occasional limits recognized in its implementation), patristic exegesis is thus neither a way of circumventing the letter nor a simple transposition of Jewish or Greco-Roman allegorism. Having dispelled these misunderstandings, we are now in a better position to clarify what spiritual exegesis is.

Spiritual Exegesis according to Origen

Origen's contribution is here decisive, for he is the first, even if other Fathers such as Justin and Irenaeus practiced such an exegesis before him, to have proposed the theory; and he himself commented on all the Scriptures. He likes to refer to the episode of the disciples at Emmaus, where it is said regarding the Resurrected One: "And begin-

22. De Lubac, "À propos de l'allégorie chrétienne," 41–42.

ning with Moses and all the prophets, he interpreted to them in all the Scriptures the things concerning himself" (Lk 24:27). He thus explores all the books of the Old Testament in order to find in it the revelation of the Word of God; the movement is twofold: from Christ toward the Scriptures (to the extent that Christ is the basis of a Christian knowledge of Scriptures); from the Scriptures toward Christ (because it is possible to find in all the Scriptures pre-figurations and prophesies of Christ).

Thus, regarding a passage of the Law, Origen writes:

> nor do I even give the name "Old Testament" to the law, if I understand it spiritually. The law becomes an "Old Testament" only for those who want to understand it in a fleshly way; and for them it has necessarily become old and aged, because it cannot maintain its strength. But for us, who understand and explain it spiritually and according to the gospel-meaning, it is always new. Indeed, both are "New Testaments" for us, not by the age of time but by the newness of understanding.[23]

The Old Testament can even be called "Gospel": before the coming of Christ, the Law and the prophets did not contain the proclamation which belongs to the definition of the gospel since he who explained the mysteries in them had not yet come. But since the Savior has come, and has caused the gospel to be embodied in the gospel, he has made all things gospel."[24] The Old Testament thus takes on a new meaning in the light of Christ; it even becomes "like a gospel." Yet this conviction calls for a whole scriptural hermeneutic, which Origen develops in book 4 of *On First Principles*.[25] To only a "literal" reading of the holy books,[26] he contrasts his theory of the meanings of Scripture; there are three meanings: the "letter," which is the immediate meaning of the text (this can be the "historic meaning," if it is a matter of a narrative; or the primary meaning of the text, if it is a matter of a legislative passage; Origen also says: the corporal meaning); the "moral

23. Origen, *Hom Nm* IX, 4.1–2; translated by Thomas P. Scheck as *Homilies on Numbers*, Ancient Christian Texts (Westmont, Ill.: InterVarsity Press Academic, 2009), 39.

24. Origen, *Com Jn* I, 33; *Commentary on the Gospel according to John*, 40.

25. For what follows, see Henri de Lubac, *Histoire et Esprit*.

26. That of the Jews who do not perceive, under the veil of the letter, the announcement of Christ; that of the "heretics" such as Marcion who, using only the literal meaning of some expressions of the Old Testament on the jealousy or the anger of God, consider that this God of the Old Testament is other than the God of kindness and love revealed by Jesus.

meaning," which is the meaning of the text for the human soul; lastly, the spiritual meaning, which is that which has treated the mysteries of the Christian faith.[27]

One notes that, with the second meaning, we are not yet at the level of the properly Christian meaning. But in fact, in his customary practice, Origen reverses the second and third meanings: the exposition of the literal meaning is soon followed by an application to Christ and to the Church (spiritual meaning), and it is only then that the application to the soul comes. As in the example of Noah's ark: Origen, first of all, examines what is said about it literally, then he comes to its spiritual meaning (Noah is the figure of Jesus Christ), and lastly, to the moral meaning (the faithful one must in his turn construct an ark, that is to say, be nourished by the Scriptures and purify his heart). The soul in question is thus the soul already permeated with the mystery of Christ.[28]

It is important to emphasize that in all this Origen is not claiming to be innovative, but he finds the foundation of his exegesis in the New Testament itself. He notably refers to 1 Corinthians 10:4: "For they drank from the supernatural Rock which followed them, and the Rock was Christ"; and also to 1 Corinthians 10:6: "Now these things happened as examples for us" (the word "examples" translates the Greek "*tupoi*," from which was later formed the word "typology"). Origen also takes the example of the allegory of Hagar and Sarah in Galatians 4:24. He is attentive to the numerous citations that, in the Gospels, highlight the fulfillment of ancient prophecies—such as the citation of Psalm 21 in Matthew 27:46 or that of Isaiah 40:3–5 in Luke 4:4–6. But it is incontestable that Origen gives a completely new scale to typological and prophetic exegesis. He thus opens the way to an immense tradition, that of the doctrine of the meanings of Scripture that will be summarized in the Middle Ages in a famous distich:

> *Littera gesta docet, quid credas allegoria,*
> *Moralis quid agas, quo tendas anagogia.*[29]

27. This presentation corresponds to the Pauline trilogy of body-soul-spirit in 1 Thes 5:23: there is a homology between the passage from the letter to the spirit and the passage from the body to the spirit.

28. Cf. Origen, *Hom Gn* II; translated by Ronald E. Heine as *Homilies on Genesis*, Fathers of the Church 71 (Washington, D.C.: The Catholic University of America Press, 2010), 72–88.

29. Cf. Henri de Lubac, "Sur un vieux distique. La doctrine du 'quadruple sens'" [About

This can be translated:

> The literal sense teaches what happened,
> The allegorical, what you should believe,
> The moral, what you should do,
> The anagogical, where you should go.

In fact, it is necessary to understand that fundamentally there are two meanings, the literal meaning and the spiritual meaning—which itself is divided into its "allegorical" meaning (the one which concerns the mystery of Christ and of the Church), its "moral" meaning (for application to the Christian life), and its "anagogic" meaning (for eschatological realities). What is important is for us to remember that Origen calls for recognizing under the veil of Scripture a more profound meaning of a "spiritual" nature. This does not mean that the letter must be lost sight of but that it is only the body of the biblical text, and it is necessary to go further in order to attain its spirit. Moreover, the letter is such that, in many cases, it indirectly invites such a deepening:

> the divine wisdom has arranged for there to be certain stumbling blocks or interruptions of the narrative meaning, by inserting in its midst certain impossibilities and contradictions, so that the very interruption of the narrative might oppose the reader, as it were, with certain obstacles thrown in the way. By them wisdom denies a way and an access to the common understanding; and when we are shut out and hurled back, it calls us back to the beginning of another way, so that by gaining a higher and loftier road through entering a narrow footpath it may open for us the immense breadth of divine knowledge.[30]

In the light of Christ, then, the reader is led to read the ancient Scriptures in a different way in order to discover in them, under the veil of the letter, the mysteries which they contain. This hermeneutic is used for various writings of the Old Testament. Thus, the first books of the Bible provide Origen with many occasions to show in this person or in that event a prefiguration or "figure" of Christ. So, for example, the exegesis of Genesis 22: Isaac asks his father: "where is the lamb for the holocaust?"; Abraham answers: "God will provide himself the lamb"; Origen comments: "He responded to his son's inqui-

---

an old couplet. The doctrine of the "quadruple sense"], in *Mélanges offerts au R. P. Cavallera*, (Toulouse: Bibliothèque de l'Institut Catholique, 1948), 347–66; *Exégèse médiévale.*

30. Origen, *On First Principles*, IV, 2, 9 [Greer 187–88; Butterworth, 285–86]. Throughout the discussion, the *Philocalia* uses "the Word of God" in place of "the divine wisdom."

ry about present things with future things. For 'the Lord himself will provide himself a sheep' in Christ."[31] Isaac is thus a "figure" of Christ, in the sense that he mysteriously announces the Son of God going toward his passion. But there is a very important difference: at the last moment Isaac is not put to death (for a ram appears and is going to be immolated in his place), whereas Christ, himself, will be crucified; Origen thus immediately follows up:

> We said above, I think, that Isaac represented Christ. But this ram no less also seems to represent Christ. Now it is worthwhile to know how both are appropriate to Christ, both Isaac who is not slain and the ram which is slain.
>
> Christ is "the Word of God," but "the Word was made flesh." One aspect of Christ, therefore, is from above; the other is received from human nature and the womb of the virgin. Christ suffered, therefore, but in the flesh; and he endured death, but it was the flesh, of which this ram is a type, as also John said: "Behold the Lamb of God, behold him who takes away the sin of the world." But the Word continued "in incorruption," which is Christ according to the spirit, of which Isaac is the image. For this reason, he himself is both victim and priest. For truly according to the spirit he offers the victim to the Father, but according to the flesh he himself is offered on the altar of the cross, because, as it is said of him "Behold the Lamb of God, behold him who takes away the sin of the world," so it is said of him: "You are a priest forever according to the order of Melchisedech."[32]

Here one sees how Origen is using the images: the ram is a figure of Christ in his passion, Isaac represents the Word of God; but this distinction must be clearly understood: the Word of God and Christ in his passion are both one and the same. Both figures are necessary in order to speak of the identity of the Word of God—in a language completely different from the subsequent language on the two natures of Christ.

One could take up many other examples from the first books of the Bible, in particular the Book of Joshua, for Joshua is eminently a prefiguration of Jesus Christ. On the other hand, Origen reflects on the numerous prophecies contained in the Old Testament. He emphasizes that the Holy Spirit expresses himself through different persons: sometimes it is by the prophet who is speaking, but sometimes it is rather by the words of the prophet that are suitable for someone oth-

31. Origen, *Hom Gn* VIII, 6; *Homilies on Genesis,*, 141.

32. Origen, *Hom Gn* VIII, 9; *Homilies on Genesis,* 145; cf. Gn 22:13; Jn 1:14; Jn 1:29; Ps 109:4.

er than the prophet, notably Christ. A major example is that of the fourth Servant Song in Isaiah:

I remember that once in a discussion with some whom the Jews regard as learned I used these prophecies. At this the Jew said that these prophecies referred to the whole people as though of a single individual, since they were scattered in the dispersion and smitten, that as a result of the scattering of the Jews among the other nations many might become proselytes.... I then adduced many arguments in the disputation which proved that there is no good reason for referring these prophecies about one individual to the whole people.... But we seemed to put him in the greatest difficulty with the words "because of the iniquities of my people he was led to death." If according to them the people are the subject of the prophecy, why is this man said to have been led to death because of the iniquities of the people of God, if he is not different from the people of God? Who is this if not Jesus Christ, by whose stripe we who believe in him were healed, when he put off the principalities and powers among us, and made a show of them openly on the cross?[33]

Origen is particularly devoted, in the end, to the Song of Songs. This book is, indeed, for him, a high point of the Old Testament. It is the drama that presents to us, through the figure of the Spouse, the Word of God making himself known to the spouse, who is herself a figure of the soul or the Church. Of course, the prophets and the Psalms had already made the voice of the Savior known; but the Song does not only do this, it additionally *represents* (in a theatrical sense) the face of the Savior who is approaching. The images of the Song are called upon in order to signify this:

"For lo, the winter is past, the rain is over and gone." We could say that the rain is the time before the Incarnation when God ordained the clouds to cause the word of the Law and of the prophets to rain down, but that this has ceased since "the Law and the prophets were until John." And the spring and the summer are after the Incarnation, for there is no longer need for rain when, thanks to Christ, "the flowers appeared upon the earth."[34]

Origen abundantly gathers the numerous images of the Word from the Song, not only the arrival of spring but also the beauty of the

33. Origen, *Contra Celsum*, I, 55; translated by H. Chadwick as *Origen: Contra Celsum*, (Cambridge: Cambridge University Press, 1953), 50–51; cf. Col 2:15.

34. Origen, *Fragm. In Sg*, trans. Luc Brésard, Henri Crouzel, and Marcel Borret, SC 376 (Paris: Cerf, 1992), 747; cf. Wis 2:10–12; Is 45:8; Lk 16:16.

Spouse when he appears, the exquisite fragrance of his perfumes, his name that is spread everywhere, "the flowers of the fields and the lily of the valleys," the "apple tree" that surpasses all the trees of the forest and the cloud upon which the Spouse is seated. The Song notably speaks of the debasement of the Word that is made flesh:

> There is yet another interpretation of these words, "Thy name is as ointment emptied out; therefore have the maidens loved Thee." The Only-begotten Son, *being in the form of God, ... emptied Himself and took the form of a servant.* The emptying out was surely out of the fullness in which He was. So those who say: *Of His fullness we all have received,* are the maidens who, receiving of that fullness of which He emptied Himself and thereby made His name as "ointment emptied out," declare: "We will run after Thee toward the fragrance of Thine ointments."[35]

The poem of the Song does not only announce the Savior; it also portrays the coming of the Spouse. It is true that between the representation of the Savior coming among us and the event of this coming there is quite a distance to overcome: the figure is not yet that of which it is the figure. The New Testament consequently has a status different from the Old: only the New Testament testifies that the Word of God has really come, that he died, and that he was resurrected. Between the Old and the New, there is a complete difference due to an event that has henceforth taken place. The two Testaments really speak of the Word of God, but the New surpasses the Old: "One would not go wrong, then, in saying that of the Scriptures which are in circulation in the churches of God and which are believed to be divine, the law of Moses is the firstling, but the gospel is the firstfruits. For the perfect Word has blossomed forth after all the fruits of the prophets up to the time of the Lord Jesus."[36] And among the Gospels, the Gospel of John occupies a preeminent place: "We might dare say, then, that the Gospels are the firstfruits of all Scriptures, but that the firstfruits of the Gospels is that according to John, whose meaning no one can understand who has not leaned on Jesus' breast nor received Mary from Jesus to be his mother also."[37] But even though the New

35. Origen, *Com Sg* I, 4, 27; translated by R. P. Lawson *as The Song of Songs, Commentary and Homilies,* Ancient Christian Writers 26 (Mahwah, N.J.: Paulist Press, 1957), 83; cf. Song 1:3; Jn 3:16; Phil 2:6–7; Jn 1:16.

36. Origen, *Com Jn* I, 14; *Commentary on the Gospel according to John,* 35.

37. Origen, *Com Jn* I, 23; *Commentary on the Gospel according to John,* 38.

Testament surpasses the Old, the dialectic of the letter and the spirit that we have seen at work in the case of the Old is still going to be at work, in another way, in the New Testament itself. Indeed, one must not understand the passage from the Old to the New Testament as a passage from the letter to the spirit; one has rather to understand that—except for the specific excellence of the New Testament—each of the two Testaments present the possibility of a passage from the letter to the spirit (or, inversely, of imprisonment in the letter alone). Origen does not back down before the paradox: in the Old Covenant there has already been a spiritual coming of Christ for humans who knew how to acquire the spirit from the letter, and on the other hand, at the time of the New Covenant, humans can remain in the letter and miss the spirit.

To this last category belong the opponents of Jesus and also those who, without properly being his adversaries, only see in him a remarkable man without discovering in him the Son of God. But believers, and above all the Apostles, are those who are not themselves limited to the revelation of the humanity of Jesus but also recognize his divinity:

> The apostles themselves saw the Word, not because they had beheld the body of our Lord and Savior, but because they had seen the Word. If seeing Jesus' body meant seeing God's Word, then Pilate, who condemned Jesus, saw God's Word; so did Judas the traitor and all those who cried out, "Crucify him, crucify him, remove such a one from the earth." But far be it that any unbeliever should see God's Word. Seeing God's Word means what the Savior says: "He who has seen me has also seen the Father who sent me."[38]

One thus cannot limit oneself to the "sensible" or "corporal" gospel; it is necessary to pass from this gospel to the "intelligible" or "spiritual" gospel: "the task before us now is to translate the gospel perceptible to the senses into the spiritual gospel. For what is the interpretation of the gospel perceptible to the senses unless it is translated into the spiritual gospel? It is little or nothing, even though the common people believe they receive the things which are revealed from the lit-

38. Origen, *Hom Lk* I, 4, translated by Joseph T. Lienhard as Homilies on Luke, Fathers of the Church 94 (Washington, D.C.: The Catholic University of America Press, 1996), 7–8; cf. Jn 14:9.

eral sense."[39] This passage to the spiritual Gospel is itself comprised of several stages: one can be more or less advanced in the spiritual interpretation of the Gospels, and Origen affirms that it is always possible to progress in this.[40] He finds indications of this progress in the Gospels themselves, thanks to the different groups that are mentioned in them: the crowd, the disciples, and some of the disciples who are more advanced than others. Thus Origen comments on the passage in which one sees Jesus explaining a parable to his disciples:

> When Jesus is with the crowds, he is not in his house, for the crowds are outside of this house; and the work of his love for humans consists in leaving the house and going to those who cannot come to him. But once he has sufficiently spoken to the crowds in parables, he leaves them and returns to his house, where his disciples join him because they did not remain with those that he left.... Thus for us, if we want not to hear Jesus like the crowds that he left in order to go into his house, let us have an attitude that distinguishes us from the crowds and let us become the close friends of Jesus so that, like his disciples, we come to him when he enters his house, that we draw near to him to ask him about the explanation of the parable.... The text of the Gospel is not only simple as some think, but to the simple it was—"according to the economy"—presented as simple, whereas, for those who want to hear in a more penetrating way and who are capable of it, there have been hidden realities full of wisdom and worthy of the Word of God.[41]

It is thus necessary to leave the crowd in order to acquire, like the disciples, a more profound understanding of the Word of God. But among the disciples themselves, some—such as those who were witnesses to the Transfiguration—go further than others in the understanding of the mysteries:

> You will ask if, when he was transfigured in front of those he led up the high mountain, he appeared to them in the form of a servant in which he was formerly.... If you wish to see the transfiguration in front of those who went up onto the high mountain, apart, with him, consider that in the Gospels Jesus is understood more simply and that he is thus said to be known "according to the flesh" by those who do not go up, by a progressive ascension in their works and

39. Origen, *Com Jn* I, 45; *Commentary on the Gospel according to John*, 43.

40. Origen emphasizes this point against the Gnostics, according to whom some humans were ineluctably enclosed in ignorance.

41. Origen, *Com Mt* X, 1; translated by Robert Girod as *Commentaire sur Matthieu*, SC 162 (Paris: Cerf, 1970), 141–45; cf. Mt 13:36.

words, on the high mountain of wisdom; on the contrary, for those who do go up, he is no longer known according to the flesh but he is looked upon as God throughout all the Gospels, and according to their knowledge he is contemplated in his divine form: it is before these, indeed, that Jesus is transfigured and not before those who are below.[42]

The Transfiguration is an exceptional moment: it is the transfiguration of the Lord at the same time as it is the transfiguration of the Gospel letter, the hidden meaning of which is more deeply penetrated by the disciples; moreover, at the side of Jesus transfigured appear Elijah and Moses, that is, for Origen, the Law and the Prophets—thus all the ancient Scripture—and as for the transfigured clothing of Jesus, these are the words and the letters with which he is clothed in the Gospels.[43] The disciples' progress thus allows them, by the same token, to contemplate Christ in his glory and to acquire the spiritual understanding of all Scripture.

Can one even go beyond this summit? Yes, for Origen, undoubtedly, with the attitude of the well-beloved disciple who rested upon Jesus' chest and whom Jesus was going to designate from his cross as the son of Mary:

But he who would be another John must also become such as John, to be shown to be Jesus, so to speak. For if Mary had no son except Jesus, in accordance with those who hold a sound opinion of her, and Jesus says to his mother, "Behold your son," and not, "Behold, this man also is your son," he has said equally, "Behold, this is Jesus whom you bore." For indeed everyone who has been perfected "no longer lives, but Christ lives in him," and since "Christ lives" in him, it is said of him to Mary, "Behold your son," the Christ.[44]

The well-beloved disciple is the one who has enjoyed that greatest intimacy with Jesus; thus it is he who is able to go the furthest in the passage from the corporal Gospel to the spiritual Gospel.

Thus in the case of the New Testament itself, there really is a dialectic of the letter and the spirit—oriented toward a more profound knowledge of the mystery of Christ who is not only man but, in his

42. Origen, *Com Mt* XII, 37; GCS 40 (Matthäuserklärung I, ed. Erich Klostermann [Leipzig: J.C. Hinrichs, 1935], 152–53); cf. 2 Cor 5:16.

43. Origen, *Com Mt* XII, 38; GCS 40, 154–55.

44. Origen, *Com Jn*, I, 23; *Commentary on the Gospel according to John*, 38; cf. Jn 19:26; Gal 2:20.

own humanity, reveals himself as the Son of God. For just as the spiritual interpretation of the Old Testament allowed reading in it not only the prefiguration of Christ but also teaching for the believer's soul, the same is true for the New Testament. This really emerges from the texts in which Origen, as we have seen, invites Christians themselves to follow an itinerary similar to that of the disciples in the Gospels. The Scriptures do not allow only knowing Christ; they light the way of those who are called to be, as Origen says, true disciples of Christ over the course of history. This implementation can take on very diverse forms. Sometimes, the knowledge of the Scriptures leads the believer to recognize his own infidelity, as when Origen meditates on the death of Jesus:

> But in whom is "Jesus dead"? Without doubt, in those who, for instance, by often repenting and again committing sin, are said to insult the death of Jesus, about whom the Apostle, writing to the Hebrews, says, "Those crucifying again the Son of God within themselves and making a public spectacle of him." Accordingly, you see that in sinners not only is "Jesus" said "to die," but also he is declared "crucified and mocked" by them. Moreover, reflect within yourself whether, when out of greed you plan and desire to lay waste to another's goods, you can say that "Christ lives in me." Or if you plan debauchery, if you are excited with anger, if you are inflamed with envy, if you are spurred on by jealousy, if you revel in drunkenness, if you are puffed up with pride, if you act with cruelty, in all these matters can you say that "Christ lives in me"? So, therefore, in this way Christ "is dead" for sinners by virtue of the fact that in them nothing of justice is at work, nothing of patience, nothing of truth, and indeed nothing of all that is Christ.[45]

On the contrary, the coming of Christ must also occur in the heart of the believer who today listens to the same story. The event of the Incarnation must find its correspondence at a point in time in an indwelling of the Word of God in this believer's soul. The Scriptures even help in grasping this coming of Christ, first of all in the form of a fortifying presence in the midst of ordeals. This is how Origen

45. Origen, *Hom Jgs* II, 1; *Homilies on Judges*, trans. Elizabeth Ann Dively Lauro, Fathers of the Church 119 (Washington, D.C.: The Catholic University of America Press, 2002), 51–52; cf. Heb 6:6; Gal 2:20. Also see *Hom Lv* VII, 2, *Homélies sur le Lévitique*, trans. Marcel Borret, SC 286 (Paris: Cerf, 1981), 309–13; *Homilies on Leviticus*, trans. Gary Wayne Barkley, Fathers of the Church 83 (Washington, D.C.: The Catholic University of America Press, 1990), 133–34.

interprets the episode in which one sees Jesus walking on the water and saving Peter from sinking: the crossing of the sea here becomes a figure, not only of Christ but of the spiritual warfare that the believer must endure in order to be with Christ.[46] The Word comes to the soul even in the ordeal, and the soul can then recognize him truthfully as the Son of God. The Christological reading of the Scriptures is thus, at the same moment, the genesis of a mystical theology. Origen does not hesitate to say it: "God wants to make us christs."[47] Christ is indeed unique, but the mysteries of Christ must be imprinted in the life of the Christian to the point that there may truly be the most intimate birth and growth of Christ in the soul; Origen emphasizes this in some remarkable formulations:

> For what does it profit if I should say that Jesus has come in that flesh alone which he received from Mary and I should not show also that he has come in this flesh of mine?[48]

> For, what profit is it to you, if Christ once came in the flesh, unless he also comes into your soul? We should pray that he will come to us each day so that we can say, "I live, now not I, but Christ lives in me."[49]

Origen's contribution, as one sees, does not lie only in his doctrine of the meanings of the Scriptures nor in its implementation through the exegesis of the two Testaments. It lies even more in the underlying theology: the certitude, received from the New Testament itself, of the connection between the Scriptures and Christ that is so profound and so intimate. This conviction can be summarized thus: on one hand, Christ is the key to the Scriptures, that means, it is by him that Christians acquire the profound understanding of all the Scriptures, the Old and the New Testaments as well as their relationship to each other; on the other, in an inverse way, the Scriptures are ways of accessing knowledge of Christ, and exegesis is in this sense the supreme way by which Christian theology is engendered. Lastly, the mysteries of

46. Origen, *Com Mt* XI, 6–7; *Commentaire sur Matthieu*, 297–301.

47. Origen, *Hom Ez* VI, 9; *Homilies 1–14 on Ezechiel*, trans. Thomas P. Scheck, Ancient Christian Writers 62 (New York: The Newman Press, 2010), 96; see SC 352, 239.

48. Origen, *Hom Gn* III, 7; *Homilies on Genesis*,, 101.

49. Origen, *Hom Lk* XXII, 3; Homilies on Luke, 93; cf. Gal 2:20. See also *Hom Jer* IX, 1; *Homélies sur Jerémie*, vol. 1, trans Pierre Nautin and Pierre Husson, SC 232 (Paris: Cerf, 1976), 379; *Homilies on Jeremiah*, trans. John Clark Smith, Fathers of the Church 97 (Washington, D.C.: The Catholic University of America Press, 1998), 85–87.

Christ, both revealed and hidden in the Scriptures, are destined to be accomplished in the very existence of believers throughout history, in a way that the reading of the Scriptures is by the same action the way of spiritual progress—a route that, moreover, is never achieved and of which Origen himself had the experience, as he confesses in the Homily on the Song of Songs:

> God is my witness that I have often perceived the Bridegroom drawing near me and being most intensely present with me; then suddenly He has withdrawn and I could not find Him, though I sought to do so. I long, therefore, for Him to come again, and sometimes He does so. Then, when He has appeared and I lay hold of Him, He slips away once more; and, when He has so slipped away, my search for Him begins anew. So does He act with me repeatedly, until in truth I hold Him and go up, "leaning on my beloved's arm."[50]

Thus the reading of the Scriptures is always associated with the search—never achieved—for Christ. It is in this sense, for Origen, the way par excellence of the Christian mystic.

It would, of course, be possible to gather further contributions to the thought on Christian exegesis made by other Fathers, in particular those of Augustine who also offered, in his *De doctrina christiana*, some major expositions on the hermeneutics of the Scriptures.[51] But what we have said of Origen suffices to demonstrate what is, in essence, the patristic doctrine of the "spiritual meaning." It is now necessary for us to reflect, more broadly, on the importance that we must today recognize in patristic exegesis.

"Both Testaments"

It is first of all important to emphasize that, if the recent documents of the Magisterium fully recognize the necessity of critical exegesis, they, nevertheless, highlight the permanent importance of patristic exegesis. Thus, in its 1993 document on "The Interpretation of the Bible in

50. Origen, *Hom Song* I, 7; Origen, *The Song of Songs*, 280. cf. Song 8:5.

51. See Augustine, *La doctrine chrétienne*, ed. Madeleine Moreau and Isabelle Bochet, Bibliothèque augustinienne II/2 (Paris: Desclée de Brouwer, 1997); *Teaching Christianity: De Doctrina Christiana*, trans. Edmund Hill (Hyde Park, N.Y.: New City Press, 1996). See the major work of Isabelle Bochet *"Le firmament de l'Écriture." L'herméneutique augustinienne* ["The Firmament of Scripture." Augustinian hermeneutics] (Paris: Institut d'Études Augustiniennes, 2004).

the Church," the Pontifical Biblical Commission declares that the Fathers of the Church have "a fundamental role" regarding the "living Tradition" that accompanies and guides the ecclesial reading of the Scriptures. Patristic exegesis "has drawn out from the totality of Scripture the basic orientations which shaped the doctrinal tradition of the Church and has provided a rich theological teaching for the instruction and spiritual sustenance of the faithful." The document recalls that in the Fathers the reading of the Bible occupies a highly valued place, that its usual place is "the Church, in the course of the liturgy," and that it gives importance to an interpretation that is "always of a theological and pastoral nature ... so as to be helpful both for the community and the individual believer." Of course, the text specifies that the Fathers' approach pays "scant attention to the historical development of revelation," that many times they "felt themselves at liberty to take a sentence out of its context in order to bring out some revealed truth," that they often have recourse to allegory, and that this allegorical interpretation "runs the risks of being something of an embarrassment to people today;" however, it concludes that "the experience of the Church expressed in this exegesis makes a contribution that is always useful" and "the Fathers of the Church teach to read the Bible theologically, within the heart of a living tradition, with an authentic Christian spirit."[52] The same document elsewhere formulates an affirmation that clearly reflects the goal of patristic exegesis: "Exegesis is truly faithful to the proper intention of biblical texts when it goes not only to the heart of their formulation to find the reality of faith there expressed but also seeks to link this reality to the experience of faith in our present world."[53]

More recently, following the Synod of 2008 on the Word of God, Pope Benedict XVI promulgated the apostolic exhortation *Verbum Domini* that contains an important passage on "the literal meaning and the spiritual meaning." It says that "a significant contribution to the recovery of an adequate scriptural hermeneutic can also come from renewed attention to the Fathers of the Church and their exegetical approach." Of course, the Fathers were ignorant of the philological

52. The Pontifical Biblical Commission, *The Interpretation of the Bible in the Church* (1993), III, B, 2, http://Catholic-resources.org/ChurchDocs/PBC_Interp-FullText.htm.

53. Ibid., II, A, 2.

and historical resources that modern exegesis has; but *Verbum Domini* highlights their attention to the different meanings of the Scriptures and, by referring to the document of the Pontifical Biblical Commission, declares that we learn from patristic exegesis to find, in accordance with the proper intention of the biblical texts, "the reality of faith there expressed."[54] The exhortation then emphasizes the necessity of the "passage from letter to spirit,"[55] and stresses that, "within the Church's great Tradition," we learn to grasp in this passage "the unity of all Scripture." It is in no way ignoring that, from the historical and literary point of view, the composition of the biblical texts took place over a very long period of time and that "its individual books are not easily seen to possess an interior unity." The fact remains that the Scriptures are "considered in their totality as the unique Word of God that is addressed to us": "the person of Christ gives unity to the 'Scriptures' in relation to the one 'Word.'"[56] The exhortation then comes to the relationship between the two Testaments, emphasizing both "the unique importance of the Old Testament" and "the newness of the Christological interpretation"—that gives meaning to "typology" that discerns in the Old Covenant the pre-figurations of what God has fulfilled in His Son.[57]

There are several studies that, in recent decades, have deepened the understanding of the importance of patristic exegesis. One of them, in particular, merits being mentioned here: the work of Anne-Marie Pelletier on the *Lectures du Cantique des cantiques* [Readings of the Song of Songs].[58] First of all, this work does not attempt to determine, like so many others, the meaning of the biblical poem but is interested in the relationship that its readers have with it. In fact, the inventory and evaluation of contemporary exegeses make clear that, if there have been so many variations in the content of these exegeses, there has been, above all, a variety of attitudes regarding the

54. Benedict XVI, apostolic exhortation *Verbum Domini* (2010), no. 37; w2.vatican.va/content/benedict-xvi/en/apost_exhortations/documents/hf_ben-svi_exh_20100930_verbum-domini.html.

55. Ibid., no. 38.

56. Ibid., no. 39.

57. Ibid., no. 41.

58. Anne-Marie Pelletier, *Lectures du Cantique des cantiques: De l'énigme du sens aux figures du lecteur* [Readings of the Song of Songs: From the enigma of the meaning to the figures of the reader] (Rome: Pontificio Istituto Biblico, 1989).

text thus commented upon. Yet patristic literature (as well as medieval literature) precisely attests that "one cannot think about the reality of the text of the Song of Songs without taking into account the reference to its readers"; what is more, according to the ancient exegeses "the reader reading the Song of Songs becomes attentive and present to a text that, itself, is entirely addressed to him as the way of understanding liturgical acts that he posits, events that he celebrates or, more generally, his spiritual identity and spiritual situation"; thus, "the goal of such a reading and 'explanatory' discourses that accompany the text is not to understand what the poem is saying but, beyond this understanding, to be able to say the words of the poem and to understand what they say."[59] This reading (formerly illustrated by Origen and other Fathers) assumes the "I" and the "you" that dialogue in the Song in such a manner that the reader himself is involved in it. Pelletier calls this "subjective reading," contrasting it with "desubjective readings" that have as their aim "the reconversion of this 'I' and this 'you' into dramatic roles in which the reader is no more than the disengaged spectator."[60] This in no way means that the meaning of the text is simply submitted to the reader's subjectivity, regardless of what is really said by this text. This does not mean that it is necessary "to set an early exegesis against a modern exegesis, one being subjective, the other objective"; early exegesis, moreover, "is far from ignoring the concern for correctly establishing the text, the investigation of sources, the search for the literal meaning"; it does not misunderstand these exigencies, even if it does not have the resources that today are at the disposal of critical exegesis.[61] Early exegesis thus does not misunderstand "objective knowledge"; but what is characteristic of early exegesis is "the subjective integration" of such knowledge: exegesis is presented here "as a complete act of reading that does not push aside or place in rivalry knowledge and subjective elaboration but, on the contrary, undertakes to articulate them and relate them to each other"; yet this synthesis later came apart, to the extent that critical exegesis was developed "outside of all subjective appropria-

59. Ibid., 415–16. Cf. also, 422–23: "The research that was undertaken allowed us to conclude that Sg existed not only in the words that comprise it but in these words augmented by what the readers made of them."

60. Ibid., 416.

61. Ibid., 421–22.

tion."[62] It is not this critical exegesis that is as such in question (on the contrary, today we benefit from its methods and its achievements); on the contrary, it becomes suspect if it is restricted to the search for an "objective" meaning by making an abstraction of the reader and his involvement in the text, and it is here that the Fathers' interpretation manifests its always real importance:

> One consequently sees the proposition of what ancient exegesis is able to set up. Not that critical exegesis be subjectivized, which would be a contradiction that would ruin its definition and project. But that critical science be re-enrolled in a comprehensive hermeneutical act; that what is learned, in the superabundance of its results, be completed and raised by the process of subjectivization that one has described. Through which the knowledge could again become a way of nourishing the collective understanding, which the present situation does not always allow it to do. One notes, in any case, such a suggestion does not consist in treating ancient exegesis as a substantialized reference. On the other hand, it sees in it a historical model that can be a powerful incentive for extending and renewing the practices of the present.[63]

That contemporary exegesis can itself be enriched by the exegesis of the Fathers—and without, for all that, circumventing the requirements of critical exegesis—is what the work of Paul Beauchamp shows in an exemplary manner. The first words of his work *L'un et l'autre Testament* presents it as "a book, not of exegesis, but of an exegete." Of course, this book "is in solidarity with the current works of biblical exegesis," and the author is "dependent upon the results, even tied to the routines of this particular science;" but he speaks at the outset in the first person and presents himself as a "reader" of the Bible: "I began in the style of an account that was to make its way through all the Bible, as if the Bible only existed to be read by a traveler who has restricted his desire to see everything with that of going farther."[64] Beauchamp gives, moreover, to his book the subtitle "an attempt at a reading." And the conclusion of this book is itself titled "The reader." If it is informed by the methods and the achievements of the exegetical discipline, the search for meaning always engages the subject that is implied in the

62. Ibid., 422.

63. Ibid., 422.

64. Paul Beauchamp, *L'un et l'autre Testament*, vol. 1, *Essai de lecture* [The one and the other Testament, vol. 1, An attempt at a reading] (Paris: Seuil, 1976), 9.

reading of the biblical text—as was true for patristic exegesis. And it is "all" the Bible that Beauchamp thus covers:

> The East of this book is the promise of the unity of the two Testaments.... The book's originality lies in the constraint it places on itself: that of reading with equal seriousness the whole text, right to the edges. This condition is necessary if we are to find the ultimate end that attracts and energizes any reading, the longed-for goal, so to speak.... The horizon is thus the whole Bible.[65]

This was also, as we have seen with Origen, the central preoccupation of patristic exegesis: the biblical texts are not explained in only an isolated manner, they uncover their meaning in the light of all the Scriptures, the Old Testament being ultimately enlightened by the New—more precisely, by the event of Christ that has "fulfilled the Scriptures." Admittedly, the first volume of *L'un et l'autre Testament* hardly explains what the Gospel brings to the reading of the Law, the Prophets, and the other writings: the author is aware of how we used to impose on the Old Testament—quite unilaterally and insensitively—the interpretations given of it by the New Testament. But habits of this kind have now, for Beauchamp, "been counteracted by a more recent tendency to set these interpretations aside, and this in a systematic fashion that is all the more radical for being almost unconscious."[66] And it is this latter tendency that today it is necessary to correct:

> Knowledge of the New Testament does not necessarily lead to distortions in our reading of the Old Testament. Such knowledge, moreover, is simply a given, both among those who adhere to the Gospel and among those who do not, and to deny such a given would be a quite unnatural contortion. But, for those who do adhere to the Gospel, the *télos-archè* they recognized in it brings to light the ancient book's truth and meaning. Thus, far from dismissing the New Testament, the reading offered here is orientated, both in general and as regards many details, to the Gospel. The reader, or even a non-Christian one, will have recognized this. This sort of choice consists in exploiting and risking the hypothesis of our faith. This faith posits that the Gospel interprets the Old Testament in terms of the Old Testament's own truth, and leads to the statement that the Gospel sheds a true light on what the Old Testament has been and is. To present the Old Testament in this light, therefore, is not to betray its true nature.[67]

65. Ibid., 11–12; we use the words "the longed-for goal, so to speak" to translate Beauchamp's metaphor "les Indes promises" [the promised Indies].

66. Ibid., 295.

67. Ibid., 295–96.

Moreover, it is necessary to add that "the light of the Gospel projected onto the past is not an object": "the Gospel also by this approach enters into the crucible of an interpretation by the subject.... The Gospel itself is enlightened by the new birth of the Old Testament."[68] The second volume of *L'un et l'autre Testament*, titled *Accomplir les Écritures*, does not yet propose a reading of the New Testament but a rereading of the Old Testament that, much more explicitly than in the first volume, is "renewed in the light of the act of Jesus, recognized as Christ."[69] It is significant that one finds in it an exposition on "exegesis according to 'figures;'"[70] one knows its importance in the patristic tradition: Beauchamp highlights the principles and the stakes of such an exegesis, showing that it is, rightly understood, essential to the understanding of Christ as "fulfilling the Scriptures." In a general manner, his exegetical work is a work that, even if it respects the results attained by critical exegesis, takes into account the most profound intuitions of patristic exegesis and by this shows its basic stakes.[71]

The Real Significance of Patristic Exegesis

Now at the end of the chapter, we can gather together the various reasons that show why today patristic exegesis is of interest and significance.[72] First of all, one will observe this fact: even apart from

68. Ibid., 296.

69. Beauchamp, *L'un et l'autre Testament*, vol. 2, *Accomplir les Écritures* [The one and the other Testament, vol. 2, Fulfilling the Scriptures] (Paris: Seuil, 1990), 11.

70. Ibid., 220–37.

71. One could also refer to Pierre-Marie Beaude, *L'accomplissement des Écritures: Pour une histoire critique des systèmes de représentation du sens chrétien* [The fulfillment of the Scriptures: Toward a critical history of the systems of representation of Christian meaning] (Paris: Cerf, 1980). From the exegetical point of view, the works of Yves Simoens are in line with the reflection undertaken by Beauchamp; see *Selon Jean. 1. Une traduction. 2. Une interprétation* [According to John. 1. A translation. 2. An interpretation] (Brussels: Éditions de l'Institut d'Études Théologiques, 1997); *Le Cantique des cantiques, Livre de la plénitude: Une lecture anthropologique et théologique* [The Song of Songs, book of the fullness: An anthropological and theological reading] (Brussels: Lumen vitae, 2004; new rev. ed., Paris: Médiasèvres, 2012); *Apocalypse de Jean, Apocalypse de Jésus-Christ* [Revelation of John, revelation of Jesus Christ] (Paris: Éditions Facultés jésuites, 2008); *Croire pour aimer: Les trois lettres de Jean* [Believe to love: The three letters of John] (Paris: Éditions Facultés jésuites, 2011); see also *Au service de Saint Jean. Lectures du corpus johannique* [In the service of Saint John. Readings of the Johannine corpus], ed. Yves Simoens, François Cassingena-Trévedy and Michel Fédou (Paris: Médiasèvres, 2012).

72. The question has been notably tackled in the issue of *Recherches de Science*

all exegetical preoccupation, many find in the Fathers' homilies and commentaries on Scripture spiritual nourishment of great value—whether it is thanks to the Office of Vigils in monasteries or personal readings in the context of the Liturgy of the Hours, or even in other circumstances. Such a fact is itself significant. It affirms that numerous patristic meditations on the Scriptures still engage today's Christian and feed his interior life. This merits being particularly highlighted at a time when one often values the traditions of Eastern religions; it is necessary to recall, in this situation, that many of the patristic texts on the Scriptures themselves transmit treasures of wisdom and spiritual experience.

But let us come to the central question that has governed the entirety of our thought: what, in spite of the decisive contributions of critical exegesis, continues to make patristic exegesis important even today? We will give several answers to this question, ending with the one that is the most fundamental.

In the first place, it is necessary to take note of the fact that regarding the Old Testament early Christian literature written in the Greek language is referring to the translation of the Septuagint and that, as a consequence, it enriches our knowledge and understanding of the biblical text.[73] Saying this in no way depreciates the work of Jerome, who deserves credit for going back to the Hebrew text in order to make a Latin translation. But the recognized primacy of the "*veritas hebraica*" does not call into question the importance of the "Bible of Alexandria:"[74] the text of the ancient Scriptures was translated into Greek before the coming of Christ, and it is to this translation that the authors of the New Testament were referring, as were the Christian writers of the Greek language that came after them. One must, of course, admit that the Septuagint has not always reproduced the true meaning of the Hebrew text; on the other hand, however, the Greek

---

Religieuse 99, no. 2 (2011) on "Exégèse critique, exégèse patristique" [Critical exegesis, patristic exegesis]; see in particular Yves-Marie Blanchard, "Les Pères de l'Église ont-ils quelque chose à dire à l'exégèse biblique d'aujourd'hui?" [Do the Fathers have anything to say to today's exegesis?], 235–47; and Christoph Theobald, "Vers une nouvelle théorie des sens?" [Toward a new theory of senses], 249–58.

73. One could make an analogous remark regarding the first Latin Fathers, whose writings allow us to know the translations of the "*vetus latina*."

74. Cf. the edition and the French translation of this "Bible of Alexandria," in the publications of Cerf.

version has enriched the Hebraic version (as is true for all translation that, as faithful as it may be to the original, necessarily brings something new to it because it appeals to the resources of another language), and the fact that the Septuagint was considered as an "inspired" translation gives even more weight to this last remark. Patristic exegesis helps us to a better understanding of the "complement of meaning" that the Bible of Alexandria thus brings to the Hebrew text—and this is even more important because, let us repeat, it is to this Bible that the authors of the New Testament were referring.

More broadly, interest in patristic exegesis makes us aware of the history of the interpretation given to the different books of the Scriptures—those of the New Testament as well as the Old. Such a contribution itself responds to a requirement of contemporary exegesis: it is more and more aware that a text is not simply clarified in an isolated manner, nor only in reference to some texts that preceded it, but that it is important to be more attentive to the subsequent "effects of meaning," that is, to the diverse ways in which it has been read and understood by subsequent eras. It often happens, of course, that the work of the exegete highlights the break between these later readings and the original meaning of the biblical text; but it also occurs that such readings bring a valuable confirmation to the research undertaken by the exegete—indeed even that they make him aware of this or that meaning of the biblical text that up to then had escaped him. Let us add that the debates internal to patristic exegesis can themselves be of great importance for the interpretation of various writings. Thus, considering only the controversy between Augustine and Pelagius, one could be tempted, through the Letter to the Romans, to understand principally Paul's vigorous emphasis on the priority and the necessity of grace; but Origen's commentary on the same epistle also places importance on the theme of liberty (counter to the Gnostics, who were tempted to rely on the Pauline text to deny free will); the comparison of these readings ultimately has consequences for the interpretation of Pauline thought, which cannot be interpreted by a unilateral meaning and rather invites a correct articulation of grace and freedom.

Another interest of patristic exegesis is, paradoxically, even due to the limitation that one has often recognized in it: the propensity to surpass, as soon as possible, the solely literal meaning of the biblical text in order to find in it hidden meanings. Of course, it is not a matter of saying that we today must not preserve the literal meaning as established by critical exegesis: we must, on the contrary, take note of this meaning (and, in its name, break with the patristic explanations that prove to be erroneous).[75] But this remark does not call into question the principle of an exegesis that additionally intends to go beyond the simple letter. We are still not here referring to the properly spiritual interpretation (of which it will be a question later), but to what recovers, in a general way, the practice of the exegesis called "allegorical." For research done in the cadre of semiotics, such as that of Tzvetan Todorov, has clearly highlighted that the linguistic sign is not univocal but polyvalent: like every text, the biblical text could thus give rise to all sorts of "allegories" or, if one prefers, "symbolic" explanations—even if it is necessary when reading patristic exegesis to speak of a "oriented polyvalence of the symbol" (de Lubac), the use of allegory being ultimately ordered to the Christian interpretation of Scriptures.[76]

From this, we again see the importance given to the reader, as he becomes involved in his reading of the biblical text, and not just in having grasped the literal meaning, but also in freely taking in its hidden harmonics. Gregory the Great had already said this in his own way, by associating the quest for meaning to the very progress of the soul. When he explained the verse from Ezekiel 1:19 ("And when the living creatures went, the wheels went beside them; and when the living creatures rose from the earth, the wheels rose"), he gave the following commentary:

> The revelations increase with the one who reads them (*divina eloquia cum legente crescunt*): the higher one directs his gaze, the deeper the meaning. The wheels do not rise if the Living Ones do not rise. If the soul of the reader does not ascend, the divine words, not understood, remain, so to speak, at ground level. When the divine text appears without fervor to whomever reads it, when the language of the Sacred Scriptures does not move his soul and in no way throws light upon his understanding, the wheel is inactive and on the ground,

75. Let us once again refer, on this point, to the works of Pierre Gibert, in particular his book *L'invention critique de la Bible* (cf. note 5 above).

76. See Tzvetan Todorov, *Symbolisme et interpretation* [Symbolism and interpretation] (Paris: Seuil, 1978), 124; the expression "polyvalence oriented to the symbol" refers to H. de Lubac, *Exégèse médiévale*, vol. 2/2:180.

because the Living One does not rise from the earth. But if the Living One advances, that is to say seeks milestones of his moral progress, and by taking a step in his heart, discovers how to take the step of good work, then the wheels advance as well: you learn to make progress in the sacred text to the extent that you yourselves became better through it.[77]

Scripture progresses with those who read it: it is precisely this idea of Gregory that P. C. Bori is referring to in his work *L'interprétation infinite.*[78] He highlights its fecundity in the history of exegesis; he also explains how its significance was minimized beginning in the twelfth and thirteenth centuries, then, above all, by some movements of the modern era that have reduced the practice and the theory of interpretation to the problem of a purely "scientific" explanation. During the same era, however, Gregory's idea was once again taken up; in any case, Pier Cesare Bori shows how Gadamer's theory on interpretation (understood as a progress of the work itself in the interpreter's present) is ultimately in line with the exegetical practice of the Fathers of the Church and in the tradition that it initiated. The stakes are clearly formulated: "to start reading a passage and to discover in it new meanings, more adapted to the actual spiritual condition, is not only to achieve a subjective progress in the face of an immobile text.... The progress does not occur within a pure subjectivity, since there are in the text objective meanings that are progressively brought to light as the reader grows."[79]

These thoughts are extremely important and today, let us note in passing, invite relativizing the traditional differences between "Antiochene exegesis" and "Alexandrian exegesis" just as the last century's discussion on the usage of the words "allegory" and "typology." Of course, such debates retain their interest and pertinence but are, in the end, secondary; for all the Fathers—whatever the diversity of their orientations—share the conviction according to which the meaning of the biblical text is not limited to the literal explanation that one can give to it nor even to the figurative meaning that the author had

77. Gregory the Great, *Homilies on Ezekiel*, VII, 8, *Homélies sur Ezéchiel*, trans. Charles Morel, SC 327 (Paris: Cerf, 1986), 245.

78. Pier Cesare Bori, *L'interprétation infinite: L'herméneutique chrétienne ancienne et ses transformations* [The infinite interpretation: Ancient Christian hermeneutics and its transformations] (Paris: Cerf, 1991).

79. Ibid., 57.

in mind—and it is exactly this idea that today contemporary hermeneutics allows recovering. Judgments about the exegesis called "allegorical" (including being "arbitrary" for which it is often reproached) must in fact be reviewed in this light: apart from the fact that this exegesis itself obeys some laws, it, first of all, illustrates the capacity of the biblical text to awaken in the reader new resonances and to do this in an infinite way—to the extent of the power of inspiration of which this text is the bearer and in the manner in which the reader himself is involved in it by his own reading. The error would clearly be to circumvent the literal meaning: one assesses the danger that there could be in substituting various allegorical interpretations for this literal meaning, and one will never say enough that this meaning must be established with all the resources that critical exegesis today places at our disposal. But patristic exegesis opportunely recalls that this does not exhaust the meanings of the biblical text: this is valid for the literal meaning itself (the explanation of which can be revitalized thanks to some discoveries), and this is valid *a fortiori* for the spiritual meaning. Gilles Dorival strongly says this at the end of an article on the "meaning of Scripture" in the Greek Fathers:

> There is not a meaning of Scripture established once and for all. The discoveries of historians and archeologists and the development of new methods of reading the texts require periodically rectifying our approach to the historical-literal meaning. And even the history of patristics teaches us that the spiritual meaning is marked by renewal. For the Fathers themselves, the search for the meaning has no end. Here, they repeat a theme outlined by Philo, according to which the sloth and the lack of perspicacity of our human nature are at issue. Origen emphasizes that Scripture is made of words; yet language cannot signify the divine perfectly; it is radically insufficient; this, however, does not mean that there may be meaning to look for outside of the Scriptures; it is in and beginning with their own text that one will be able to discover "what is according to Scripture" (1 Cor 4:6), in a sudden illumination that will be given to us one day by God. Gregory of Nyssa created the concept of epektasis in order to think about this unending tension of man toward God.[80]

Yet, as these last words have suggested, Christian allegory does not only respond to a general law of hermeneutics—the necessity of not

80. Gilles Dorival, "Sens de l'Écriture—Pères grecs" [Senses of Scripture—Greek Fathers], in *Supplément au Dictionnaire de la Bible* [Supplement to the Bible Dictionary], vol. 7 (Paris: Letouzé & Ané, 1996), col. 441–42.

just considering a single meaning—but it is ordered to the very search for God. More precisely, what characterizes it as "Christian allegory" is that it is intrinsically linked to the revelation of Christ—and this is so both because it is founded on this revelation and because it contributes to making it known to us. We are here reaching what constitutes the most fundamental significance of patristic exegesis. De Lubac spoke of a "polyvalence oriented to the symbol": in fact, the use of allegory is, in the Fathers, "oriented" by the faith of the God of Jesus Christ. On one hand, patristic exegesis is indeed rooted in the conviction that Christ is the key to the Scriptures and that, in his light, the texts of the Old Testament unfold their most profound meaning; it considers, on the other hand, in an inverse sense, that these texts of the Old Testament themselves cause us to acquire a more profound knowledge of Christ and the mysteries revealed by him.

It is important to emphasize that the Christian faith is here presupposed. Lacking this, one would give the impression that patristic exegesis starts with ancient texts and, on this basis, "proves" the mystery of Christ and the Church. It is, of course, necessary to recognize that, in many cases, Christian apologetics has thus appeared to "demonstrate" Christian faith based on ancient Scriptures—at the risk of not respecting the right of Judaism to claim another reading of what Christians call the "Old Testament." It is even more necessary to explain what was in fact the presupposition of patristic exegesis: even when it seemed to establish the Christian faith on the foundation of the ancient Scriptures, it is in reality this faith that produced it, and it is by its light that it reread the Old Testament—that then, for its part, opened up a more profound understanding of the New. Thus understood, the Christian reading of the ancient Scriptures does not claim to impose itself on the Jews. It is, nevertheless, legitimate—and even necessary from the point of view of the Christian faith, taking into account Jesus' position regarding the Scriptures of Israel: by his life, and even more by his Paschal mystery, he leads these Scriptures to their fulfillment; and when he walks with the two disciples on the road to Emmaus, he opens their eyes to their profound meaning: "And beginning with Moses and all the prophets, he interpreted to them in all the scriptures the things concerning himself" (Lk 24:27).

The biblical texts, thus reread and explained in the light of faith, in return contribute to shedding light upon the Christian mysteries. Allegory is itself committed to this objective, even when it appears to us to be totally arbitrary (as when Origen, regarding the propitiatory pure gold in Exodus, sees in the "pure gold" an allusion to "the holy and pure soul of Jesus," and, in reading that this propitiation is "two and one-half cubits in length," discovers here a symbol of the soul of Christ who "is the mediator between God and man"; the allegory, as arbitrary as it may be in itself, is, however, meant to enlighten the mystery of the Word made flesh).[81] Above all, the faith's presupposition of Christ's "fulfilling the Scriptures" is the foundation for the patristic use of typology and prophetic argumentation (which, let us recall, were already practiced by Paul and the other authors of the New Testament); more broadly still, it directs the central vision of the relationship between the two Testaments, of their unity or—as Irenaeus says—of their "symphony." Such a view of the Scriptures, of course, cannot be imposed and, let us repeat, must never be substituted for the search for the literal meaning as it can be established by critical exegesis. It is, however, required for every *Christian* reading of the Bible which must take into account the revelation of Jesus who "fulfilled the Scriptures" and started with these Scriptures themselves in order to open up the understanding of his own mystery. It is to this conviction that patristic exegesis bears witness, and it is what today gives to it its continuing significance.

81. Cf. Origen, *Commentary on the Epistle to the Romans*, III, 8, 4–5; trans. Thomas P. Scheck, Fathers of the Church 103 (Washington, D.C.: The Catholic University of America Press, 2001), 218–20. This allegory is in fact suggested by Rom 3:25: "whom God put forward as an expiation by his blood, to be received by faith. This was to show God's righteousness."

CHAPTER 6

The Contribution of the Fathers to Christian Thought

We have attempted, in the preceding chapter, to specify the meaning and the stakes of patristic exegesis. It is now necessary for us to return to the difficulties that from the point of view of human sciences, philosophy, and theology (leaving aside the questions raised by "contextual" theologies, which will be examined in the next chapter) seem to create an obstacle to the project of a "patristic theology." We would like to show that these difficulties, as important as they may be, do not constitute decisive objections. They must be taken into consideration, of course, but they cannot deter a work of patristic theology that, on the contrary, today remains necessary.

Patristics and Human Sciences

We have mentioned above a first set of questions principally linked to the development of the human sciences: must not patristic texts, or more broadly Christian literature of Antiquity, be considered first as subjects of philosophical, sociological, and historical study? Do they not above all else call for the implementation of the methods proper to these latter disciplines, and is there not the risk of some theological reflections unduly interfering with such approaches? One would, of course, admit that the theologian is interested in the history of doctrines, but, one could ask, is he justified in drawing on patristic writings in his own task as theologian? Does he not call into question, by his personal engagement as a believer, the goal of "objectivity" that the study of the early texts requires? In fact, must not the historical and cultural distance between the patristic era and our own dissuade the expectation of today developing a theological thought "based on the Fathers"?

It is necessary, of course, to acknowledge the partial truth that is contained in these questions; in particular, the theologian must endeavor to respect the procedures of each discipline and to gather the fruits of the research undertaken by all those who in the fields of philology, history, and other sciences contribute to shedding light upon the texts of early Christianity. Not, moreover, that this research itself can be lacking in all presuppositions nor bear the mark of a personal engagement: it is also important to denounce, even in the field of science, the myth of a perfect "objectivity." At the least, the theologian cannot study the Fathers without being informed, as much as possible, by the contributions that are made by researchers in various disciplines and that enrich both. The patristic "subject" lends itself more than ever to such an interdisciplinarity and receives very valuable insights from it.

Having recognized this, it is nonetheless legitimate—and, we believe, necessary—that the literature of early Christianity also gives rise to a properly theological work, not only in the sense of an inquiry into the history of doctrines but also in the sense of an actual reflection *on* the thinking of the Fathers, indeed *based* on this thinking. It would be serious if a narrow conception of "objectivity" were to lead to a confiscation of patristics by the human sciences to the detriment of theology. This would not only be a form of exclusion (reversing in some way the former situation in which patristics, on the contrary, risked being the special possession of theologians); it would also be contrary to the Fathers' own intention to the extent that they wrote precisely as Christians and intended to contribute to the understanding of the faith. Lastly, and above all, it would be depriving contemporary theology of what, today as yesterday, must contribute to founding it and nourishing it.[1]

1. Dominique Bertrand has emphasized, in this sense, the "theological weight" of the collection Sources Chrétiennes very well; all the while recognizing the contribution of "culturalist" works on Christian Antiquity, he correctly argues for not being limited by the "understanding of ancient eras" but recognizing "the understanding of the persons themselves who have shaped the eras"; such is precisely the "job" assigned "to the Sources Chrétiennes and to the movement that it supports": "the more one scientifically studies the Fathers, the

This last remark in no way means that it is not necessary to recognize the distance between the Fathers' era and ours or to acknowledge the discontinuities at the very heart of early Christianity. Rather, it is important to take note of this, but without its calling into question the possibility of thinking, even today, *on* the Fathers or even *based on* them. We have mentioned above the difference in the viewpoints that formerly appeared between Michel de Certeau and Henri de Lubac—the one placing greater stress upon the "ruptures," the other emphasizing the essential continuity of Tradition. Yet patristic theology today must prove that it is capable of honoring both points of view and, even more, of reconciling them.

For this purpose, it is possible to draw on some considerations concerning the hermeneutics of the ancient texts—for example, those that Edward Schillebeeckx developed in his book *L'histoire des hommes, récit de Dieu* [Church: The human story of God]. The author recognizes that the experience of faith in Jesus has been communicated since the Christian beginnings in greatly different worlds: "In each instance we have a culture-specific appropriation of the message of the gospel." The discontinuities are thus real, depending upon whether the faith is being expressed in the Aramean world, or in the Hellenistic world, or even in other worlds. And yet there is "the corresponding relationship between the original message ... and the situation, then and now, which is different each time," so that there is really "a fundamental unity and identity." This identity is expressed through connecting the two "relationships": just as Jesus' message arose in a given sociohistorical context, an analogous relationship was manifested between the "patristic understanding of the faith" and the "socio-historical context then." Thus, "the equal proportion of relationships down through the

---

more their overall Christian value ... becomes apparent as an 'achievement for all time'"; it is a matter of "making understandable the writings and not the ideas," of "passing from various states of the authors' faith ... to a renewed encounter with the authors," of "working on a consideration of the future of the Church at the same time more humanist and more divine in the midst of the history of mankind"; see "Poids théologique de la collection des Sources Chrétiennes" [Theological significance of the Sources Chrétiennes collection], *Esprit & Vie*, no. 168 (2007): 10, 11. Also see, by the same author, "Les Pères de l'Église et la rencontre des cultures" [The Fathers of the Church and the encounter of cultures], in *Penser la foi. Recherches en théologie aujourd'hui, Mélanges offerts à Joseph Moingt* [Thinking the faith. Essays in honor of Joseph Moingt], ed. Joseph Doré and Christoph Theobald (Paris: Cerf—Assas Éditions, 1993), 473–86.

Christian tradition of faith is a norm, an orientation, and an inspiration; it is the model on the basis of which now, loyal to the gospel, we can, nevertheless, also make its message comprehensible here and now." The recognition of discontinuities thus does not prohibit upholding "the Christian identity, which is one and the same," even if it "is never complete identity, but proportional identity."[2] We understand as well that, if it is not a matter of underestimating the distance between the patristic era and our own, a hermeneutical work no less allows laying out the way in which the Fathers thought about the faith in the various situations of their time and finding in it inspiration for thinking analogously about the faith in the situation of our own times.

Independent of these considerations, the awareness of a fundamental continuity is, in any case, required by an essential conviction of Christian theology: that of the Spirit's action in history, whatever the diversity of places and of times. This conviction, here expressed in its most general form, is valid in an eminent way for the Fathers of the Church to the extent that they have most especially contributed to the transmission of the Gospel and to the understanding of the Christian mystery. It, of course, does not amount to ignoring that they expressed it in necessarily particular languages. It even more does not amount to accepting everything that they held, nor to closing our eyes to what, from the patristic era, occasionally appears to deform or contradict the Gospel message. This conviction is no less based on the understanding of the living Tradition itself, understood as the way in which the God of Jesus Christ does not cease to inspire, by His Spirit, words and actions that bear witness to the Gospel. Christian theology cannot doubt such a continuity that, despite the difference in times, or rather through it, attests to the permanence of God's gift to his Church as well as to all humanity. Such a continuity—that is first the work of the Spirit, as it is received in history—is not only an assurance of the patristic tradition's link to the source of Revelation; it is also what allows Christians of subsequent eras, in their turn, to commune with the Fathers, and this is what gives the theologian the assurance of being able

2. Edward Schillebeeckx, *Church: The Human Story of God*, trans. John Bowden (New York: The Crossroad Publishing Company, 1992), 40–42. Also see the earlier reflections of Claude Geffré on theology as hermeneutics, in *Le christianisme au risque de l'interprétation* [Christianity at the risk of interpretation] (Paris: Cerf, 1983), 65–90.

today, regarding the different disciplines as well as the awareness of the historical discontinuities, to maintain a vital relationship with the patristic texts, to allow himself to be inspired by them and thus in his turn to advance in his own understanding of the Christian mystery.

Philosophical Stakes

What is currently the situation of the questions concerning the philosophical language of the Fathers and the basic orientations that are linked to it? On this subject, we have recalled the recurrent reproach against the "Hellenization" of Christianity, as well as the distancing that has often occurred from a way of thinking that is qualified as "onto-theological" or that belongs to a "metaphysical" age now past.

Before considering these questions in themselves, we must recall that "philosophy" holds a very important place in patristic literature. In Antiquity, the word designated a very high ideal—not only an ideal of thinking, but also, and indeed first of all, an ideal of life.[3] Pierre Hadot, in particular, has clearly shown how philosophy was a veritable "spiritual exercise" in thinkers such as Marcus Aurelius.[4] In any case, for the Fathers of the Church since Justin, the search for the truth was inseparable from an existence "according to the *Logos*," led in a manner "worthy of God." Concerning the doctrines themselves, it is clear that some Christian authors knew the philosophical movements of the previous centuries and of their own time very well, that their writings show the influence of the fundamental debates with thinkers such as Plotinus, Porphyry, or Proclus (as one sees, for example, in Augustine or Dionysius the Areopagite), and that their own attempts at understanding the faith—corresponding to what we designate as "theology"—widely integrate the resources of Greco-Latin conceptuality.[5]

Having recognized this, is it legitimate to find fault with patris-

3. See Anne-Marie Malingrey, *"Philosophia." Étude d'un groupe de mots dans la littérature grecque, des présocratiques au IVᵉ siècle après J.-C.* ["Philosophia." Study of a group of words in Greek literature from the Presocratics to the fourth century A.D.] (Paris: Klincksieck, 1961) (the word "philosophy" could also designate, in particular, the monastic life).

4. See Pierre Hadot, *Exercices spirituels et philosophie antique* [Spiritual exercises and ancient philosophy] (Paris: Institut d'Études Augustiniennes, 1981; new ed., Paris: Albin Michel, 2002).

5. See Pierre Hadot, *Études de patristique et d'histoire des concepts* [Studies in patristics and the history of concepts] (Paris: Les Belles Lettres, 2010).

tic literature for having "Hellenized" (or "Latinized") Christianity in its own way by referring to ancient philosophy? The fecundity of this literature already invites placing this in great doubt and leads rather to emphasizing the remarkable effort that was made by the Fathers in order to think about the Christian faith—an effort so powerful that some contemporary philosophers have themselves benefitted from it, whether by repeating the insights of some ancient author or by finding in them, sometimes because they were in line with them and sometimes because they were distant from them, ways for developing their own thought. It is a fact, in any case, that the in-depth reading of the Fathers has profoundly influenced various philosophers, whatever might, moreover, be the orientations of their respective thinking; this is most of all borne out regarding Augustine, whose importance for philosophers as different as Étienne Gilson, Hannah Arendt, Paul Ricoeur, Jean-Luc Marion, or Jean-Louis Chrétien[6]—to cite only a few names—is known. Of course, there is a partial truth in the suspicion against the "Hellenization" of Christianity: not only does it rely upon an undeniable fact (early Christianity did in fact encounter Greek thinking and borrowed many concepts from it), but it correctly warns against the risk of deforming or of quite simply forgetting, in the name of such a "Hellenization," the biblical message in its original form. However, in addition to the Hebrew Scriptures having been translated into the Greek language since the Hellenistic Era and the New Testament, from the outset, having been transmitted in this same language (the word *logos*, in particular, is already found in the Gospel of John, even if the clarification of its meaning is first based on the prior biblical tradition), the risks noted above must not be considered as inevitable. In order not to succumb to them, it suffices to be attentive to the particularities inferred by the "translation" of the biblical message into the philosophical language of the Greeks and to be aware that this "trans-

6. See Étienne Gilson, *Introduction à l'étude de Saint Augustin* [Introduction to the study of Saint Augustine] (Paris: Vrin, 1929; new ed., 1987); Isabelle Bochet, *Augustin dans la pensée de Paul Ricoeur* [Augustine in Paul Ricoeur's thought] (Paris: Éditions Facultés jésuites, 2003); Jean-Luc Marion, *Au lieu de soi. L'approche de Saint Augustin* [In the place of oneself. The approach of Saint Augustine] (Paris: PUF, 2008); Véronique Albanel, *Amour du monde. Christianisme et politique chez Hannah Arendt* [Love of the world. Christianity and politics according to Hannah Arendt] (Paris: Cerf, 2010) (this work emphasizes the importance of the reference to Augustine in the thinking of Arendt); Jean-Louis Chrétien, *Saint Augustin et les actes de parole* [Saint Augustine and the acts of speech] (Paris: PUF, 2002).

lation" necessarily implies a distance from the first formulations of the biblical message—a distance that must not necessarily be evaluated in a negative manner but that, in the best of cases, allows understanding, by the use of philosophical language, an explanation or a transposition of what belongs to Revelation. The risk, in any case, is inherent in what is required of every presentation of the biblical mystery in a given cultural context: one must indeed recognize in what way such a "translation" modifies or impoverishes the original, but one must also recognize what it brings on its own, beginning with the resources that belong to a specific culture.

Thus, on one hand, it is right to emphasize that the translation of the divine Name (Ex 3:14) by the Greek expression *egô eimi ho ôn* no longer reproduces the exact meaning of the Hebrew expression *asher eyeh asher* and that it risks implying that God is only a "being" among others, although the supreme Being. But, on the other hand, it is also by this translation that the divine Name was really able to be understood in the philosophical language of the Greeks—even if it were necessary at the same time to emphasize (as the Fathers have precisely done) that God is not, for all that, comparable to one being among others but that He absolutely transcends all creatures. It is necessary in an analogous way to interpret the recourse to the word *homoousios* at the Council of Nicaea in order to talk about the equality of "substance" between the Son and the Father. On one hand, this word clearly had limits: apart from the fact that it was not explicitly used in the New Testament, it did not take into account what is so strongly indicated by the hymn of the Letter to the Philippians, namely, that the Son "did not count equality with God a thing to be grasped" (Phil 2:6) and that it is precisely by his "kenosis" that, paradoxically, the profundity of his divine filiation was revealed. But, although insufficient by itself, it no less represented an attempt to say, in philosophical language, what was precisely rejected by Arians and what, however, emerged from the Gospel revelation: "I and the Father are one" (Jn 10:30).

Moreover, the reproach against the "Hellenization" of Christianity forgets that the Fathers did not do this in order to adopt concepts available from Greek philosophy but to transform their meaning in light of the biblical Revelation. Regarding the Council of Nicaea, Aloys Grillmeier formerly emphasized this: the "Hellenization" of the language thus has for its counterpart a "de-Hellenization" of its content.[7] Some analogous remarks can be made regarding many ideas developed by the Fathers, and it is necessary, in many of these cases, to recognize those that give a totally new meaning to philosophical words: thus for the word "hypostasis," which, first of all, means "substance" but that, because of the reflections conducted in the context of the Trinitarian doctrine, came to designate the "act of subsisting" and could thus be applied to what individually distinguishes each of the Three—the Father, the Son, the Spirit. Some new concepts appeared, such as that of "enhypostasis" and "perichoresis," for Christian theology needed them in order to express what Greek thinking had up to then not been able to formulate—the very paradox of the *Logos* made flesh, the mystery of a God one and triune. What one calls the "Hellenization" of Christianity is actually what, in the best of cases, allowed introducing, in the conceptual language of the Greeks, the newness of the Christian faith.

But, will one ask, was this "Hellenization" not done in a way that can, from the philosophical point of view, be legitimately contested? On this subject, we have recalled an orientation that is today quite widespread: the Heideggerian project to overcome "metaphysics" and to return to "things themselves" that leads to a distancing away from the "onto-theological" language of which patristic writings often bear the mark. One, however, observes that this orientation has a positive counterpart: the "post-Heideggerian" reading of some ancient works, in particular from a phenomenological perspective, has shown their significance from a new point of view—as the studies of Michel Henry, Jean-Luc Marion, Emmanuel Falque, and Joseph O'Leary show.[8] It is

7. Aloys Grillmeier, "De Jésus de Nazareth 'dans l'ombre du Fils de Dieu' au Christ, image de Dieu" [From Jesus of Nazareth in the shadow of the Son of God to Christ, Image of God], in *Comment être chrétien? La réponse de Hans Küng* [How to be a Christian? Hans Küng's answer], ed. Jean-Robert Armogathe (Paris: Desclée de Brouwer, 1979), 128: "Nicaea is not the Hellenization but the de-Hellenization, or the liberation, of the Christian image of God from the dead-end and divisions into which Hellenism had landed it. It was not that the Greeks made Nicaea; it is rather that Nicaea moved beyond the Greek philosophers."

8. Cf. Michel Henry, *Incarnation. Une philosophie de la chair* [Incarnation. A philosophy of the flesh] (Paris: Seuil, 2000), 180–95 (about Irenaeus and Tertullian); Marion, *Au lieu de soi* (on Augustine); Emmanuel Falque, *Dieu, la chair et l'autre. D'Irénée à Duns Scot* [God, the flesh, and the other. From Irenaeus to Duns Scotus] (Paris: PUF, 2008) (on Irenaeus, Tertullian, Origen, and Augustine, and some medieval authors); Joseph Stephen O'Leary, *Christianisme et philosophie chez Origène* [Christianity and philosophy by Origen] (Paris: Cerf, 2011).

in fact legitimate that some patristic texts be reread according to such an option; these texts have proven to be in a position to be meaningful to the reader today and, even more, to contribute to the renewal of his thinking.[9] This, moreover, does not mean that other options are not equally legitimate. Without here having to take a position on the internal debates of contemporary philosophy, we, for our part, think that the Fathers' thinking merits being studied according to diverse perspectives. Not only do the phenomenological readings not do away with the need for hermeneutical works concerned with placing early texts in their historical context and, in return for this effort, with bringing out the meaning for our own time,[10] but one must also take into consideration the "metaphysics" of the Fathers, which, grasped in all its depth, does not fall under the blow of critics that one is often tempted to use on it. Thus, the fact that God is presented as "the One who is" in no way amounts to, for Gregory of Nyssa or for Augustine, considering him as a "being" among others (even if the greatest), as these Fathers, on the contrary, greatly emphasize his radical transcendence regarding every creature. An even stronger reason is the case of Dionysius the Areopagite, who did not avoid using extreme formulations in order to signify the overwhelming challenge that the human spirit is called to overcome in the presence of the Mystery. In fact, if it is legitimate to read the philosophical texts of the Fathers according to this or that contemporary option (whether "metaphysical," "existential," "hermeneutical," or "phenomenological"), does one not first simply have to reflect "beginning with the Fathers," allowing them to guide by their own concepts and, above all, by the profound movement of their research? These are rich enough to awaken and stimulate our own research, and one must in any case hope that the in-depth reading of the Cappadocians, Augustine, Dionysius, and Maximus the Confessor will, as such, also contribute to the future tasks of Christian thinking.

9. Cf. Falque, in his introduction to the work previously cited: "The concepts of *Dieu, la chair et l'autre*, of course, belong, and in an exemplary way, to the field of contemporary phenomenology, but they find in the corpus of patristic and medieval philosophy not only what grounds them but also what renews them" (*Dieu, la chair et l'autre*, 12).

10. On this point, see Henri-Jérôme Gagey, "La théologie entre urgence phénoménologique et endurance herméneutique" [Theology between phenomenological urgency and hermeneutical endurance], *Recherches de Science Religieuse* 98 (2010): 31–57 (even if this article does not specifically bear upon the relationship between philosophy and patristics).

The "Authority" of the Fathers

Lastly, we previously have presented the state of some questions that have been raised in the cadre of theology. They are so diverse that here it is not possible to respond to every one of them; as we have stated, those questions that are connected to "contextual" theologies are referred to in the next chapter, and others will be taken up in the second part of this book according to the particular themes to which they are connected (thus, we will tackle the attitude of the Fathers regarding "heresies" when we treat the stakes of patristics for ecumenical dialogue; and we will come back to the question of "anti-Judaism" in the context of the chapter on religions). Here we would like to limit ourselves to a fundamental reflection: what, in spite of the historical distance and despite what in the early Church today appears questionable to us, continues to be legitimate, and even necessary, for a patristic contribution to the theology of our times?

This necessity could first be based on some traditional considerations regarding patristics as a "theological place." Here, the "Fathers of the Church" is being limited to the narrow meaning, without considering in its entirety the literature of early Christianity; it is a matter of taking up the traits that one has customarily recognized in these "Fathers," which is to say, orthodoxy, holiness, approval by the Church, and antiquity, and showing how they help to define the importance of patristics for theology—with the condition that some clarifications are now needed –; it is, in other words, a matter of highlighting what constitutes, even today, the "authority" of the Fathers.

The first trait is that of orthodoxy: one expects from a Father of the Church that he correctly teaches the faith, that he allows discerning the doctrines faithful to Christian Revelation and those that clarify it, which help to advance in the understanding of the Christian mystery. This clearly does not mean that all the Fathers were orthodox on every point. The trait must rather be understood thus: a Father of the Church is a Father of the Church to the extent that he thinks in a correct manner—that is, more precisely, in a manner conforming to the preaching received from the apostles and the living Tradition of the faith.

The second characteristic, that of holiness, must be associated as well with the first. It has become popular to emphasize the coherence that must exist between words and actions, between doctrine and practice, or—to use language dear to liberation theologies—between orthodoxy and "orthopraxy"; this also invites emphasizing all the more the importance of the second trait that was formerly recognized in the Fathers. Some examples easily support this: what makes an Ignatius of Antioch a Father is not only that he spoke so well of Christ and the Church, it is that his practice was also coherent with what he taught (he was faithful to the Gospel up to enduring martyrdom in its name); or even, what makes Basil of Caesarea a Father is not only that he contributed in such a remarkable way to the deepening of the Trinitarian doctrine, it is also that he preached to the rich the love of the poor and that he even founded an asylum where lepers and other unfortunates could find refuge. Of course, counter-examples also exist, and further on we will take them up when we mention the shadows of the patristic era and the discernment that it calls for today. The trait of holiness is, nevertheless, essential to the definition of what it is to be a Father of the Church: the Fathers are "Fathers of the Church" *to the extent* that they have realized such an ideal.

The third trait, the approval of the Church, is equally important but calls for still more clarifications. If some Christian authors have been the object of such an "approval," it was imposed on the basis of an ecclesial consensus—that was notably expressed by the lists of "Fathers" enumerated by popes and councils. Even more, one must keep in mind the completely paradoxical case of Origen, who was condemned on the eve of the Council of Constantinople II! But this was a condemnation of some doctrines called "Origenist" that, for the most part, had nothing to do with the true thinking of the Alexandrian, and he has been widely rehabilitated by studies such as those of Balthasar, Daniélou, de Lubac, and Crouzel: his work is actually a preeminent work and, no less than that of Augustine, merits "the approval of the Church." The case of Origen thus does not refute this latter criterion but, in its own way, confirms it. Such criteria correspond to the exigency of a consensus by which the Christian community agrees to recognize a Christian author as a "Father of the Church."

As for the last trait, that of antiquity, it in no way means that the heritage of patristic literature impedes innovation in theology; one keeps in mind the warning of Congar on this subject:

> What the Fathers achieved in proclaiming and explaining the Gospel according to the *logos* of ancient civilization must be done today, too, and will be necessary again tomorrow for other cultural periods. In this respect, the Fathers had a role which was historically conditioned and defined and which must not be allowed to render sterile or impossible other analogous historical roles, but should on the contrary inspire and stimulate them. In order the better to fulfil these roles, the Church at all times and in every century remains as full of vigor and promise as it was in the fourth and fifth centuries.[11]

We have additionally recalled that, if the period of the "Fathers" is traditionally understood as ending in the seventh and eighth centuries, the name "Father" was also given to a medieval author such as Bernard of Clairvaux. The fact remains that, by their antiquity, the "Fathers of the Church" hold a completely particular position that does not simply place them at the beginning of a list continuing through the Middle Ages and then the modern era but that locates them in this specific period in which the Christian Revelation, for the first time after the generations of the apostles and their immediate successors, inspired new practices and languages outside of Palestine and as far as the ends of the then-known world.

For a Patristic Theology

It, however, does not suffice to return to and reinterpret the characteristics that one traditionally attributes to the Fathers of the Church, all the more so since patristic literature, as we have emphasized, is not limited to the writings of the properly called "Fathers" but covers, even more widely, all Christian writings of Antiquity. It is also important to show what, in Europe's present situation, gives a more specific foundation to patristic theology.

First of all, faced with the objection according to which the writings of early Christianity are more and more foreign to European civilization, we must recall that this civilization was grafted upon, among other things, what occurred all around the Mediterranean Basin during the first centuries of the Christian era; and it would be difficult to question the fact that patristic literature had exercised an influence,

11. Yves Congar, *La Tradition et les traditions*, 2:199; *Tradition and Traditions*, 443–44; see chap. 3, pp. 68–69.

certainly not exclusive, but nevertheless very real, on the literary, philosophical, and religious culture of subsequent centuries. Saying this is not to deny nor even to relativize the great transformations that marked Europe—particularly beginning in the sixteenth century. It is also not to deprecate the criticism of the *Aufklärung* regarding some forms of traditionalism or dogmatism nor its vigorous emphasis on the responsibility of modern humanity that must not rely on the past in order to protect itself from the future but that must rather assume, in the present moment, the commitment of its own liberty. What we want to emphasize, in contrast, is that theology—or here more specifically, European theology—would have no future whatsoever if it were to lose the *memory* of its roots. We already know this at the anthropological level: mankind only constructs its future if it truly accepts its past. Yet this is also very valid for theology itself.[12] If it were to forget the Fathers of the Church, not only would its past cease to be present to it, but it would also be incapable of imagining or constructing its future.

But, one may say, we must also be aware of what makes the Christian heritage ambiguous, this past in which the wheat and the chaff were mixed. This remark, assuredly well-founded, does not, however, constitute an objection against the preceding argument; it, on the contrary, invites complementing it: to remember early Christianity, and here more precisely, patristic literature, is today a task that is inseparable from a discernment of the past. Thus, has not Origen's great theology suffered unjustly, even in the heart of the Church, from misunderstandings and condemnations that, for their part, most often were not equitable? Even more, but on the contrary, can the beautiful theology of Cyril of Alexandria itself justify the dramatic conditions in which the Council of Ephesus took place? It is not a matter of accusing men

12. Cf., in another context, the reflections of Johann Baptist Metz on "memorial reason": the criticism of the Enlightenment was justified, but it forgot that reason necessitates memory—a memory that, faced with the economic-technical world, becomes a "dangerous memory." "Of course, Christianity has preserved in its cult the memorial character of its identity ('Do this in memory of me'), but it has failed to carry through this reference to memory at the cultural level, and to defend it against modernity's abstractive reasoning. But only if Christianity succeeds in doing this can it intervene in the crisis of the European spirit with healthy—indeed salvific—criticism"; Jean-Baptiste Metz, "Une liberté solidaire. Crise et mission de l'esprit européen" [A freedom in solidarity. Crisis and mission of the European spirit], *Concilium* 240 (1992): 126.

from the past—judgement does not belong to us—but of humbly confessing the shadows by which the patristic era itself is marred.

Must one even add that, for all that, these admissions highlight the best of the patristic heritage, that is, what makes the Fathers of the Church truly recognized as such. Taking up the examples already given, just because Origen was unjustly attacked after his death, one must, once the misunderstandings are dispelled, not fail to welcome him as an eminent witness of the Christian faith; nor should the painful circumstances of the Council of Ephesus prevent recognizing the full orthodoxy of Cyril of Alexandria (even if orthodoxy could also be expounded in the language of the "Antiochene" theologians, as was shown, two years after Ephesus, by the act of union between Cyril and John of Antioch). Thus, even if it is not necessary to give a totally idealized version of past history, it is no more necessary to present it only from a negative point of view; rather, we are invited to acknowledge both the truth and the error, the light and the shadow,—knowing, once again, that the ultimate judgement does not belong to us. The history of early Christianity keeps its ambiguity, but it is rightly against this background that the greatness and the beauty of the patristic heritage stand out.

The memory of this heritage can from then on find a major expression in the form of *narration*. It is a matter of transmitting the *story of the Fathers*. By this we mean both the story that the Fathers transmitted to us and the story that we make of it in our turn. The story that the Fathers have handed on to us is what the Fathers have said, written, thought, accomplished (their numerous contributions being as fragments of a long story spread out over seven centuries); the story that we make of it is the manner in which we today transmit the heritage of the Fathers (a story that is thus not limited to knowledge but that is the testimony of witnesses). Why assign to European theology the task of relating to the Fathers of the Church, among others, according to this modality of the story? First, because the story is what allows remembering and this "remembering" is, as we have said, an essential condition of theological invention. Next, because the story, if it tries to be faithful to history, reveals both its shadows and its lights, and thus it responds to the exigencies from a present look at the early centuries. Let us add, anticipating the next chapter, that the emphasis on the story is, moreover, justified by the situation of the non-European theologies that, on one hand, cannot forget the patristic heritage, and that, on the other, have to find original ways for their own expression. For the story is really referring to a particular history that one is intent on relating and, at the same time, has the characteristic of not imposing itself: it is only proposing itself or exposing itself to others, inspiring the free reaction of its readers. The story is located between description and prescription:[13] it does not just describe what has happened (for it pronounces on the meaning of the narrated history), but for all that it does not mean to prescribe to others what they must do. By relating to the Fathers of the Church according to the modality of the story, European theology thus allows non-European theologies to have access to the tradition of the Fathers, but in a way that allows them freedom to discover the particular ways that understanding the faith must take in the context of their various continents.

However, being limited to this narrative perspective would risk implying that the story of the Fathers is only one story among others. We have, of course, specified that European theology itself is committed to this story: the interpretation that it gives to early Christianity is, as we said, the testimony of witnesses. But this must be correctly specified: it is not a matter of only recognizing what, in the heritage of patristic literature, is a source of inspiration for contemporary theology (by distinguishing it from what, in this same heritage, seems to us today to be of less interest, indeed, ambiguous or even questionable); it is also a matter of selecting what, in the history of early Christianity, has a *normative* value for our own understanding of the faith.

This exigency notably calls for the consideration of the ecumenical councils that, since the Council of Nicaea in 325, specified the fundamental statements of the Christian faith. This presents the opportunity to return here to an objection that we have noted above and that today receives quite a lot of support: the ecumenical councils should first of all be understood as political events or, if one wishes, ecclesial-political events: they were responding to the pressure of emperors, concerned with obtaining an agreement on the doctrinal

13. Terminology used by Paul Ricoeur in another context; cf. the exposition "Entre décrire et prescrire: raconter" [Between describing and prescribing: Telling], in *Soi-même comme un autre* [Self as an other] (Paris: Seuil, 1990), 180–93.

questions then being debated and thus able to assure the peace of the Empire. Thus formulated, this objection is not acceptable. In no way is it a matter of denying the role of emperors (it is they themselves who, in fact, convoked the councils, and they expected much from them for their own political interests—as one sees in the case of Constantine, Justinian, and still others). But it is not these imperial interventions that, by themselves, explain the adoption of this or that dogmatic definition during the Councils of Nicaea, Chalcedon, or Constantinople III. If the conciliar Fathers came to formulate these definitions, it was not first in order to respond to the will of the emperors but because what was at stake was fundamental for the faith: the doctrine of the Son "consubstantial" with the Father, at Nicaea, had to respond to the Arian doctrine that saw in the Son a simple creature; the formula of Chalcedon had to specify the identify of Christ against the two opposing errors that were formulated regarding him, that of Nestorius who did not grant enough to the unity of the Word made flesh, and that of Eutyches who, on the contrary, implied a sort of absorption of Christ's humanity by his divinity; the definition of Constantinople III was to emphasize, against the "Monothelite" movements, that the union of God and man in Jesus Christ did not prevent attributing to him a human will distinct from his divine will—otherwise the humanity of Christ would not be fully recognized. The definitions of the ecumenical councils were not the fruit of political decisions but of an awareness of what, in such circumstances, the fidelity to the "rule of faith" implied. This, moreover, is confirmed by, *a contrario*, the ordeals endured by some Fathers in the very name of such fidelity: when an emperor himself became a partisan of Arianism, the bishops Athanasius of Alexandria and Hilary of Poitiers went on to experience exile; and later in the seventh century, Maximus the Confessor had to endure terrible tortures for having defended the doctrine of the two wills of Christ, and this despite the political and ecclesial pressures that were exercised upon him. One may object with the case of the emperor Justinian who, himself being a theologian, directed the decisions of Constantinople II in the sense that it attempted to reconcile the "Monophysites" with the "Chalcedonians." Even in this case, however, the objection must be overcome; of course, Justinian's influence was decisive, but it does not suffice to explain a doctrinal orientation that was in fact prepared by several theologians in the first decades of the sixth century and that, independent of its interest in the ecclesial politics of the emperor, was itself very fundamental: it was the desire to reinterpret Chalcedon in a manner that took into consideration the concern, formerly so central for Cyril of Alexandria, for clearly establishing the unity of the *Logos* become flesh.

It is necessary as well to return to other objections that are also raised: even if one agrees to recognize that the ecumenical councils cannot simply be explained by pressures from the political order, was their doctrinal language not necessarily conditioned by the era of the Fathers? Was it right to claim to impose it upon the entirety of the Christian world, and, *a fortiori*, how can it be normative for us today? What is more, does this language not risk being misleading to the extent that it does not always seem to respect the form of the Gospel Revelation—for example, by introducing the word "consubstantial" that runs the risk of leading to forgetting that Jesus declares his Father "greater" than himself (Jn 14:28), or even by starting "from above" (the Son consubstantial to the Father) in order then to evoke the Incarnation, whereas the Gospel stories, first of all, invite considering Jesus, and from there, to being open to the recognition of his divine filiation (as today the "Christologies from below" emphasize)?

To begin with this last objection, it is important to keep in mind that no conciliar definition must be considered in isolation. On one hand, it must be placed within a precise context in which it was a matter of responding to this or that doctrinal error: thus, the definition of Nicaea was not attempting to say everything but was principally making a statement on the doctrine of Arius—so the recourse to the word "consubstantial," of course, did not mean to call into question the Gospel saying "The Father is greater than I" but was designed to eliminate the comparison of the Son with a simple creature. On the other hand, the conciliar definitions are mutually complementary and enriching: if Nicaea affirms the equality of "substance" between the Son and the Father, the Council of Chalcedon completes this affirmation by emphasizing that the Son is also "consubstantial with us in humanity." If this latter council places a special emphasis on the distinction of the natures (all the while specifying, moreover, that there is "only one Christ"), the Council of Constantinople II rather emphasizes the union of God and of man to the point of recognizing the legitimacy of the "one single nature" language that was so dear to Cyril of Alexandria. It is true, moreover, that the point of view adopted by these conciliar definitions corresponds to what in our day one calls a "descendant" Christology; but, apart from the fact that such a point of view was already that of the Johannine prologue, the Fathers were not ignoring that, according to the witness of the Gospels, it was necessary to discover in Jesus' own humanity the revelation of his divine identity. In this way, as was already the case for the Johannine prologue, the Gospel story was assumed in their affirmations on the Son of God become man—even if, in the historical situation that was theirs, they had above all to pronounce on some questions such as the equality of "substance" between the Son and the Father or the understanding of the connection between the "natures" of Christ.

What remains, assuredly, is the question of the particularity that marks the language of conciliar definitions and, before that, the language of the Fathers that prepared for the conciliar definitions or that commented upon them. It cannot be denied: this particularity was inevitable. But we no longer have to deprecate it. We will emphasize, along the lines of what was said above, rather the Fathers' effort to find in the Greek language words and concepts capable of expressing the Christian mystery—through, as we have seen, a conversion of their primary meanings. Of course, it is necessary to add that, unfortunately, one was tempted to impose some forms of expression on others: Cyril of Alexandria wished that one spoke of "a single nature of the Word made flesh" (at least until 433, when he recognized the legitimacy of the language of "two natures" that the theologians of Antioch preferred). And if it is true that later Christians called "Nestorians" continued to reject the Council of Ephesus or that "Monophysite" Christians rejected the Council of Chalcedon, in numerous cases some were not, for all that, followers of what one calls "Nestorianism" but did not accept Cyril's attitude at Ephesus, and others, for their part, did not take up Eutyches's error but did not accept the language of "two natures" that had been imposed by Chalcedon. However, it would be excessive to infer that it was these councils that had, as such, provoked the divisions among Christians; what provoked such divisions was, on one hand, the doctrinal deviations and, on the other, the attempts to impose on others a language itself orthodox but that was not the conciliar definitions themselves. Indeed, these definitions are formulated in necessarily particular languages, but in their own particularity they intend to respond to an exigency of the faith that, itself, is valid for all Christians—including those of today—even if the same goal of faith must also be translated into other languages and cultures.

It was necessary to focus on the importance of the conciliar definitions (themselves made possible by the doctrinal thought of the patristic era) in order to complete our preceding exposition on the "story of the Fathers." Such a "story" is today necessary, for the reasons that we have said; but this story is not only that of one literature among others, for it gives access to some doctrinal developments that (in the very particularity of their formulations and in spite of the often dramatic events of ecclesial history) constitute a major reference and even have a normative value for all Christian theology.

This—is it necessary to be specific?—in no way limits the task of reflection that is the theologian's, and, on the contrary, very much, stimulates it. In a more general way (therefore, beyond conciliar statements and the patristic thought of which they are the fruit), the Christian writings from Antiquity are for the theologian an inexhaustible resource for his thinking. If we are interested in the Fathers even though their era is no longer ours, it is not just to understand the first centuries of Christian history better, it is also because we believe that they can and must aid us in reflecting upon the same questions that are ours today. Karl Rahner, as we have seen, said this remarkably well: the early texts must be read in a manner so that they "say to us something about the question itself, something about what *we* up to the present have not yet reflected upon or only insufficiently":

> one associates with an ancient thinker, in the end, not simply to know his opinion but to learn something of the question itself. Because historical theology is too often merely a connection and too rarely a *syntheologein*, one most often only learns from it the fragment from the past that, otherwise, is already conserved in the theology of today, but not the fragment, from our past, that forms our future.[14]

14. Rahner, "Essai d'une esquisse de dogmatique," 20; "The Prospects for Dogmatic Theology," 10, trans. modified. See chap. 3, pp. 75–76.

If it is possible that patristic work is to have such a fecundity, it is because the Fathers of the Church are precisely "fathers" and because, by reason of their own fidelity to Scripture, they have engendered, fashioned, and structured the practice and the understanding of the faith: today, theology, in its own effort to accomplish its proper task, is indebted to this.

The metaphor of "paternity" must here be understood in all its profundity. In the Old Testament, the book of Malachi ended with the announcement of the coming of Elijah before the arrival of the day of the Lord; for Elijah, said Yahweh, "he will turn the hearts of the fathers to their children and the hearts of children to their fathers" (Mal 3:24).[15] The statement was to be repeated at the beginning of the Gospel of Luke (1:17), applied to John the Baptist who had, like Elijah, to turn the heart of the fathers toward their children and the disobedient to the wisdom of the just. Now there is also, since the coming of Christ and in the time of the Church, a distinction between the Fathers and those who follow: on one hand, the generation of the Fathers, in the first centuries of Christian history; on the other, the generation of sons, that is all those who have engendered the faith since the end of the patristic era up until our present history—itself open to the future. And just as the Old Testament expressed an exigency of reconciliation between fathers and sons, similarly one can understand that there is analogically, in Christian history itself, an exigency of communion between the generation of the Fathers and the following generations. Communion does not mean identity nor uniformity: contemporary theologies must necessarily be original and new: not only different among themselves but different from early theologies that were developed at the time of the Fathers. But it is necessary that these theologies be, in their very innovation, in communion with the witness of faith that the Christian authors of the first centuries produced. This profundity does not dissociate patristic theology from contemporary, even less does it place them in opposition: actually theology, at the point when it accepts its heritage from the Fathers, must contribute to what allows new generations in their turn to engender an understanding of the faith according to the newness of places and times.[16]

15. In the RSV, Mal 4:6.

16. See our study "Sources Chrétiennes," esp. 794–95.

And of course, this engendering is the work of the Spirit. But the Spirit acts in history and through it: the engendering of the faith is not immediate, it itself happens through a relationship of paternity and filiation in the very history of Christianity, and the relationship of the Fathers of the Church precisely attests that this relationship of paternity and filiation is found inscribed in the very constitution of Christian theology.

CHAPTER 7

Patristics in the Age of Globalization

The preceding chapter attempted to show why today patristics must, in spite of the difficulties and objections that from the point of view of human sciences, philosophy and even theology have been able to be raised, still contribute to the understanding of the faith. But are these responses themselves sufficient with regard to the questions that are asked outside of Europe? As we stated above, it is now necessary for us to tackle the questions linked to the theologies that are called "contextual." To the extent that these theologies are being developed in lands other than those where patristic literature was formed, in what way can it be profitable, indeed necessary, for them? Here we are not thinking about North America (where, moreover, studies on the Fathers have seen a remarkable development for several decades) but about Latin America, Africa, Asia and Oceania, for this is where the question is asked in all its acuity: could patristic literature be so conditioned by the geographical, historical, and cultural context of the "Mediterranean world" (in the broadest meaning of this expression) that, all the while recognizing in it a real importance for European theology, one must doubt its significance and pertinence for the theologies developed on these other continents?

We will show that in reality some of the problems raised by these theologies not only must not dissuade working with patristics but can, on the contrary, actually be enlightened by it—as we will see for Latin America, Africa, and Asia. This first approach will be followed by a more fundamental reflection that will attempt to specify and justify the type of connection that "contextual" theologies must maintain with patristic literature. Lastly, it will then be necessary for us to return to European theology, to the extent that it henceforth finds itself more distant from its "Mediterranean" sources and thus, in its own way, becomes similar to the situation of "contextual" theologies.

Latin America, Africa, Asia

It must first of all be noted that in the past several decades, outside of Europe and North America, there has been a real boom in patristic works—whether it be in translations of Greek and Latin authors or in studies devoted to one or another of them. This fact, undoubtedly, concerns a relatively limited number of researchers, but it is no less revealing of an interest in the Fathers and in their writings.[1]

However, these works in themselves are not what we want to consider. Our question rather bears upon the way in which some non-European theologies can effectively benefit from patristic literature. We will respond to it by briefly focusing on the cases of Latin America, Africa, and Asia.

For Latin America, one can first of all recall the support that formerly some theologians found in the Fathers in order to denounce some forms of colonization and Christianization that in their eyes were unacceptable with regard to the Gospel; thus, for this purpose, Bartolomeo de Las Casas invoked John Chrysostom, Ambrose, Augustine, and many more.[2] In modern times, in any case, various orientations of Latin American theology have been—could still be—able to benefit from the patristic heritage. This is, first of all, true for the thought undertaken in the context of base ecclesial communities beginning in the 1960s. These communities were above all committed to the reading of biblical texts that, in the context of situations marked by poverty and injustice, encouraged Christians to be involved in the

1. One could here mention Latin American, African, and Asian patrologists who speak during international colloquies, in particular in the framework of the conferences that are held every four years at Oxford (see the publication of *Actes* in the collection Studia Patristica), or even, some journals that originated on their continents: as, in Tokyo, the publication *Patristica*, which is the journal of the Japanese Society for Patristic Studies.

2. Cf. the texts collected by Marianne Mahn-Lot in *Bartolomeo de Las Casas. L'Évangile et la force* [Bartolomé de Las Casas. The Gospel and the force], 3rd rev. ed. (Paris: Cerf, 1991), 99 ff. (see, for example, 116–20; 127; 191).

liberation of their people; from this experience was born the movement of "liberation theologies" that, whatever were the limits or excesses that one has sometimes recognized in them, have had the value of emphasizing the importance of the context in which theological reflection is developed and, especially, of vigorously keeping in mind that the Christian faith calls for an engagement for justice or, as one later said, a "preferential option for the poor." Now patristic literature deserves to be read from this perspective: some of its writings attest to the experience of Christian communities that by listening to the Word drew from it the source for an engagement with society—an engagement that could take the form of a radical witness in favor of the poor, as one particularly sees in Basil of Caesarea and John Chrysostom.[3]

It is true that Christians of Latin America were also confronted by very different questions, not only because of the difficulties encountered by liberation theologies but for other reasons as well: the attention to the heritage of the Amerindian cultures; the awareness of ecological problems; even more, the challenge that the rise of evangelical Churches represents and their impact on the Catholic Church itself, etc. But all these questions, even if they are asked in an original way in Latin America, could only benefit from being enlightened by the patristic tradition. We have already suggested this, regarding Christianity's connection to cultures, by mentioning de Las Casas's thought on the way to announce the Gospel on this continent (a reflection precisely echoed by Gustavo Gutiérrez in one of his books).[4] Thought on ecology, for its part, could benefit from some patristic contributions on the place of mankind on this earth and on mankind's responsi-

3. Here we are not referring to other "liberation theologies" that were developed outside of Latin America: it would be necessary to make analogous considerations to those that we are proposing here, but by taking into account these theologies' own characteristics (according to their different contexts in North America, Africa, or Asia). A special remark is required, nevertheless, for "feminist theologies": on one hand, these theologies call for a critical look at the history of early Christianity, to the extent that it was able to support or even give its approval to some forms of discrimination toward women; on the other, however, they must also receive the light of some patristic writings—whether these writings, placed in the context of their time, demonstrate a profound sense of the equality between man and woman created "in the image of God," or whether they highlight the meaning of Mary in the history of salvation or the testimony of holiness given by women at the heart of the Christian community, or lastly, whether they emphasize the transcendence of God in relationship to the masculine and feminine representations that one can have of Him.

4. Gustavo Gutiérrez, *Dieu ou l'or des Indes occidentales, 1492–1992* (Paris: Cerf, 1992).

bility toward what one today calls the "safeguarding of creation." As for problems linked to the growth of evangelical Churches, they call for some basic theological reflections for which the literature of the Fathers would, once again, offer numerous resources. Some major questions can be formulated for this purpose: what allows discerning the "charisms" to which the diverse communities testify and what must an authentic theology of the Spirit be? What is the ecclesiality, or at least the degree of ecclesiality, of such a Church separated from the main Churches that originated during the Reformation as well as from the Catholic Church? What is the Catholic Church able to learn from the growth of evangelical Churches, and what can it select for its own way of practicing and understanding the liturgy or, more broadly, ecclesial life? What must finally be the relationship between the Catholic Church and the other Churches or Christian confessions from the perspective of the communion to which the disciples of Christ are called? *Mutatis mutandis*, these were some of the questions with which the Fathers were themselves confronted in the ecclesial situation of their time, and their contribution would, without a doubt, contribute to shedding light upon the thought of Christian communities in Latin America.

African Christianity, also, can greatly benefit from patristic literature. In the first place, one will not fail to recall that during the first centuries of our era, North Africa was influenced by the presence of important Christian communities. These communities, which sometimes experienced great trials—they had several martyrs—were also the milieus in which great theologies, such as those of Tertullian, Cyprian, and, above all, Augustine, were developed. In addition to this past, the memory of which must remain alive, African Christianity can today be interested in the Fathers under several aspects. Without here focusing on the liberation theologies that have found specific forms on this continent, we will, above all, mention the attempts undertaken in sub-Saharan Africa in order to "inculturate" the Gospel message and to give to Christianity meaningful expressions in the context of traditional customs and religions. These attempts have taken shape in the context of the liturgy, catechesis, and theology itself. Thus some theologians have recourse to words such as "ancestor," "elder," and "healer" in order to apply them to Christ; by doing this, they are aware that these designations, so important in African tradition, cannot be transposed as such—Christ being, according to François Kabasélé's expression, "beyond models."[5] Nevertheless, it is possible, even if it means giving these words a new importance, to use them so that the Christian mystery is presented in a way that speaks to African Christians. Yet such attempts, which must be pursued, correspond to the effort that Christians formerly made in order to announce the Gospel and to think about the faith in the "cultures" of their time. To study patristic literature from this angle is not to attempt to reproduce in Africa the languages from the Greek or Latin world, but it is to find inspiration today for carrying out a work analogous to that of the Fathers—with everything that this work implies about, on one hand, attention to the local languages and cultures and, on the other, fidelity to the Gospel as well as to the Tradition of the Church.

It is, of course, undeniable that in our day, after the enthusiasm that marked the first attempts of "inculturation," African Christianity also finds itself confronted by the famous problem of the "double belonging"—entrance into the Church and participation in the sacraments sometimes being accompanied by practices inherited from traditional religions and that, in some cases, are not compatible with the Christian faith. But on precisely this very point, it would be quite fruitful to discover how Christianity formerly confronted similar problems (as with the evangelization of Gaul) and to gain from it enlightenment on the pastoral discernment that such situations require today. More broadly, it is important for Christian communities to be interested in the very way in which the Gospel was formerly announced on lands then known. What here is at issue is in no way an imitation of early Christianity's "Mediterranean" or "European" history; it is rather the appeal to know what was great in this history as well as its shadows and its dramas so that the Churches of Africa can profit from them in their own way of conceiving and practicing the announcement of the Gospel on their own continent.

Other challenges are assuredly to be taken into account. Thus, how to conceive of the encounter of traditional African cultures with

5. Cf. François Kabasélé, "L'au-delà des modèles" [Beyond the models], in *Chemins de la christologie africaine* [Ways of African Christology], ed. François Kabasélé, Joseph Doré, and René Luneau, rev. ed. (Paris: Desclée, 2001), 245–67.

modernity? How to face the questions that (as in Latin America) the increasing popularity of the evangelical communities raise? How can the Church help in overcoming ethnic and political conflicts, as well as the tragedies to which they have given rise? This is not the place to focus on all these questions nor on the other real challenges of evangelization in Africa.[6] But what we are highlighting is that, like the problems relating to "inculturation," some of these questions are able to inspire new research in the field of patristic literature. African Christianity can find in it not some immediate solution to the problems of the Church on this continent but nonetheless some points of reference and a source of inspiration likely to encourage its own theological and pastoral reflections.

If we lastly turn to Asia, we will begin by recalling that during the patristic era Christianity penetrated into some of its lands—from Persia as far as India in the south as well as China. But we would like, above all, to emphasize that during the contemporary era the Fathers of the Church have more than once been invoked in order to reflect upon the announcement of the Gospel on the Asian continent. It is itself significant that Henri de Lubac, author of so many works on the Fathers, also devoted three books to Buddhism; one of these books compares several Buddhist themes with Christian themes that are apparently close, and, in order to do this successfully, precisely relied upon some patristic texts.[7] It is no less significant that Jules Monchanin—the priest who in 1939 left for India to found there a Christian *ashram*—had been profoundly influenced by the heritage of the Fathers. Thus he wrote: "What Saint Justin, a martyr, and Clement of Alexandria, a philosopher, said of Greece, can also be applied to India. The *Logos* mysteriously prepared the way for his coming, and the Holy Spirit was stimulating from within the quest of the purer among the Greeks sages. The *Logos* and the Holy Spirit are still at work, and in a similar way, in the depths of the Indian soul"; Monchanin added that "the Indian wisdom is marred by errors," but he noted that this was equally true of Greek wisdom before it had received "the Easter mes-

6. See, on this point, Léonard Santedi Kinkupu, *Les défis de l'evangélisation dans l'Afrique contemporaine* [The challenges of evangelization in contemporary Africa] (Paris: Karthala, 2005).

7. See de Lubac, *Aspects du bouddhisme*.

sage of the resurrected Christ."[8] Other texts of Monchanin show how he was influenced by the theology of the Greek Fathers, who inspired him to make comparisons between the Trinitarian doctrine of Christians and the Hindu approach to the Absolute; his knowledge of ancient monastic literature also led him to make valuable comparisons between the Hesychast tradition and the practice of yoga.[9]

More recently, it is true, Asian theologians have warned against the ambiguities of some approaches developed in the West and that, all the while being interested in the cultural traditions of Asia, do not take the religious traditions of this continent enough into account. It is in this sense that Aloysius Pieris has contested the "models of Greco-Roman inculturation." Such models, he writes, are inapplicable to Asia: "the patristic tradition was consistently negative in its assessment of other religions," and the Fathers consider that "only the *culture* of Rome and the *philosophy* of Greece were worth being assumed by the Church"; yet, continues the author, this is not transposable to the Asian situation because, in this latter case, "to pluck a philosophy out of its soteriological context is to deprive it of its life."[10] But whatever one thinks of this judgment,[11] it is important to observe that Pieris does not leave it there but shows how Asian Christianity can profit from other "models" selected from tradition. He first mentions the "North European model of Christianization," which was connected to the encounter of Christianity with the "cosmic" religions in the High Middle Ages (a "model" that, according to us, was in fact present in the last centuries of the patristic era): there, he writes, is found a useful analogy for understanding what is at stake in the encounter with the tribal societies of Asia. It is true that this analogy, in its turn, remains of limited importance, for the "cosmic religions," except in the Philippines and in some regions in India and Southeast Asia, had been

8. Jules Monchanin, *Écrits spirituels* [Spiritual writings], intro. Édouard Duperray (Paris: Centurion, 1964).

9. Monchanin, *Mystique de l'Inde, mystère chrétien. Écrits et inédits* [Mysticism of India, Christian mystery. Writings and unpublished], intro. S. Siauve (Paris: Fayard, 1974), 40; 109–17; 126–27; 133.

10. Aloysius Pieris, "Western Models of Inculturation: Applicable in Asia?" in *An Asian Theology of Liberation* (Edinburgh: T & T Clark, 1988), 52–53); translated by Joseph Feisthauer as *Une théologie asiatique de la liberation* (Paris: Centurion, 1990), 95–108.

11. We will tackle the questions that themselves touch upon the attitude of the Fathers regarding religions, see chap. 13.

supplanted even before the arrival of Christianity by "metacosmic religions" such as Hinduism, Buddhism, and Islam. However, in the situation thus created, Asia can greatly benefit from another model that early Christianity brings with it: the "monastic model." It indeed shows a "gnosis" in the positive sense of the term (thus distinct from what one usually means by "Gnosticism"), and this "gnosis," which in Christianity is inseparable from "*agapè*," offers as such a fecund point of contact between the West and the East: "even within Christian orthodoxy itself, which has always been agapeic, there was a legitimate line of gnosticism, whereas the 'heretical' gnoses 'were only as it were the embroidery along the edge of this continuous line.' Similarly the gnostic religions, especially Hinduism and Buddhism, are not without their own versions of agapeic (*bhakti*) religiousness."[12] The Church, concludes Pieris, "is not competent to converse with Asia if it does not learn from its own Christian monastics the language of *gnosis* spoken by Asia's non-Christian monastics, and also the language of *agape*, the only one that the Asian poor can really understand."[13]

These are far from being the only issues of the evangelization of the Asian continent. As in the case of Latin America and Africa, it would be necessary to identify other major challenges with which the Church finds itself confronted on this continent and to ask questions, from this viewpoint, of some writings of early Christianity. Here are some examples of quite different natures: the problems posed by the caste system can inspire research on the way in which the Fathers of the Church gave their opinions on the forms of social inequality of their time; works on the "inculturation" of Christianity in the "Confucian" context call for reflections on the way in which Christian authors formerly were in dialogue with the wisdoms of Antiquity; or even, in a completely different order, the situation of the Church in China invites discovering the debates that animated the third and fourth centuries when Christians from Italy and North Africa deliberated reconciliation with those who, for a time, had been separated from the "main Church."

Whatever may be the case in Asia, Africa, and Latin America—

12. Pieris, "Western Models of Inculturation, 56 (quoting Louis Bouyer).

13. Ibid., 57. Also see Aloysius Pieris, *Love Meets Wisdom: A Christian Experience of Buddhism* (Maryknoll, N.Y.: Orbis Books, 1988).

having limited ourselves to these three continents,—we hope to have suggested at least some specific reasons for which non-European theologies can today be interested in patristic literature and find in it an inspiration for their respective tasks. It is necessary for us, however, to return to the question at a more fundamental level and to explain what, in one way or another, justifies such an interest in the patristic tradition by these non-European theologies.

Patristics and "Contextual" Theologies

Of course, as we have already emphasized, the theologies that are being developed outside of Europe cannot as such repeat the heritage of patristic literature. If it is true that European theology itself feels the historical and cultural distance that separates it from the Fathers (and we will return to this later), *a fortiori* the remark is valid for other continents and, in particular, for Asia. One understands that, in these lands, some theologians want to distance themselves from the languages and schemas of thought formerly "imported" from the West (all the more so as this "importation," in past centuries, is not without links to the history of colonization). On the positive side, one must agree with their attempt to present the Christian faith by taking into consideration their specific contexts. Moreover, this was so for theologies that originated during the era of the Fathers: these themselves varied depending upon whether they were elaborated in Alexandria, Rome, Carthage, Antioch, or in Persia, etc. It is fortunate that similarly new theologies appear today, and they are more varied than ever because they are no longer limited to the areas surrounding the Mediterranean Basin, the Middle East, and Northern Europe but are consequently being developed in many other lands.

In this very context, it is, however, essential that non-European theologies maintain a vital relationship with the heritage of early Christianity and thus with, among other things, patristic literature. In order to justify this affirmation, it, first of all, can be useful to recall the reflection that Pope John Paul II proposed in his encyclical *Fides et ratio*. He emphasizes that today's Christians, above all "those from India," must draw from their own cultural patrimony "elements compatible with their faith," but that, for this work of "discernment," they must take into account some "criteria"; after having mentioned a first "criterion" (namely "the universality of the human spirit, whose basic needs are the same in the most disparate cultures"), John Paul II added:

> The second, which derives from the first, is this: in engaging great cultures for the first time, the Church cannot abandon what she has gained from her inculturation in the world of Greco-Latin thought. To reject this heritage would be to deny the providential plan of God who guides his Church down the paths of time and history. This criterion is valid for the Church in every age, even for the Church of the future, who will judge herself enriched by all that comes from today's engagement with Eastern cultures and will find in this inheritance fresh cues for fruitful dialogue with the cultures which will emerge as humanity moves into the future.[14]

John Paul II's thinking in fact warns of two opposing pitfalls. One would be to believe that it suffices to transpose the heritage of European Christianity as it is, or at least to adapt it, without taking into account the original resources that Christianity can find in the patrimony of other continents and that are likely to enrich the catholicity of the Church. But the other pitfall would be to believe that, in the very name of such a cultural context and of what comprises its specificity, it would suffice to read Scripture in this context forgetting what occurred between the era of the New Testament and our own. One would, at the very least, recognize that the heritage of early Christianity was (in the best of cases) profitable for the Christians of Europe but would consider that it no longer had importance for Christians of other continents. The passage of *Fides et ratio* that we have cited correctly clarifies this last position. Of course, it is vital that non-European Churches read the Scriptures in a new way in the context of their respective continents, and one must, in any case, agree with their rejection of purely and simply reproducing what was said

14. John Paul II, encyclical letter *Fides et ratio* (1998), no. 72; http://w2.vatican.va./content/john-paul-ii/en/encyclicals/documents/hf_jp-ii_enc_14091998_fides-et-ratio.html. John Paul II adds a last criterion: "Thirdly, care will need to be taken lest, contrary to the very nature of the human spirit, the legitimate defense of the uniqueness and originality of Indian thought be confused with the idea that a particular cultural tradition should remain closed in its difference and affirm itself by opposing other traditions." And the pope further adds: "What has been said here of India is no less true for the heritage of the great cultures of China, Japan, and the other countries of Asia, as also for the riches of the traditional cultures of Africa, which are for the most part orally transmitted."

or done in the history of "Mediterranean" Christianity (and, above all, of what in the past was unfaithful to the Gospel). On the other hand, it would be illusory and dangerous to imply that this history can be put in parenthesis and that it must no longer be taken into consideration outside of Europe. In addition to such a position amounting to misunderstanding the contributions of the patristic era to the universal Church, it would not grant an essential characteristic of Christianity: its historicity.

Indeed, it is really this historicity of Christianity that is here at issue (and the text cited above gives to it a theological significance by mentioning "the providential plan of God who guides his Church down the paths of time and history"). The catholicity of any Church is connected not only to the fact that this Church receives the Gospel in its local, regional, or continental context. It is connected as well to history because it is in history that God communicates with humans—whatever may be the response that humans make to this gift.

Two exigencies follow: one for European Christianity itself, the other for the Churches on other continents. European Christianity must, above all, remember what were its patristic sources, not in order to impose "models" that must be repeated as such, nor just to be informed on what happened during the first centuries of the Church's history, but in order to bear witness to the gift that it has been given and to the way in which Christians formerly responded to it. Thus, we will recall what we previously said about the "story of the Fathers."[15] We have explained that this is, to the extent that it "remembers" the tradition, an essential condition of theological work and that by its very nature it allows revealing both the shadows and the lights of the past—according to what an equitable look at these early centuries requires. And above all, we have added, even if those who transmit a story make a pronouncement on its subject, they do not claim to prescribe to others what they must say or do. For these considerations are especially important from the perspective that is here ours. European theology certainly must not dictate to other theologies the ways that they must undertake; but it has the responsibility of maintaining the memory of the patristic era and of today transmitting its story.

15. See chap. 6, pp. 160–61.

The other exigency concerns the Churches of other continents, called to listen to what is thus narrated to them, not just in order that they may imitate or reproduce it on all points, but because it is important for them to understand the announcement of the Gospel such as it was formerly transmitted and such as it was, according to whatever was the case, received or rejected. What is here at stake is—at least in an analogous way—a transposition of what happened at the beginning of Christianity between the Christians that came from the Gentiles and the Christians that came from Israel: on one hand, of course, the Jews converted to Christ had to tell the people of the "Gentiles" what God had done for them and how they acted toward him; on the other, the Gentiles had to hear and welcome this story in order to invent, in communion with those who had preceded them in the faith, their own way of being disciples of Christ. What is at stake is a relationship that is in some ways the same as regards the patristic heritage. Just as European theology has the responsibility of making this heritage known—but without it being a substitution for the other theologies that must be developed in their respective contexts—these theologies of other continents must inversely listen to the story of the Fathers and allow themselves to be instructed by it for the benefit of their own tasks—otherwise they would be threatened by the self-importance formerly denounced by Paul in the Letter to the Romans (Rom 11:16–24): that of Christians toward Israel (the wild olive scorning the olive upon which it had been grafted), or more directly that of some Christians toward other Christians (the believers from the Gentiles being tempted to judge or to scorn the believers who remained attached to the ancient traditions of the Jewish world).

The "Story of the Fathers": Its Importance Outside Europe

The preceding reflections, however, call for some supplemental details and explanations, which will further contribute to establishing the importance of patristics from the very perspective of theologies developed outside of Europe. In the first place, what we have said above regarding Latin America, Africa, and Asia calls for a more general reflection on the importance of the work formerly carried out by the

Fathers. The Christians of these other continents, as we said, are in search of theologies that are faithful to Scripture and that in their own situations take into account the faith; yet we want to emphasize that, in doing this, they are in the same situation as the Romans, Gauls, Germans, Syrians, and Persians who formerly had to think about the Christian mystery in their respective worlds. We are dealing with situations of genesis on both sides. One cannot thus say: since the Fathers of the Church developed theologies that are culturally influenced and thus particular, there is no reason whatsoever to be interested in them outside of Europe. It is necessary to affirm the opposite: precisely because the Fathers of the Church have developed particular theologies (but through which the message of a salvation offered to all nations is expressed), it is important that non-European theologies are able to know what were the first "inculturations" of the Gospel in the countries around the Mediterranean Basin. For it was a matter of true "inculturations," not simply of superficial adaptations: while in contemporary Europe, we have often spoken of "inculturation" in Africa or in Asia as if it were primarily our task (forgetting that it must first and foremost be the work of African and Asian Christians),[16] the Fathers of the Church—in most cases at least—themselves came from these nations that had to be evangelized. Origen, because he was Alexandrian, could truly contribute to creating an Alexandrian Christian theology; Augustine, because he was perfectly fluent in the heritage of the Latin language and culture, was able to contribute to creating an authentic Latin theology. Yet this task that the great creators of early theologies carried out is exactly what must be realized today, on their own continents, by the theologians of America, Africa, Asia, and Oceania. We are not able to accomplish it in their place, but, from this point of view, what the Fathers of the Church have done so well is a remarkable example of what must be done in our day in other contexts. Also, it is important that among non-European theologians there are some who actually specialize in patristic studies; more broadly, it is important that Christian communities are able to have access to some writings from early Christianity, in particular those that are more apt

16. This clearly does not exclude the contribution of Christians coming from Europe, who help autochthonous Christians in the work of inculturation and who, even more, embody by their own presence a communion with the Christian communities of Europe.

to enrich the knowledge of the faith in the situation of this or that country outside of Europe. In this regard, one cannot over emphasize what is at stake regarding the translations of these writings into various languages. The significance of such translations, moreover, was already recognized in Antiquity. Thus, many of the patristic writings in the Greek language were translated into languages such as Armenian and Georgian. And Rufinus of Aquileia spent much time translating for the Latin West numerous works of Origen that otherwise would have been lost: in this way he contributed to the development of all medieval theology that, beyond the cultural transformations of the High Middle Ages, was going to be deeply nourished by the exegesis of Origen.

On the other hand, even if we have emphasized the importance of the story—for European theologies that must remember the patristic heritage and for the theologies of other continents that must incorporate this heritage for the benefit of their specific tasks—we must repeat here that the "story of the Fathers" is not only one story among others. We have already explained this when, in a general way, we reflected upon the relationship between patristics and contemporary theology: it is not a matter of simply gathering information on early Christianity, on its shadows as well as it greatness; it is also a matter of gathering what, in the heritage of the patristic era, has normative value for our own understanding of the faith. This exigency is valid for all theology, whatever the context of its elaboration. This in no way denies the particularity of the languages in which Christian doctrines are expressed, such as they were notably presented by the ecumenical councils from the first millennium. But a hermeneutical work permits correctly discerning and retaining what, in spite of or through this particularity, takes into account the faith received from the apostles. The fidelity here required in no way limits the ability of non-European theologies to formulate the Christian mystery in their own languages. In fact, the patristic era itself already attested to a capacity to express the same faith in quite diverse ways (as when Ephrem expressed in the Syriac language a theology that, at the core, was fully coherent with the Nicaean doctrine on the "substantial" equality of the Son and the Father); and today some "contextual" theologies testify to an analogous creativity (for example, when, in the Chinese world, the mystery of Jesus

Christ "true man and true God" is formulated with the help of Confucian or Taoist categories).[17] But such a creativity precisely requires the adherence to this same faith that the Fathers formerly expressed in their own way and which today's theologians must attempt to take into account in the languages of their respective traditions.

This confirms that, from this point of view, patristic literature has not just to be related but must as such contribute to engendering the understanding of the faith in our times. This exigency is valid not just for European theology: it is also valid for the theologies that are developed as well outside of Europe, whatever the diversity of their contexts. What is at stake, after all is said and done, is the exigency of catholicity. The new theologies that are developed outside of Europe must, even in their variety, be in communion with one another; they must assuredly be local (in the sense in which theologians from diverse continents are called to take into account the same faith, although in contexts that are necessarily different); but they can thus be in communion locally only if they are, in the continuum of time, in communion with the Fathers of the Church—to the extent that they have contributed in a decisive way to the understanding of the Christian mystery and are still today our "Fathers in the faith," they must continue to inspire and to make fruitful, from the West to the East, the always new tasks of Christian theology.

Is not what we have here expounded also valid, in another way, for Europe itself?

A Return to Europe

In fact, we cannot conclude this chapter without returning to European theology, to the extent that it is being elaborated in partially new contexts. Paradoxically, it is the very attention to the new forms of theology on the other continents that can help in becoming aware of this. For several decades, Europe has experienced some very important changes: a new culture is taking shape—or rather new cultures, since this continent is so diverse. These changes are assuredly of var-

17. See Aloysius B. Chang Ch'un-shen, *Dann sind Himmel und Mensch in Einheit: Bausteine chinesischer Theologie* [Then heaven and man are in unity: Building blocks of Chinese theology] (Freiburg: Herder, 1984).

ious kinds; they are due to demographic, economic, and political developments; they are also due to technological innovations that mark our age of globalization; they are also linked to the worldwide transformations on the cultural and religious landscape (characterized, on one hand, by the strong presence of "agnosticism" or "indifference" in religious matters, and, on the other, by the expansion of Islam and, to a lesser degree, Eastern religions—to which it is necessary to add the importance of the new religious inclinations and the "New Age Nebula"). From the point of view that we here maintain, it is necessary, above all, to emphasize that there has been a widening of the distance from the ancient world, and therefore from the patristic tradition. This is verified at the properly cultural level: Greek and Latin are taught less and less; the "Classics" of ancient literature are often not well known, and many have great difficulty in interpreting the meaning of the paintings and sculptures that, nevertheless, in the museums of Europe so frequently refer to the ancient world (whether it is a matter of the Greco-Roman world or the world of the Bible). The developments are such that, consequently, European theologies are apparently found in a situation comparable to that of African or Asian theologies: they must themselves be developed in contexts that are largely new.

For this very reason, we here will be able to repeat what we previously said regarding other continents: if Latin American, African, and Asian theologies cannot break with the heritage of the patristic tradition but need to benefit from referring their own tasks to it (as we have shown), this must also be true for the theologies developed in Europe. However, rather than repeat the arguments already given and that would apply as well in the present case, we will draw attention to several particular traits from the European situation and then to some specific exigencies of theologies that are being developed on this continent.

The first point to emphasize is that, even if these theologies can or must become in their turn "contextual" theologies, they are not exactly (despite the similarity raised above) in the same position as the theologies from other continents—at least in their relationship to the patristic tradition. Of course, the large decrease in the number of Christians in Europe sometimes leads to asking if, in the past, this continent was truly "evangelized," or rather, if the Gospel formerly announced there was actually received (just as some argue, in this sense, for a "first evangelization"). The fact remains that, whatever were the ambiguities or even the faults of Christianity in history, the Gospel really penetrated the areas encompassing the Mediterranean world, in the West as well as in the East, and that since the end of the patristic era, it has also left its imprint on lands farther away, such as those of Northern Europe. This penetration of the Gospel is thus inscribed in the early history of the continent. Additionally, as well as having contributed, in some aspects, to the developments of Western modernity, this penetration accounts for Christianity's remaining as the most widespread religion under the European sun, and it additionally is attested to by the multiplicity of churches, crosses, statues, paintings, and sculptures that bear witness to the Christian faith in the countries of Europe. Patristic literature itself is a part of this heritage, and one sees the impact of this on European theology that cannot refer to this heritage as if to a foreign heritage but that must rather find in it its roots—or more precisely, to discover through it how the Gospel formerly took root in the Mediterranean and European arena. Not that this past is not often forgotten; here the exigency is to reveal accurately what is buried, or at the least not well known, and to demonstrate the inspirational power that is connected to these testimonies of early Christianity, always capable of inspiring and nourishing the understanding of the faith.

Beyond this first remark, European theology has a very special responsibility for making the history of Christian doctrines known and for demonstrating the permanent meaning of what was "defined" by the ecumenical councils on the essential points of the faith—that necessitates knowledge of the Fathers to the extent that they prepared and commented upon these conciliar definitions. This, of course, assumes, as we have said above, a hermeneutical work, capable of revealing the profound goal of the early texts in spite of or through the particularity of their formulations; and such a task, as we have also said, is not the prerogative of European theology (in fact, the Mediterranean arena of Antiquity included Egypt, Palestine, Syria, and Asia Minor as well as Greece, Italy, and Gaul). The fact remains that this task is especially called for by European theologians, taking into account the close link that connects their continent to its Mediterranean sources. We have spoken here of "responsibility": precisely, European theology must not only inform about what was said and thought by the Fathers on the essential points of the faith, it must itself "be responsible to them"—not, of course, in the sense in which it would close its eyes to what in the early history bore the mark of error or to the behaviors of intolerance or exclusion that were sometimes manifested in the very name of the "true religion," but in the sense that it must select, take on, and transmit patristic thought to the extent that this thought has been able to bring to light the Christian faith and deepen its meaning.

The responsibility of European theology toward the patristic tradition is also connected to the situation of the Churches and the exigency of ecumenism. Of course, it was during the era of the Fathers that the divisions between "Chalcedonians," "Monophysites," and "Nestorians" arose—the long-lasting effects of these divisions remaining until our day. But it is all the more necessary to study the causes of these divisions and to recognize the misunderstandings that, at least in part, have caused the ruptures of the past. The patristic works that have been undertaken in this direction have already borne fruit: and so Christological agreements have been reached in recent decades between the Roman Catholic Church and some Churches of the East.[18] One can hope that a better knowledge of history will allow covering still more territory, and European theology must notably contribute to it for the same reason that we mentioned above: the direct link that connects it to its Mediterranean sources. Above all, the great divisions that occurred after the patristic era—first of all the separation between the West and the East in the Middle Ages, then the separations between the Protestant Churches and the Roman Catholic Church in the sixteenth century—invite theologians from the various Churches to come together, not only on Scripture, but also on their common heritage of the Fathers, and to find in it impetus and inspiration for overcoming the divergences that remain between them. The ecumenical advances of these past decades have already benefitted from such work, and it is important that it can produce new fruit in the future.

18. See chap. 12, pp. 289–93.

This exigency quite especially falls to European theology due to the separations in question having originated in Europe itself, indeed more precisely in Western Europe (for the divisions that arose in the sixteenth century). This continent was directly implicated in the subsequent history of relationships between the Catholic Church and the other Christian Churches or confessions—even if the heritage of their divisions is equally present on other continents.

In the end, the current cultural and religious situation of Europe invites emphasizing a last aspect of its responsibility toward the patristic tradition. For an era in which other religions are more present on this continent—not only Islam but Eastern religions as well, in particular Buddhism—for an era also in which new forms of religiosity or even forms of wisdom filled with a search for transcendence are increasing, it more than ever becomes essential to make known and appreciate the immense richness of the spiritual literature that has been transmitted to us by the Fathers. Already in 1955, in one of his books on Buddhism, de Lubac wrote these lines:

> In our day, a form of lethargy is undermining some Christian consciences. As to their own spiritual tradition, it, alas, allows only indifference or contempt. Will the one who, by chance, finds himself so affected, not experience the renewal of an interest in themes that he thought hackneyed by discovering them in their Buddhist transposition? Will he thus not begin to appreciate better the value of some interior approaches? By piquing his curiosity, will this detour through the Far East not rekindle his taste?[19]

Today, of course, there is not necessarily "indifference" or "contempt" toward the spiritual tradition of Christianity: most often, it is simply ignorance, and many experience the deep attraction of Eastern spiritualities (or at least are moved by some form of spiritual quest) without realizing that they can find in patristic literature a very profound nourishment, capable of transmitting to them the desire for God and of guiding them in the itinerary of their own life. Whether through exegesis called "spiritual," or through the most profoundly "mystical" pages of a Gregory of Nyssa, or through the writings of the desert Fathers or by many other writings, a considerable patrimony

19. Henri de Lubac, *Amida* (Paris: Seuil, 1955), 9; reprinted as de Lubac, *Aspects du bouddhisme*, 169–70.

has thus been bequeathed to us; and it has a very great importance for our time. By making it known and appreciated, European theology will contribute to the fact that some patristic texts might actually be perceived as "sources." This is really what must be taken into consideration in the cultural and religious situation of its own continent. First of all, the nourishment needed by Christians in order to ground and nourish their personal and ecclesial life is at stake; it additionally is an essential condition so that their dialogue with other believers may not be impoverished, but rather that, in this very dialogue, they can demonstrate the spiritual profundity of their own tradition.

To Read the Fathers Today: this is, after all is said and done, the exigency to which the route proposed in the first part of this work refers. We would precisely like to show, in the second part, how the reading of patristic writings is proving to be fruitful in the different fields of theology. We will not devote a specific chapter to the exegesis practiced by the Fathers, this question having already been treated in chapter 5; but one will have to keep in mind (and we will, moreover, have the opportunity to repeat it) that the reference to Scripture holds an essential place in the very constitution of patristic thinking. We will not claim to cover all the questions that it would be possible to tackle; but we will hope at least to present a sufficiently large range—from ecclesiology to spiritual theology, including anthropology, ethics, Christology, and Trinitarian theology, ecumenism, and a reflection on the religious traditions of humanity.

Part Two

Reading the Fathers Today

The Present Tasks of Patristic Theology

CHAPTER 8

The Church of the Fathers

The expression "the Church of the Fathers" is the title of a study by John Henry Newman, whose theological itinerary was—as recalled above—profoundly influenced by his in-depth reading of the Fathers of the Church. Actually, Newman almost apologized for thus titling one of his works; he wrote in the foreword: "The following Sketches … do not, as the author is very conscious, warrant a title of such high pretension as that which was there prefixed to them and is here preserved." However, added Newman: "But that title will at least show the object with which they were written, namely, to illustrate, as far as they go, the tone and modes of thought, the habits and manners of the early times of the Church."[1] The pages that follow would simply like to set out the bases for a study on this "Church of the Fathers" and to make clear the value of such a study for theology's current situation.

One recalls Balthasar's characterization of patristic literature as "that intimate journal written by the Church when she was seventeen years old." Of course, we know that the Church is no longer seventeen years old and that patristic writings cannot today give a direct response to all our questions. These writings are no less of great interest for a contemporary ecclesiology, and we would like to show this by focusing on some traits that contribute to characterizing the Church of the Fathers: the constitutive role of the reading of the Scriptures; the development of ecclesial practices and institutions; the concern for announcing the Gospel in all places; the recognition of a legitimate plurality in the heart of the Church (independent of questions asked by the struggle against "heresies"—questions that we will treat in another chapter).

1. Newman, *Historical Sketches*, 2:ix.

The Reading of the Scriptures

It is first of all important to emphasize the central importance of the Scriptures or, more precisely, the reading of the Scriptures for the genesis and growth of the Church herself. The experience of "Bible study groups," which have been developed since Vatican Council II, draws our attention exactly to this point. The first goal of these groups is to come together around this or that scriptural text and, under the direction of a leader, to allow themselves to be taught and nourished by the Word of God. For the participants, it is then a matter of a profoundly ecclesial experience. In the best of cases, such groups effectively allow "being formed and animated by the inspirational power conveyed by Scripture," which ought to produce effects on the personal and collective commitments of their members—and, among others, their pastoral commitments.[2] One could also mention a major phenomenon that became widespread throughout Latin America (but that has spread to other continents), that of the "base ecclesial communities," at the juncture of a real solidarity with the poor and an active reading of the Scripture.

Yet the experience corresponding to what we call "Bible study groups" was very important during the era of the Fathers—as one sees, for example, with Origen and Jerome, who extensively used the reading of the Scriptures to form Christians. It is not a matter of simply repeating what they said about the Bible; the issue is rather that we grasp their lively manner of proceeding, that we learn from them to scrutinize the scriptural text in order to discover in it not only the literal meaning but the "spiritual" meaning in the light of Christ, and that we reflect on the very act that is thus involved in the reading of the Bible and on its impact on the life of the Church—since this act is what we still need to set out.

It is true that in Bible study groups one is not concerned with what

2. Cf. Christoph Theobald, "Lire les Écritures dans un contexte de mutation ecclésiale: À propos du chapitre VI de *Dei Verbum*" [Reading the Scriptures in a context of ecclesial change:About chapter 6 of *Dei Verbum*], in *La Bible sans avoir peur* [The Bible without fear], ed. J.-F. Bouthors (Paris: Lethielleux, 2005), 263–91; repr. in *"Dans les traces..." de la constitution "Dei Verbum" du concile Vatican II. Bible, théologie et pratiques de lectures* ["In the Footsteps ..." of the constitution "Dei Verbum" of the Second Vatican Council. Bible, theology and reading practices] (Paris: Cerf, 2009), 163–86 (see notably 183–84).

Origen or Augustine said on Exodus or the Gospel of John; rather one reads the scriptural text itself. Consequently, the objection already mentioned comes to mind:[3] what interest would there be in additionally referring to the Fathers since Christians, for several decades, have had such a fruitful experience in the common reading of biblical texts? At best, one would admit that the return to the patristic sources was historically valuable for returning to the scriptural sources; but beginning at the point when Christians are in more direct contact with Scripture, how can the texts of the Fathers of the Church bring "more" to them?

The objection must, however, be overcome. Clearly not in the sense that patristic exegesis must interfere with the reading of Scripture such as it ought to be implemented in Bible study groups (indeed, it is necessary that today the members of these groups themselves have the experience of reading the Bible and of allowing themselves to be engaged by the Word of God). But the practice of these groups, from the perspective that we here envisage, invites rediscovering how the patristic reading of Scripture was itself an ecclesial experience, capable of inspiring Christian communities and enriching their understanding of the faith. Thus the meditation on the Exodus of the Hebrew people and on the crossing of the Red Sea nourished the catechetical and doctrinal reflection on Baptism; similarly, the meditation on the manna in the desert nourished the understanding of the Eucharist, and one could more broadly show the importance of the "typological" reading of the Old Testament for Christian life and in particular for the sacramental life. Let us recall what Jean Daniélou wrote on this subject in the book *Sacramentum futuri*, devoted to the origins of biblical typology:

> The Old Testament gave us an eschatological interpretation of the Exodus, by showing it to us as a figure of the messianic times. The New Testament declared to us this typology realized in the mystery of Christ, who accomplished the New Exodus, announced by the Prophets, by liberating mankind from the power of the devil. The Fathers of the Church, all the while maintaining these two interpretations, are, above all, going to show in the Exodus the figure of the great events of the life of the present Church, that is of the sacraments by which the power of God continues to accomplish the liberation of mankind, represented in the Exodus and substantially acquired in Jesus Christ.[4]

3. See chap. 4, p. 104.
4. Daniélou, *Sacramentum futuri*, 152.

And the author then explained "how the Fathers see in the crossing of the Red Sea, followed by the eating of the manna, the figure of Baptism and the Eucharist received on the anniversary of the exit from Egypt, then how this interpretation is extended to the whole of the Exodus."[5]

Indeed, quite a lot of patristic texts—from Irenaeus to Augustine, including Origen, Cyril of Jerusalem, and John Chrysostom—attest to the fecundity of such a typology for the understanding of Baptism and the Eucharist. But the patristic reading of the Bible contributes, more broadly, to forming the understanding of the Christian mystery in its entirety. This quite particularly pertains to the work of Irenaeus, so profoundly shaped by his meditation on the Scriptures that in his case is an actual matrix for the understanding of the ecclesial faith. This also pertains to other works written by the Fathers, including those among them who were more influenced by the heritage of philosophy and who were, first and foremost, no less readers and commentators on Scripture. We do not need to repeat here all our previous thoughts on what today gives to patristic exegesis its intrinsic importance.[6] One point, on the other hand, must be emphasized in the context of this chapter: from the point of view of Christian theology, the reading of Scripture cannot be truly ecclesial if it disregards the testimony of the Fathers. It is worthwhile to recall what Vincent of Lérins had already written in 434: "Here, perhaps, someone may ask: Since the canon of the Scripture is complete and more than sufficient in itself, why is it necessary to add to it the authority of ecclesial interpretation?" And he answered:

> Holy Scripture, because of its depths, is not universally accepted in one and the same sense. The same text is interpreted differently by different people so that one may almost gain the impression that it can yield as many different meanings as there are men.... Thus, because of the great distortions caused by various errors, it is, indeed, necessary that the trend of the interpretation of the prophetic and apostolic writings be directed in accordance to the rule of the ecclesiastical and Catholic meaning.[7]

5. Ibid.

6. See chap. 6, pp. 133–46.

7. Vincent of Lérins, *The Commonitories*, 2 [Morris, 269–70]. See also Vincent of Lérins, *Tradition et progress*, 25–26.

In this light, one understands that our ecclesial situation can itself open a new access to patristic texts. For today we know, as in the preceding centuries, a problem analogous to the one formerly formulated by Vincent de Lérins: how to proceed when one is faced with different and sometimes contradictory exegeses? Of course, on one hand, the work on scriptural texts alone can help in overcoming the difficulties, by means of the resources of textual criticism and other disciplines; but a Christian interpretation of the Scriptures implies as well, in order to resolve some debates, an appeal to "the rule of the ecclesiastic and catholic meaning"—this "rule" that precisely the Fathers have contributed to formulating.

We have said above that the reading of the Bible has notably contributed to the genesis and development of ecclesial practices; it is now important to consider this aspect on its own, taking into account its stakes for contemporary ecclesiology.

Ecclesial Practices and Institutions

If, in fact, the writings from early Christianity have much to offer contemporary ecclesiology, it is by the way in which they draw our attention to the history of ecclesial practices and institutions, as well as to how they were thought about in different places in the Mediterranean world. Considerable works have been carried out during the past fifty years on ancient liturgies and catecheses, on the way in which the "mysteries" or "sacraments" were celebrated and understood, on the ministries to communities, on the attitude toward those who were separated from the Church and wished to be re-admitted to it, on the relationships between Christian communities, etc.[8] All of this is of great value for the theologian, even regarding questions that are asked about the Church today.

8. In addition to some works of de Lubac, Congar, and other theologians who have already been mentioned in chapter 3, some older studies, still very valuable, can here be mentioned: Gustave Bardy, *La Théologie de l'Église*, vol. 1, *De saint Clément de Rome à saint Irénée* [The theology of the Church, vol. 1, From Saint Clement of Rome to Saint Irenaeus] (Paris: Cerf, 1945); vol. 2, *De saint Irénée au concile de Nicée* (From Saint Irenaeus to the Council of Nicaea] (Paris: Cerf, 1947); Josef Andreas Jungmann, *La liturgie des premiers siècles jusqu'à l'époque de Grégoire le Grand* [Liturgy of the Christian early period up to Gregor the Great] (Paris: Cerf, 1962); Louis Bouyer, *L'Église de Dieu. Corps du Christ et Temple de l'Esprit* [The Church of God. Body of Christ and temple of the Spirit] (Paris: Cerf, 1970), 17–44.

Of course, it is important to avoid the presentation of a "golden age" of Christian Antiquity, whether to justify current situations by invoking such antiquity or, on the contrary, to challenge them in the name of a supposedly ideal past. History reveals rather the complexity of the patristic period, in which the Church was, of course, marked by remarkable innovations but equally lived through crises and conflicts. On the other hand, the very concept of "genesis" must be used with caution: it is not because this or that practice appears that it is itself foundational. It is necessary, in any case, to recognize that some developments of patristic ecclesiology, whatever were the reasons for them at the time, themselves showed a distancing away from the language of the New Testament: thus when the distinction between the Levitical priesthood and the rest of the people was transposed to the Church in the form of a differentiation between "clerics" and "laics" or when, beginning in the third century especially, Christians re-appropriated the "priestly" categories in order to describe the ministry of the bishop and the priest.[9] But the work of the theologian is precisely to bring out, amidst the very complexity of the developments, the elements of significance for our own time's ecclesiological reflection. Sometimes it will be a matter of recovering the original meaning of this or that practice (for example, the meaning formerly given to presidency at the Eucharist; or, again, to the way in which one understood "chrismation" or "confirmation"). Sometimes it will be a matter of understanding the faults that on some points affected the life of the Church (as when the links with imperial power proved to be ambiguous, even leading to supporting unjust behaviors vis-à-vis persons and groups). Sometimes it will be a matter of noting the forms of ecclesial life that

9. See André de Halleux, "Ministère et sacerdoce" [Ministry and priesthood], in *Patrologie et œcuménisme. Recueil d'études* [Patrology and ecumenism. A collection of studies] (Leuven: Leuven University Press, 1990), 710–65; Alexandre Faivre, "La question des ministères à l'époque paléochrétienne. Problématique et enjeux d'une périodisation" [The Issue of ministries in the Paleochristian era. Problematic and stakes of a periodization], in *Chrétiens et Églises. Des identités en construction. Acteurs, structures, frontières du champ religieux chrétien* [Christians and churches. Identities under construction. Actors, structures, boundaries of the Christian religious field] (Paris: Cerf, 2011), 115–50. Beyond the single question of ministries, the apostolic constitutions are a good source for the developments that marked the ecclesiology of the first centuries; see on this point Joseph Gerard Mueller, *L'Ancien Testament et l'ecclésiologie des Pères. Une lecture des Constitutions apostoliques* [The Old Testament and the ecclesiology of the Fathers. A reading of the apostolic constitutions] (Turnhout, Belgium: Brepols, 2004).

existed for a period of time but that were later extinguished (such as the "ministry" of deaconesses and widows in the ancient Church) or even to question more broadly if patristic ecclesiology does not contain teachings, later forgotten, that merit being given new attention.

On this latter point, one can, for example, consider the question of the pastoral attitude vis-à-vis remarried divorcés. It is clear that the Fathers of the Church fully adhered to the words of Christ on the indissolubility of marriage; but must one in every case exclude from communion those who have remarried after a divorce? Texts from the third and fourth centuries allow catching a glimpse of the discipline that was then in effect: in principle, the Church could readmit to communion all those who had failed, once they had fulfilled the required penance; Origen and Cyprian considered that this was a pastoral question, falling under the judgment of the local bishop. Of course, Novatian and his followers felt that the Church must not grant her pardon in such situations (no more than in the situation of the "*lapsi*" who had not held up during the persecutions); but the Council of Nicaea declared about them: "they will promise in writing to be conformed to the teachings of the catholic and apostolic Church and to make it the rule of their conduct, that is, they must commune (*koinônein*) with those who have been married twice (*digamoi*) and with those who have lapsed under persecution, but have done penance for their faults."[10] The era of the Fathers never, let us repeat, abandoned the teaching on the indissolubility of marriage, but, on the other hand, it helped to make understood that, without placing in question this exigency, it would be possible for the Church (in some cases at least and through a "penitential" approach) to readmit remarried divorcés to the Eucharistic communion.

10. Council of Nicaea, can. 8; other trans.: "it is fitting that they give a written undertaking they will accept and follow the decrees of the catholic church, namely that they will be in communion with those who have entered in a second marriage and with those who have lapsed in time of persecution, and for them a period [of penance] has been fixed and an occasion [for reconciliation] allotted," *Decrees of the Ecumenical Councils*, vol. 1, ed. Norman P. Tanner (London: Sheed and Ward, 1990), 9–10. See Charles Munier, "La sollicitude pastorale de l'Église ancienne en matière de divorce et de remariage" [The Church's pastoral concern for divorce and remarriage], *Laval théologique et philosophique*, 44 (1988): 29; repr. in Charles Munier, *Autorité épiscopale et sollicitude pastorale. II*[e]*–VI*[e] *siècles* [Episcopal authority and pastoral concern. Second–sixth centuries], "*Variorum*" (Aldershot: Gower House, 1990).

Thus patristic ecclesiology, in its very diversity, provides ample material for reflection for our time. One cannot, in any case, overly emphasize the remarkably inventive capacity shown by Christian communities during the first centuries: this in itself is a teaching for today's Church in that, even if she does not have to reproduce everything that originated between the second and eighth centuries, she is at least called upon to identify, with the same freedom, her own ways of being faithful to the Gospel.

This fidelity to the Gospel does not occur only with the reading of the Scriptures and the development of ecclesial practices in which the faith of the Christian community can be expressed. The Church of the Fathers appears to us also as a Church that, initially constituted by Israel and the Nations, brings with her a concern for announcing the Gospel to the ends of the world.

The Announcement of the Gospel

Indeed, the Church of the Fathers must not only be considered in her internal development but also in her relationship to the world—a world in which she has a vocation to announce the Gospel.

This dimension was notably rediscovered, as one has seen, by the theologians of the twentieth century, who drew attention to the patristic theme of the "seeds of the Word" and who emphasized its importance for the understanding of Christian missions. Strongly emphasized in the writings of Henri de Lubac and Jean Daniélou, it took shape in the experience of a man such as Jules Monchanin, whose project of a "Christian *ashram*" in India was nourished by a deep meditation on patristic literature; in 1939 he wrote: "The immense task to which we are called is to rethink all of India as Christian and Christianity as Indian. Just as the Greek Fathers grafted Revelation into Hellenic thought, so today we must try to graft Revelation onto Indian thought."[11] Of course, the patristic era's frame of reference for its evangelizing action was cultural contexts that are no longer ours. But the Church of the Fathers, as a "missionary" Church, had already

11. *Théologie et spiritualité missionnaires* [Missionary theology and spirituality], ed. Édouard Duperray and Jacques Gadille (Paris: Beauchesne, 1985), 194. On Jules Monchanin, see also chap. 7, pp. 173–74.

crossed some frontiers. She developed within the sphere of influence of the "passage to the Nations" that was so strongly characteristic of the writings of the New Testament, in particular in the letters of Paul and in the Acts of the Apostles. The Church of the Fathers was this communion of Churches that took form and substance all around and beyond the Mediterranean Basin—in Greece, Egypt, Italy, North Africa, Gaul, in the land of the "Britons" who were on the other side of the sea (the inhabitants of our Great Britain), in Asia Minor, Syria, Persia, and even as far as China where some Nestorian Christians went to announce the Gospel in the course of the seventh century.

It is true that today one comes up against an objection mentioned above:[12] the announcement of the Gospel calls for an "inculturation" of the Christian message, yet this "inculturation" does not consist only in an adaptation of Christianity to the cultural values of Africa or of Asia; it must be, above all else, implemented by Africans and Asians themselves thanks to the experience that they have of their own cultures. These cultures must, of course, be open to the Gospel, but in a new and original way. Consequently, will one ask, do the new perspectives of the mission not run the risk of being contradictory to the patristic heritage, to the extent that it would be too conditioned by cultural contexts that are no longer ours—or that, in any case, are not those of the Christian communities in Africa and Asia?

And yet, as we have shown above,[13] the objection must be overcome. Of course, the actual contexts have changed, but it is necessary to consider more closely what was at stake in the missionary practice and theology of the patristic era. It is, first of all, necessary to take into account the fact that, in many cases, the Fathers were themselves born in the countries in which they announced the Gospel: their witness has more importance for Africans and Asians who, in their turn, must announce the Gospel on their own continents. As for the witness of other Christian authors, that is, those who left their countries of origin in order to announce the Gospel on other lands, it too retains all of its importance: still today Christians announce the Gospel in countries in which they were not born; their presence as such expresses the link between the Churches, and thus, from this point of view, it

12. See chap. 4, pp. 109–10.
13. See chap. 7, p. 179, and following.

is worthwhile to recall the Fathers' experience and thought. In any case, whatever the forms of the Christian mission may be, patristic texts confront us with highly significant questions. Thus, how were the Fathers of the second and third centuries able to give an account of their faith in the heart of a world where Christianity was so much in the minority? Did the Christian authors purely and simply dismiss the cultural and religious traditions of the Greek and Roman worlds, or did they rather rely upon some of these traditions in order to devise a new theological language, in conformity to the rule of faith at the same time as respecting the ways in which the Greeks and the Romans were able to have access to the mystery of God revealed in Jesus Christ? Was there not, moreover, among them, diverse tendencies as to the way of practicing and conceiving this relationship of Christianity to cultures? How did the non-Christians react? What reception did they give to the Church's missionary initiative, or with what resistance did they, on the contrary, oppose it? How was this action altered once the empire became Christian? And what happened when the "Barbarians" progressively expanded into this empire? All these questions merit being asked for the benefit of a theological reflection on mission. As the Church has the responsibility of announcing the Gospel, the writings of the Fathers help us to reflect on the Church—or more precisely on the relationship of Christianity to the religious traditions of mankind, as we will clarify later.[14]

Unity and Diversity

A last theme must be tackled here. In spite of what we have said on the genesis of ecclesial practices during the patristic era, as well as on the concern for announcing the Gospel in all places, is not the Church of the Fathers often perceived as a Church more or less uniform and monolithic, or at least as a Church that did not take pluralism enough into consideration, as is often claimed in our day? More radically, does one not denounce the "exclusivism" and the "imperialism" that marked the attitude of the Fathers toward "heretics," in contrast to what today is required by a respectful dialogue with other Christians?

14. See our chapter 13, "Patristics and the Theology of Religions."

We will provisionally leave aside the second of these questions, which will be treated in another chapter;[15] the first, on the other hand, calls for some reflections here.[16]

Of course, the contemporary appeal for pluralism would not at all be honored if the Church of the Fathers appeared as a uniform and monolithic Church. But the Church of the Fathers actually has quite diverse aspects. It is important, first of all, to take note of the testimony of Irenaeus, who, all the while strongly affirming the unity of the Church, himself referred to the diversity of the Churches:

> Though the languages throughout the world are dissimilar, nevertheless the meaning of the tradition is one and the same. To explain, the churches which have been founded in Germany do not believe or hand down anything else; neither do those founded in Spain or Gaul or Libya or in the central regions of the world. But just as the sun, God's creation, is one and the same throughout the world, so too the light, the preaching of the Truth, shines everywhere and enlightens all men who wish to come to the knowledge of the Truth.[17]

The unity of the Church is thus manifested through the very difference of languages and peoples. Irenaeus also writes: "It is within the power of all, therefore, in every Church, who may wish to see the truth, to contemplate clearly the tradition of the apostles, manifested throughout the whole world."[18] This, of course, assumes that these diverse Churches be in mutual communion; and Irenaeus indicates that this communion must notably be manifested in the agreement with a particular Church: "the Church that is very large, very old, and known to all and that the two glorious apostles Peter and Paul founded and established in Rome": "For it is a matter of necessity that every Church

15. See chap. 12.

16. For what follows, see our study: "Diversité ecclésiale et communion dans la foi: le témoignage de la littérature patristique" [Ecclesial diversity and communion in faith: The testimony of patristic literature], in *L'Église catholique dans le monde: entre unité et diversité* [The Catholic Church in the world: Between unity and diversity], ed. M. Fédou (Paris: Médiasèvres, 2002), 77–104 (esp. 78–92).

17. Irenaeus, *Against the Heresies*, I, 10, 2, trans. Dominic J. Unger, Ancient Christian Writers 55 (New York, N.Y.: Paulist Press, 1992), 49. Cf. 1 Tm 2:4. Another trans., *Contre les hérésies*, translated by Adelin Rousseau (Paris: Cerf, 1984), 66.

18. Irenaeus, *Against the Heresies*, III, 3, 1. In *Apostolic Fathers, Justin Martyr, Irenaeus*, ed. Alexander Roberts, James Donaldson, and A. Cleveland Coxe, *The Ante-Nicene Fathers* 1 (1885); repr. Grand Rapids, Mich.: Eerdmans, 1996), 415. Irenaeus, *Against the Heresies*, Book 3, trans. Dominic J. Unger, Ancient Christian Writers 64 (New York, N.Y.: Paulist Press, 2012), 32; *Contre les hérésies*, 279.

should agree with this Church, on account of its preeminent authority, that is, the faithful everywhere, inasmuch as the apostolic tradition has been preserved continuously by those [faithful men] who exist everywhere."[19] The emphasis, throughout all these texts, is very much placed on communion; but communion that is manifested as such in a great diversity of cultural expressions, spiritual movements, traditions and customs, and theologies. The same Irenaeus, whose emphasis on the unity of the Church we highlighted, interceded with Pope Victor in order to dissuade him from excommunicating the Churches of Asia that celebrated Easter on 14 Nisan (whether or not it was a Sunday); here is what he wrote "in the name of the brothers that he supervised in Gaul": "This variety of observance did not originate in our time, but much further back, in the times of those before us.... Yet none the less they all lived in peace, and we live in peace, with one another; and the difference concerning the fast enhances the unanimity of our faith."[20] As understood by Irenaeus, the particular observance that here is in question in no way presents an obstacle to unity; it even "confirms" it, for this unity is all the more profound because of its achievement being shown through the diversity of practices! The Church of the Fathers must thus help us in reflecting on such a diversity that is not opposed to unity but that is rather, according to Congar, the "internal value of unity."[21]

So what happened in the subsequent centuries, after the conversion of Constantine? Beginning at that time, Christianity, which previously was not recognized in the Empire (and was even at times the object of persecutions), was tolerated as a legitimate religion and then, toward the end of the fourth century, recognized as an official religion.

It is incontestable that there were, in this new period, processes of standardization of the Church; this can be seen in liturgical customs and canonical legislation, as well as in theology itself taking into

19. Irenaeus, *Against the Heresies*, III, 3, 2; *Apostolic Fathers, Justin Martyr, Irenaeus*, 415–16. See also Ancient Christian Writers 64, 32; *Contre les hérésies*, 279–80.

20. According to Eusebius of Caesarea, *The Ecclesiastical History*, V, XXIV, trans. Hugh Jackson Lawlor and John Ernest Leonard Oulton (London: Society for Promoting Christian Knowledge, 1927), 170. See Yves Congar, *Diversité et communion: Dossier historique et conclusion théologique* [Diversity and communion: Historical record and theological conclusion] (Paris: Cerf, 1982), 37.

21. Congar, *Diversité et communion*, 64.

account dogmatic formulations that were approved by ecumenical councils, such as those of Nicaea and Chalcedon. However, the question must be asked: was this standardization as important as has often been believed? Was it not, to some extent, the subject of a particular reconstruction from the Middle Ages and perhaps even more so in the modern era? Has there not been a tendency to present a very unified image of post-Constantine Christianity in order subsequently to justify a particular understanding of the Church and her missionary expansion?

Actually, the post-Constantine Church, even if she were marked by processes of standardization, herself knew a true diversity. It is possible to show this, first of all, regarding theologies themselves. Whatever the importance of the dogmatic formulations of Nicaea or Chalcedon, there was not *one* but *some* post-Constantine theologies. One can give the example of the Greek and Latin Fathers who, all the while in full communion with the faith defined at the time of the councils, did not repeat the actual language of these councils. Thus, the Council of Nicaea had said in 325, against the doctrine of Arius, that the Son of God is not a simple creature but that he is "consubstantial" with the Father—in Greek, *homoousios*; but some Fathers of the Church preferred to express the same faith without relying upon this concept: this was the case for Hilary of Poitiers in his *De Trinitate*. The concept was certainly important to his aim (it was a matter of saying that the Son of God is not a creature, but eternally engendered by God, of the same "substance" as He), but, apart from the fact that it was not scriptural, it did not allow saying that the Son is, from another point of view, "below" the Father (to the extent that he is the Son and that he assumed the human condition). This is why Hilary, all the while maintaining the aim of the Council of Nicaea (he was even exiled for this!), stated the mystery in another way:

> The Father therefore is greater, because He is Father; but the Son, because He is Son, is not less. By the birth of the Son the Father is constituted greater: the nature that is His by birth, does not suffer the Son to be less. The Father is greater, for the Son prays Him to render glory to manhood He has assumed. The Son is not less, for He receives back His glory with the Father. Thus are consummated at once the mystery of the Birth, and the dispensation of the Incarnation. The Father, as Father, and as glorifying Him Who now is Son of Man, is greater:

Father and Son are one, in that the Son, born of the Father, after assuming an earthly body is taken back to the glory of the Father.[22]

The aim of the Council of Nicaea is intact, but the theological language is not that of *homoousios*: a good example of what one would today call a theological pluralism; the same faith can be said in different languages. One could give other examples: thus, over the course of the fourth century, Gregory of Nazianzus and Basil of Caesarea do not use the same language regarding the divinity of the Holy Spirit. Gregory says that "the Spirit is God," but Basil, all the while being in agreement with the substance, prefers other, more scriptural language and says that, with the Father and the Son, the Spirit receives all adoration and glory. And later, in the fifth century, two theologians who were initially adversaries—Cyril of Alexandria and John of Antioch—agree to recognize that their different languages regarding Christ are equally legitimate. Even though Cyril, up until then, always spoke of a single nature of Christ and John of Antioch spoke of two natures of Christ, Cyril admits in 433 that the language of John is well-founded. He recognizes that one can indeed speak of two natures of Christ, since one clearly maintains the unity of the Word who was made flesh "according to the hypostasis." Thus the patristic era gives us examples of a legitimate diversity of theological languages—and we will see, moreover, that, in our day, the ecumenical dialogue finds in it a powerful foundation in its search for a communion within the Church that might grant certain diversities.[23] Other examples could be borrowed from the Syriac language of the East. Thus, during the same era when the Greek and Latins Fathers affirmed the identity of Christ as true man and true God, some Eastern Fathers such as Ephrem and Aphraates stated the

22. Hilary of Poitiers, *On the Trinity*, IX, 56, in *Hilary of Poitiers, John of Damascus*, trans. E. W. Watson, L. Pullan, and others, A Select Library of Nicene and Post-Nicene Fathers of the Christian Church, 2nd ser., 9 (Edinburgh: T & T Clark; repr. Eerdmans, 1997), 175; *The Trinity*, trans. Stephen McKenna, Fathers of the Church 25 (Washington, D.C.: The Catholic University of America Press, 1954), 379. See Corbin, *La Trinité ou l'excès de Dieu*, 143.

23. The examples of Hilary (as well as Athanasius), Basil, and Cyril of Alexandria were mentioned by Pope Paul VI in the context of his dialogue with the Patriarch Athenagoras; cf. his address to Patriarch Athenagoras, July 25, 1967, *La Documentation catholique* 1499 (1967), col. 1382; they have been used by the Groupe des Dombes in its document *Pour la conversion des Églises. Identité et changement dans la dynamique de communion* [For the conversion of the Church. Identity and change in the dynamics of communion], nos. 57–63 (Paris: Centurion, 1991), 40–42; see chap. 12, pp. 302–3.

same faith in a completely different way in the heart of their own tradition. Their writings, which for a long time remained unrecognized in the West, today cause us to realize that, even after the conversion of Constantine and in spite of the process of standardization that marked this period, a true plurality of theological languages really existed. Unity was not sacrificed for all that: Ephrem and Aphraates were profoundly committed to the faith of the Church; but they took it into consideration in an original way, drawing upon the resources of their own language and more broadly upon their tradition.

The diversity of the post-Constantine Church is seen even more at the level of ecclesial practices. Here again several examples can be given. Thus, the practices of fasting were different in Italy: in Rome one fasted on Saturday, but not in Milan. On this subject, it is worthwhile to cite a letter from Augustine, recalling Ambrose's response to him regarding the practice of fasting:

> There are things that differ according to place and region.... These things are left to the liberty of observances. There is no better way of behaving for a wise and prudent Christian than to conform to the customs of the Church in which one finds oneself. For what is neither against the faith nor against good morals must be considered as indifferent and observed for the sake of those with whom one lives in society.[24]

One can also take the example of Pope Gregory the Great, to whom the question had been asked: "Is it necessary to baptize by a single immersion or by three?"; he responds: "If there is a unity of faith, a difference of custom in no way harms the holy Church."[25] Above all, he writes in July 601 to Augustine of Canterbury who, accustomed to the Roman liturgical practices, had asked the question: "Even if there is only one faith, [why] is there in the Church varied practice, a way of saying the Mass for the Holy Roman Church, and another for that of the Gauls?" Gregory responds:

> My brother, you know the customs of the Roman Church in which, of course, you were brought up. But it is my wish that if you have found any customs in the Roman or the Gaulish church or any other church which may be more pleasing to Almighty God, you should make a careful selection of them and

24. Augustine, *Letter* 54; PL 33, 200 (Vivès, 4:450).
25. Gregory the Great, *Registri epistolarum*, I, 43; PL 77, 497; this response dates from 591.

> sedulously teach the Church of the English, which is still new in the faith, what you have been able to gather from other churches. For things are not to be loved for the sake of a place, but places are to be loved for the sake of their good things. Therefore choose from every individual Church whatever things are devout, religious, and right. And when you have collected these as it were into one bundle, see that the minds of the English grow accustomed to it.[26]

The same Gregory the Great writes to the Abbot Mellitus that Christians must not destroy the temples to idols in Britain:

> For if the shrines are well built, it is essential that they should be changed from the worship of devils to the worship of the true God. When this people see that their shrines are not destroyed, they will be able to banish error from their hearts and be more ready to come to the places they are familiar with, but now recognizing and worshipping the true God. And because they are in the habit of slaughtering much cattle as sacrifices to devils, some solemnity ought to be given them in exchange for this. So on the day of the dedication or the festivals of the holy martyrs, whose relics are deposited there, let them make themselves huts from branches or trees around the churches which have been converted out of shrines, and let them celebrate the solemnity with religious feasts.[27]

There is a remarkable concern for taking into account the tradition of a given country and of inventing practices that, all the while being authentically Christian, are significant for the people of the place—the corollary being that these practices are necessarily different from those that are adopted in other places.

Of course, we will have to consider in a later chapter another form of diversity, that which is due to the divisions between the Catholic Church and other ecclesial groups; it will then be necessary to ask how to interpret the heresiology of the Fathers, because for several decades the Catholic Church has favored an attitude of ecumenical dialogue with other Christians. But here it was a matter of showing that, independent of this question, the Church of the Fathers knew forms of diversity that fully agreed with communion in the faith. The theolog-

26. Cited in Bede, *The Ecclesiastical History of the English People*, ed. Judith McClure and Roger Collins (Oxford: Oxford University Press, 1994), 43. See also Bède le Vénérable, *Histoire ecclésiastique du peuple anglais*, I, 27, trans. Pierre Monat and Philippe Robin, SC 489 (Paris: Cerf, 2005), 211–13. The attribution of the letter to Gregory has been contested but is once again accepted—although today the question is still not entirely settled.

27. Cited in Bede, *Ecclesiastical History* I, 30; McClure and Collins, 57, *Histoire ecclésiastique*, 249.

ical languages and the liturgical traditions that have been mentioned could be quite varied from the West to the East; however, they were no less compatible with each other and in themselves implied no dissidence or any ecclesial separation whatsoever.

A Church formed by the reading of the Scriptures; a Church marked by the genesis and the development of practices and institutions through which the faith of Christian communities could be explained; a Church concerned with announcing the Gospel among the nations and to the ends of the known world; a Church in which communion took place with a legitimate diversity of theologies and practices: such are some of the traits that characterized the Church of the Fathers, and they remain of great importance for the ecclesiological thought of our time.

CHAPTER 9

The Stakes of Patristic Anthropology

A quick glance at the twentieth century is sufficient to be convinced that, during this century, the anthropology of the Fathers made major contributions to the renewal of Christian theology.[1] One is particularly thinking about the debates on the supernatural: to a large extent it is the reading of the Fathers that allowed Henri de Lubac to develop his view of the human being as a being who is naturally oriented toward God (the inscription of his book *Le mystère du surnaturel* is the phrase *Fecisti nos ad te*, that is, the first words of Saint Augustine's famous statement: "Thou hast made us for Thee and our heart is unquiet till it finds its rest in Thee").[2] Furthermore, patristic anthropology's fecundity for the twentieth century is borne out by the ecclesial event of Vatican Council II: one notably perceives this in the great constitution *Gaudium et spes*, for example, with its number 12 on humanity in the image of God.

It would, of course, be possible to present these contributions of patristic anthropology to the theology of the twentieth century in detail. But our purpose is rather to show how patristic anthropology can

1. This chapter repeats, with some modifications, a study that we published under the title "La passion de l'humanité. Enjeux de l'anthropologie patristique pour la théologie contemporaine" [The passion of humanity. The stakes of patristic anthropology for contemporary theology], in *Avec les Pères de l'Église, penser l'homme devant Dieu*, vol. 2, *Figures d'hier, questions d'aujourd'hui* [With the Fathers of the Church, thinking of man before God, vol. 2, Figures of yesterday, questions of today] (Paris: Médiasèvres, 2002), 133–57.

2. Augustine, *Confessions*, I, 1; Bourke, , 4; see Augustin, *Les Confessions*, I, 1, trans. E. Tréhorel and G. Bouissou, Bibliothèque augustinienne 13 (Paris: Institut d'Études augustiniennes, 1992), 273.

today still be fecund for our theological work; this, in any case, will be the subject of the present chapter.

Athens, Rome, Jerusalem

Patristic anthropology is, first of all, filled with a profound sense of the universal: the Fathers of the Church show concern for being interested in every human being, in all human beings, whatever their age, their condition, their language, or their country of origin. This sense of the universal clearly does not mean that the Fathers welcomed every reality; as we will reiterate, they were often in conflict with traditions inherited from the ancient world, and one knows Tertullian's famous phrase: "What has Athens to do with Jerusalem?"[3] But one knows as well that this was to some extent refuted by Tertullian's own practice that borrowed greatly from the tradition of which he was the heir; and if, in any case, one considers the entirety of patristic literature, one will rather come to realize that the Fathers' anthropology is shaped by both the heritage of Israel and the heritage of the Nations—which can rightly be symbolized by the title of this first part: "Athens, Rome, Jerusalem."

The Fathers were, in the first place, filled with the concern to reach every human being. Their vision from this point of view is in continuity with the writings of the New Testament, which, as it is always necessary to keep in mind, came to us in Greek (that is, in the language that was then most common) and in which some texts establish in a very explicit manner the universal importance of announcing the Gospel. One of these texts can be considered as particularly significant: Paul's discourse at the Areopagus in Athens. Werner Jaeger writes on this subject:

> That was the decisive moment in the encounter of Greeks and Christians. The future of Christianity as a world religion depended on it. The author of Acts saw this clearly when he let the apostle Paul visit Athens, the intellectual and cultural center of the classical Greek world and the symbol of its historical tradi-

3. Tertullien, *Traité de la prescription contre les hérétiques*, VII, 9, trans. Pierre de Labriolle, SC 46 (Paris: Cerf, 1957), 98; see also *Apologétique*, 46, 18, trans. Jean-Pierre Waltzing (Paris: Les Belles Lettres, 1929), 97–98.

> tion, and preach on that venerable spot, the Areopagus, to an audience of Stoic and Epicurean philosophers, about the unknown God. He quotes the verse of a Greek poet, "We are his offspring"; his arguments are largely Stoic and calculated to convince an educated philosophical mind. Whether this unforgettable scene is historical or was meant to dramatize the historical situation of the beginning intellectual struggle between Christianity and the classical world, the setting of the stage reveals clearly how the author of Acts understood it. This discussion required a common basis, else no discussion would be possible. As such a basis Paul chose the Greek philosophical tradition, which was the most representative part of that which was alive in Greek culture at the time.[4]

This episode from Acts is also significant for another reason: Paul, in his presentation of the Gospel, refers to Christ using only the expression "a man": "The times of ignorance God overlooked, but now he commands all men everywhere to repent, because he has fixed a day on which he will judge the world in righteousness *by a man* whom he has appointed, and of this he has given assurance to all men by raising him from the dead" (Acts 17:30–31). This tells us how Christian anthropology is linked to Christology—amply testified to by the Fathers, as we will subsequently see. But in the framework of this first exposition, we will especially keep in mind the openness to the universal that is expressed through Paul's discourse in Athens and that, in its turn, permeates patristic literature.

In fact, the concern for reaching every human does not just shed light on the importance of mission that is one of the most impressive aspects of the Church's history in the first centuries. It also governs the very language of the Fathers, their schemas of thinking, the images and categories to which they have recourse in order to address themselves to the "Nations." Of course, sometimes the Fathers may directly echo biblical anthropology: the work of Irenaeus is a remarkable witness to this. But the Fathers are not afraid of repeating notions that held an important place in the Greek tradition, even if it meant giving them new meanings—as, for example, one sees with the Alexandrians. This is valid first and foremost for the concept of *logos* (that actually was passed down from the Johannine literature), but it is also valid for the manner of thinking about the human being (body and soul, or spirit and

4. Werner Jaeger, *Early Christianity and Greek Paideia* (Cambridge, Mass.: The Belknap Press of Harvard University Press, 1961), 11.

soul and body—according to what was already found in 1 Thes 5:23) and more broadly for the use that was made of Greek concepts (Platonic, Stoic, and others) in order to address Greeks in the language of the Greeks. The Latin-language Fathers, beginning with Tertullian, will do the same with their tradition. This is not simply a strategy but arises from the concern for reaching every human being such as he is (thus including his cultural heritage), and the Fathers are more than aware of this as they are themselves, for the most part, from cultures in which they endeavor to speak and think about their faith.

Having said this, we are not ignoring the suspicions that, since Harnack, have often concerned the "Hellenization of Christianity" nor the response that was formulated by A. Grillmeier: Hellenization would have affected only the form of the preaching of the Gospel, whereas there would actually have been a "de-Hellenization" of its content.[5] But it is necessary to move beyond this debate for several reasons. One of these is that patristic literature is clearly not limited to the Greek Fathers, nor even to the Latin Fathers: there is also a Syriac, Coptic, and Ethiopian patrology, etc., which preclude going no further than the traditional discussions on the "Hellenization of Christianity." The other reason is that, even when there were intense contacts with Greco-Roman traditions, Christianity was often in conflict with these traditions (as had already happened to Paul, whose discourse at the Areopagus had, it seems, little success). Speaking the language of others does not mean that those being spoken to, in fact, allow themselves to be convinced; but the hearers can correctly give their opinion with full knowledge of the facts on the proposition of the Gospel only if this Gospel is available to them in their own language. For this is really what the Fathers of the Church understood: of itself, their anthropology is not less Christian because it is expressed with the help of Greek or Latin or Syriac categories; it rather reveals, in this very way, to what point it is governed by the concern to reach every human being such as he is and in the tradition that is his.

Furthermore, this universal goal is itself grafted onto a concept of the unity of the human race. Such a unity is both the condition and the effect of the Gospel: the condition, because the Gospel message

5. See Grillmeier, "De Jésus de Nazareth," notably 128.

can be received in every place because all human beings have in common the power to receive it; the effect, because the Gospel message, to the extent that it is received, renews the links between human beings and gives to them their being in communion in Christ.

This vision of the unity of the human race, of course, benefitted from Stoic influences, and above all it could rely upon the biblical concept of mankind created in the image of God (all human beings thus having in common being created), or even Paul's exposition on the solidarity between human beings (let us think about the correspondence he established between Christ and Adam, his exposition on the theme of "Israel and the Nations" or his thought on the Church as body). However, Paul himself "had no concern, because he did not feel any need for it, to formulate a theory of human unity throughout all history."[6] It is above all beginning at the end of the second century that such a doctrine is found broadly expressed, with authors such as Irenaeus and Clement of Alexandria.

Clement, in particular, often makes use of the word *anthrôpotès*. The term first of all means, in him, similarity, community, equality of nature between human beings. Thus, Clement writes (in a text in which he repeats Stoic expressions):

> the individual whose life is framed as ours is, may philosophize without Learning, whether barbarian, whether Greek, whether slave—whether as an old man, or a boy, or a woman.... And we admit that the same nature exists in every race, and the same virtue. As far as respects human nature [*pros tèn anthrôpotèta*], the woman does not possess one nature, and the man exhibit another, but the same: so also with virtue.[7]

Here the word *anthrôpotès* designates the human species in the abstract sense; but most often it designates the concrete human race, the

6. Claude Mondésert, *Clément d'Alexandrie. Introduction à l'étude de sa pensée religieuse à partir de l'Écriture* [Clement of Alexandria. Introduction to the study of his religious thought from Scripture] (Paris: Aubier-Montaigne, 1944), 191; see more broadly pp. 190 ff., which we follow in the present exposition.

7. Clement of Alexandria, *The Stromata, or Miscellanies*, IV, 8, in *Fathers of the Second Century: Hermes, Tatian, Athenagoras, Theophilus, and Clement of Alexandria*, ed. Alexander Roberts and James Donaldson, rev. A. Cleveland Coxe, Ante-Nicene Fathers 2 (Edinburgh: T & T Clark; repr. Grand Rapids, Mich.: Eerdmans, 1994), 419; see Clément d'Alexandrie, *Stromate IV*, 8, 58, 3–59, 1, trans. Claude Mondésert, SC 463 (Paris: Cerf, 2001), 153–55. Cf. Gal 3:18; see Mondésert, *Clément d'Alexandrie*, 192.

whole of mankind, and Clement is aware of the fact that they all participate in the same historic destiny, "not as a sum of individuals embarked on the same ship but as a whole that subsists above its parts and possesses a kind of personality."[8] From Clement's work emerges the story of concrete humanity: created by God as the most beautiful of his works. Loved by God, humanity strayed from him and fell into all kinds of evil; but the *Logos* of God, by which humanity had been created, did not abandon it. He called it to himself, working as a teacher in order to rectify it, then he himself became flesh, in order to be able to better lead it toward God, allowing humanity to become a new creature and to attain the status of children. Let us cite some sentences from this narrative:

> the good Instructor, the Wisdom, the Word of the Father, who made man, cares for the whole nature of his creature; the all-sufficient Physician of humanity, the Savior, heals both body and soul....
>
> Both the laws served the Word for the instruction of humanity [*eis paidagôgian tès anthrôpotètos*], both that given by Moses and that by the apostles....
>
> the greatest and most regal work of God is the salvation of humanity.[9]

This concept of the "concrete personality of humanity," writes Claude Mondésert, "can today appear banal to us"; however, during Clement's era, it "begins not only to be formed but to be expressed"; and of course, "it is an innovation that was prepared for by the philosophy of the day," but it "rises much higher with its own certain boldness, emphasizing the reading of the Bible and the new interpretation of the Old Testament inaugurated by the New."[10]

One could undoubtedly assert that, in our era, it became necessary not only to emphasize the unity of the human race but also to highlight, above all, that this unity itself sets out or includes differences: for example, the difference between Westerners and Asians, or more

8. Mondésert, *Clément d'Alexandrie*, 193.

9. Clement of Alexandria, *The Instructor* (*Paedagogus*), I, 2; III, 12; I, 12. In *Fathers of the Second Century*, 210, 294, and 235. See Mondésert, *Clément d'Alexandrie*, 194–95.

10. Mondésert, *Clément d'Alexandrie*, 195. Of course, this does not prevent the Fathers' anthropology from being dependent on cultural representations that are no longer ours today, and we have distanced ourselves from some of their expressions—those, for example, that convey the ancient representation of an "inferiority" of women compared with men. But it is more important to see that these representations were already "labored" to a certain point by the very awareness of the unity of the human race.

broadly cultural differences. This emphasis is clearly important, and it is necessary to recognize that the authors of Christian Antiquity were less aware of it than we because, in some ways, their situation was the inverse of ours: the Greco-Roman world was a world that, at least in its ancient traditions, placed primary importance on particularities (above all, those of each city and the customs or *nomoi* that were connected with them); this tendency certainly began to be blurred thanks to the thought of philosophers (notably with Stoic cosmopolitism) and thanks to the processes of political unification (with Alexander the Great and Augustus), but it is truly Christianity that, on the basis of biblical Revelation, placed in the forefront the unity of the human race and of human history. For this itself represents, also for us, a decisive contribution of patristic anthropology. For as legitimate and necessary as our awareness of the differences may be, we are also threatened by the risk of schisms or ruptures: some ways of unilaterally highlighting cultural particularities could cause losing sight of the fundamental unity of the human condition—for it is this unity that formerly was so strongly brought to light by the Fathers of the Church.

The perspective of the Fathers is not, for all that, one of an abstract universalism that would disregard the particular destiny of Israel. Of course, on this point, we are today urged to reread tradition critically. It is indisputable that some patristic texts are very harsh vis-à-vis Jews (even if this can in part be explained by the literary genre of such writings and by the forms of proselytism to which Christians themselves were subjected during the first centuries). It is equally true that Christian authors, even if they were heavily nourished by the Old Testament tradition, found it more difficult to think about the meaning of the existence of the Jewish people after the coming of Christ (with exceptions, as one will soon say).

Having recognized this, it is none the less equitable to emphasize the manner in which the Fathers, or in any case some of them, defended the tradition of Israel against the contempt and the attacks to which it sometimes fell victim in the world of their day. One can here invoke the example of Origen faced with the philosopher Celsus, who was defending a certain type of universalism and enumerated the people who shared the same tradition, but failed to take into account the Jews among these peoples. This is what Origen writes:

> Thinking that *between many of the nations there is an affinity* in that they *hold the same doctrine*, Celsus names all the nations which he supposes to have held this doctrine originally. Bur for some unknown reason he misrepresents the Jews alone, and does not include their race in the list with the others; nor does he say of them either that they *took part in labors* equal to theirs and *had the same notions* or that they *held similar doctrines in many respects*.... See then the willfulness of the man who believes some particular nations to be *wise* while he condemns others as *utterly stupid*. Hear Celsus's words: *There is an ancient doctrine which has existed from the beginning, which has always been maintained by the wisest nations and cities and wise men*. And he would not speak of the Jews as being *a very wise nation* on a par with the *Egyptians, Assyrians, Indians, Persians, Odrysians, Samothracians*, and *Eleusinians*.[11]

Origen then presents, in contrast to Celsus's attitude, that of other authors who knew how to include the Jewish people:

> How much better than Celsus is Numenius the Pythagorean, a man who showed himself in many works to be very learned and who by studying several doctrines made from many sources a synthesis of those which seemed to him to be true. In the first book of his work on *The Good* where he speaks of the nations that believe God to be incorporeal, he also included the Jews among them, and did not hesitate to quote the sayings of the prophets in his book and to give them an allegorical interpretation. It is said also that Hermippus in his first book on "Lawgivers" related that Pythagoras brought his philosophy to the Greeks from the Jews. Moreover, a book about the Jews is attributed to Hecataeus the historian, in which the wisdom of the nation is emphasized even more strongly—so much that Herennius Philo in his treatise about the Jews even doubts in the first place whether it is a genuine work of the historian, and says in the second place that if it is authentic, he had probably been carried away by the Jews' powers of persuasion and accepted their doctrine.
>
> I am surprised that Celsus numbers the *Odrysians, Samothracians, Eleusinians*, and *Hyperboreans* among the *most ancient and wise nations*, and yet does not reckon the Jews worth including with the wise or the ancient.... Celsus seems to have said these things not because they are true but out of mere perversity, with a view to impugning the origins of Christianity which depends on the Jews.[12]

Later, Origen comes across this sentence of Celsus: *The Jews were runaway slaves who escaped from Egypt; they never did anything important,*

11. Origen, *Contra Celsum*, I, 14; Chadwick, 16–17; *Contre Celse*, I, 14; trans. Marcel Borret, SC 132 (Paris: Cerf, 1967), 113–15. We are following the convention of Chadwick and Borret who put in italics the extracts from Celsus's *Discours véritable*.

12. Origen, *Contra Celsum*, I, 15–16; Chadwick, 17–18; *Contre Celse*, SC 132, 115–19.

nor have they ever been of any significance or prominence whatever. And he replies:

> If he thinks that he can argue that they were never of any significance or prominence from the fact that *nothing about their history is to be found among the Greeks*, we will say that if anyone were to study carefully their society in their early days when the law was given, he would find that they were men who manifested a shadow of the heavenly life upon earth. Among them none was regarded as God other than the supreme God.... There was a law among them as follows: "Do not break the law and make for yourselves a graven image, any figure that is a likeness of male or female, a likeness of any beast of those that are in the earth, a likeness of any winged bird which flies under heaven, of any creeping thing which creeps upon the earth, a likeness of any fish that is in the waters under the earth." ... It was possible to see an entire nation studying philosophy; and in order that they might have leisure to hear the divine laws, the days called Sabbaths and their other feasts were instituted. And why need I mention the appointment of their priests and sacrifices, which contains countless symbols which are explained by those who are learned?[13]

Admittedly, a little later, Origen mentions the shadows that have also marked Jewish history, and in his work he often returns to Israel's "transgression" or "faux pas" at the time of Jesus. In his *Commentary on the Epistle to the Romans*, he at least shows a quite remarkable attention to the vocation of the elect people and to the hope of its salvation, according to Paul's perspective in Romans 11.[14] As to whatever may be the case concerning this last point, (that no other Father, to our knowledge, develops to such a degree and that many patristic texts even seem to ignore), it is above all necessary to remember here the concept of the universalism that Origen contrasted to that of the philosopher Celsus, and with which other Fathers later opposed Porphyry and the Emperor Julian: a universalism that does not misunderstand Israel's particular situation, and that, positively, grants the "election" of this people. From this point of view, if patristic anthropology is very much governed by the concern for reaching every human, it is not, for all that, a question of an abstract universalism

13. Origen, *Contra Celsum*, IV, 31; Chadwick, 207–8; *Contre Celse*, SC 136, 261–63; cf. Dt 4:16–18.

14. See Origen, *Commentary on the Epistle to the Romans*, 2:155–90; see also Origène, *Commentaire sur l'épitre aux Romains*, VIII, 6–12, trans. Luc Brésard and Michel Fédou, SC 543 (Paris: Cerf, 2011), 499–589.

that would forget the Jewish race.[15] Of course, the position of the philosopher Celsus itself intended to be universal, but it was only superficially so; its expression was: "all peoples except one." Origen's expression was rather stated thus: "all peoples without exception, including the Jewish people," and what is more, this is the people that the Lord chose, the "portion of the Lord."[16] It is much more a matter of going from Jerusalem to the "Nations," provided that the "Nations" do not cause forgetting Jerusalem.

Patristic anthropology was, to a large extent, developed at the confluence of the biblical source and the Greco-Roman heritage. Is this merely a fact from the historical order, or is it rather necessary to think of this fact as itself having a stake for contemporary thought? In order to respond to this question, we will refer to a reflection of Henri-Irénée Marrou. He points out that the Christians of the first centuries did not create their own religious schools in the Greco-Roman world; on the other hand, they did create them "whenever the Church was set up in a 'barbarian' land, that is, one that had not assimilated classical culture;" in Egypt, in Syria, and in Mesopotamia, Christianity enlivened the local languages and caused the flowering of literature and education in Coptic and Syriac; Christians also promoted Ethiopian as a literary language, as well as Armenian and Georgian, and much later Slavic (with Cyril and Methodius).

> But, I repeat, there was nothing like this in the original Graeco-Latin cultural area. Never throughout the whole of antiquity, except for a few particular cases, did the Christians set up their own special schools. They simply added their own specifically religious kind of training—which, as we have seen, came from the Church and the family—on to the classical teaching that they received along with their non-Christians fellows in the established schools.

This is a surprising and significant fact: "from very early times a connection was established between classicism and Christianity—a connection that the historian knows to have been very enduring." "Deplorable or providential," continues Marrou,

15. This is also evidence of the commitment of the Fathers of the Church to scrutinize tirelessly the letter of the First Testament.

16. Cf. Dt 32:9 (in the Septuagint).

the fact is very clear: Christianity was born in Hellenistic Palestine and developed in the midst of Graeco-Roman civilization—and it was everlastingly affected by it. Even when the Gospel is preached to the Chinese or the Bantus it is impossible to forget that it was first written in Greek. This is as inescapable as the fact that Buddhism made its first appearance in India or that the Koran was first written in Arabic.

Why this fact? One can think of a first explanation: Christianity is above all a religion and not, first of all, a cultural ideal; and it pursued what was most urgent by building up dogmas, a morality, a canonical discipline, and a liturgy (rather than creating from the beginning Christian schools). There is, moreover, a phenomenon of "cultural osmosis"; the adoption by Christians of Greek and Latin schools is a remarkable example of this:

precisely because they were living in a classical world, the Christians of the early centuries accepted the fundamental category of Hellenistic humanism as "natural" and self-evident—the view of man as an unconditioned source of value existing before any particular specification took place in him. It might be said that before one can be a Christian one must first be a man, mature enough on the purely human level to be able to perform an act of faith and acts of morality.[17]

For, continues Marrou, since classical education "had developed its own admirable technique for producing a perfectly developed type of human being," why look for another system of education?

However that may be, the moment arrives when on the fully human being it becomes necessary to graft the purely religious shoot of a supernatural Gift. In some way the unchanging technique of classical humanism made it marvelously apt for having the golden branch of the order of grace grafted on to it. A man educated to classical standards could become an orator or a philosopher, whichever he liked; he could choose the life of action or the life of contemplation. He was now offered a further choice, with the announcement of the Good Tidings: besides these things he could now lay himself open to grace, to faith, could receive the sacrament of Baptism, could become a Christian.[18]

17. Henri-Irénée Marrou, *A History of Education in Antiquity*, trans. George Lamb (New York, N.Y.: The New American Library of World Literature, 1956), 425; *Histoire de l'éducation dans l'Antiquité*, 2nd rev. ed. (Paris: Seuil, 1950), 422–23. The preceding excerpts are taken from pages 423–24 in the English translation (pp. 420–21 in the French edition).

18. Marrou, *A History of Education in Antiquity*, 426; *Histoire de l'éducation dans l'Antiquité*, 423.

Of course, as Marrou immediately clarifies (and as we ourselves have recalled above), this does not mean that there were not difficulties nor conflicts between Christianity and the Greco-Roman world. All apologetic literature is evidence of this. But the fact remains that Christianity found in or chose from the Greco-Roman view of the world and of humanity some traits upon which it was rightly able to rely in order to transmit the message of the Gospel. From this point of view, the link between early Christianity and this Greco-Roman culture is not able to be simply considered as accidental or circumstantial; or more exactly, through its very contingency, it says something essential that all contemporary anthropology must in its own way take into account—not only in the West but also in India and the Far East.[19] This is what we would like to clarify by showing how the anthropology of the Fathers proves to be an essential reference for thinking about the world of humanity and humanity in the world.

The World of Humanity

We will first enumerate three traits that characterize the world of humanity according to the Fathers, the first two being expressed in a negative way, the third in a positive one. For the Fathers, the world in which mankind's existence unfolds *is not an illusion*. We perceive the importance of this remark in the context of the intercultural and interreligious debates of our day. For Hinduism, the world is maya, illusion; and every effort of the sage consists in rightly freeing oneself from this world in order to become one with Brahman (the Absolute) and, in this way, to escape the cycle of rebirths. Even more radically, Buddhism considers that mankind is itself in the illusion when it recognizes a "self" capable of becoming one with the Absolute: the way of awakening actually consists in the deliverance from this very illusion. Yet patristic anthropology testifies to another view of this world of humanity. Admittedly, the Fathers knew very well that the form of this world must pass away. They sometimes (as, for example, Gregory of Nyssa in his *Homélies sur l'Ecclésiaste*)[20] comment on the famous

19. This, of course, does not mean that Western Christianity ought to impose all its language on the theologies developed outside of the West!

20. Cf. Grégoire de Nysse, *Homélies sur l'Ecclésiaste*, I, 3 ff., trans. Françoise Vinel, SC 416 (Paris: Cerf, 1996), 113 ff.

verses from Qoheleth on the vanity of things here below; and the desert Fathers show a remarkable lucidity on all the ways that human beings can have of giving to the world an absolute weight that it does not have. The fact remains that the world is not an illusion; it has the solidity and the consistency of what has been created, of what is received from God. And even if it is destined to pass away by death, it today has the weight of the reality that God has given it; and it is also the very place that the human being can, in various ways, leave his own imprint.

Secondly, the world of humanity as the Fathers presented it to us is a world *that does not experience the succession of cycles* over the course of which the same things would be indefinitely repeated. The Fathers were here in opposition to some movements from the Greco-Roman tradition. They indeed knew that one finds, in Pythagoreanism and in other schools, the idea of a periodic re-beginning of the same things. Celsus wrote: "The period of mortal life is similar from beginning to end, and it is inevitable that according to the determined cycles the same things always happened, are now happening, and will happen."[21] It is true that this theory is also refuted by all that, from this same Greco-Roman world, supports an affirmation of history, with the idea that the events of this history are not repeated as such (neither in this life nor in another) and that they, on the contrary, give way to the totally new, to the newness of the unexpected. But the Fathers precisely took up this idea; they contrasted it with theories of successive cycles. They wanted to substantiate the history of salvation as the Bible taught it to them and, more than this, the great innovation that the coming of the Son of God into our world and his resurrection from the dead represented for them. Thus Augustine writes in *The City of God*:

> It was this controversy [the controversy over the beginning of the things of time] that led the natural philosophers to believe that the only way they could or should solve it was by a theory of periodic cycles of time according to which there always has been and will be a continual renewal and repetition in order of nature, because the coming and passing ages revolve as on a wheel....
>
> Far be it from us ... to believe this.
>
> For, Christ died once for our sins; and "having risen from the dead, dies now no more, death shall no longer have dominion over him" ...

21. According to *Contra Celsum*, IV, 65; Chadwick, 236; *Contre Celse*, SC 136, 347.

> Therefore, with these hypothetical rotations brought to a stop [*circuitus illi iam explosi sunt*], we need not suppose that the soul will return to its former misery.[22]

From this perspective, the patristic view of the world has a meaning that is more relevant than ever for a time when Christianity finds itself faced with Eastern traditions that, in their cosmological and anthropological bases, assume a cyclical vision of the world and its unfolding.

Lastly, the world as the Fathers present it to us is precisely the world of the *human being*, that is, a world in which the human being holds a central place and for which he must exercise a major *responsibility*. No patristic text has said this as powerfully as what is written in *To Diognetus*:

> To put the matter simply, what the soul is in the body, this is what Christians are in the world. The soul is spread throughout all the limbs of the body; Christians are spread throughout the cities of the world. The soul lives in the body, but it does not belong to the body; Christians live in the world but do not belong to the world. The soul, which is invisible, is put under guard in the visible body; Christians are known to be in the world, but their worship of God remains invisible. The flesh hates the soul and attacks it, even though it has suffered no harm, because it is hindered from indulging in its pleasures. And the world hates the Christians, even though it has suffered no harm, because they are opposed to its pleasures. The soul loves the flesh that hates it, along with its limbs; Christians love those who hate them. The soul is imprisoned in the body, but it sustains [or constrains] the body; Christians are detained in the prison of the world, but they sustain [or constrain] the world. The soul, which is immortal, dwells in a mortal tent; Christians temporarily dwell in perishable surroundings but await that which is imperishable in the heavens. The soul grows stronger even when mistreated by what the body eats and drinks; Christians increase daily even when punished. God has appointed them to such a position, and it would not be right for them to abandon it.[23]

22. Augustine, *The City of God*, XII, 14 and 21, trans. Gerald G. Walsh and Grace Monahan, Fathers of the Church 14 (Washington, D.C.: The Catholic University of America, 1952), 267–69, and 287. See also Augustin, *La Cité de Dieu*, XII, 14 and 21, trans. G. Combès, Bibliothèque augustinienne 35 (Paris: Desclée de Brouwer, 1959), 191, 195, and 227.

23. *Epistle to Diognetus*, 6, trans. Bart D. Ehrman, in *The Apostolic Fathers*, vol. 2, Loeb Classical Library 25 (Cambridge, Mass.: Harvard University Press, 2003), 141–43. See also *À Diognète*, VI, trans. Henri-Irénée Marrou, 2nd. ed., SC 33 (Paris: Cerf, 1965), 65–67.

Here let us not denounce a dualism of the soul and the body! This would be missing an essential point: the paradoxical condition of Christians who, without being "of this world," are truly "in the world" and "preserve the world." This last expression, which one finds in other forms in other patristic writings, above all echoes the words of Jesus in the Sermon on the Mount: "you are the salt of the earth … you are the light of the world" (Mt 5:13 and 14). This notably stands out in Clement's homily *Who Is the Rich Man that Shall Be Saved*?:

All the faithful then are generous and give honor to God, worthy of the name that they wear as a diadem. However, from now on, some are elected from among the elect, and they are all the more so for not trying to attract attention, withdrawing in some way from the tempests of this world and taking refuge in a safe place. They do not wish to seem to be saints, and they blush from thus being called. They hide the ineffable mysteries in the depths of their mind, and they disdain causing their nobility to be seen in the world. The Word calls them *the light of the world and the salt of the earth.* It is the seed, the image and likeness of God, His true son and heir, sent here below as if in a strange land for a great harmonious design of the Father. By his intermediary, the visible world and the invisible world have been created, either for service, or for training, or for formation. For as long as this seed remains here below, everything remains coherent, but, once it has been harvested, all will be very quickly dissolved.[24]

One could object that the position thus recognized in mankind amounts to assigning to it a place of too much importance: would it not hide, under the cover of the reference to mankind created in the image of God, an anthropocentrism completely unjustified? In fact, the objection was already raised in Antiquity. Celsus thus attributed to the Jews and the Christians the following statements:

God shows and proclaims everything to us beforehand, and He has even deserted the whole world and the motion of the heavens, and disregarded the vast earth to give attention to us alone; and He sends messengers to us alone and never stops sending them and seeking that we may be with Him for ever. There is God first, and we are next after Him in rank since He has made us entirely like God, and all things have been put under us, earth, water, air, and stars; and all things exist for our benefit, and have been appointed to serve us.[25]

24. Clément d'Alexandrie, *Quel riche sera sauvé?* 36, 1–3, trans. Patrick Descourtieux, SC 537 (Paris: Cerf, 2011), 193–95; cf. (in addition to Mt 5:13–14) Gn 1:26, Ti 1:4; Rom 8:17.

25. According to Origen, *Contra Celsum*, IV, 23; Chadwick, 199–200; *Contre Celse*, SC 136, 239.

Later Celsus accused Christians of asserting "that God made all things for man" and, in describing animals, claimed to show that "everything was made just as much for the irrational animals as for men."[26] But Origen responded precisely to these objections. On one hand, he said, Celsus attributes to us "statements which we do not make. For we both read and know that God 'loves everything that exists and hates nothing that He has made'" (Wis 11:24); "How can we say that *God has left the motion of the heavens and the whole world, and has disregarded the vast earth to give attention to us alone*?"[27] On the other hand, Celsus did not understand the difference between "image" and "likeness": "However, if he had realized the difference between man being made in God's image and being made in His likeness, and that though God is recorded to have said 'Let us make man in our image and likeness' God only made man in the image of God, but not yet as His likeness, then he would not have made us say that *we are like God in every way*."[28] What is more, the Stoics themselves place humanity, and in general rational nature, above all beings without reason: "providence primarily cares for the rational beings, while the fact that the irrational animals also share in what is made for men has been a subsidiary result."[29] And the fact that mankind is weak on some points was precisely for him the occasion to exercise his intelligence, which is superior to all the powers of beasts.[30] Origen concludes: "I think I have shown by what has already been said how all things have been made for man and every rational creature; for all things have been created primarily on account of the rational being."[31] The objection formerly expressed by Celsus undoubtedly reflected a basic difficulty that has only become more pronounced in the contemporary era: the increased knowledge that we have of the infinitely great and the infinitely small but also our new attention to nature and to some developments of ecology, which easily lead to an extreme relativization of

26. Origen, *Contra Celsum*, IV, 74; Chadwick, 242–43; *Contre Celse*, SC 136, 367–69; see the exposition up to IV, 99.

27. Origen, *Contra Celsum*, IV, 28; Chadwick, 203; *Contre Celse*, SC 136, 251.

28. Origen, *Contra Celsum*, IV, 30; Chadwick, 205; *Contre Celse*, SC 136, 255.

29. Origen, *Contra Celsum*, IV, 74; Chadwick, 243; *Contre Celse*, SC 136, 369.

30. Origen, *Contra Celsum*, IV, 76 and 78; Chadwick, 244–46; *Contre Celse*, SC 136, 375 and 379.

31. Origen, *Contra Celsum*, IV, 99; Chadwick, 262; *Contre Celse*, SC 136, 433.

humanity and its place in the universe. But it is at this very place that patristic anthropology remains a source for our reflection. One could say, in stepping back from the debate between Origen and Celsus, that this patristic anthropology grants to the human being a place that is neither absolute nor exclusive but that is both central and subordinate. A place neither absolute nor exclusive: the Fathers well know that an individual is not the Absolute (otherwise, the result would be self-idolatry), and that he is surrounded by a multitude of beings—moreover, not only irrational animals but also angelic creatures.[32] And, nevertheless, a central and subordinate place: central in the sense that the other things on the face of the earth are made for humanity; subordinate in the sense that these things are given to mankind not so that it may use them egotistically but so that, by them, it glorifies its Creator. There is a responsibility proper to humanity in the world, but this is so that God Himself may be glorified.[33]

From there, what remains is to clarify what, according to the Fathers, justifies the place of the human being in the universe. If the world is truly the world of humanity, what then is humanity that it holds such a position and exercises such a responsibility?

Humanity in the World

One could respond concisely: what, for the Fathers, gives this importance to humanity in the world is that it is created in the image of God. But the question rebounds: what content to give to this expression; in what way does this content interest us today? We will respond by bringing out three essential characteristics of the patristic vision of humanity and highlighting their stakes.

Humanity is first understood as *a being of reason and speech*. Unfortunately, it is necessary for us to use here two words where the Greeks Fathers used only one; they said: humanity is *logikos*, it participates in the *Logos*.

32. For the Fathers, the existence of angels calls the human being to, among other things, humility, that of a being that cannot claim the pretense of being the only rational creature.

33. One thinks about the views of Teilhard so aware, on one hand, of the infinite multiplicity of things that make up the universe but so conscious, also, of the unique place of the human being and his responsibility in the evolution toward the Omega point.

One has sometimes held that the Fathers' anthropology put the accent on rationality, on intellectuality, on abstraction, and that it was in this way contaminated by the Greek heritage. This suspicion lies, in fact, on two ambiguities. On one hand, one is projecting onto the Fathers some erroneous trends of what one later called rationalism, to the point of making them responsible for what was later to be wrongly perpetuated in the name of reason; yet, as much as it is necessary to be lucid and critical about the erroneous trends in question, it is as important to recognize the truth that is being spoken through the determination of mankind as a rational being. That mankind so often perverts the use of reason does not put into question the fact that reason is offered to him as a gift. On the other hand, the suspicion consists in forgetting that the Fathers, at the same time as they took up the heritage of the Greek *logos* as reason, claimed to follow the biblical tradition of the *logos* as word. It is not necessary to imply that their reprise of the concept of *logos* was, itself, an infidelity to the biblical tradition of the word. Actually, the Fathers found in this word *logos* the possibility of saying at the same time reason and word. When apologists speak of the seeds of the *Logos* spread throughout the universe, they mean by this the seeds of Reason *and* of the Word, both being identified actually in the *Logos* of God who is himself Word and Reason: the Word is Reason, the Reason is Word. Therefore, to say of the human being that he is *logikos* is to say that he is inseparably a being of reason and a being of speech. Instead of being tempted to separate these two notions, or to contrast them with each other, we have to understand, throughout the writings of the Fathers, a vision that highlights the unity of the human being as that of a being called to speak in a reasonable and sensible manner, and to show his reason in his very way of inhabiting the language and addressing the word to others.

The second contribution of the Fathers to contemporary anthropology consists in their emphasis on *freedom*. To be in the image of God is to be free. One cannot overly stress this point, all the more remarkable as the Fathers lived in a world believed to be governed by gods or by various forms of destiny (with all the kinds of fatalistic beliefs that could result from them). The Fathers' anthropology is, to a large extent, an homage made to the freedom of the human being.

It is true that this homage could appear to be contradicted, up to a certain point, by the thought of Augustine and his emphasis on grace; but (even though it is necessary not to project onto Augustine the various subsequent doctrines of "Augustinianism") it is here necessary to recognize that the bishop of Hippo had to react against the position of Pelagius and his followers who, in the extreme, made the gift of God superfluous. In fact, in his own response to Pelagius, Augustine did not fail to speak to a large extent on the importance of human freedom. Be that as it may, the controversies on grace and freedom in the West must not lead to forgetting the Fathers' emphasis, throughout the patristic era, on humanity's freedom.

One can at least recall two particularly significant names. First, that of Irenaeus, who against the Gnostics develops a very high concept of human freedom:

> But man is endowed with reason and, in this respect, similar to God, created free and master of his actions, he is himself the cause of his becoming sometimes wheat and sometimes chaff....
>
> This statement: "how often would I have gathered your children together and you would not" (Mt 23:37) clearly illustrated the ancient law of the freedom of mankind. Because God made man a free agent possessing from the beginning his own faculty to make decisions, even as he does his own soul, to follow the advice of God voluntarily and without duress from God. Coercion, indeed, in no way is with God, but good advice is always present with Him. And this is why, on one hand, He does give good counsel to all; on the other, He has placed the power of choice with mankind....
>
> God has given that which is good ... and they who do it shall receive glory and honor because they have done that which is good when they could have not done it, whereas those who do not do it will be subjected to the just judgment of God for not having done the good that they could have done.... All are of the same nature, able both to keep and to do what is good, also being able to reject it and not to do it....
>
> Mankind is free to make decisions since the beginning—for God also is free to make decisions, He in whose likeness man was precisely created—also, at any time, he is advised to keep the good, which is accomplished by obedience to God.[34]

34. Irénée, *Contre les hérésies*, IV, 4, 3; 37, 1; 37, 4; Rousseau, 414, 545, 546, and 548; *Against the Heresies*, 466 and 518–19.

The second name to mention is that of Maximus the Confessor, who in the seventh century fought with all his might the position called Monothelite, according to which Christ could have had only one will (his human will being as such absorbed by the divine nature); Maximus opposes this with Christ's being free even in his agony: Jesus said "if it be possible, let this cup pass from me," and it is with all his freedom that he added "nevertheless, not as I will, but as thou wilt" (Mt 26:39). Christ's submission to the will of his Father does not mean that he was not free, but that in his freedom he precisely made the choice to abandon himself unreservedly to this will of his Father.[35] This Christological reflection shows at the same time what true humanity is: Christ would not have been truly man if he had not had such a human will, for the possession of such a will (and of the freedom that accompanies it) is an essential mark of humanity.

Lastly, the patristic view of the human being is that of a human being as *person*. This word "person," of course, is only progressively imposed over the course of the patristic era; first in the context of the Trinitarian and Christological debates that were carried out to clarify the meaning of the Greek term *prosôpon*, and, especially, the term *hypostasis*; but it was exactly in this very way that it made a major contribution to anthropology. With this concept can be associated several notions of great importance. In the first place, the notion of dignity: we will return to it in the next chapter when we mention the Fathers' homilies on esteem and love for the poor and their exhortations to promote social justice. In the second place, person includes unicity. Indeed, the notion of *hypostasis* is understood in relation to that of "essence" (*ousia*) and of "nature" (*physis*). Human nature is what all humans have in common and what distinguishes them from beings that belong to other orders; the person, in contrast, is what makes each human being different from the others. In each person, nature, all the while preserving what makes up his essence (the *logos* of his nature, according to Maximus), receives a singular mode of existence (*tropos*, again according to Maximus). And John Damascene writes: "the subsistences do not exist one within the other, but each one individually and separately, that is to say, each is constituted according to itself

35. See Maxime le Confesseur, *Opuscules théologiques et polémiques*, trans. Emmanuel Ponsoye, Les Pères dans la foi 64 (Paris: Cerf, 1996).

with quite numerous traits that distinguish it from others: space separates them, a point in time distinguishes them; a life choice separates them as well as strength, shape and appearance, habits, temperament, way of living, in short, all the properly characteristic traits and, above all, the fact that they exist in one another but separately."[36] The Father's anthropology here makes an important point, in particular in view of the debates with the cultures of India and the Far East. This does not mean that the concept of person can be immediately translated into Chinese or Japanese, but this does mean that there would not be a Christian anthropology in China or in Japan (nor a Christology either) if one did not find, in these very cultures, ways of expressing an equivalent notion. Another connotation of the concept of person must still be raised, that of relationship. Here once again is seen the contribution of Trinitarian theology to anthropology: the Greek Fathers, beginning with Basil, deepened the meaning of the intra-Trinitarian relationships; and this was later also going to be reflected in anthropology and to promote the understanding of the human person as a relational being.

A being of reason and speech; a being of freedom; a personal being: these are three essential aspects of humanity according to the view of the Fathers of the Church, and these aspects can be held to be constitutive of a Christian anthropology. We hope to have thus confirmed the thesis stated above: the anthropology of the Fathers, heir to the biblical tradition and the Greco-Roman tradition, remains an important reference for thinking about the world of humanity and humanity in the world, including the intercultural and interreligious debates of our times. But what was just said still does not suffice to characterize the anthropology of the Fathers nor its contribution to contemporary theology. What indeed remains is to highlight that this anthropology has to be understood above all by its Christological reference: because Christ was truly human and perfect man, it is in the end this reference to Christ that gives a foundation to the patristic view of the human being. We have already suggested this when we mentioned Christ regarding other themes (as that of freedom); this

36. Jean Damascène, *La Foi orthodoxe*, I, 8, trans. P. Ledrux, SC 535 (Paris: Cerf, 2010), 183–85; cf. J.-C. Larchet, *Pour une éthique de la procréation. Éléments d'anthropologie patristique* [For an ethics of procreation. Elements of patristic anthropology] (Paris: Cerf, 1998), 155.

aspect presently deserves to be developed for itself: according to the Fathers, it is very much the relationship with Christ, and the belonging to Christ, that is ultimately constitutive of the human being.

The Belonging to Christ

The Fathers are very aware that mankind, such as it is concretely, does not respond to its original vocation. The work of Christ is presented from this perspective as a work of rebuilding, of the restoration of humanity to its dignity, of healing, or quite simply of "salvation." This then is an essential aspect of patristic anthropology: one cannot consider the human being according to his single vocation; one must also consider him such as he is concretely in history, namely a being affected by evil (in various forms), by violence, by sin, and that Christ comes precisely to free him and to give back to him his true humanity.

But it does not suffice to repeat today the contributions of patristic thought on sin and redemption such as were notably developed by Augustine. It is also important to recognize the view that the Fathers set out more broadly on the mystery of evil and the way in which they expressed the compassion of Christ toward humanity thus wounded. Let us cite, as an example, the interpretation that Origen proposed for the Parable of the Good Samaritan:

> On account of the half-dead man, this Samaritan set out not "from Jerusalem to Jericho," like the priest and the Levite who went down. Or, if he did go down, he went down to rescue and care for the dying man.... So, when he had come to the half-dead man and seen him rolling about in his own blood, he had pity on him. He drew near to him, in order to become his neighbor. "He bound his wounds, poured in oil mixed with wine." ... The Samaritan is that man whose care and help all who are badly off need. The man who was going down from Jerusalem and fell among thieves, who was wounded and left by them half-alive, needed the help of this Samaritan most of all.[37]

Thus the Samaritan is the figure of Christ in his compassion for a wounded human; yet this compassion is in fact exercised toward all humanity:

37. Origen, *Hom Lk*, XXXIV, 5–6. *Homilies on Luke*, 139–40. See also Origène, *Homélies sur Luc*, trans. Henri Crouzel, François Fournier, and Pierre Périchon, SC 87 (Paris: Cerf, 1962), 407. Cf. Lk 10:25–37.

You should know that, according to God's providence, this Samaritan was going down to care for the man who had fallen among thieves. You learn that clearly from the fact that he had bandages, oil, and wine with him. I do not think that the Samaritan carried these things with him only on behalf of that one, half-dead man, but also on behalf of others who, for various reasons, had been wounded and needed bandages, oil, and wine.... He cleans the wounds with oil, to reduce the swelling of the wounds, but also with wine, adding in something that stings. And the man who had been wounded "he placed on his own beast," that is, on his own body, since he deigned to assume a man. This Samaritan "bears our sins" and grieves for us. He carries the half-dead man, and brings him to the *pandochium*—that is, the Church, which accepts everyone and denies its help to no one. Jesus calls everyone to the Church when he says, "Come to me, all you who labor and are burdened, and I shall refresh you."[38]

It is truly a matter, throughout this text, of sin and salvation, but it is even more a matter of humanity affected by evil and healed by the compassion of Christ—and we can think that such language particularly has something to say to a contemporary anthropology. The parable represents for Origen the situation of every human: it is every human who in one way or another is "half dead" and abandoned on the side of the road; and it is this wounded human that the Samaritan has just picked up and cared for—the Samaritan, that is, the Son of God in person who has "deigned to assume our humanity" so that our wounds may be healed and that the image of God may be restored in us. Such is the passion for humanity in God, a passion that leads Him to meet with the wounded being in order to return him to his true humanity—through which he himself will receive a part in the divine filiation.

Ecce homo, "Here is the man!" said Pilate in presenting Jesus to the crowd (Jn 19:5): Christ is not less a human at the hour of the Passion, he is never more so—not, of course, because of the Passion as such but because through this Passion is expressed the profundity of a gift that gives its utmost and that is constitutive of true humanity (at the same time that it expresses the very life of God). Henceforth, the believer is himself called to follow Christ, and it is in giving himself in his turn that he accomplishes his human existence. The anthropology

38. Origen, *Hom Lk*, XXXIV, 6–7; *Homilies on Luke*, 140. See also *Homélies sur Luc*, 407–9. Cf. Mt 8:17 (Is 53:4); Mt 11:28.

is, again in this sense, very determined by Christology, and one finds evidence of it in some of the writings of Christian Antiquity. The acts of the martyrs, in particular, present men and women who have given their utmost in their relationship with Christ—as far as the gift of their life—and who from that have realized their vocation as men and women created in the image of God. One of the most remarkable expressions of this theme is, however, found, not in these acts, but in a letter from Ignatius of Antioch who is preparing himself to experience torture and who, prior to it, asks not to be diverted from his way:

> *I would rather die* and come to Jesus Christ than be king over the entire earth. Him I seek who died for us; Him I love who rose again because of us. The birth pangs are upon me. Forgive, brethren; do not obstruct my coming to life—do not wish me to die; do not make a gift to the world of one who wants to be God's. Beware of seducing me with matter; suffer me to receive pure light. Once arrived there, I shall be a man. Permit me to be an imitator of my suffering God. If anyone holds Him in his heart, let him understand what I am aspiring to; and then let him sympathize with me, knowing in what distress I am.[39]

This text of Ignatius in fact associates death and life, implying how following Christ up to the total gift of oneself is, paradoxically, the entrance into true humanity. Yet this last theme is also developed for itself in patristic literature. It emerges from all the writings on the resurrection, understood as a resurrection of the flesh—as distinguished from the simple immortality of the soul, as well as from reincarnation. A simple immortality of the soul would mutilate the future of humanity by depriving it of what is so essential for it: its capacity to be in relationship. A reincarnation, despite its ties to resurrection, would not adequately recognize humanity's vocation as Gregory of Nyssa explains it:

39. Ignatius of Antioch, *To the Romans*, VI, 1–3, trans. James A. Kleist, Ancient Christian Writers 1 (Westminster, Mass.: The Newman Bookshop, 1946), 83. See also Ignace d'Antioche, *Aux Romains*, VI, 1–3, trans. Pierre Thomas Camelot, 2nd. ed., SC 10 (Paris: Cerf, 1998), 113–15. One also reads in another letter, regarding Christ himself: "There is only one doctor, physical and spiritual, begotten and unbegotten, come in flesh, God, in death true life, born of Mary and born of God, first passible and now impassible, Jesus Christ our Lord"; *Aux Éphésiens*, VII, 2; translated into French, SC 10, 65). The phrase "come in the flesh, God" can rather be understood as follows: "became in the flesh God," an expression that must clearly not be taken in an adoptionist sense but that draws attention to the fact that the "flesh" (and thus also the crucified flesh) was for Jesus himself the way of his divine holiness.

Some insult humanity by invoking a community [of nature]. They decree that the soul is the same, in turn in the human and in the beast. It would change bodies as clothing, always passing into what pleases it, becoming, after having been human, a winged, aquatic or terrestrial animal, after which it would again return to human nature....

... this amounts to thinking that everything is confused, that the nature in beings is unique, everything mixed into a blurred and confused unity; no particular trait would distinguish one nature from another.[40]

Resurrection, such as it is revealed by Scripture, is thus understood as that which alone gives to humanity a true future. By it, writes Gregory of Nyssa, "God will lead ... our nature toward the first state of mankind":

He has one goal: when the complete fulfilment of our nature will have been achieved in each human, while some will have been without delay purified from sin in this life, others will have been, after this life, healed by fire for as long as is necessary, and still others, here below, will not have experienced neither good nor evil, then [God] will offer to all to take part in that which is good in Him and of which Scripture says that the eye does not see, that the ear does not hear and that thought does not understand. This is nothing other than, according to my judgment, to be in God Himself, for the good which is inaccessible to the ear, the eye, and the heart can only be that which is located above the universe.[41]

Thus, on the foundation of the resurrection of Christ, the resurrection of the dead is thought of as the fulfillment of humanity beyond death. A perspective that was already Irenaeus's: "The glory of God is the living human, and the life of the human is the vision of God."[42] The anthropology of the Fathers thus passes on to contemporary theology the task of thinking about the resurrection as the fulfillment of the becoming-man beyond death, and this on the same foundation that has already been revealed through the resurrection of the "the first-born from the dead" (Col 1:18).

40. Gregory of Nyssa, *L'âme et la résurrection* [The soul and resurrection], 89 and 92, trans. Christian Bouchet, Les Pères dans la foi 73 (Paris: Migne, 1998), 83 and 85; cf. 1 Cor 2:9.

41. Gregory of Nyssa, *L'âme et la résurrection*, 127 and 128; Bouchet 113–14.

42. Irénée, *Contre les hérésies*, IV, 20, 7; Rousseau, 474; other trans.: "The glory of God is a living man; and the life of man consists in beholding God," *Against Heresies*, 490. For a detailed presentation of the eschatology of the Fathers, see Brian Daley, *The Hope of the Early Church: A Handbook of Patristic Eschatology* (Cambridge: Cambridge University Press, 1991).

But the saints already offer us a kind of anticipation of this fulfillment, and it is thus finally to the experience of holiness in history that we are referred. The anthropology of the Fathers is nourished not only by the reference to the new humanity that was Jesus Christ on this earth but by the reference to those who in the present time incarnate this new humanity that they receive from their belonging to Christ and that makes them as intermediaries between earth and heaven: some human beings who are, in their very humanity, "temples of the Spirit"—already realizing, at least within the limits of our world, the figure of living mankind such as it is called to be, beyond death, in the light of God.

Patristic anthropology is thus inspired by the "passion of humanity"—this is at the same time out of esteem for mankind, concern for each human, the desire to accept the best heritage of human traditions, interest in the world that is the dwelling of mankind, the awareness of what causes the singularity and the dignity of mankind in this world, and lastly, the recognition of the gift manifested by God vis-à-vis humanity and the call that He addresses to mankind so that, in his Son, it may achieve the perfect fulfillment of its humanity—a fulfillment that coincides with communion with the divine life, of which the experience of holiness already represents the anticipation at the very heart of our history.

Of course, one will ask, what authorizes placing at the fore, a "passion of humanity," when one additionally knows the importance that some Fathers gave to the experience of "impassibility" (*apatheia*)? These Fathers assuredly had a high ideal of such an "impassibility," which means for them the surpassing of numerous mythological representations regarding the *pathos* attributed to divinities and the freedom from all sorts of passions that divert from union with God. But *apatheia* is not the last word of patristic anthropology; it is rather what makes possible the surpassing of impassibility itself for a new form of "passion": the passion that is itself the gift of the love for the other or, in biblical terms, *agapè*.

It remains to suggest that the "passion of humanity," thus understood, is in some manner inscribed in the eternity of God. One could here recall that Origen, who could not be suspected of calling into question the ideal of impassibility, however, did not fear saying that "the Father himself is not without suffering."[43] One could also recall the theme of the divine *philanthropia* from Clement of Alexandria to Maximus the Confessor. But Denys the Areopagite is undoubtedly the one who knew how best to express this deep-rootedness, in God even, of a "passion of humanity"—not hesitating moreover, to qualify this "passion" by appealing to the language of amorous desire (*erôs*):

> This divine yearning brings ecstasy so that the lover belongs not to self but to the beloved.... This is why the great Paul, swept along by his yearning for God and seized of its ecstatic power, had this inspired word to say: "It is no longer I who live, but Christ who lives in me." Paul was truly a lover, and, as he says, he was beside himself for God, possessing not his own life but the life of the One for whom he yearned, as exceptionally beloved.
>
> And, in truth, it must be said too that the very cause of the universe in the beautiful, good superabundance of his benign yearning for all is also carried outside of himself in the loving care he has for everything. He is, as it were, beguiled by goodness, by love, and by yearning.[44]

Nothing, in this, undermines the perfect transcendence of God; but quite the contrary, it is all the more extraordinary that the perfectly transcendent God, paradoxically, "leaves Himself" for love of humanity.

> [He] is enticed away from his transcendent dwelling place and comes to abide within all things, and he does so by virtue of his supernatural and ecstatic capacity to remain, nevertheless, within himself. That is why those possessed of spiritual insight describe him as "zealous" because his good yearning for all things is so great and because he stirs in men a deep yearning desire for zeal. In this way he proves himself to be zealous for the creatures for whom he provides. In short, both the yearning and the object of that yearning belong to the Beautiful and the Good. They preexist in it, and because of it they exist and come to be.[45]

Here we grasp how the anthropology of the Fathers finds its deep-rootedness first and ultimately in *theologia* in the strongest meaning of the word. If *apatheia*, which is victory over the passions, is in its turn

43. Origen, *Homilies 1–14 on Ezechiel*, 93.

44. Pseudo-Dionysius, *The Divine Names*, 4, 13, in *The Complete Works*, trans. Colm Luibheid, Classics of Western Spirituality (Mahwah, N.J.: Paulist Press, 1987), 82. See also the French translation of Maurice de Gandillac, *Les noms divins*, in *Œuvres complètes du Pseudo-Denys l'Aréopagite* (Paris: Aubier-Montaigne, 1943), 107; and of Ysabel de Andia, *Les noms divins*, SC 578 and 579 (Paris : Cerf, 2016), 475–77.

45. Pseudo-Dionysius, *The Divine Names*, 4, 13 (Luibheid, 82).

conquered by the passion of humanity, it is that this passion exists in God Himself as a superabundant love for mankind. Patristic literature does not ask us only to think today about the passion of humanity but also to contemplate at length the ineffable Source from which it proceeds—in this original place where it is no longer a matter of thinking about mankind before God but of God's own look at mankind.

CHAPTER 10

The Contribution to Christian Ethics

Patristic anthropology, as presented in the preceding chapter, necessarily leads to presentations on what must be considered as "good" or as "bad" for the human being. We must now consider this aspect in itself and show how patristic literature makes its own contribution to ethical thought. We will, of course, only be able to do this in a limited way, as the subject is so vast.

We will begin with some general remarks on the place of ethics in the writings of the Fathers; we will then focus on three specific areas in which their thought is employed: first, in questions relating to procreation and the end of life; then, in questions affecting connections with the State or, more broadly, the commitment of Christians as citizens; lastly, in questions concerning the use of wealth and the attitude toward the poor.

The Place of Ethics in the Writings of the Fathers

Ethics is very much present in the literature of early Christianity, and one can be convinced of this by considering some texts from quite diverse genres that, each in its own way, place great emphasis on it. It is already the case in the earliest writings, such as Clement of Rome's letter to the Corinthians: on the occasion of a crisis that arose among the Christians of Corinth (namely the dismissal of some "presbyters"), the author develops long paraeneses against envy and jealousy, which are the cause of the dissents, as well as exhortations on humility, concord, and unity. The instruction as it is given refers to biblical models and, above all, to the example of Christ himself; in this way, the Corinthians are precisely invited to be converted in order to live in harmony and peace. The writing of Clement must be read from the same perspective as the paraeneses that conclude Paul's epistles: the moral exhortations must not be detached from the instruction on the faith but are intimately linked to it.

The same could be said about numerous letters that have come to us from the patristic era. Let us think about, for example, those of Cyprian, Basil, John Chrysostom, Jerome, and Augustine: one very often finds in them expositions on questions of morality, but these expositions (whatever may be their possible relationship with doctrines from Greek or Latin moralists) must furthermore be understood in the light of what these same authors say on the Revelation of the God of Jesus Christ and on its importance for human existence. Being perceived in this way avoids the suspicion of "moralism"; because for the Fathers, what is at stake through the practice of the good is, after all is said and done, actual conformity to Christ and fidelity to his Spirit. This deep connection with Revelation appears quite particularly in some of the writings from the homiletic genre: meditations occasioned by biblical passages that, in this instance, call for teachings on this or that virtue or vice and on the way in which Christians must behave in their personal, social, and ecclesial life.

The same connection is confirmed by some treatises on moral questions, a remarkable example of which is *The Paedagogus* of Clement of Alexandria. This work follows upon the *Protrepticus*, in which the "*Logos*" exhorted turning away from idolatry to salvation; now, he is addressing converts who have entered the Church:

> being at once curative and preceptive, following in His own steps, He makes what had been prescribed the subject of persuasion, promising the cure of the passion within us. Let us then designate this Word appropriately by the one name *Tutor* (or *Pedagogue*, or *Instructor*).
>
> The Instructor being practical, not theoretical, His aim is thus to improve the soul, not to teach, and to train it up to a virtuous, not to an intellectual life.[1]

1. Clement of Alexandria, *The Instructor* (*Paedagogus*), I, 1: *Fathers of the Second Century*, 209.

The stage of "science," that is, of a deeper knowledge, will in fact come later: Clement will treat it in the *Stromata*. The subject of the work *The Pedagogue* is itself the telling of how the *Logos* educates the human being who has become a Christian. Book I treats the subject in a fundamental way by highlighting the goodness of God and his love for mankind (his *philanthrôpia*). It shows how this goodness is expressed in creation, then in the coming of the *Logos* in our humanity: it is this *Logos*, perfect Image of the Father, that Christians are to reproduce precisely in their souls. Books II and III then give what one can call a "treatise on practical morality." They show how the indwelling of the *Logos* must take shape, concretely, in Christian existence—and this even in the most mundane occurrences: eating and drinking, sleep, work, leisure, etc. Thus, in the mind of Clement, are the reference to the Revelation of Christ and the requirement of a moral life connected. In this very way, the work gives a key for correctly interpreting a number of subsequent treatises on ethical questions. Even when it will not be explicit, one must always presuppose the reference to Christ and his holiness; this is the holiness that the baptized are called to live, to the extent of their fidelity to the Gospel and the way in which they themselves become, by the Spirit, "the image and likeness of God."

The importance of ethics is also shown, and in a central way, in the area of what is properly called exegesis. We have already alluded to this regarding some homilies, but it is above all necessary to recall that the patristic doctrine on the interpretation of the holy books, formulated for the first time by Origen, distinguished several meanings of Scripture, and among them, a "moral meaning" (or "tropological meaning"). Of course, the Jewish exegete Philo of Alexandria already looked for the meaning of the biblical texts for the human soul and for ethical behavior, and, on this point, Origen himself submitted to Philo's influence. However, in Origen the "moral meaning" takes on a new importance by reason of its connection to the Christian mystery. Indeed, even though, in his theoretical exposition of *On First Principles*, he locates this "moral meaning" between the literal meaning and the spiritual meaning, he usually gives to it a different—and very significant—place in his own practice of exegesis: the exposition on the literal meaning is, in this latter case, followed rather by the exposition on the spiritual meaning (that is, on the meaning of the biblical text in the light of Christ), and the exposition on the moral meaning only comes third.[2] What emerges is that this "moral meaning" is itself directed by the spiritual meaning; in other words, for Origen it is a matter of highlighting the importance of the biblical text for the behavior of those who, being Christians, must be conformed to Christ in the entirety of their lives. Thus, we find as well in the field of exegesis what we have seen with Clement's *The Pedagogue*: here also, the teachings with moral significance refer to the Christian mystery and are elucidated by its light.

However, this does not mean that there never was any contact between ethics thus developed and that which one might encounter, during the patristic era, in Greek and Latin philosophers. On the contrary, some Fathers very much took up explanations or exhortations that they found around them, as they appeared to them to be consistent with the biblical tradition. One has particularly emphasized, quite rightly, what they borrowed from the Stoics: all the while rejecting their concept of the world and their pantheist doctrine, the Fathers were often inspired by their reflections from the ethical field.[3] More broadly, the Fathers, for their part, take up all that, in the common morality, corresponds to the values advocated by the biblical tradition. The example of the Apologists in the second century is particularly revealing. On one hand, they, of course, strongly denounce some mores, such as the practice of "exposing newborns" or various forms of prostitution;[4] but on the other, they appeal to the moral conscience witnessed to by the wisdom of the Nations and draw from it an argument for defending Christ's disciples against their adversaries[5] (emphasizing as well, it is true, the unique value of the teaching given in the Sermon on the Mount).[6] Moreover, it is significant that, in the second half of the second century, the philosopher Celsus formulated a schol-

2. Cf. Henri de Lubac, *Histoire et Esprit*, 139–50.

3. See Michel Spanneut, *Le stoïcisme des Pères de l'Église, de Clément de Rome à Clément d'Alexandrie* [The Stoicism of the Fathers of the Church, from Clement of Rome to Clement of Alexandria] (Paris: Seuil, 1957).

4. Thus Justin, "Apology on Behalf of Christians," 27, in *Apologies*, ed. Denis Minns and Paul Parvis, Oxford Early Christian Texts (Oxford: Oxford University Press, 2009), 153–57.

5. See Justin, "The Second Apology," II, 11; *Apologies*, 315–17.

6. See Justin, "The Second Apology," I, 15–16; *Apologies*, 113–21.

arly grievance regarding Christians: their morality is "commonplace" and "in comparison with the other philosophers contains no teaching that is impressive or new."[7] Origen, in the response that opposes Celsus, himself recognizes that all humans have "in accordance with the universal ideas ... a sound conception of moral principles," and he then adds: "There is therefore nothing amazing about it if the same God has implanted in the souls of all men the truths which He taught through the prophets and the Saviour; He did this that every man might be without excuse at the divine judgment, having the requirement of the law written in his heart."[8] Of course, like Justin before him, Origen also shows how, in the area of morality, the teaching of Christ surpasses all the doctrines that appeared before him. He insists no less that this teaching was already "sown in the souls of all humans." The theme is related to the famous doctrine of the *Logos spermatikos*—an expression that Justin had borrowed from Stoicism while giving it a new meaning: the *Logos* of God was already present, in some way, in the centuries that preceded the coming of Christ.[9] This same doctrine is repeated by Clement of Alexandria and Origen in order to take into account what, from the world of the Nations, already attests to some participation in the true God; yet for them, as for Justin, the "seeds of the *Logos*" are notably revealed through the behavior of humans, who, without having known Christ, endeavored to live with honesty, justice, and holiness. Origen's sentence that we have cited above reveals at the same time the scriptural foundation of this concept: the passage from the Letter to the Romans on those of the Nations who "have not the Law" but "do by nature what the Law requires" and "show that what the Law requires is written on their hearts" (Rom 2:14–15). Origen, indeed, makes a major contribution to the thought on the subject of the "law of nature": by which he means, in particular, the ethical exigency of what in it is universal—an exigency that thus serves as a critical authority regarding the "law written by cities":

When the written law does not contradict the law of God it is good that the citizens should not be troubled by the introduction of strange laws. But where

7. According to Origen, *Contra Celsum*, I, 4; Chadwick, 8; Marcel Borret translates into French: their morality is "*banal*" (the Greek word is *koinon*); see *Contre Celse*, SC 132, 85.

8. Origen, *Contra Celsum*, 8–9; *Contre Celse*, SC 132, 85–87.

9. Cf. Justin, "The Second Apology," I, 46, 3; II, 7, 1 and 3; *Apologies*, 201, 297 and 299.

the law of nature, that is of God, enjoins precepts contradictory to the written laws, consider whether reason does not compel a man to dismiss the written code and the intention of the lawgivers far from his mind, and to devote himself to the divine Lawgiver and to choose to live according to His word, even if in doing this he must endure dangers and countless troubles and deaths and shame.[10]

The notion of "natural law" will later give rise to numerous expositions in the cadre of moral theology. It is all the more important to identify it at its source and to discover how it was first utilized by the Fathers—and in particular Origen. It allowed them to speak of the presence of the ethical exigency in the human conscience and thus also of its universality; it also led them to emphasize the status of such an exigency that is irreducible to customs like written laws, and that can, according to the case, be honored or transgressed by them. What the "law of nature" considers, at this depth, is nothing other than the "law of truth" and the "law of God."[11]

Another contribution from patristic literature to moral theology merits being emphasized: that which comes from what is experienced within the framework of monastic life. Of course, the writings of the first Fathers already bear witness to an ethical thought that was strongly rooted in Christian spirituality: as we have seen with Clement of Alexandria, the disciple of Christ ought to reproduce in the entirety of his life the holiness of his master, and this was possible for him to the extent that he was open to the Spirit of God. But the experience of the anchorite and the cenobitic life, as it developed beginning in the third century in the deserts of Egypt, Palestine, Syria, and Asia Minor, caused a remarkable deepening of this life in the Spirit and, as a result, produced some very important fruits in the field of ethics itself. Confronted by a true solitude (above all in the case of the anchorite) and left, so to speak, to their own devices—or rather put into the hands of the One for whom they had left all—the monks with a rare profundity discovered that fidelity to God did not happen only in a battle against the exterior manifestations of idolatry (such as the veneration of statues representing divinities), but, more radically, in a

10. Origen, *Contra Celsum*, V, 37; Chadwick, 293; *Contre Celse*, SC 147, 111–13.

11. Cf. Origen, *Contra Celsum*, I, 1 and V, 37; Chadwick, 7 and 293; *Contre Celse*, SC 132, 81; and *Contre Celse*, SC 147, 113.

battle against the evil spirits that gave rise to all kinds of "passions" or "vices." They learned to recognize the traps into which they could be ensnared, at the same time, as the ways that allowed them to avoid or be delivered from them. The literature of the "Fathers of the Desert" collects the teachings of what was thus lived and, by this fact, represents a major contribution to moral thought—a thought that here, more than elsewhere, is inseparable from an attention to the properly spiritual experience.

A number of writings could be considered from this angle: the *Life of Antony*, the *Apophtegmata* of the Fathers, the treatises of Evagrius Ponticus, the *Conferences* of Cassian, the *Rule* of Saint Benedict, and many more (to which it would be necessary to add the writings of some Fathers who, although not monks or had ceased to be—such as John Chrysostom) have largely contributed to the diffusion of the teaching of monasticism. A special mention can be made of Evagrius, for he is the one who, in his treatise *On the Practical Life*, gave us the first list of the most serious vices: the eight "generic thoughts" that are gluttony, fornication, avarice, sadness, anger, acedia, vain glory, and pride; it is this list that, translated into Latin by John Cassian, will be repeated by Gregory the Great in his *Moralia*, then by the medieval authors.[12] It really is a matter of "thoughts": Evagrius does not warn against only the concrete attitude of gluttony or some other vice but against the interior disposition of the intellect that, giving in to evil spirits, allows itself to be drawn to evil. For him, indeed, the "demons" do not just attack the "impassioned part of the soul" but also harass its "rational part." Evagrius explains as well what must be done to combat these "demons": first, it is important to identify them; it is also necessary to cut short the evil thoughts that they inspire, to analyze the way in which they seek to deceive, to allow the hatred toward them to increase, so as to find or recover the vision of God.

12. Cf. Évagre, *Traité pratique*, 6, in *Traité pratique*, vol. 1, trans. Antoine and Claire Guillaumont, SC 171 (Paris: Cerf, 1971), 507–9; John Cassian, *The Conferences*, , trans. Boniface Ramsey, Ancient Christian Writers 57 (New York: Newman Press, 1997), 183; *The Institutes*, trans. Boniface Ramsey, Ancient Christian Writers 58 (New York: Newman Press, 2000), 117; see also Cassien, *Conférences*, V, 2, trans. E. Pichery, SC 42 (Paris: Cerf, 1955), 190; *Institutions cénobitiques*, V, 1, trans. Jean-Claude Guy, SC 109 (Paris: Cerf, 1965), 191. See A. Solignac, "Péchés capitaux" [Deadly sins], in *Dictionnaire de spiritualité*, vol. 12/1 (Paris: Beauchesne, 1984), col. 853–62.

Analogous themes are developed in all the monastic literature. In it, it is not a matter of a strict moralism; it is much rather taking the moral life into account in all its complexity and, above all, at its very root that is from the spiritual order—the choice of good over evil, coming from, above all, obedience to the Spirit of God, as it is manifested through the discernment of thoughts and the combat against "demons."

What remains is to emphasize that the teaching of the Fathers in matters of morality was developed in the context of debates and conflicts, themselves very instructive for our own reflection today. Independent of the opposition to the "pagan" world, of which we have already spoken above, several kinds of controversies can here be raised. In the first place, the Fathers had to fight against some puritanical movements that, among other things, disparaged marriage and unilaterally exalted the ideal of continence (thus the "encratites" whom Clement of Alexandria fought against). On the other hand, they had to be opposed to the Gnostics who, in order to explain the problem of evil, maintained the intrinsic inequality of created beings: some, said these Gnostics, were forever trapped in the world of "matter" and had no possibility of having a part in redemption. Authors such as Irenaeus and Origen were directly opposed to this concept, emphasizing that every human being has the possibility of progressing from evil toward good and thus receiving salvation. The Fathers, beginning in the fourth century, also fought against another doctrine that was spreading all around the Mediterranean Basin: Manicheism. This was notably the case of Augustine, who, for about ten years, was himself a follower of this doctrine, but who, later, undertook to refute it.[13] Even though, for the Manicheans, evil was a principle that was superior to mankind, concurrent with the good, and that necessarily imposed itself on some humans, Augustine affirmed that God was not the author of evil, that He had created mankind free, and that sin was explained by a bad use of this freedom. Lastly, it is necessary to emphasize the very special importance of the controversies caused by Pelagius and Julian of Eclanum who, in the first decades of the fifth century,

13. See Alban Massie, *Peuple prophétique et nation témoin: Le peuple juif dans le* Contra Faustum manichaeum *de saint Augustin* [Prophetic people and witness nation: The Jewish people in Augustine's *Contra Faustum*] (Paris: Institut d'Études Augustiniennes, 2011).

considered the human being as capable of meriting salvation by his forces alone. Augustine was strongly opposed to this doctrine and, in contrast, affirmed the necessity of grace. By this, he did not mean to deny freedom, for, for him, grace itself gives to mankind free will; but it is true that, in the framework of the polemic against Julian of Eclanum, Augustine accentuated his statements on the radical inability of mankind and, what is more, developed an idea of predestination that risked undermining the affirmation of freedom. Augustine's position gave rise, in any case, to reactions, and the debates continued to the end of the patristic era and through the Middle Ages. They rebounded again in the sixteenth century with the Protestant Reformation, then in the seventeenth century in the context of the Jansenist controversy. One cannot overly emphasize the place of this debate on "grace and freedom" in the tradition of the West—even in our day. Such a debate is not only important in itself but has a direct impact on the concept of morality; it all the more calls for a rereading of the writings of the Fathers on the subject (not only, moreover, those that appeared in the context of the Pelagian controversy but also other writings that, in the East as in the West, bear witness to the different positions on this subject).

Patristic literature, as one sees, offers extensive material for reflection in the field of ethics. On the basis of the preceding, we would now like to focus on three sets of questions that have more specifically held the attention of the Fathers.

The Respect for Life

For what affects the beginnings of life, it goes without saying, we are today confronted with questions that were unknown to the ancients: along with advances in science have appeared new techniques (those that make possible medically assisted procreation, those that allow interventions on the embryo and the fetus, etc.). The recourse to these techniques raises ethical problems of great complexity and that obviously cannot find direct answers in the writings from the past. However, as new as they may be, these specific problems are connected in some way to some of the more fundamental questions that, themselves, were tackled and discussed during the era of the Fathers: such as questions on the meaning of sexuality, on the place of procreation in the life of the couple, or even on the representation of human nature and the human person. It is thus valuable to obtain light from patristic literature on these very points.

First, as to what concerns procreation, the writings of the Fathers bear witness to two different perspectives. According to one of them, procreation is presented as the essential goal of sexuality (so think some Greek Fathers, in particular Clement of Alexandria, and the greater part of the Latin Fathers). This perspective was developed as a result of Christian authors having to respond to several challenges: that of countering the gnostic movements (some of which condemned marriage as incompatible with the Christian life and, consequently, compelled celibacy or demanded total sexual abstinence of spouses); also, that of opposing pagan mores (to the extent that the use of sexuality was found to be perverted). According to another perspective, procreation, on the contrary, does not appear as the sole justification for marriage. This position is encountered more in the Greek Fathers of the fourth century: John Chrysostom, for example, presents the recourse to sexuality as also being a kind of rampart against lust, and above all, positively, he maintains that marriage has as its goal realizing a form of communal life based on the love of the spouses and their children. In all cases, the Fathers consider that the man and the woman must not act under the influence of a passion that diverts them from God, that they must not treat their own person or another person as a simple instrument of pleasure (that is, reduce the person to an object), and that the use of sexuality must be, on the contrary, governed by the mutual respect of the spouses and by the love that they have for one another—their union itself being a "mystery" in which the union of Christ and the Church takes shape (Eph 5:32).

On abortion, the Greek and Latin Fathers have, in principle, one and the same position: they denounce this practice that must have been (as that of abandoning newborns) quite widespread in the pagan world. The fundamental reason is that, to the extent that the fetus is a living being, the use of abortive practices amounts to transgressing the prohibition against killing. Other reasons were added during the era of the Fathers: the connection that abortive practices often have to sorcery and magic; their use by prostitutes; and even, the dangers of these practices for the health of the mother. On this basis, however, different judgments come to light due to the fact that all Christian authors do not have the same ideas on the formation of the embryo and on the stages of its development. Thus Tertullian considers that even if the embryo has a soul from conception, it is a human being only when it achieves its final form; and Augustine, in his turn, repeats the distinction between the unformed and the formed embryo. This theory of delayed hominization (that notably is based upon Ex 21:22–24 according to the Septuagint) implies that the abortion of an unformed fetus is not the same as a murder.[14] The Greek Fathers, themselves, prefer the theory of immediate animation: from its conception, the embryo is considered to be a human person. This then leads them to an irrevocable denunciation of every form of abortion at whatever stage; but paradoxically this very firm attitude will be accompanied, in the subsequent tradition, by a principle of "economy": the concern for taking into consideration the concrete situation of the persons and of showing the Church's compassion toward them.

For the Fathers, the respect for human life must also prevail at every stage of existence, even its last phases. Of course, patristic literature mentions some cases of Christians who, at the era of the great persecutions, went to their death in order to escape lengthy tortures;[15] some women did the same in order to escape the threat of rape;[16] lastly others, confronted by a strong temptation to which they risked giving in, preferred to give themselves to death in order not to succumb to this temptation. However, such cases are altogether rare enough; and even though the Fathers praise the martyrs for their eminent witness of courage and faith, they, in a general way, consider that martyrdom must not be sought out nor provoked. It must only be accepted in the situations in which it represents the only alternative to apostasy. If this were not the case, martyrdom would become a form of

14. Cf. Tertullien, *De anima*, 25, 2 and 27, 2, in *Opera II, Corpus Christianorum, Series Latina* 2 (1954; repr. Turnhout, Belgium: Brepols, 1996), 819 and 832; Augustin, *Questions sur l'Heptateuque*, II, 80, in *Œuvres complètes de saint Augustin*, vol. 7 (Paris: Vivès, 1870), 579–80; see Larchet, *Pour une éthique de la procréation*, 82–83.

15. See Eusebius of Caesarea, *The Ecclesiastical History*, VIII, 12, 2, Lawlor and Oulton, 267.

16. Cf. ibid., VIII, 12, 3–4, Lawlor and Oulton, 267; see other references in Jean-Claude Larchet, *Une fin de vie paisible … sans douleur sans honte* [A peaceful end of life … without pain or shame] (Paris: Cerf, 2010), 29–30.

suicide; yet Clement of Alexandria precisely took to task some people who "have misunderstood the Lord" and who claim that the martyr is "a murderer of himself and a suicide." He responds to them that such a comparison is unwarranted because the goal of martyrdom is not death but the witness of the faith.[17] Apart from these exceptional situations, the dignity of human life must be preserved until the end. This means, in the mind of the Fathers, that a person cannot put an end to his days out of fear of illness or death. In no way is this fear unnatural, to the extent that such ordeals contradict the aspiration of every human being to life. Maximus the Confessor recognizes it in Christ himself at the moment when he begins his prayer at Gethsemane; this prayer shows that Jesus "truly took on flesh that dreaded death," for it is the lot of flesh to dread death and to feel agony from this perspective.[18] However, Christ, by his Passion and his Resurrection, gives to the human person the strength not to be so overcome by fear as to be carried away by evil, but to face this fear victoriously—with faith, patience, and humility, and by benefiting from the sacramental life as well as the help given by the members of the community. On the other hand, it is important to do everything possible in order to diminish physical suffering: the Fathers, of course, could not foresee the resources in this area that today are at our disposal, but they themselves considered it necessary to employ the treatments of their times in order to relieve the suffering of people affected in their bodies. The concern for human dignity was in any case primordial in their eyes, and this dignity had to be respected until the end—the very dignity of the human being who ought to be conformed to Christ throughout his life, and even in the ordeal of illness and death.

What is in fact underlying the Fathers' positions on these ethical questions is above all else their understanding of human nature and the human person—and it is undoubtedly because of this understanding that their writings today also provide essential reference points for

17. Clément d'Alexandrie, *Stromate IV*, 17, 1–3; SC 463, 85–87: "We also say that those who rush to death … put themselves in peril without giving witness, although they may be officially punished; for they do not keep the characteristic mark of the believer's witness, not having acquired the knowledge of the true God; and they give themselves over to a vain death, as the Indian gymnosophists to the useless fire" Cf. Larchet, *Une fin de vie paisible*, 33).

18. Maxime le Confesseur, *Opuscules théologiques et polémiques*, 24, Ponsoye, 263.

Christian ethics, whatever may be the newness of the questions that confront us.

It is thus necessary to return briefly to these important notions from patristic anthropology,[19] taking into account their impact on moral theology. Of course, the notion of nature is not just Christianity's. The Fathers here took up a concept from the philosophical tradition: human nature (or the human essence) defines all human beings by what is common to them—thus by what distinguishes them from other species. But the Fathers connect this notion with God; thus Maximus the Confessor, in speaking of the *logos* of human nature, considers this in its spiritual origin and in its spiritual end. The human being is the one who, according to the words of Scripture, is created "in the image of God" and who has a vocation to achieve perfect "likeness" with God. Since this last definition is applied to human nature itself, all beings who possess such a nature are recognized as being fundamentally equal in their provenance and their destiny: it follows that they have the same dignity. Human nature in its entirety, and each person in particular, thus receives an eminent value (by being related to God Himself); and this value is inalienable because the characteristic of being "in the image of God" is, for the Fathers, constitutive of the human being himself. Of course, human nature is wounded by sin and its consequences; however, as Maximus also says, the results of sin undermined the *tropos* of this human nature, that is, its mode of existence, but not its *logos*, that is, what constitutes it in its origin and in its end. The ethical exigency, in addition to its intrinsic justifications, is ultimately based on this theological vision: whatever may be his age, his physical or moral state (and, as we will say later, his social situation), every human being must be the object of an absolute respect because his very relationship with God is at stake. Therefore, all that is accomplished for another is also accomplished for God, and inversely all that is committed against another is equally committed, by the same deed, in opposition to God.[20]

19. See chap. 9, pp. 211–13 and 227–28.

20. This reasoning is supported by, among others, the parable of Mt 25:31–46, which the Fathers have commented upon abundantly: all that is accomplished for the least is accomplished for the "Son of man" himself; this is a major foundation for action toward the poor, which we will mention at the end of this chapter.

This reflection on human nature is accompanied, in the Fathers, by a reflection on the "person" (or "hypostasis") that, as we have said above, was above all developed beginning in the fourth century in the cadre of Trinitarian theology and Christology but that rebounds on the understanding of the human being and that also has ethical consequences. While human nature describes what is common to all human beings, person designates this man or that woman by what is proper to him (the place of his birth, traits of his temperament, the way of leading his life, etc.). Using Maximus's words: even if all human beings possess in themselves the *logos* of their nature, that is, what constitutes their common essence, they each have a particular *tropos*, a mode of existence that distinguishes them from others. Furthermore, a person is not characterized only by the fact that he is, as such, "singular" and thus irreplaceable. Christian authors emphasize more precisely the person's capacity not to be subjected entirely to biological, psychological, and social determinations, his aptitude for freedom, his faculty to be open to transcendence, his vocation to receive the gift of God and to live in it—this, in an always unique way. Such a conception of the human person thus contributes to establishing the Fathers' position on the ethical questions that affect the origin and the end of life. It constitutes, at the same time, an essential reference in regard to some questions that they clearly could not have foreseen, as those that today arise from the risks of genetic manipulations. It forcefully recalls that each human being is unique, that he cannot be treated as a simple object, and that he, on the contrary, must be respected in his absolute value—itself rooted, according to faith, in the mystery of God the Creator and Savior.

The Commitment of the Citizen

Another area of thought greatly occupied the Fathers owing to its ethical as well as theological implications: that of the commitment of the citizen, and particularly relationships with power. If one pays attention to the time period of the patristic era (about seven centuries), as well as to the diversity of the situations encountered by the Fathers (not only in time but also in place), one will not be surprised to find a great variety of positions in the Christian authors who spoke about the State or the attitude regarding "politics." It is true that two major landmarks generally come to mind: the conversion of Constantine in the second decade of the fourth century, and toward the end of that same century, the recognition of Christianity as a religion of the Empire. There thus would have been a before and an after: the before, the situation of a Christianity that was in the minority and was regularly persecuted; the after, the situation of a Christianity that was dominant and, at the same time, was tempted to confiscate political power for its own purpose.

Things, however, are far from being so simple. It is, of course, not a matter of underestimating the importance of the "Constantinian revolution" but of recognizing that each of the two periods (delimited in this way) is itself complex and that each has in any case given rise, from the Christian side, to different, and sometimes even opposing, positions.

First, as to the second and third centuries, it is undeniable that some Christians showed themselves to be very critical toward the State or that they even expressed a true rejection of it. To the extent that Rome advocated a cult of the divinized emperor or that persecutions were sometimes initiated against the disciples of Christ, they were led (along the lines of the *Apocalypse*) to formulate severe judgments on political power. Thus Hippolytus of Rome saw the imperial State as an incarnation of the Antichrist. On the other hand, however, Christians also kept in mind the words of Jesus: "Render therefore to Caesar the things that are Caesar's ..." (Mt 22:21). The letter of Clement of Rome to the Corinthians contains as well a prayer for those who govern mankind.[21] One even sometimes finds the idea that the empire can serve the design of God (in that it, notably, promotes a wider diffusion of Christianity). In the third century, when Origen comments on the beginning of Romans 13, he does not hesitate to say that the secular judge is "a minister of God" and that the State itself has moral duties (to the point that, in many areas, the Church does not need to judge the attacks on the natural law, this judgment being normally assured by the secular authorities).[22]

21. *First Clement*, 61, 1–2, in *The Apostolic Fathers*, vol. 2, trans. Robert M. Grant and Holt H. Graham (New York: Thomas Nelson & Sons, 1965), 95–96; see also Clément de Rome, *Lettre aux Corinthians*, 61, 1–2, in *Épître aux Corinthiens*, trans. Annie Jaubert, SC 167 (Paris: Cerf, 2000), 199–201.

22. Origen, *Commentary on the Epistle to the Romans*, IX, 26–29; Fathers of the Church

What happened after the conversion of Constantine? Of course, Eusebius of Caesarea gives complete support to the emperor who became a Christian and does not hesitate to see in him an image of the *Logos* of God on earth. Constantine, he says, governs "in imitation of the All Powerful," he is "adorned in the image of celestial royalty."[23] This way of justifying the imperial power is laden with serious ambiguities, which will reappear more than once in the subsequent history of the medieval West and the Byzantine East. But it would be erroneous to consider only this aspect. It is first necessary to recall that, from a merely historical point of view, the "Constantinian revolution" was not imposed everywhere and that it even encountered strong resistance (as during the reign of Julian called the "Apostate," a little after the middle of the fourth century). On the other hand, independent of these oppositions, some Christians were concerned with defending the spiritual freedom of the Church. Augustine assuredly draws the ideal portrait of the Christian emperor, but he especially emphasizes that the "city of God" is not to be confused with the earthly city. And the pope Gelasius clearly distinguishes the power of the State and that of the Church (all the while hierarchizing them, for, in his eyes, there must be a subordination between them, even as there is a subordination of the body to the soul and of the earthly to the heavenly).[24] The distinction thus made has a critical importance for any temptation to confuse the political and the spiritual order—a confusion that, in the sixth century, was notably going to affect the ideology of the Eastern Emperor Justinian.

The actual behavior of Christians toward political life reflects, in its very diversity, the orientations of thinking that we just mentioned. Some, in the second half of the patristic era, do not back down before

---

104, 223–26. Cf. also *Commentaire sur l'Épître aux Romains, Livres IX–X*, vol. 4, SC 555 (Paris: Cerf, 2012), 167–76; see Hugo Rahner, *L'Église et l'État dans le christianisme primitif*, 58–60; translated by Leo Donald Davis, SJ, as *The Church and State in Early Christianity* (San Francisco: Ignatius Press, 1992). Origen also came to imagine the eventuality of a situation in which all Romans would become Christians, as if he sensed in some way the evolution that would later lead not, of course, to a conversion of all Romans but at least to an official recognition of Christianity; cf. *Contra Celsum*, VIII, 69; Chadwick, 505–6; *Contre Celse*, SC 150, 335.

23. Eusèbe de Césarée, *Louanges de Constantin*, I, 6; III, 5, in *La théologie politique de l'empire chrétien* [The political theology of the Christian empire], trans. Pierre Maraval (Paris: Cerf, 2001), 87 and 96.

24. See Hugo Rahner, *L'Église et l'État dans le christianisme primitif*, 185–87 and 203–9.

major responsibilities in the heart of the empire or more modestly assume some of the powers in their regions or their localities. Others, on the contrary, refrain from such commitments, and sometimes even deliberately break with the world in order to seek God in the solitude of the deserts. It is above all right to emphasize the spiritual meaning of early anchoritism and cenobitism; but they can, under other aspects, equally have value as political protest. According to Athanasius, Antony "did not make much of the documents" that Constantine and his sons addressed to him, and he asked them to consider that "Christ alone is the true and eternal King."[25] More radically, Sulpicius Severus tells how Martin one day encountered a man dressed as an emperor ... but it was in fact the Devil who appeared to him thus![26]

The attitude of the Fathers of the Church toward "politics" is thus, altogether, extremely complex. This complexity is due, on one hand, to the diversity of the situations but also, more profoundly, to the paradox that results from the New Testament itself: Jesus says to "give to Caesar" what he is owed (Mt 22:21); the apostle Peter exhorts both to "fear God" and to "honor the king" (1 Pt 2:17). Beyond the specific problem of the attitude toward the State, the paradox is above all rooted in the vocation of the disciples whom Jesus calls "the salt of the earth" (Mt 5:13), but who, while being "in the world," must not be "of the world" (Jn 17:14–16) because their true homeland is elsewhere. No patristic writing has better highlighted this paradox than the writing *To Diognetus*, from which it is necessary to recall at least these lines:

> To put the matter simply, what the soul is in the body, this is what Christians are in the world. The soul is spread throughout all the limbs of the body; Christians are spread throughout the cities of the world. The soul lives in the body, but it does not belong to the body; Christians live in the world but do not belong to the world.... The soul grows stronger even when mistreated by what the body eats and drinks; Christians increase daily even when punished. God has appointed them to such a position, and it would not be right for them to abandon it.[27]

25. St. Athanasius, *The Life of Saint Antony*, trans. Robert T. Meyer, Ancient Christian Writers 10 (Westminster, Mass.: The Newman Press, 1950), 86–87; see also *Vie d'Antoine*, 81, 2 and 5, trans. G. J. M. Bartelink, SC 400 (Paris: Cerf, 1994), 341 and 343.

26. Sulpice Sévère, *Vie de saint Martin*, 24, 4, trans. Jacques Fontaine, SC 133 (Paris: Cerf, 1967), 307–9.

27. *Epistle to Diognetus*, 6, 1–2 and 9–10, *The Apostolic Fathers*, 2:141–43. See also *À Diognète*, VI, 1–2 and 9–10, SC 33, 65–67. See above, chap. 9, p. 221.

The Concern for the Most Vulnerable

The commitment of the citizen notably occurs, for the Fathers, by attention to social justice. It is thus important to focus on this latter aspect, and more particularly on the question of the attitude vis-à-vis the most vulnerable—a theme to which patristic literature gives a quite remarkable importance.

We will show this through the example of a Cappadocian Father, Basil, the bishop of Caesarea during the fourth century. Not only did this man personally divest himself of all his goods in favor of the poor, but he intervened with the public powers in several situations. He drew the magistrates' attention to various injustices, he attempted to bring about the reduction of the taxes that in his eyes were excessive, he endeavored to shield the guilty from the harshness of some laws.[28] He himself took initiatives benefitting the unfortunate of his time: he devoted himself, as one wrote about him, to "the organization of charity."[29] Even before his episcopacy, in 368, he had improvised relief for the poor: when a famine had severely distressed the city and region of Caesarea, he set up the equivalent of what one would today call "soup kitchens." Above all, once he became bishop, he founded a charitable establishment that in the fifth century would receive the name of "Basiliade." This foundation, located on the outskirts of Caesarea, was first designed for foreigners, the homeless, and vagrants; it later became a hospice where one welcomed the sick and notably lepers.[30]

Such action for the benefit of the most vulnerable first found its

28. See Stanislas Giet, *Les Idées et l'Action sociales de saint Basile* [The social ideas and action of Saint Basil] (Paris: Gabalda, 1941), notably 356–99; see also Yves Courtonne, *Un témoin du IVe siècle oriental. Saint Basile et son temps d'après sa correspondence* [A witness of the Eastern fourth century. Saint Basil and his time] (Paris: Les Belles Lettres, 1973), chap. 6, "Le défenseur des faibles" [The defender of the weak], 360–423. Here we are repeating some of the elements of our article "'Boire à son propre puits.' Des mystiques chrétiennes de l'action sociale hier et aujourd'hui" ["We drink from our own wells." Mystics of social action yesterday and today], in *Aux sources de la charité. Les spiritualités* [To the sources of charity], ed. Paul Huot-Pleuroux (Paris: Cerf, 2003), 61–80 (on Basil: 70–77). See also Peter Brown, *Through the Eye of a Needle: Wealth, the Fall of Rome, and the Making of Christianity in the West, 350–550 A.D.* (Oxford: Oxford University Press, 2012); translated by Béatrice Bonne as *À travers un trou d'aiguille. La richesse, la chute de Rome et la formation du christianisme* (Paris: Les Belles Lettres, 2016).

29. Giet, *Les Idées et l'Action sociales de saint Basile*, 417.

30. Ibid., 417–23.

inspiration in the Holy Scriptures. It suffices, in order to be convinced, to pay attention to the biblical references that are made in the *Homilies on Wealth*, or even the *Homily on Psalm 14*. In them Basil comments on the parable of the rich man who wanted to construct larger granaries and whose life was suddenly taken; he also recalls the story of the young man who was asked to sell his belongings but went away sad; and he even refers to the famous parable of the last judgment in Matthew 25.[31] Thanks to these references, and also to many other passages scattered throughout Basil's *Homilies* and correspondence, it is possible to identify some major themes that, in the eyes of the Cappadocian bishop, contribute to establishing the exigency for social and charitable action.

First of all is the dignity of the human being. Basil, who more than once comments on the texts of the Bible on creation, loves to emphasize the grandeur of mankind as God wanted him to be; and he relies upon this consideration in order to comfort the unfortunate:

> You are in a humble and inglorious condition: poor, born impoverished, without home, without city; you are weak and lack your daily food, trembling before the powerful, fearful before all because of the very humility of your life, because *the poor*, says Scripture, *are defenseless against threats*. Do not be discouraged and be careful, because you have nothing that is worthy of envy, not to abandon all hope but raise your soul toward the goods that God has given to you, and wish for those that, according to His promise, the future holds for you.[32]

To the theme of human dignity are linked those of equality and unity. Here we find again what we said regarding questions affecting the origin and end of life: to the extent that all human beings share the same nature and are created in the image of God, each of them must not be despised nor rejected. This is precisely what escapes the rich man in the parable of Luke 12: he wanted to build larger granaries, but "he forgot that we all have the same nature, he did not think that he ought

31. Cf. Lk 12:16–21; Lk 18:18–23; Mt 25:31–46. See Basile de Césarée, *Homélies sur la richesse*, édition critique and exégétique [Homilies on wealth. A critical and exegetical edition], ed. Yves Courtonne (Paris: Firmin-Didot, 1935); also see *Riches et pauvres dans l'Église ancienne* [Rich and poor in the ancient Church], ed. Adalbert-Gautier Hamman (Paris: Desclée de Brouwer, 1982), 67–102; rev. ed. (Paris: J-P. Migne, 2011), 87–132.

32. Basile, *Hom. III*, 6 (with a citation of Prv 13:8), cited in Giet, *Les Idées et l'Action sociales de saint Basile*, 26.

to give over his surplus to the poor."[33] The unity of mankind is fundamentally due to their common condition as creatures. In his treatise *On the Holy Spirit*, Basil indeed writes that "in mankind no one is a slave by nature"; there certainly exists a form of servitude that is imposed on human beings, but it is due to their condition as creatures and, by this very fact, is the lot of all: "if one is called master and the other servant, we are all, by 'the equality of honor' between us and as 'the possession' of the One who has made us, 'companions in slavery.'"[34]

"Companions in slavery" (*homodouloi*): the word runs the risk of surprising the modern reader who, at best, will speak of a "dependence" or of a "submission" of creatures toward their Creator. But in fact, by its very force, the term chosen by Basil allows him to speak of the intrinsic equality of all creatures before God. And this affirmation has as such a social importance. It is because all humans are created by God—all "companions in slavery"—that one can also truly say: "in mankind no one is a slave by nature." Elsewhere Basil writes: "we know ourselves, and we know that nature places every human, in regard to all, in the same equality of honor."[35]

It is not here simply a matter of a "humanist" consideration, such as one could encounter in this or that moralist of Antiquity. Or more precisely, if social action is truly based on a general notion of humanity and on the equality between all its members, it has its ultimate source in the mystery of God as it is revealed through Holy Scripture. Indeed, the Bible bears witness to the generosity of the Creator and to the prodigality of his gifts; in this light, Basil is denouncing the attitude of those who concentrate wealth in their hands and hold on to it rather than share it with the poor:

> Go! Distribute generously your fortune, be liberal and magnificent in your expenditures for the indigent. Have said of yourself also: *He acts with largesse, he gives to the poor, his justice abides always*. Do not exploit distress by increasing prices: do not wait for a food shortage before opening the granaries. *The people curse the one who sells his wheat with scales of gold*. Do not wish for famine in order to be enriched by it, nor for public misery for your particular interests.

33. Basile, *Hom.* 6, 2, in Hamman, *Riches et pauvres dans l'Église ancienne*, 68.

34. Basile, *Traité du Saint-Esprit*, XX, 51, in *Sur le Saint-Esprit*, 2nd ed., trans. Benoît Pruche, SC 17 (Paris: Cerf, 1968), 427 and 429.

35. Basile, *Lettre* 202, 1, cited in Giet, *Les Idées et l'Action sociales de saint Basile*, 33.

Do not become a trafficker in human catastrophes, do not make the anger of God an occasion for increasing your fortune. Do not inflame the wounds of the unfortunate that the whips have lacerated.

You contemplate your gold, and you have no concern for your brothers! You know every kind of money and you know how to distinguish the counterfeit from the real, but your brother who is in need, you totally ignore.

The brightness of gold dazzles you, but the moaning that the unfortunate raise behind you, leaves you indifferent. How can you not see the distress of the poor?[36]

Holy Scripture, the revelation of the largesse of God, teaches us the extent to which God has gone, out of his love for humanity—sharing our own condition and giving his life for all. Basil notably emphasizes that at the heart of the teaching of Christ is found the exigency for fraternal love; in a significant way, he uses the following words for the heading of his *Moral Rules*: "The first and the greatest commandment of the Law is, according to the testimony of the Lord, to love God with all one's heart; and the second, to love the neighbor as oneself."[37] And elsewhere he writes:

Who does not know, indeed, that the human is a gentle and social being, and neither solitary nor savage? Nothing is more proper to our nature than to enter into the society of others, to need others, to love what is of our species. After having given us these seeds that he instilled in our hearts, the Lord came to harvest the fruits, and he said: *I give you a new commandment: it is to love one another.*[38]

Or even:

As the foot has one faculty but lacks another, and as, without the assistance of other members, it does not find in itself the power to subsist, nor help in order to obtain what is lacking, thus, in the solitary life, what we have is useless, and we are without care in order to (receive) what we lack: for God, our Creator, decided that we would have need of each other, *so that*, as it is written, *we may be united with each other.*[39]

36. Basile, *Homélie 6*, 3, in Hamman, *Riches et pauvres dans l'Église ancienne*, 71; cf. Ps 111:9 and Prv 11:26.

37. Basile, *Moralia*, III, 1, cited in Giet, *Les Idées et l'Action sociales de saint Basile*, 34); cf. Mt 22:37 and 39.

38. Basile, *Regulae Fusius tractatae*, 3, 1, cited in Giet, *Les Idées et l'Action sociales de saint Basile*, 34); cf. Jn 13:34.

39. Basile, *Regulae Fusius tractatae*, 7, 1, cited in Giet, *Les Idées et l'Action sociales de saint Basile*, 37).

The unity of which Basil is speaking can rightly happen only through social action and the practice of charity toward all, including the most vulnerable. The reference to the parable of the last judgment in Matthew 25 is here decisive:

> As to the goods that have been entrusted to your management, you have hoarded them. The one who has fleeced a man of his clothes will be called a pillager. And the one who does not clothe the nakedness of the beggar, although he can, does he deserve any other name? To the starving belongs the bread that you store. To the naked man, the coat that your coffers contain. To the tramp, the shoes that are rotting in your house. To the destitute, the money that you keep buried. Thus do you so greatly oppress the people that you could have helped....
>
> How can I make you see the torments of the poor, so that you know on what groaning you amass your treasure? Ah! How precious will this saying, on the day of judgment, seem to you: *Come, O blessed of my Father, inherit the kingdom prepared for you from the foundation of the world; for I was thirsty and you gave me drink, I was a stranger and you welcomed me, I was naked and you clothed me*. Shivers, cold, dark sweats will overcome you at the news of this judgment: *Depart from me, you cursed, into the eternal fire prepared for the devil and his angels; for I was hungry and you gave me no food, I was thirsty and you gave me no drink, I was a stranger and you did not welcome me, naked and you did not clothe me.*[40]

Basil is not the only one to make such strong statements. One cannot fail to mention another very remarkable example, that of John Chrysostom who, first in Antioch, then as the bishop of Constantinople, quite energetically denounced the serious abuses and injustices that occurred because of some uses of wealth. This was so when he evoked the presence of the sinful woman before Jesus, at the meal given by Simon the Pharisee (Lk 7:36–50); this episode inspired quite an exposition on the reception of the poor at the table of the rich:

> Chase away the parasites, and bring to your table Christ. If you share your salt and table, he will be indulgent with you at the Judgment; he knows how to respect a shared table. If robbers know how to, how much more the Master. Think of the way in which he justified the prostitute around a table, and for whom he reproached Simon by saying to him: You did not embrace me. If he fed you

40. Basile, *Homélie 6*, 7–8, in Hamman, *Riches et pauvres dans l'Église ancienne*, 76–77; Cf. Mt 25:34 and 39.

although you did not do it, for a stronger reason will he give you his reward if you do it. Do not consider that the poor one who approaches you is dirty and filthy; but think that it is Christ who through him penetrates into your house and so cease this cruelty.[41]

It is true that the episode of the anointing at Bethany could here cause difficulty, since, faced with the disciples' objection to the use of the perfume that would have been more valuable if sold for money to give to the poor, Jesus had declared "For you always have the poor with you, but you will not always have me" (Mt 26:11). John Chrysostom, however, was not hindered by this difficulty: Jesus, he says, is only expressing this in order to defend the accused woman, and one cannot thus rely upon this speech in order to relativize the exigency of care that must be reserved for the poor.[42] But there is more: John Chrysostom does not hesitate to say that the giving of alms is "something more necessary" than virginity.[43] When elsewhere he places much emphasis on this ideal of virginity, the parable of the ten virgins paradoxically leads him to stress that service to others, and notably the care of the poor, is superior to such an ideal. This parable indeed shows that the state of life of these virgins does not, as such, guarantee their salvation (since the foolish virgins actually miss the coming of the spouse); what is essential, on the contrary, is to keep the lamps lit—that is, according to Chrysostom, to be useful to others. Thus he exclaims: "There is nothing colder than a Christian who does not save others"; and he then evokes the foolish virgins, who certainly were "pure, well-behaved, and chaste" but were not "useful to anyone": "Such are those who have not fed Christ. Notice, indeed, that among them no one is deserving of reproach for personal sins, neither fornication, nor perjury, nor anything else; but only for not having been useful to others. Such was the one who hid the talent, who certainly led an irreproachable life, but without being useful to others. How

41. Jean Chrysostome, *Homélie 48 in Mt*; PG 58, 494; cited by Catherine Broc-Schmezer, *Les figures féminines du Nouveau Testament dans l'œuvre de Jean Chrysostome* [The female figures of the New Testament in the work of John Chrysostom] (Paris: Institut d'Études Augustiniennes, 2010).

42. Cf. Broc-Schmezer, *Les figures féminines*, 161–62.

43. Jean Chrysostome, *Homélie 50 in Mt*, § 3; PG 58, 510; cited in Broc-Schmezer, *Les figures féminines*, 440.

can someone like this be a Christian?"[44] Of course, here as elsewhere, the writings of the Fathers must be placed in their historical context. The abuses to which they were bearing witness explain, among other things, their concern for so forcibly protesting against usury, which was then a particularly widespread blight on society;[45] they also explain their quite marked emphasis on the sharing of goods (an emphasis that, moreover, contrary to what one has sometimes thought, did not exclude in their mind a legitimate right to private property).[46] One cannot, however, in the name of these considerations, underestimate the importance of their statements. Basil of Caesarea, John Chrysostom—and even others, such as Gregory of Nazianzus and Gregory of Nyssa, or even, in the Latin Fathers, Ambrose and Augustine—have clearly perceived the ethical impact of Revelation in the area of society. They have taken seriously the biblical teaching on the equality of human beings, created in the image of God, as well as the words of Christ on love for neighbor and the attitude toward the most vulnerable. They have drawn strength from them to denounce, with a remarkable freedom, the individual and social manifestations of greed, egoism, and oppression inflicted on the poor. They understood that fidelity to the Gospel must be a part of the relationships between humans, calling for the conversion of some practices and directing modes of life to conformity to the exigency of charity.

Such a contribution—being added to those that we have previously raised—confirm the importance of patristic literature in the field of ethics. The Fathers do not only provide fundamental reference points on human behavior. They take part in the situations of their time—whether procreation, the attitude toward suffering and death, connections with political power, social inequalities, or relationships between the rich and the poor. If their writings do not respond to every current problem, they, nonetheless, shed light on the discernment of Christians who, today as yesterday, have to recognize the impact of

44. Jean Chrysostome, *Homélie 20 in Acts*, § 4; PG 60, 162; cited in Broc-Schmezer, *Les figures féminines*, 441.

45. In the periods in which food was lacking, workers had recourse to usurers and borrowed from them; but the interest rate charged by the creditors was considerable, and these creditors thus became rich to the point of little by little monopolizing lands and riches.

46. See Pierre Bigo, introduction to Hamman, *Riches et pauvres dans l'Église ancienne*, 7–16.

the biblical message on the questions of human life and life in society. They emphasize with the greatest force the exigency for the respect that must be given to every person, from the beginning to the end of his destiny. They, all the more, highlight the exigency for social behaviors that, in the cities of this world, are able to incarnate love of neighbor and, in particular, of the neediest—for in this way is prepared, in complete conformity to the Gospel, the city awaited and hoped for at the end of history, this city that Basil henceforth invites contemplating:

> If, sometimes, during a quiet night, fixing your eyes on the inexpressible beauty of the stars, you have thought about the author of the universe [by asking yourself] who, with these flowers, has embroidered the firmament ...; if, on the contrary, you have, during the day, considered with a reflective mind the marvels of the day and, by visible beings, conjectured invisible beings, you come as a listener who is prepared and merits to complete this venerable and fortunate assembly.
>
> Come then: as one takes by the hand and leads in the cities those who do not know them, thus will I myself lead you as strangers toward the mysterious marvels of this great city.[47]

This great city to which Basil leads his audience is "the entire universe become, by fraternal love and social solidarity, the City of God."[48]

47. Basil, *Homélies sur l'Hexaéméron*, VI, 1, Giet, SC 26, 327–29.
48. Giet, *Les Idées et l'Action sociales de saint Basile*, 37.

CHAPTER 11

The Contribution to Christology and Trinitarian Theology

No matter what the Fathers of the Church borrowed from the ideas of the Greco-Latin world, it was the primary content of the confession of the Christian faith that above all illuminated their anthropological and ethical concepts and that continued to be deepened through their work. In fact, Christology and Trinitarian doctrine hold a considerable place in the writings of the Fathers. Refuting heterodox positions on these subjects, meditating on the Scriptures, and meeting the catechetical and pastoral needs of their time led to a deepening of their understanding of the Christian mystery. It is, therefore, important to ask to what extent their Christological and Trinitarian thought is today still fecund for the work of theologians.

The standard manner of tackling the question would begin by taking into consideration criteria on the Fathers of the Church from the traditional definition: orthodoxy, holiness, approval by the Church, antiquity. One would then say: Christological and Trinitarian thought must allow itself to be inspired by Christian authors from the past in as much as they respond to these four criteria—to the extent, thus, that they presented an orthodox doctrine, that they witnessed to Christ by the holiness of their life, that their doctrine has been approved by the Church, and that a specific authority is recognized in them by their very antiquity. But as we have seen above,[1] these criteria cannot be implemented in a very direct or uniform way. If they provide important reference points, their application, in some in-

1. See chap. 6, pp. 156–58.

stances, can be difficult, sometimes even impossible. It is incumbent upon us rather to ask ourselves how the Fathers may actually contribute to engendering our understanding of the faith—and specifically, here, of faith in Christ and in the God of Jesus Christ; to the extent that they make such a contribution, they are actually "Fathers"—even in the cases where they were not orthodox nor holy on all points and even in the case where they were not the subject of the Church's solemn approval.

We will briefly recall how patristic writings have influenced thought on Christ and the Trinity, first in the years 1930–60, then after Vatican Council II; and we will also mention the difficulties in this field that have sometimes been raised regarding the theology of the Fathers. But we will above all show that, in some of its characteristics, what is at stake is essential for the deepening of the Christological and Trinitarian faith.

The Heritage of the Twentieth Century

As early as the end of the nineteenth century, the work of Théodore de Régnon, *Études de théologie positive sur la Sainte Trinité*, had shown the great importance of patristic studies for Trinitarian doctrine. It was equally so, a little later, for the work of Jules Lebreton, *Histoire du dogme de la Trinité des origines au concile de Nicée*.[2] The writings of the following generation—that of Henri de Lubac, Jean Daniélou, Hans Urs von Balthasar—quite particularly illustrated the fecundity of the patristic renewal for what one today calls "Christology," and it is possible to verify this on several essential points.

The reading of the Fathers first helped with considering Christ in his connection with Holy Scripture. Of course, this was not absent from theological treatises on the Word Incarnate, though it was above all "utilized" as a justification for or an illustration of doctrinal theses; but the rediscovery of the Fathers once again focused attention on the way in which the Old Testament speaks of Christ and gives us access to his mystery. It was to recover the importance of what is said regarding Jesus in the Gospel of Luke: "beginning with Moses and all

2. See chap. 2 above, sec. "'Return to the Fathers': The Meaning of This Expression."

the prophets, he interpreted to them in all the Scriptures the things concerning himself" (Lk 24:27). Balthasar, for example, emphasized how much Irenaeus's Christological view was shaped by his reflection on the concord and harmony of the two Testaments. It is significant that another writing by this same theologian, first titled "The *mystérion* of Origen," finally received the title of "Word and Mystery in Origen": indeed, Balthasar showed how Origen had meditated on the Word of God—the *Logos* having first been revealed by Scripture before his coming in the flesh. One finds a comparable reflection in de Lubac, expounding in *Histoire et Esprit* the diverse "incorporations of the *Logos*" according to Origen; more broadly, the attention paid by this theologian to the Fathers of the Church, whether Irenaeus, Origen, Augustine, or other Fathers, led him to a profound understanding of Christ as fulfilling the Scriptures—as one can see through a number of his writings. Let us again recall the important works of Daniélou on Judeo-Christianity, his exploration of biblical typology, and his concern for making known the original languages on Christ in the cultural situation of the first centuries.[3]

The return to the Fathers had another impact on Christology: it allowed restoring to its central place the view of Christ as the center and fulfillment of history. This view (that, in another way, found a famous expression in the writings of Teilhard de Chardin) was indeed supported by some great theologians in the twentieth century who were also patrologists. It was broadly connected to the preceding point: to the extent that Christ was understood as fulfilling the Scriptures and that they were not speaking only of Israel but of humanity in its entirety, it was natural to highlight the place of Christ within universal history. The theology of some Fathers especially supports this view, in particular that of Irenaeus with his theme of "recapitulation," but also those of Origen, Gregory of Nyssa, and Augustine. Patristic literature, examined from this angle, contributed to founding a true theology of history oriented to and centered around the central event of Christ.

3. Cf. Hans Urs von Balthasar, *La Gloire et la Croix, II/1*, 27–84; *Studies in Theological Style*; "Le *mystèrion* d'Origène," 38–64; Henri de Lubac, *Histoire et Esprit*, 336–73; *History and Spirit*; Jean Daniélou, *Sacramentum futuri*; *Théologie du judéo-christianisme*; *Message évangélique et culture hellénistique aux IIe e IIIe siècles* (Desclée, Paris-Tournai, 1961); *The Theology of Jewish Christianity*; *Gospel Message and Hellenistic Culture*. See chap. 3.

Thirdly, the return to the Fathers promoted the renewal of an important field of research: the history of dogmas. The fifteen hundredth anniversary of the Council of Chalcedon in 1951 was, from this point of view, a major date. One name, among others, illustrates this fecundity of the return to the Fathers for the genesis and development of Christological doctrines: Aloys Grillmeier (who was born in 1910—thus, a few years after de Lubac and Balthasar). Patrologists acquired a more exact knowledge of this history and, above all, made advances in the hermeneutics of the early texts, with the concern for locating conciliar statements within their context in order to give to them an interpretation that is pertinent for today.

The following decades have also shown the fecundity of patristic work for Christology and Trinitarian theology. This was owing to, on one hand, some editions and translations of particularly important texts on the subject (such as the *Contre Eunome* of Basil; the *De Trinitate* of Hilary; and many more writings). On the other, the history of Christological dogma, which had found a new momentum at the beginning of the 1950s, later gave rise to some major works; above all, that of Grillmeier, *Le Christ dans la tradition chrétienne*, the volumes of which constitute a major reference,[4] and also other publications, such as those of Joseph Moingt, Basil Studer, Bernard Sesboüé, Joseph Wolinski, and Luis Ladaria.[5] Lastly, it is necessary to mention the numerous monographs on the Fathers from the point of view of their Christology or their Trinitarian doctrine: those of Moingt (on Tertullian), Sesboüé (on Basil of Caesarea), Michel Corbin (also on Basil and on Gregory of Nyssa), Goulven Madec (on Augustine), and numerous others.

Let us add, that henceforth—and we will subsequently return to it in this chapter—the study of the early doctrines on the God of Jesus Christ made clear its fecundity for the field of philosophy as well. This is witnessed to by Michel Henry's book *Incarnation* that, in the cadre

4. See chap. 4, pp. 90–91.

5. See Basil Studer, *Dieu sauveur. La rédemption dans la foi de l'Église ancienne* [God the Savior. Redemption in the faith of the ancient Church], trans. Joseph Hoffmann (Paris: Cerf, 1989); Moingt, *L'homme qui venait de Dieu* (the author offers, in the first part, a lengthy review of the history of Christological dogma, on which he had formerly taught with the concern for bringing out the "logic" governing the elaboration of this dogma); Sesboüé and Wolinski, *Le Dieu du salut*; Sesboüé, *Jésus-Christ dans la tradition de l'Église*; Luis Ladaria, *Mystère de Dieu et mystère de l'homme*, vol. 1, *Théologie trinitaire* [Mystery of God and mystery of man, vol. 1, Trinitarian theology], trans. Philippe Curbelié (Paris: Parole et Silence, 2011).

of phenomenological thought, devotes several pages to Irenaeus and Tertullian—who radically took seriously the "becoming flesh" of the Son of God; and even Emmanuel Falque's book, *Dieu, la chair et l'autre*, which notably treats Irenaeus, Tertullian, Origen, and Augustine.

However, some difficulties have appeared in recent decades. Without repeating everything that was said on this subject in the first part of the book, let us at least recall three of these difficulties that directly affect Christology and Trinitarian theology. On one hand, one reproaches the Fathers' typological exegesis for being facilely arbitrary or, in any case, for often manipulating the literal meaning of some biblical texts; this exegesis then risks being considered, at best, as a monument of the past, of course venerable but henceforth outdated, and one asserts that Christology must be built on other bases and by other methods.

On the other, the research on the "Christologies from below" (formulated in the 1960s and 1970s), but also other research by contemporary theology (such as that of taking into greater consideration the Passion of Christ and the revelation of a "crucified God"), seem to contradict the dominant current of thought on Christ in the fourth and fifth centuries and the statements by which this thought was then expressed. Thus, Jürgen Moltmann expressly contests the language of Chalcedon on the "two natures"; as for Moingt, he emphasizes that today it is no longer possible to be satisfied with an approach that presupposes the consideration of the Word of God and that it is rather necessary to begin with the Gospel "narrative" of the man Jesus of Nazareth—even if it then means showing how and in what sense Jesus must be recognized as Son of God. Some reflections were also developed based on other points of view, for example, that of feminist theology for which patristic literature, by the very fact of Jesus' belonging to the masculine gender and by the use that it makes of the name of "God," maintains a domineering language vis-à-vis women, which risks by this very thing supporting a position of inferiority for women in society and in the Church.

Lastly, another difficulty is due to the particularity that influences the Fathers' Christology and Trinitarian doctrine by the very fact of their rootedness in their culture, essentially limited to the area surrounding the Mediterranean Basin. On this subject, one can recall the divergence that, beginning in the 1950s, appeared between Jules Monchanin and Henri Le Saux in the context of India. The former considered that it was, of course, necessary to speak of Christ and the Trinity in a way that was meaningful for Indians but that this necessarily implied the rejection of some symbols and schemas of Hindu thought. The latter thought, on the contrary, that it was possible to venture further and to go as far as being freed from the conceptual distinctions that are characteristic of Christology and Trinitarian dogma in order to envisage, in Christ himself, a radical experience of non-duality between his "I" and that of his Father. More broadly, what is suspected in the Fathers' Christology and Trinitarian doctrine is often linked to the denunciation of their being too closely connected to Greek conceptuality; and for other civilizations, especially Asian, other approaches to the mystery would be recommended, in particular taking account of the experience and the priority given to the symbol rather than to the concept.

Let us add, as we emphasized above, that this awareness of cultural particularity is also increasing in Europe, in light of the changes that for several decades have characterized the European continent, and, more generally, the phenomenon of globalization. Such a development is reinforced by the very fact that early Christianity is henceforth less known: some cultural references that were obvious at the time of Vatican II have faded into the background as memories (while all the information is available on the Internet!). From this point of view, we are in a totally new situation in Europe: the question is no longer one of only taking a position regarding Christology or the Trinitarian doctrine of the Fathers (whether to emphasize its real importance or to challenge some formulations), it is first that of the very access to a heritage that, if it is known by specialists, no longer informs the memory and the consciousness of our contemporaries.

However, in spite of the difficulties that were just mentioned—or rather, thanks to taking these difficulties into serious consideration—it is today possible to note the emergence of new issues that have great promise for the fecundity of patristics in the field of Christology and Trinitarian theology.[6]

6. In what follows, we will rely in part upon our study "La théologie anténicéenne: quelles ressources pour la christologie?" [Ante-Nicene theology: What resources for

The Reference to Scripture

A first issue concerns *the reflection on Christ and on the God of Jesus Christ, in the context of a reading of the Scriptures within the Christian community*. It is indeed one of patristic literature's fundamental contributions: to remind dogmatic theology that its source is the Word of God, transmitted by the Scriptures and the living Tradition of the Church. Of course, beginning in the fourth century especially, the exigencies of the debate with some philosophical movements, and even more the necessity of refuting this or that heterodox doctrine (beginning with Arianism), constrained the Fathers of the Church to some expositions that, all the while taking some support from Scripture, were not directly inspired by meditation on the holy books. The development became even more pronounced in the sixth and seventh centuries, as one sees through the debates that divided the Chalcedonians, the Monophysites, and the Nestorians. Nevertheless, even during this second half of the patristic era, great doctrinal works found their fundamental inspiration in Scripture—thus the *De Trinitate* of Hilary, *On the Holy Spirit* of Basil, and even (for at least one part) the *De Trinitate* of Augustine. And during these centuries, one also saw an increase in homilies and commentaries on Scripture that, by referring to this or that verse, made important contributions to Christological and Trinitarian thought. Going further back, one, in any case, notices that the ante-Nicaean Christologies are to a large extent biblical Christologies, or at least Christologies directly dependent upon the Scriptures and their ecclesial interpretation; the same remark is valid, more broadly, for the writings that treat Christian doctrine on the subject of God. It suffices to recall here the last three books of Irenaeus's *Against Heresies* or even some of Tertullian's writings such as *Against Marcion* and *Against Praxeas*. It is true that Origen's *On First Principles*, itself, treats God and his Son in the cadre of a doctrinal synthesis and that this was able to be compared (but, in fact, excessively) to a kind of "theological summa" before it existed. Even in this, however, refer-

Christology], in *De Jésus à Jésus-Christ*, vol. 2, *Christ dans l'histoire* [From Jesus to Jesus Christ, vol. 2, Christ in history], ed. Joseph Doré (Paris: Mame-Desclée, 2011), 189–207; but we will also treat Trinitarian doctrine, and we will, furthermore, consider the entirety of the patristic period.

ence to the Scriptures holds an important place; and the work precisely culminates, in book 4, with an exposition on the way of interpreting these Scriptures. By this, it reveals what must be the fundamental source of thought on the faith, and, furthermore, one precisely knows that Origen was, above all, a reader of and commentator on the Bible.

Patristic literature thus recalls the essential importance of Scripture in the very development of Christology and Trinitarian theology. It is clearly not necessary to deduce from this that these must necessarily be developed in the cadre of a biblical theology; but this does mean that all the other forms of Christian dogmatics must at least presuppose the effort (constantly being reworked) in order to take into account the faith in the God of Jesus Christ beginning with the Scriptures and their reception by the Church. This, today, assuredly implies a great attention to the contributions of historians regarding Jesus, as well as to the exegetical research that, in a number of cases, no longer authorizes repeating some of the Fathers' interpretations but does allow obtaining a more correct first meaning of the biblical texts. But these exigencies, henceforth required by critical exegesis, do not dispense with receiving the fundamental intuitions that exist in the reading of the Christian authors of the first centuries on the Scriptures for the Christological and Trinitarian faith.

Two of these intuitions are particularly important. The first emerges from texts written in the first decades of the second century, during the era when the word "Scriptures" designated above all what today one understands by "Old" or "First Testament." This is so in the apostolic Fathers as well as in Justin himself. The historical time to which we are referring highlights a point of great importance: what is primary is not, first of all, the relationship between a category of new texts (the Gospels and the Epistles) and the whole of the Scriptures called "Old" (the Law, the Prophets, and the other Writings); it is rather the relationship between an event and the Scriptures inherited from Israel—the event being, in this instance, the act of Christ who brought these Scriptures to their fulfilment (as it emerges as well from the Gospels themselves). Of course, the necessity of establishing the canon of the Scriptures led quite rapidly to identifying a corpus of texts titled "New Testament": the development was essentially completed in the last decades of the second century, as the work of Irenaeus shows.

But this development should not place into question the preceding remark. In the strictest terms, it is not the New Testament that fulfills the Old, but it is rather Christ who fulfills the Scriptures (that is our "Old Testament"); as for the New Testament, its meaning is nothing other than giving witness to the act of Christ thus fulfilling the Scriptures.

The other fundamental intuition of which we have to take note concerns typology and prophetic argumentation, constantly employed by the Christian authors of the patristic era and used to good advantage throughout the Middle Ages. Of course, one must not hesitate to recognize the arbitrary way in which the Fathers often used typology, due to their conviction that all the Scriptures spoke of Christ; and positively, it is necessary again to stress here the irreversible knowledge that henceforth critical exegesis produces. However, it is also important to keep in mind what the development of contemporary thought on language has highlighted: a text cannot be reduced to its function of making known this or that content in some sort of demonstrable way. It does not exist only in an "objective" way, with meanings that science allows clarifying; it also exists, and even above all, for the "subject reader" who receives it and appropriates it. Above all, the denunciation of "patristic allegorism" (as being a way to circumvent the letter of the Scriptures) does not place into question the recourse to "allegory," understood in its properly Christian meaning—the one that connects it to the word "typology": a Christian reading of the Scriptures is entitled to interpreting this or that person or episode from biblical history as a "figure" of the mystery revealed in the New Testament; it cannot shirk from today's exigency of saying how the mystery of the God of Jesus Christ is found "prefigured" in the ancient Scripture and how it can be said to be "fulfilled" by him. Such a reading clearly does not fall into the category of an "objective" knowledge; it first presupposes an option of faith (and it is completely legitimate for others, starting with Jewish readers, not to choose the same option in their reading of what we call the Old Testament). But the believing reader's involvement does not mean that his reading is for all that not acceptable. This reading has its own logic, and it is in any case required, from the Christological point of view, by what emerges from the New Testament itself and by what the Fathers were intent upon honoring as much as possible. Christ is revealed as such through his very way of fulfilling what was written about him. As to prophetic argumentation, despite appearances, its true meaning is not to prove the Christian mystery based on ancient predictions (since a Jewish reading of these same predictions as well interprets them otherwise). Like typology, it proceeds from the Christian faith that, by turning towards the writings of the Old Testament, perceives in them announcements of the mystery henceforth revealed in Christ. Inversely, these announcements, due to the very fact that they appear as henceforth "fulfilled," contribute to making Christ, who has thus led them to their fulfillment, better known, and the faith of the believer, in its turn, finds itself confirmed and deepened.

Thus understood in their profound meaning, typology and prophetic argumentation retain all their pertinence. Of course, Christology and Trinitarian theology must, let us repeat, take into account the knowledge henceforth achieved by critical exegesis. But once this exigency is honored, it cannot renounce assuming the task that was so essential for the Fathers of the Church: to expound the meaning that the ancient Scriptures assumed in the light of the New Testament, to show how Christ brings them to their fulfilment and how its figures and prophecies reciprocally contribute to a better knowledge of his mystery. From this point of view, patristic exegesis is revelatory and inspirational for what today can be a reading of the Scriptures in the light of Christ, and, at the same time, a meditation on Christ by the light of the Scriptures considered in their unity and their totality. Christology will be in this same way honored in its properly spiritual importance since it is in the Spirit of Christ that the Christian reads the Scriptures and draws from them food for his own life.

The Contribution to Philosophical Thought

A second issue must be emphasized: the contribution that patristic thought can here make to philosophy. A good example of this is given by the meditation of Michel Henry on the concept of the Incarnation. The author indeed relies upon Irenaeus and Tertullian in order to think about the "birth," the "flesh," and their necessary "correlation." In his eyes, these Fathers, through their controversy with Marcion, testify to a decisive modification of the concept of the human body, which is no longer thought of as an "objective body" but as a "suffering flesh"; and this flesh must be interpreted as "a phenomenological matter of life," as it also emerges quite particularly in Irenaeus's battle against gnosis:[7]

> The unconditional allocation of the flesh to Life, from which it receives its pathetic effectuation, finds in Irenaeus an extraordinary deepening. The whole context of the problem proves in the first place that the life of which it is a question is really the absolute phenomenological Life. It is that life, the Life of God self-revealed in his Word, that is made flesh. To the Gnostics' question of knowing from where the flesh of Christ proceeds ..., Irenaeus knows the answer written in the Word that, more than any other, fascinates him. The flesh in which the Word comes, itself comes from the Word, that is from Life.[8]

Irenaeus's Christology thus helps in thinking about the immanence of Life in the flesh:

> Irenaeus's extraordinary affirmation—one that is implicit also in the Johannine Word—is the *cogito* of the flesh or, if one prefers, the Christian *cogito*.... In Irenaeus, the polemical denunciation of the contradictions proper to the gnostic theses that he has in view ... is the obverse of a phenomenology that is positive. That the Life is present in all flesh as that which reveals the flesh to itself, making of it a particular flesh and giving to it Life—this is that to which, in all flesh, the Life attests by the radical self-attestation which is his absolute self-revelation.[9]

Another example can be borrowed from Emmanuel Falque, who, in addition to his own studies on Irenaeus and Tertullian, highlights the contribution of Augustinian theology to a thinking on relationship. Since, on one hand, an understanding of the three divine Persons in terms of "substances" would lead to tritheism, but, on the other, one cannot substitute "pure substantiality" with a "pure accidentality" (without placing divine immutability into question), a new problem is imposed; and it is correctly suggested to Augustine by the concept of relationship, itself inspired by the Revelation of the triune God:

> It is not relationship that is first discovered in order then to be applied to the Father, to the Son, and to the Holy Spirit; but it is on the contrary the necessary connection of the three (Father, Son, and Holy Spirit) that requires the relationship, itself then existing, and later, regarding mankind. "Person" (*persona* or

7. Henry, *Incarnation*, 180 ff.
8. Ibid., 190.
9. Ibid., 193–95.

hypostasis) makes of God "someone" not that by this one applies to Him what in Him is human in order to then transfer it to the divine. It is the inverse; because God is totally whole and "relational" in His nature, precisely in the cadre of Trinitarian Christianity, the "movement towards" (*ad aliquid*) takes its meaning first inside the Trinity itself.[10]

Falque also maintains, it is true, that Augustine's thought does not draw all the implications from the discovery thus effected: the schema of substance "does not cease to exercise its power over the bishop of Hippo, as if metaphysics had always to innervate theology, and to impose on it by cohabiting with it."[11] A "tension" thus exists between the "metaphysical" (to which the language of "substance" belongs) and the "theological" (which the problem of relationship intends to honor more). But even this, adds the author, is of great importance for philosophy, which must always speak in an inadequate language—"as if words never could suffice, in particular when it is a matter of speaking of God."[12]

Such studies show, each in its own way, how the patristic expositions on Christ and the Trinity themselves contribute to the thought of contemporary philosophers. But if the examples given were borrowed from works that are written within the phenomenological movement, it is important to emphasize that other movements of thought ought equally to benefit from patristic literature (for example, within the hermeneutic tradition).[13] Indeed, in reading the Fathers according to a single orientation (whether Hegelian, Heideggerian, or another), we would be risking simply projecting onto them what we already think, instead of taking their writings as themselves a source for our philosophical reflection. Yet it is necessary to make sure that the writings of the Fathers do not become a kind of pretext (analogous to what they sometimes were for Scholastic thought). Actually, the fecundity of these writings for a philosophical reflection will first depend upon the way in which one sets about listening to the Fathers in order to learn from them how to think.

10. Emmanuel Falque, *Dieu, la chair et l'autre*, 58–59.

11. Ibid., 70.

12. Ibid., 84.

13. Here we are referring to the remarks that we made more generally on the relationship between philosophy and patristics, see chap. 6, pp. 151–55.

Patristic literature has from this point of view considerable resources. First, because some Fathers undertook a powerful reflection, properly philosophical, on the identity of Christ and on the doctrine of God: thus for the Greek Fathers between the fourth and seventh centuries, from the Cappadocians to Maximus the Confessor, as well as for Latin thinkers such as Augustine and Boethius. It is during this period, in particular, that the Christological and Trinitarian meanings of the fundamental concepts of "nature," of "person" and "hypostasis," of "hypostatic union," of "composite hypostasis," of "enhypostasis," and of "perichoresis"[14] were specified. The debates from the patristic era have, on all these points, opened some extremely important paths—first, of course, for theology but also for anthropology; thus the notion of the "hypostasis-person" regarding Christ flowed back onto the understanding of the human being and onto what makes up its unity: "One could doubt that left to itself anthropological reflection would have progressed as clearly in this direction (in spite of the recognition of the soul's preponderant role in the human composite) if Christology had not pointed out the way for it."[15] Of course, one has reproached such concepts for supporting an abstract and purely "speculative" thought; but this is because one has, in this case, taken them simply as completion points, losing sight of the philosophical inventiveness or, if one prefers, the act of thinking that had given birth to them. Yet it is this very act of thinking that needs recovering if we want to profit from patristic literature during our time.

But it is not only the most speculative writings of the fourth through eighth centuries that are fecund for a philosophical reflection on Christological and Trinitarian questions. In their own way, the writings of the first three centuries also are fecund, less by the use of very elaborate concepts than by the implementation of schemas of thought and modes of thinking that also can inspire our own reflection. One can here take the example of "subordinationism" imputed to the ante-Nicaean Fathers (an example that, in fact, also concerns dogmatic theology but that we present here due to its importance for

14. See George Leonard Prestige, *Dieu dans la pensée patristique*, trans. D. M. (Paris: Aubier-Montaigne, 1955); *God in Patristic Thought* (London: Heinemann, 1936).

15. Bernard Meunier, "Conclusion," in *La personne et le christianisme ancien* [The person and ancient Christianity], ed. Bernard Meunier (Paris: Cerf, 2006), 339.

philosophical thought). The Fathers of the first centuries often use a language that seems "to subordinate" the Son of God to the Father, notably authorizing this by the words of Jesus "the Father is greater than I" (Jn 14:28). Often this "subordinationism" was used as a reproach against them because one saw in it the influence of a contamination by "Platonic" philosophies, and, at the same time, an anticipation of what would be the Arian heresy in the fourth century. But in fact, this language of "subordination," as it is expressed in the Fathers of the first three centuries, ought rather to open us to a thought that, without in any way tending towards Arianism, takes into account the "kenosis" assumed by the Son—that which is due to his very filiation (the Son receives himself from the Father), and, even more, that which is due to the Incarnation (the Son "did not count equality with God ...": Phil 2:6). This does not put into question the importance of the Council of Nicaea, affirming that the Son is consubstantial with the Father—which was then necessary for opposing Arianism; but the faith in the Son of God "of the same substance as the Father" must not prohibit considering the Word made flesh as the One who receives himself from the Father and who emptied himself for us—which is what the Christology of the first three centuries helps us to understand correctly, by its way of emphasizing the subordination of the Son to the Father. There was thus, by this very way, an essential contribution from the ante-Nicaean Fathers to the doctrine of God.

It is finally all patristic literature that opens up horizons to a true work of thought—including some writings that are expressed above all by means of images and symbols (such as the hymns of Ephrem, the poems of Gregory of Nazianzus, and the hymns of Ambrose). It is thus not a matter of subscribing to this or that philosophical movement in order to attempt to illustrate or justify it by some patristic citations. It is a matter, more radically, of profiting from the resources that are offered to us by the writings of the Fathers. It is a matter of thinking with them and, from the experience that one will thus have, of learning to think better, even today, about the One who is a "scandal for Jews" and "folly for Greeks" but who is, for those who are called, "the power of God and the wisdom of God"—for "the foolishness of God is wiser than mankind and the weakness of God is stronger than mankind" (1 Cor 1:25). It is a matter of learning, by contact with the Fathers, how always to venture further in the discovery of the mystery of God revealed in His Son, a mystery that the human mind must always endeavor to take into account and that, nevertheless, always surpasses it because of its immensity.

The preceding expositions have already introduced us to a last issue that is of a particular importance and that it is now necessary to tackle for itself: the contribution to *dogmatic theology*.

The Contribution to Dogmatic Theology

That the Fathers' Christology and Trinitarian doctrine has, from this point of view, a very great importance has always been recognized during the modern era: the first centuries of the Christian era were indeed marked by intense debates regarding Christ and the Trinity, and during this era, doctrinal formulations were developed that were going to be an essential reference for theologians of subsequent times. And today, as yesterday, Christian dogmatics must necessarily refer to the heritage of the Christological and Trinitarian doctrines. It would be possible to justify such an exigency by some fundamental considerations, as we have attempted to do more generally in the first part of this book, by showing that it is essential for contemporary theology to undertake an active relationship with the tradition of the Fathers—not only in order to be informed about it or in order to find in it sources of inspiration but also because some doctrines developed during the early era have a normative value for all Christology and all Trinitarian theology. It would also be possible to take some examples in order to illustrate, on this or that point, the Fathers' contribution to Christian dogmatics—as we have already done, in the preceding section, with the question of "subordinationism." We will, however, give priority to some different points of view, by indicating the importance of patristic literature for the debates with the religious traditions of humanity, then by showing what else is at stake for the current tasks of Christology and Trinitarian theology.

It is first important to mention questions relating to Judaism. We are not placing ourselves here in the realm of actual relations between Christians and Jews (relations that, unfortunately, have in some cases been marked by very harsh controversies) but rather in the properly doctrinal realm. We are also not considering all the questions on which patristics can contribute to the understanding of the connections between Christianity and ancient Israel or between Christianity and Judaism as it developed beginning in the first century of our era. We simply want to emphasize the interest that, in the context of the debates with Judaism, is present in the Fathers' argumentation on the subject of Jesus Christ: this argumentation is often strongly illuminating for today, for, even if it is true that contemporary debates often bring in other questions such as the connection to the law and the meaning of the practices inherited from the tradition, one cannot deny that the separation between Christians and Jews was first occasioned by their divergences on the subject of Jesus of Nazareth and his identity.

It is then necessary to mention the questions touching upon the divine filiation of Christ and "Trinitarian monotheism" in the context of the debate with Islam. The Koran opposes this article of faith with the doctrine of the divine unicity: according to it, God cannot have a Son, for He is the only God. But the Fathers of the Church produced numerous writings in order to justify the affirmation of Christ's divine filiation. They, of course, essentially did it before the appearance of Islam and thus in quite different contexts. (For them, it was rather a matter of the controversies with Arianism—except in the very last phase of the patristic era, when one sees John Damascene debate with Muslims.[16] What is more, the analogy with the past clearly does not mean that it is necessary to repeat the polemical language that sometimes characterized the Christian authors' statements against the Arians!). The Fathers' argumentation is no less enlightening from this same perspective for the doctrinal debate with Islam. It helps in understanding why Christians believe in Jesus Christ as "Son of God"—and this without lapsing into a form of "associationism" that would be perceived as a new form of polytheism. The expositions of Hilary of Poitiers, Basil of Caesarea, and Gregory of Nyssa on the divine filiation of Christ remain, from this point of view, a very valuable source for contemporary Christology.

Above all, patristic literature offers great resources for reflecting

16. Cf. Jean Damascène, *Écrits sur l'islam*, collected and translated by Raymond Le Coz in SC 383 (Paris: Cerf, 1992).

upon a totally crucial question in the present field of "theology of religions": that of the unicity of Christ. Such a question is asked, for example, in the context of the debate with Hinduism, which is ready to recognize Christ as a manifestation (or "avatar") of the divine but only as "one among others" within the Hindu pantheon. But the same question is also raised, in another way, in the context of some "pluralist" theologies, according to which religions are more or less equivalent ways, with each leading toward the "ultimate Reality." Moreover, one knows that, in addition to these movements, the position here evoked is equally encountered in the form of a quite widespread relativism: "all religions have the same value...." Thus the question is this: without lacking respect vis-à-vis those who believe otherwise, how, nevertheless, to maintain, from the Christian point of view, the unicity of Jesus Christ in the history of humanity? Patristic literature powerfully helps to resolve this question, which is undoubtedly one of the central questions, if not the major question, of future Christology.[17] On one hand, the Fathers of the first three centuries were indeed directly confronted by the existence of other religious practices and beliefs, regarding which it was necessary for them to speak and think about the unicity of the way of Christ. On the other, even after the conversion of Constantine and the official recognition of Christianity, the Fathers still had to justify this unicity of Christ vis-à-vis those who rejected it (among other things, in the context of their debates with Neoplatonic philosophers). And it was especially the work of thought that they had to do in order to deepen it within the Christian world, because of the Christological controversies, that led them to clarify in what sense the Christian community confesses Jesus Christ as "unique" within universal history.

One could also mention some of the questions connected to some beliefs that are notably held by Eastern religions, such as the belief in reincarnation. The challenge is the following: how to account for the confession of faith regarding Christ in which Christians do not say

17. Cf. Bernard Sesboüé, *Les "trente glorieuses" de la christologie (1968–2000)* [The "glorious thirty" of Christology (1968–2000)] (Brussels: Lessius, 2012), 454: "The issue here is as important for the Faith as were the issues at the great early councils, from Nicaea to Chalcedon. During these it was Christ's divinity, and his unity as both a human being and as God, that were being debated. It may be that the great theological debate of the twenty-first century will be about whether or not Christ is the unique and only savior of humanity."

that he was reincarnated but that he was resurrected? What is at stake does not, moreover, concern only Eastern religions but also many beliefs that, in the West, have assimilated the belief in reincarnation—even if it is given a different meaning. Yet this challenge was taken up by the Fathers of the Church, at least by some of them who had to take a position regarding the beliefs of "metempsychosis" or the "transmigration of souls," and who, faced with this, endeavored to bring to light the proper meaning of the resurrection of Christ.

Lastly, we live in a world where the Christian faith is sometimes combined with traditions that are more or less ancestral, very diverse in origin and nature: thus in the countries of Africa, Asia, and Oceania, everywhere that Christianity has taken shape in situations strongly influenced by the heritage of traditional beliefs; equally as well in the countries of Europe themselves (through some expressions of "popular religion" or various forms of "syncretism"). It is very illuminating to reread, from this perspective, patristic writings that show what Christianity's presence was in the regions influenced by such traditions—for example in ancient Gaul—in order thus to reflect upon the announcement of the Gospel in such situations and on the necessary discernment between what is compatible with the faith and what, on the contrary, risks compromising a true adherence to the Gospel.

Here we have placed the emphasis on the contribution that the Fathers' Christology and Trinitarian doctrine can make to some of the debates of our time. It would, of course, be possible to emphasize as well some other contributions of patristics to Christian dogmatics—thus in the field of pneumatology (as we will say in another chapter, regarding the procession of the Spirit and the debates on the *Filioque*). But rather than enumerate all these contributions, here it is important to respond to some potential objections and, by this very way, to clarify what are the issues from patristics for Christology and Trinitarian theology.

One of these objections would consist of highlighting the shadows of an era during which Christians were sometimes divided and fought over some theological concepts—whether the matter of the Arian crisis in the fourth century, or the separation among Nestorians, Chalcedonians, and Monophysites in the fifth century, or the separation with the Monothelites in the seventh century. It is clearly not a matter of denying the dramas that were thus produced. Such dramas, however, do not authorize discrediting the history of Christological and Trinitarian dogma in its entirety; this would be misunderstanding all that, in this history, attests to a remarkable deepening of the confession of the Christian faith. The heirs of the patristic tradition—and so we are—precisely have the responsibility of today relating what thus happened, so that we may learn from this past how the mysteries of Christ and the Trinity were deepened in spite of the threat that the heterodox doctrines represented—and, let us add, in spite of the counter-testimony that in our eyes represents the harshness of some behaviors sometimes adopted against "heretics." To relate this to others (even heirs of civilizations completely different from the Mediterranean civilization) is not to impose on them accepting in their turn the very same ways, but it is to transmit to them the memory of the ways by which the truth of the Christological and Trinitarian faith came to us. For such a truth is not communicated otherwise than by the history, and this knowledge must help future generations to receive the faith from the early generations at the same time as it protects us from doctrines that in some way distort the meaning of Revelation.[18]

Another objection is sometimes raised: is not patristic literature too conditioned by its Greco-Latin sources to help us to think about Christ and the God of Jesus Christ in the present context of globalization? It is undeniable that, if the Fathers were confronted by all kinds of religious practices and beliefs, these were most often rooted in the areas surrounding the Mediterranean Basin, whereas today Christianity is being faced with a much more radical otherness—in particular that of Asian civilizations and their multi-secular traditions, and also that of the current European civilization, due to its cultural and religious changes. One is consequently faced with the argument that, even if the Fathers contributed much to the Christological and Trinitarian thought of their day, they can no longer provide an analogous function in our own time. But this objection is in no way decisive. We, on the contrary, would like to emphasize that patristic literature remains of great interest for the present tasks of Christology and Trinitarian theology—and this, not *in spite of* the particularity of its Med-

18. One can refer to what we developed at greater length in the first part, see above chap. 6.

iterranean sources but, paradoxically, because of and *thanks to* them.

This particularity is, first of all, less narrow than the objection seems to presuppose. As said above, not only are the writings of the Greek and Latin Fathers themselves quite varied, but we are little by little discovering an Eastern patristic literature—in the Syriac language (as in Ephrem) and in other languages such as Coptic, Armenian, Georgian, Arabic, etc. This is exactly one of the reasons why this literature is of interest: because it shows us how the Christian faith was stated in different languages and according to quite different schemas of thought, and in this very way the careful study of it can be inspirational for whomever is interested in the genesis of new theological languages in particular cultural spheres.

What is more, in the field of Greek and Latin patristics, the Christological and Trinitarian doctrine testifies to an effort of exceptional inventiveness that, as such, can today inspire theologians attempting to present the Christian faith in the context of their own cultures. Some Fathers can be cited: thus Justin, applying for the first time to the *Logos* the qualifier "preexistent";[19] Irenaeus, with his doctrine of Christ "recapitulating" all things;[20] Tertullian, with his expositions on the flesh of Christ and his explanations regarding the Trinity,[21] or even the author of the *Refutation of All Heresies*[22] and his profound theology of the *Logos*; Origen, meditating on the Wisdom present in God from the beginning and, in this same beginning, conceiving in it the "reasons" for the world to come,[23] etc. Let us, for example, focus on the

19. A. Lukyn Williams translates: "He existed beforehand"; cf. Justin Martyr, *The Dialogue with Trypho*, trans. A. Lukyn Williams (London: Society for Promoting Christian Knowledge, 1930), 96; trans. G. Archambault as *Dialogue avec le juif Tryphon*, 48, 2 (Paris: Picard, 1909), 1:215.

20. See Bernard Sesboüé, *Tout récapituler en Christ. Christologie et sotériologie d'Irénée de Lyon* [Recapitulating everything in Christ. Christology and soteriology of Irenaeus of Lyons] (Paris: Desclée, 2000).

21. See Jérôme Alexandre, *Le Christ de Tertullien* [The Christ of Tertullian] (Paris: Desclée, 2003); Moingt, *Théologie trinitaire de Tertullien*.

22. One does not know with certitude who this author is (Hippolytus? Josipus?); cf. *Philosophoumena ou Réfutation de toutes les hérésies*, X, 33, trans. Auguste Siouville, vol. 2 (Paris: Rieder, 1928), 223–28; and see our study "La redécouverte des anténicéens et ses enjeux pour la théologie trinitaire," in *Les sources du renouveau de la théologie trinitaire au XXe siècle* [The sources of the renewal of Trinitarian theology in the twentieth century], ed. Emmanuel Durand and Vincent Holzer (Paris: Cerf, 2008), 59–73.

23. Cf. Origen, *On First Principles*, I, 4, 4–5; Butterworth, 42–43; Origène, *Traité des principes*, vol. 1, *Livres I–II*, trans. Henri Crouzel and M. Simonetti, SC 252 (Paris: Cerf, 1978), 171–73.

case of Tertullian; faced with the "unitarian" doctrine of Praxeas (who feared that the difference of the Father and the Son led to affirming "two gods"), he gives us this remarkable exposition of Trinitarian theology:

> I declare that I recognize two of them: God and his Word, the Father and His Son. For the root and the tree are two things, but united; the spring and the stream are two realities but indivisible; the sun and the ray are two forms, but form one. Everything that goes out from another is necessarily second to that from which it goes out, but it is not for all that separate. For where there is a second, there are two, and where there is a third, there are three. For the third is the Spirit that proceeds from God and from the Son, just as the third from the root is the fruit that goes out from the tree, the third from the spring is the stream that goes out from the river, and the third from the sun is the light that goes out from the ray. Each of them, however, is not foreign to the principle from which it draws its properties.[24]

This is the very same Tertullian who created the theological use of the word "person" in order to express the unity of God and man in Jesus.[25] One readily grasps, through such examples, the appearance of languages attempting to take account of the Christological and Trinitarian faith. Those are the moments of genesis, the knowledge of which is important not just for historical study but also for the theological task itself. But this is valid not only for the ante-Nicaean period; the following centuries themselves also testify to a very great creativity in the matter, which was all the more necessary for taking up the challenge of Arianism or for taking a position in the context of the Nestorian and Monophysite controversies: one could here mention Athanasius, Hilary, the Cappadocians, Cyril of Alexandria, Leo the Great, and many others, including Maximus the Confessor and John Damascene.[26]

What is at stake is important for the "contextual" theologies that

24. Tertullian, *Adversus Praxean*, VIII, 6–7 (Corpus Christianorum, Series Latina 2, 1168).

25. Ibid., XXVII, II (Corpus Christianorum, Series Latina 2, 1199).

26. See, for example, *Dieu Trinité d'hier à demain avec Hilaire de Poitiers (actes du congrès-colloque du Futuroscope de Poitiers, 15 au 17 November 2002)* [God Trinity from yesterday to tomorrow with Hilary of Poitiers. Proceedings of the congress-colloquium of Poitiers's Futuroscope], ed. Dominique Bertrand (Paris: Cerf, 2010); or also Bernard Sesboüé, *Saint Basile et la Trinité. Un acte théologique au IVe siècle. Le rôle de Basile dans l'élaboration de la doctrine et du langage trinitaires* [Saint Basil and the Trinity. A theological act in the fourth century. The role of Basil in the development of Trinitarian doctrine] (Paris: Desclée, 1998).

today are being developed outside of Europe: these theologies can discover in the Fathers forms of understanding the faith that are likely to inspire them in their own work of doctrinal development, for they, in their respective cultural spheres, also have to choose images and concepts in order to account for the Christian mystery. But it is, moreover, essential for European theology itself to pass along these moments of genesis, to discover in some way the process by which the Fathers were able, upon the foundation of the New Testament, to deepen the meaning of the faith of the God of Jesus Christ and to draw from that a new inspiration for the tasks of thinking that are essential for our times.

One will add that, if patristic literature depends a great deal upon Greco-Latin culture, this culture ought not to be considered only from the point of view of what in our eyes represents obstacles (such as, for example, the tendency towards a kind of depreciation of corporeality) but also from the point of view of what, in itself, helps receiving and thinking about the revelation of Christ—for example, the meaning of history (that emerged little by little, despite concurrent representations, such as those of cyclical time) or even the meaning of the human person and his dignity (so well attested to by certain characters from Homer and the Greek tragedies). There is here an anthropological base that, in spite of all the ambiguities and all the dramas of Greco-Roman civilization, was in the end—to repeat an expression of Eusebius of Caesarea—like an "evangelical preparation" and that is, in any case, presupposed by the thought of the Fathers of the Church on Christ. Of course, such representations are not as widespread as one formerly believed (Hinduism and Buddhism, in particular, rest upon other conceptions of the world and the human being). But precisely, do these representations not speak to us of something that is universal, a kind of "possession for all time" (as Thucydides said in a completely different context),[27] a good that is, in any case, required so that one can truthfully account for the "economy of salvation," of the personal identity of Christ, and of what he was "once for all" in the history of the world? If such is the case, the particularity that patristic literature receives from its Greco-Latin rootedness is not an obstacle

27. Thucydides, *History of the Peloponnesian War*, vol. 1 (London: William Heinemann, 1928), 41.

but contributes, on the contrary, to highlighting the importance of this literature for thinking about Christ (and it would be necessary to reason in an analogous way for the representation of the Trinity)—for, in our age of globalization, dialogue with the religious traditions of humanity more than ever returns us back to, even beyond doctrinal considerations, a debate on the representations of the world, history, the human being, and his relationship to the Absolute.

Thus it does not suffice to affirm the major importance of Christological and Trinitarian doctrines for the patristic era. Nor does it suffice to recognize how much these doctrines were determinative for the theology of subsequent eras. We hope to have shown that today the writings of the Fathers still remain a reference and a source for all reflection on Christ and the Trinity. The cultural and religious situation of our time gives us new reasons for rereading these writings in a particularly enlightening and fruitful way. In this field, as in others, patristic literature is not simply what opened the way to the theology of the Middle Ages and modern times. It is also that to which we must always return, not just to repeat everything that was said then, but in order to find, in contact with the Fathers, light and inspiration for our own effort today to account for the faith of the God of Jesus Christ.

CHAPTER 12

Patristics and Ecumenism

In the first part of this work, we have already highlighted that some theologians in particular recognized the importance of the study of the Fathers for reflection upon the unity of Christians—thus Johann Adam Möhler in the nineteenth century and Yves Congar in the twentieth. We have also recalled that, according to its original plan, the collection Sources Chrétiennes was, above all, to make the Greek Fathers known to French-speaking readers and, by this, make a contribution to the "union of the Churches." Thus, it is important to tackle the question of the connections between patristics and ecumenism: in what way is the study of the Fathers important for the search for full communion between Christians?

In our chapter on the Church, we have already given one element of the answer: patristic literature, through some of its writings, attests to the exigency for a communion within diversity (one recalls Irenaeus's intervention regarding the controversy on the date of Easter or even the statements of Augustine and Gregory the Great on the variety of liturgical usages).[1] Such testimonies are of great importance from the perspective of a communion of Churches that would not imply a standardization of practices but would make a place for legitimate differences. Without returning to this point (that, moreover, is valid not just for the relationships between Churches but also asks each Church to recognize a real diversity *ad intra*, provided that this does not harm the communion), we would rather like to consider, in the present chapter, the differences that were or that still are recognized as divisive and to show in what way the writings of the Fathers can here be very valuable for advances in ecumenical dialogue.

1. See chap. 8, pp. 202–6.

An objection could be raised at the outset: does not patristic literature bear witness to the sometimes violent controversies with those traditionally described as "heretics," and can one, consequently, rely on it in order to make progress in dialogues that today must be undertaken with mutual respect? This objection here calls for a first exposition on the notions of "orthodoxy" and "heresy," very much discussed for several decades, and on the way in which the texts of the Fathers can be reread from the perspective of ecclesial communion. We will then see how, in recent decades, patristic literature has indeed led to important advances in the ecumenical project. We will show this by successively considering the dialogue with the Churches of the Nestorian and Monophysite tradition, the dialogue with Orthodoxy, and the dialogue with the Churches coming from the Protestant Reformation. Looking at these dialogues will allow identifying some major areas in which future ecumenical reflection also ought to be able to benefit from in-depth work on the writings of the Fathers.

"Orthodoxy" and "Heresy"

It is first necessary to face the objection according to which the literature of Christian Antiquity, because of the significance of the controversies with the "heretics" and the way in which they were sometimes treated, could not be rightly invoked in the cadre of a contemporary ecumenical reflection. Of course, patristic literature contains many writings against Christians presented as "heterodox": Marcion, Montanus, Arius, Apollinaris, Nestorius, Eutyches, and many others. Furthermore, some of these "heretics" were the object of punishments that today appear to us unacceptable (but it is equitable to state that in an inverse way some "orthodox" Christians were themselves also severely punished by their adversaries—such as Athanasius, exiled several times—or were the object of a real persecution—as Maximus the Confessor). The heresiological literature of Christian Antiquity, therefore, raises the question: did not the Catholic Church affirm its identity by a process of exclusion vis-à-vis "others"—namely those who were denounced as "heretics" (to say nothing here of Jews and "pagans")?

In order to shed light on this question, it is first important to recognize how the problem of the connection between "orthodoxy" and "heresy" has been addressed during the modern era and in our time. One can distinguish several stages in the thought on this subject. Traditionally, until the first decades of the twentieth century, one repeated the version formerly given by the historian Eusebius of Caesarea: orthodoxy was the teaching given by Jesus to his apostles and transmitted to the bishops; heresies, themselves, were the incursion of dangerous errors into the Christian tradition, under the influence of this or that "pseudo-Christian." This traditional representation was little by little weakened in the nineteenth century and at the beginning of the twentieth century because advances in historical science allowed establishing that the earliest so-called "heretical" practices and ideas did not truly come after orthodoxy but that they were rather contemporary to the doctrines described as orthodox. Then came a second stage, represented by a work of Walter Bauer.[2] He reversed the traditional thesis and explained that, contrary to what the early authors had implied, heresies did not appear as dissidences toward an already constituted orthodoxy. Actually, he said, there were a number of doctrines, often contradictory, that claimed to follow the Gospel; and it is only little by little that some of them were imposed as "orthodox." More recently, Alain Le Boulluec took up the question in his work *La notion d'hérésie dans la littérature grecque. IIe–IIIe siècles.*[3] He compares the two preceding approaches: both indeed presuppose that one can identify orthodoxy and heresy in isolation, either to say that orthodoxy preceded the heresies (that was the traditional thesis) or to say (with Bauer) that heresy precedes orthodoxy. Yet, for Le Boulluec (whose work reflects the type of approach developed in other fields by Michel Foucault), orthodoxy and heresy are not to be understood first as "things," or as "essences," but as "notions" that must always be defined in connection with each other. The author recalls that originally the Greek word *hairesis* simply designated a "choice" and in this

2. Walter Bauer, *Rechtgläubigkeit und Ketzerei im ältesten Christentum* [Orthodoxy and heresy at the beginning of Christianity] (Tübingen: Mohr, 1934); the first edition was dated 1930; translated by Philippe Vuagnat as *Orthodoxie et hérésie aux débuts du christianisme* (Paris: Cerf, 2009).

3. Alain Le Boulluec, *La notion d'hérésie dans la littérature grecque. IIe–IIIe siècles* [The notion of heresy in the Greek literature. Second–third centuries] (Paris: Institut d'Études Augustiniennes, 1985).

way served to describe a group having affinities of ideas, theories, and common practices, without this word having the least pejorative connotation. He maintains that Justin in the second century represents a decisive turning point. It is indeed in his work that the word *hairesis* came to designate a party or sect that held itself to be outside of the established or recognized tradition, thus a "heretical" group in the pejorative sense that it would acquire; Le Boulluec writes: "it falls to Justin to have invented heresy."[4] A new stage was introduced by a Jewish researcher, Daniel Boyarin, in a book published in 2004 titled *Border Lines* and translated into French under the title *La partition du judaïsme et du christianisme*.[5] The author maintains that the patristic discourse on heretics quite especially contributed to defining the Christian identity, and even to constructing Christianity, not only by locating it in relation to "heresies" but also, and even more so, by locating it in relation to the practices and doctrines of Jews; he, moreover, shows that a heresiological discourse was simultaneously developed among the Jews in the second and third centuries (the Jews considering Christians as *minim*).

In view of these latter works, we must indeed recognize that heresiological statements (and also statements on Jews and "pagans") have themselves contributed to Christians becoming aware of what constituted their doctrine and their practices. However, it is here necessary to make some important clarifications.

First of all, even if it is true that the critical and often polemical discourse on "the heretics" has historically contributed to the awareness of the "Catholic" identity, it is necessary to maintain that basically the Fathers of the Church had the conviction of being faithful to the Tradition received from the apostles. In this sense, the idea of an "invention" of heresy or of orthodoxy must not lead to a misunderstanding. One can, of course, say that the notion of orthodoxy and the notion of heresy were developed together, and each by the other, but even if this phenomenon appeared particularly beginning with Justin

4. Ibid., 110.

5. Daniel Boyarin, *Border Lines. The Partition of Judaeo-Christianity* (Philadelphia: The University of Pennsylvania Press, 2004); translated by Jacqueline Rastoin as *La partition du judaïsme et du christianisme* (Paris: Cerf, 2011).

in the second century, it is noticeable prior to Justin, with the New Testament itself. Jesus already warns against those who will detract from the truth and from the true life, and the Epistles of Paul demand fleeing from error and becoming attached to the teaching of the Lord.

On the other hand, a reflection on the truth cannot be satisfied with only a historical or sociocultural approach. This approach is, of course, necessary and valuable, but it is not decisive: it is not because Christian authors made use of heresiological discourse in order to better affirm their Christian identity that what they said was in itself erroneous. A simply historical or sociocultural perspective would in fact expose itself to a risk of relativism. Boyarin, of course, avoids this risk, for at the outset he affirms his own convictions. But one could be tempted to believe that, if the affirmation of one's own identity is first nourished by discourse against others, there would be no more convincing reasons for being an orthodox Christian than a Marcionite or an Arian one. That the affirmation of the Christian identity, like that of the Jewish identity, was developed even with the help of heresiology is an incontestable fact, which history and sociocultural analysis allow us precisely to understand better. However, in the matter of the relationship to the truth, one cannot rely upon this fact in order to say that no belief or doctrine is itself preferable to another. Thus, the fact that Tertullian was himself so violently opposed to Marcion does not mean that basically he was not right to affirm, in light of the confession of faith, the perfect humanity of God become man. Or even, the fact that Cyril of Alexandria had such a contestable attitude during the Council of Ephesus does not prohibit recognizing that this same Cyril developed, in conformity to the hymn of the Letter to the Philippians, an admirable reflection on the kenosis of the Word Incarnate.

After all is said and done, patristic literature, from the perspective from which we are examining it, testifies to two orientations that in practice have often been mixed: on one hand, one cannot deny that, in at least a number of cases, it is in polemicizing against others, indeed in giving proof of intolerance toward them, that the Christian authors of Antiquity affirmed what they held to be true; but on the other, their will to formulate "orthodox" doctrines in matters of faith must be fully recognized: it attests to their concern for fidelity to the Gospel and to the tradition received from the apostles. And this dual acknowledgement sheds light on the way in which the ecumenical dialogue must today be allowed to be enlightened by the Fathers. Of course, the relations between Christians must no longer be contaminated by any form of intolerance; they must be, on the contrary, marked by goodwill, esteem, and respect. But it is no less necessary to attempt to express the Christian faith in a manner that is as correct and as true as is possible—and from this point of view the contribution of patristic literature remains of major importance.

It would, besides, be a serious error to retain from this literature's heritage only the heresiological discourse and the intolerance that sometimes marked it. It is also actually possible to find, in the first Christian centuries, remarkable examples of "ecumenism" before it existed, as we will have the occasion of specifying later. It is, in any case, a fact that the testimony of patristic literature has already enabled some important advances in the dialogue between Christians. We would like to show this through some significant examples, beginning with the relations between the Catholic Church and the Churches of the Nestorian and Monophysite tradition.

The Dialogue with the Churches of the Nestorian and Monophysite Traditions

The Council of Chalcedon (451) had spoken of the "two natures" of Christ; but some Christians denounced this "dyophysite" language and continued exclusively to support the formula formerly favored by Cyril of Alexandria: "a single nature of Christ." Other Christians, partisans of the "dyophysite" language, never had accepted the condemnation of which Nestorius was the object during the Council of Ephesus (431); and in spite of the act of union of 433 (by which Cyril had recognized the legitimacy of the "two natures" language), they considered that the traditional language of Cyril could in no way be accepted. Such was the origin of the Monophysite and Nestorian Churches that developed in the East in the last part of the patristic era and of which some Churches are today heirs.[6]

6. We will not here tell the history of the controversies that are at the origin of the ecclesial divisions; we refer to the expositions of Aloys Grillmeier in his work *Christ in Christian Tradition* (cf. chap. 4, pp. 90–91). For a reevaluation of the early controversies

Yet, in recent decades, a deeper knowledge of the patristic texts has enabled the success of several agreements of great importance. A good example of this, from the cadre of the relations with the Churches of the Nestorian tradition, is given to us by the declaration signed in 1994 by Pope John Paul II and His Holiness Mar Denkha IV, catholicos-patriarch of the Assyrian Church of the East. One reads this in it:

> Therefore our Lord Jesus Christ is true God and true man, perfect in his divinity and perfect in his humanity, consubstantial with the Father and consubstantial with us in all things but sin. His divinity and his humanity are united in one person, without confusion or change, without division or separation. In him has been preserved the difference of the natures of divinity and humanity with all their properties, faculties, and operations. But far from constituting "one and another," the divinity and humanity are united in the person of the same and unique Son of God and Lord Jesus Christ, who is the object of a single adoration.[7]

The first lines of this paragraph principally emphasize the difference of the two natures, in conformity with the language favored by the Churches of the Nestorian tradition (and that is also, let us recall, the language of Chalcedon). At the same time, from these first lines, it is clear that the two natures are not understood as separated nor even juxtaposed: the divinity and the humanity are "united in one person," and the text once again stresses this in the last sentence, by specifying that the two natures do not constitute "one and another." "Dyophysism" thus does not exclude the union between the divinity and the humanity. The declaration thus respects the equilibrium of the

with respect to contemporary ecumenism, see the work of André de Halleux, *Patrologie et œcuménisme. Thèmes, contextes, personnages* [Patristics and ecumenism. Themes, contexts, people], ed. Cristian Badilita (Paris: Beauchesne, 2010). Let us additionally point out, regarding the specific conflict between Cyril of Alexandria and the Antiochians, the study of Jean-Noël Guinot, "Rétablir l'unité après la déchirure: Cyrille d'Alexandrie et Théodoret de Cyr, des modèles pour le dialogue entre les Églises?" [Restoring unity after tearing: Cyril of Alexandria and Theodoret of Cyrus, Models for the dialog between the Churches], in *Les Pères de l'Église dans le monde d'aujourd'hui* [The Fathers of the Church in today's world] (Paris: Beauchesne, 2006), 183–208; repr. Jean-Noël Guinot, *Théodoret de Cyr exégète et théologien*, vol. 2, *Un théologien engagé dans le conflit nestorien (431–451)* [Theodoret of Cyrus exeget and theologian] (Paris: Cerf, 2012), 373–97.

7. John Paul II and Mar Denkha IV, "The Common Christological Declaration between the Catholic Church and the Assyrian Church of the East" (1994), http://vatican.va/roman_curia/pontifical_councils/chrstuni/documents/rc_pc_chrstuni_doc_11111994_assyrian-church_en.html.

Christological formula by taking account of the famous expressions of the Council of Chalcedon: "without confusion or change, without division or separation." This means that one can in no way impute to the Assyrian Church of the East the heresy known by the name of "Nestorianism": the declaration shows that there is actually agreement on the doctrine regarding Christ. This is what the beginning of the following paragraph confirms: "Christ therefore is not an *'ordinary man'* whom God adopted in order to reside in him and inspire him, as in the righteous ones and the prophets."[8] Such an agreement in the faith, nevertheless, does not exclude a difference of language, but this is no longer recognized as a source of separation:

> The humanity to which the Blessed Virgin Mary gave birth always was that of the Son of God himself. That is the reason why the Assyrian Church of the East is praying the Virgin Mary as "the Mother of Christ our God and Savior." In the light of this same faith the Catholic tradition addresses the Virgin Mary as "the Mother of God" and also as "the Mother of Christ." We both recognize the legitimacy and rightness of these expressions of the same faith, and we both respect the preference of each Church in her liturgical life and piety.[9]

This passage is of a particular importance if one recalls that the Nestorian controversy erupted in 428 precisely regarding the expression "Mother of God" (*Theotokos*): Nestorius did not accept this expression, whereas Cyril of Alexandria, on the contrary, went to its defense. Placed in the context of its time, the debate around the word *Theotokos* had a properly Christological stake: as Cyril clearly saw, the rejection here of this word undermined the unity of the Word made flesh (Mary is called "Mother of God" clearly not in the sense that she would be the mother of the divinity but in the sense that her son Jesus is none other than the Word of God become man). But the agreement with the Assyrian Church of the East shows that it fully recognizes the divinity of Christ; from now on, according to the declaration, there is no reason to impose on it the use of the expression "Mother of God" since its preferred expression ("Mother of Christ our God and Savior") sufficiently speaks of the divine identity of Christ. This is a beautiful illustration of what one calls in ecumenical language a "differentiated

8. Ibid.
9. Ibid.

consensus": inasmuch as the partners agree upon the essentials of the faith, the diversity of their languages can be recognized as completely legitimate.

Some analogous agreements were equally concluded with the Churches of the Monophysite tradition. Thus, in 1973, Pope Paul VI signed a declaration with the Coptic Patriarch Shenouda III:

> We confess that our Lord and God and Savior and King of us all, Jesus Christ, is perfect God with respect to His divinity, perfect man with respect to His humanity. In Him, His divinity is united with His humanity in a real, perfect union without mingling, without commixtion, without confusion, without alteration, without division, without separation. His divinity did not separate from His humanity for an instant, not for the twinkling of an eye. He who is God eternal and invisible became visible in the flesh, and took upon Himself the form of a servant. In Him are preserved all the properties of the divinity and all the properties of the humanity, together in a real, perfect, indivisible, and inseparable union.[10]

As one sees, the text particularly emphasizes the union of the divinity and the humanity: one was never separated from the other, "not for the twinkling of an eye." But this emphasis, dear to the Monophysite Churches, in no way implies the idea of a "confusion" of the divinity and the humanity (this same idea that one had rightly denounced, in the fifth century, in the monk Eutyches). In fact, the declaration explicitly says that the union of the divinity and the humanity is "without confusion." Of course, it does not repeat the language of the "two natures"; indeed, the Catholic Church considers that there is no reason whatsoever to impose this "dyophysite" language on a Church of the Monophysite tradition since it, without using such language, no less recognizes the difference between the divinity and the humanity. The end of the sentence clears up all ambiguity on this point by repeating the formula of Chalcedon: in Christ "are preserved all the properties of the divinity and all the properties of the humanity." It is thus clear that the doctrine of the Orthodox Coptic Church, without being "dyophysite," can in no way be compared to the thinking of Eutyches and that, whatever may be its own emphases, it is in communion with

10. "Common Declaration of Pope Paul VI and the Pope of Alexandria Shenouda III" (1973), http://vatican.va/roman_curia/pontifical_councils/chrstuni/anc-orient-ch-docs/rc_pc_christuni_doc_19730510_copti_en.html.

that of the Catholic Church. Other examples could still be mentioned: thus, in 1984, the agreement of Pope John Paul II and His Holiness Moran Mar Ignatius, Syrian patriarch of Antioch and all the East; or even, in 1996, the agreement reached with His Holiness Karekin I, catholicos of all the Armenians.[11]

Undoubtedly, it is necessary to make two important clarifications. On one hand, as we have indicated in passing, the Christological agreements that were thus signed do not mean that the controversies of the fifth century were based on simple misunderstandings. This remark is clearly valid for Eutyches whose Monophysitism was not acceptable with regard to the Christian faith. It is also valid, to a lesser degree, for Nestorius himself to the extent that his thinking, although unjustly exaggerated by his adversaries, does not give enough credit to the unity of the Word made flesh. It additionally can be valid, up to a point, for some theologians of the Nestorian and Monophysite Churches in the following centuries; at least there is a debate on this point—thus regarding Severus of Antioch and his Monophysitism that Joseph Lebon and other patrologists have rehabilitated, but of which Jean-Claude Larchet maintains that, all the while being "moderated" compared with that of Eutyches, it cannot be considered as fully orthodox.[12] On the other, as important as they may be, the Christological agreements do not suffice to restore the communion between the Churches; in fact, as the declaration with Patriarch Shenouda III says, the theological differences have been "nourished and widened by non-theological factors," and the rapprochements effected in the doctrinal realm do not bring to an end the separations that are also connected to the political circumstances of the past as well as to the changes of the diverse Churches throughout history. The fact remains that these rapprochements, in their way, already attest to the fecundity of patristic work for the relations of the Catholic Church with the Churches of the Nestorian and Monophysite traditions.

11. "Common Declaration of Pope John Paul II and His Holiness Mar Ignatius Zakka I Iwas" (1984), http://vatican.va/roman_curia/pontifical_councils/chrstuni/anc-orient-ch-docs/rc_pc_christuni_doc_19840623_jp-ii-zakka-i_en.html; "Common Declaration of John Paul II and Catholicos Karekin II" (1996), http://vatican.va/roman_curia/pontifical_councils/chrstuni/anc-orient-ch-docs/rc_pc_christuni_doc_19961213_jp-ii-karekin-i_en.html.

12. Cf. Jean-Claude Larchet, *Personne et nature. La Trinité–Le Christ–L'homme* [Person and nature. The Trinity–Christ–man] (Paris: Cerf, 2011), 99–132.

The Dialogue with Orthodoxy

It is in the last centuries of the first millennium that divergences were deepened between the "Latins" and the "Greeks"—divergences that were going to lead to the schism of 1054. We are here in the presence of a separation that, even if it is the culmination of a long historical process, does not go back as far as the patristic era. This already suggests the benefit that there is in examining the literature of the Fathers from the perspective of the dialogue between the Catholic Church and the various Orthodox Churches.[13] More precisely, one ought to expect much from Greek patristics that (with the exception of Origen)[14] is a common reference for all these Churches. This, in particular, is what the very significant studies that André de Halleux collected in his work *Patrologie et œcuménisme* show; the author writes in its preface: "that the mutual recognition of the Fathers resisted schism, even in the darkest moments, has, since that time, inspired all the attempts at rapprochement and reconciliation. Only, indeed, the patristic 'auctoritas' is able to provide the two Churches, in their dialogue as well in their polemics, a common reference and a common criterion for the interpretation of the mystery revealed in the Holy Scriptures."[15] Of course, the same author recognizes that often in history the references to patristics by Catholic and Orthodox theologians may have been diverted to purely partisan ends: one would then have used this or that citation in order to defend one's own positions or to attack the positions of others. But the ecumenical dialogue rightly calls for a totally other way of relating to the writings of the Fathers:

> By maintaining the patristic testimony in its real context, which is that of an era preceding the "heretical" dissensions and the schismatic isolations between Catholics and the Orthodox, one contributes to making of this testimony the instrument of reconciliation. The apparently opposed points of view henceforth turn out to be non-contradictory approaches, rather complementary, or

13. Here we are giving priority to the Catholic Church's point of view, but the Churches coming from the Reformation, as well as "Latin" Churches, themselves participate in the dialogue with Orthodoxy and must as well examine the writings of the Fathers from this perspective.

14. On this point, see p. 300.

15. Halleux, *Patrologie et œcuménisme*, xiii.

even convergent, of the same unfathomable mystery of God and his economy, that each of the two Churches tackles according to its own "charism."[16]

The fecundity of such an approach is verified—for one part only, it is true, but, nevertheless, in a significant way—regarding two questions that are among the most important in the dialogue between the Catholic Church and Orthodoxy: the question of the *Filioque*, and that of the ministry of communion between the various Churches.

From the point of view that we hold here, the question of the *Filioque* was notably tackled by de Halleux, in 1978, in the context of a paper that argued "for an ecumenical agreement on the procession of the Holy Spirit." In it he expressed the wish for a common reference to the writings of the Fathers:

> This common reference would lead the Orthodox and the Catholics to the period prior to the schism, when the Trinitarian theologies of the Greek East and the Latin West peacefully coexisted even in their pluriformity. No longer would either of the two Churches henceforth require that the subsequent clarifications of its own theology be held by the other to be a norm of faith; but each of the two would as well recognize in the other the legitimacy of its particular theological developments.[17]

De Halleux added that such a return to patristic literature would also have the advantage of "recalling theology to a greater sobriety": in fact, even though the "Pneumatomachi" spoke of the Spirit as a creature—otherwise, they thought, one would be obliged to say that the Spirit "was engendered" as a brother of the Son—the Fathers of the fourth century only "negatively defined the procession" (the last word meaning that the Spirit is neither created nor engendered). Moreover, even when the patristic tradition appealed to some philosophical notions as those of "principle" or of "cause," it did not give them absolute value.[18] In the rest of his paper, de Halleux made very important clarifications on the early doctrine. On one hand, the statement of the Creed of Constantinople on the Spirit who "proceeds from the Father" means above all that the Spirit is not a creature; as such, it does not involve taking a

16. Ibid.

17. André de Halleux, "Pour un accord œcuménique sur la procession de l'Esprit Saint et l'addition du 'Filioque' au Symbole" [Toward an ecumenical agreement on the procession of the Holy Spirit and the addition of the "Filioque"], in *Patrologie et œcuménisme*, 434.

18. Ibid., 435.

position on the way in which the Spirit "proceeds from the Father," and one thus cannot invoke it against the Latin affirmation of the *Filioque*. On the other, if this last affirmation was developed by the Latins, it must above all be understood in the context of the opposition to Arianism: by associating the Son with the Father, one clearly meant that the Son is consubstantial with the Father. The addition of the *Filioque*, thus understood, does not place into question the affirmation of the "divine monarchy" to which the Greek Fathers are very attached (and that Augustine himself honors by recognizing that the Spirit proceeds from the Father *principaliter*—that is, "as from the unique principle").[19] De Halleux thus asks for recognizing the complementarity of the two traditions, and he concludes by pointing out what was perhaps "the only way for an honorable agreement": the Catholic Church could recognize the intrinsic truth of "monopatrism," whereas, for its part, the Orthodox Church would in the same way recognize the authenticity of the *Filioque*, understood as an equivalent of the traditional formula "the Spirit proceeds from the Father through the Son."[20]

In 1995, an important document from the Pontifical Council for the Unity of Christians took note of the results that patristic studies had thus achieved. This document affirms that no profession of faith can contradict the doctrine taught by the indivisible Church and that found its expression in the Creed of Constantinople: "the Spirit proceeds from the Father." The Latin formula (*ex Patre Filioque procedit*) is no less legitimate, but, apart from the fact that the Latin verb *procedere* has a broader meaning than the Greek verb *ekporeuesthai* (that is itself reserved for the procession of the Spirit from the Father), it expresses the consubstantiality of the Son with the Father and, from this point of view, does not prevent recognizing the "original relationship that the Holy Spirit maintains as person with the Father."[21]

It is true that this Roman document has not been received equally by Orthodox theologians. If it was widely praised by Olivier Clément, it also sparked reservations and even, sometimes, basic objections. So

19. See ibid., 436–40.

20. Ibid., 442.

21. Pontifical Council for Promoting Christian Unity, "The Greek and Latin Traditions about the Procession of the Holy Spirit: Clarification" (1995), http://ewtn.com/library/CURIA/PCCUFILQ.HTM.

it is that Jean-Claude Larchet, all the while recognizing the positive contribution of the text, himself reproaches the reduction of the question of the *Filioque* to a simple linguistic misunderstanding. More fundamentally, he reproaches it for disassociating the procession according to the person (that would be emphasized principally by the Greek Fathers) and the procession according to the nature (especially emphasized by the Latin Fathers). Actually, he affirms, the Spirit proceeds "from the Father alone" not simply according to the hypostasis but also according to the essence. Larchet additionally considers the idea of the mediation of the Son in the procession of the Spirit as unacceptable. This, he says, would cause confusion between the "economical" plan (by which one may actually speak of the Spirit as sent by the Son) and the plan of "theology" (for which one must maintain the procession of the Spirit from the Father alone).[22] It is clearly not possible here to go back over these questions that would call for lengthy expositions on Trinitarian theology. In any case, Larchet's objections show that, if patristic studies have already made possible important advances on the question of the *Filioque*, this is still not entirely resolved. One may hope that new studies will allow going further in the sense of an ecumenical consensus, in such a way that the Catholic Church and Orthodoxy, whatever the diversity of their traditions may be, agree in depth on the procession of the Spirit.

The other question that we mentioned above, that of the ministry of communion between the Churches, itself also requires significant work on patristic literature. This work, in fact, has already borne fruit. It would be possible to show this through the document of the Groupe des Dombes on "le ministère de communion dans l'Église universelle" [The ministry of communion in the universal Church] (for, even if this document emanates from a group for dialogue between Catholics and Protestants, it puts forward some propositions that are also valid for the Churches of Orthodoxy; and it does this notably thanks to a journey through the history of the first millennium). But here

22. Cf. Jean-Claude Larchet, "La question du *Filioque*. À propos de la 'Clarification' proposée par le Conseil pontifical pour la promotion de l'Unité des chrétiens" [The issue of the *Filioque*. About the "clarification" proposed by the Pontifical Council for Promoting Christian Unity], reprinted as an article published in 1997 in *Le Messager orthodoxe*), in *Personne et nature*, 11–63.

it is above all necessary to mention the document "Ecclesial Communion, Conciliarity and Authority" that was produced by the Joint International Commission for the Theological Dialogue between the Roman Catholic Church and the Orthodox Church during its meeting in Ravenna in October 2007.[23]

This document distinguishes three levels of ecclesial institutions: that of the local Church around its bishop, that of a region comprised of several local Churches, and that of the "inhabited land" (*oikoumenè*) that encompasses all the local Churches. Between the East and the West, there are not (from the point of view of synodality and authority) significant differences on what the local Church is. On the contrary, one finds them more at the regional level, for here the exercise of conciliarity is clearly more influential in the East than in the West; the differences are equally appreciable at the universal level, but in this latter case it is in the West that the exercise of conciliarity is the most accentuated. But the document emphasizes the importance that the ecumenical councils have had in history, reuniting bishops "from all regions," and in particular "those of the five major sees, Rome, Constantinople, Alexandria, Antioch, and Jerusalem, according to the ancient order."[24] The two parties that signed this document agree to speak of the importance of such a conciliarity; they additionally state that the Churches, up to the ninth century, recognized a series of prerogatives for those who are the "first" (*protoi*)—this being valid not only for the bishop at the level of the local Church and for the "first" of the bishops at the level of a province, but also for the bishop of Rome as "first" among the patriarchs.[25] The document here refers to the testimony of the patristic era:

23. The Joint International Commission for Theological Dialogue between the Roman Catholic Church and the Orthodox Church, "Ecclesiological and Canonical Consequences of the Sacramental Nature of the Church: Ecclesial Communion, Conciliarity and Authority," http://vatican.va/roman_curia/pontifical_councils/chrstuni/ch_orthodox_docs/rc_pc_chrstuni_doc_20071013_documento-ravenna_en.html. See also Frans Bouwen, "Ravenne 2007. Xe Session plénière de la Commission mixte internationale pour le dialogue théologique entre l'Église catholique et l'Église orthodoxe" [Ravenna 2007. Tenth plenary meeting of the International Joint Commission for Theological Dialogue between the Catholic Church and the Orthodox Church], *Proche-Orient Chrétien* 58 (2008): 59–78.

24. Joint International Commission,"Ecclesiological and Canonical Consequences," no. 35.

25. Ibid., no. 44.

These relations, among the bishops themselves, between the bishops and their respective *protoi*, and also among the *protoi* themselves in the canonical order (*taxis*) witnessed by the ancient Church, nourished and consolidated ecclesial communion. History records the consultations, letters, and appeals to major sees, especially to that of Rome, which vividly express the solidarity that *koinonia* creates.... Both sides agree that this canonical *taxis* was recognized by all in the era of the undivided Church. Further, they agree that Rome, as the Church that "presides in love" according to the phrase of St. Ignatius of Antioch (*To the Romans*, prologue), occupied the first place in the *taxis*, and that the bishop of Rome was therefore the *protos* among the patriarchs.[26]

The document adds that it is true that all are not in agreement with the manner of interpreting the early texts on the prerogatives of the bishop of Rome as *protos*. Nevertheless, it says, "Conciliarity at the universal level, exercised in the ecumenical councils, implies an active role of the bishop of Rome, as *protos* of the bishops of the major sees, in the consensus of the assembled bishops." From the Catholic position, this point can be recognized as an important advance that is not just unilateral because, at the same time, the text emphasizes the synodal dimension to which Orthodoxy is especially attached. Both aspects are maintained with a perfect equilibrium: "Primacy and conciliarity are mutually interdependent. That is why primacy at the different levels of the life of the Church, local, regional, and universal, must always be considered in the context of conciliarity, and conciliarity likewise in the context of primacy."[27] Of course, the session at Ravenna was also marked by a serious incident: the delegation of the patriarch of Moscow withdrew because he did not accept the presence of the official delegates from the Church of Estonia. Such an incident inevitably reflected upon the reception of the text adopted at Ravenna. It is, indeed, not certain if all the formulations of this text would have been accepted by the delegation from Moscow.[28] The subsequent sessions were, moreover, marked by a certain reticence regarding what seemed to be established by the document of Ravenna. But it is all the more necessary to emphasize that, on this question of the ministry of communion in the universal Church, the study of

26. Ibid., nos. 40 and 41.

27. Ibid., no. 43.

28. It is, in any case, what the reservations formulated by Bishop Hilarion of Vienna imply; see Bouwen, "Ravenne 2007," 75–76.

patristic texts remains indispensable for new advances in the dialogue between Catholics and the Orthodox.

There are also other domains in which the study of the Fathers ought to contribute to such advances, notably in what concerns the understanding of the Church and the questions relating to the validity of the sacraments. Independent of these questions, it is necessary to wish that each of the Churches may be increasingly open to some of the patristic works that in the past have often been neglected or, in other cases, unjustly depreciated, even though they made an essential contribution to the understanding of the faith. This was, let us recall, one of the raisons d'être of the Sources Chrétiennes in its beginnings: to make more known in the West the treasures of Greek patristics, to which Orthodoxy is so legitimately attached. And conversely, one wishes that the Orthodox Churches may sometimes be less severe in their judgment on the Augustinian tradition (whatever its limits may have been). Above all, it would be equitable if Orthodoxy came to recognize more broadly the grandeur of Origen, whose thinking was unduly assimilated to that of the "Origenist" monks of the fourth and fifth centuries, and who, however (if one disregards his hypothesis on the "preexistence of souls") today merits being recognized as one of the greatest geniuses of early Christianity.

The Dialogue with Protestantism

As with the preceding case, the Churches arising from the Protestant Reformation can find in patristic literature a reference that on the whole they share with the Catholic Church. Of course, unlike Orthodoxy, they above all rely on sources from Latin Christianity and quite particularly on Augustinian doctrine. Moreover, their traditional emphasis on "*sola scriptura*" causes them not to give as much importance to the patristic tradition as does the Catholic Church and the Orthodox Churches. However, Protestant historians and theologians are more and more interested in patristic literature, and for several decades the ecumenical dialogue has greatly benefitted from it. From this angle, we can show this by glancing over some of the documents of the Groupe des Dombes, which brings together Catholics, Lutherans, and Reformed.

The 1976 document on the episcopal ministry already devotes a section to the "ministère de l'épiscope après l'époque des apôtres" [The ministry of the episcopacy after the era of the Apostles]: here references to Clement of Rome, Ignatius of Antioch, and Irenaeus make clear "a convergence toward a ministry of the episcopacy exercised by one person and considered as a gift from God to his Church but that in no way destroys the collegiality previously attested to."[29] The following document, on "l'Esprit-Saint, l'Église et les sacrements" [The Holy Spirit, the Church and the sacraments] (1979), also relies upon the testimony of the Fathers. Augustine is invoked several times (regarding the Word capable of purifying "even the child who cannot believe in his heart and confess with his mouth"; regarding the sacramental action that is not the personal act of the "ministers" but the act of Christ himself); John Chrysostom is mentioned as well in the section on the Eucharistic epiclesis.[30]

The subsequent documents place an increasing importance on the historical journey and, in this framework, broadly appeal to the writings of the Fathers. This is the case, first, with the 1985 text on "le ministère de communion dans l'Église universelle" [The ministry of communion in the universal Church]. One finds in it a first exposition on the "Ante-Nicaean Church," which treats the tradition of the apostles, the "marks" of unity (the canon of the Scriptures, the confessions of faith, the celebration of Baptism and the Eucharist), as well as the ministerial authorities (with the diffusion of the episcopal structure and the primacy recognized in the see of Rome, whose bishop is the "first among bishops"). A second exposition covers the period from Nicaea I (325) to Nicaea II (787): the text evokes the authority of the ecumenical councils, the affirmation of a universal authority for the

29. Groupe des Dombes, *Le ministère épiscopal. Réflexions et propositions sur le ministère de vigilance et d'unité dans l'Église particulière* [The episcopal ministry. Reflections and proposals on the ministry of vigilance and unity in the particular Church], no. 30; repr. Groupe des Dombes, *Communion et conversion des Églises. Édition intégrale des documents publiés de 1956 à 2005* [Communion and conversion of the Churches. Full edition of documents published from 1956 to 2005] (Montrouge: Bayard, 2014), 102 (see nos. 24–30, 100–102). This document, like other documents of the Groupe des Dombes, was presented by Bernard Sesboüé in his book *Pour une théologie œcuménique*.

30. Cf. Groupe des Dombes, *L'Esprit-Saint, l'Église et les sacrements* [The Holy Spirit, the Church and the sacraments], nos. 107, note 33; 108, note 34; 109, note 35; 116; in *Communion et conversion des Églises*, 159–61. Also see the citation of Serapion of Thmuis regarding the epiclesis in the priestly ordination, no. 124 (*Communion et conversion des Églises*, 163–64).

pope, the structuring of the Churches of the East with the sees of the metropolitans and, above them, the patriarchal sees of Jerusalem, Antioch, Alexandria, and Constantinople (the apostolic see of Rome is for its part the only patriarchate in the West, but, because of its primacy of honor, is considered as the first of the five sees).[31] This historical journey, which, moreover, is continued up to the modern era, is of great importance for the entire document. It contributes to establishing the bases for the subsequent expositions on the three dimensions (communal, collegial, and personal) that ought to characterize the ministry of communion. It also helps to identify, in the case of the bishop of Rome, the traditional distinction between the "patriarchal" authority that he exercised in the ecclesiastical provinces of the West and the "primacy of honor" that he used vis-à-vis the patriarchs of the East (a primacy that itself confers "the solicitude of the unity in the faith and the communion in charity")[32]—yet "in as much as the distinction between these two functions will not be made visible in the living organization of the Church, the necessity of the ministry of communion exercised by the bishop of Rome will not be acceptable to our Orthodox, Anglican, and Protestant brothers."[33]

The document *Pour la conversion des Églises* [For the conversion of the Churches], published in 1991, invokes in its turn several significant accounts from the era of the Fathers: that of Athanasius who, as attached as he was to the confession of the Nicaean faith regarding the Son "consubstantial" (*homoousios*) with the Father, recognized the possibility of expressing the same doctrine in another language; that of Basil of Caesarea who, in order to affirm the divinity of the Spirit, preferred to stand by the formulations conforming to Scripture (because "it was necessary to avoid the disaster of a profession of the faith leading to the division of the Church"); that of Cyril of Alexandria who, after the Council of Ephesus, recognized the right of the Antiochian bishops to speak of "two natures" of Christ. The document recalls that these examples had already been invoked by Pope

31. Groupe des Dombes, *Le ministère de communion dans l'Église universelle* [The ministry of communion in the universal Church], nos. 13–29, in *Communion et conversion des Églises*, 174–82.

32. Ibid., no. 29, regarding Pope Gregory the Great (*Communion et conversion des Églises*, 182).

33. Ibid., no. 143 (*Communion et conversion des Églises*, 219–20).

Paul VI in the framework of his dialogue with the Patriarch Athenagoras; it emphasizes its importance for a conversion that may engage not only persons but also the Churches themselves (for the Fathers mentioned above were bishops who "learned well to engage their community and the communion of the Churches").[34] This exposition is additionally followed by a few paragraphs on the "conversions" of Saint Augustine—"conversions" that themselves benefitted from the "conversion of the Church," which sparked "a process of renewal for the early Churches of the East and the West" and which exercised "a decisive influence on the Latin Church of the following centuries and in particular on the Protestant reformers."[35]

The document on "Marie dans le dessein de Dieu et la communion des saints" [Mary in the design of God and the communion of saints], which appeared a few years later, includes an important section on the early Church.[36] It first recalls the place of Mary in the confession of faith—that Catholics and Protestants have rightly shared. It then collects the principal contributions from patristic literature, by above all emphasizing that "the Marian theology of the early Church is a Christology" and that the statements on the virginal conception and on Mary "Mother of God" (*Theotokos*) must be understood in this light; such a clarification is, in fact, essential from the perspective of the dialogue with the Churches of the Reformation. The text, in this section, also tackles other subjects that have been the subject of controversies in the modern era (such as that of the Immaculate Conception and that of the invocation of Mary). But at the end it formulates the two exigencies that on the whole emerge from patristic literature and from which the ecumenical dialogue must today benefit: "It is appropriate to look at Mary in this way, which does not detract from her Son but on the contrary is part of the contemplation precisely of the mysteries

34. Groupe des Dombes, *Pour la conversion des Églises*, nos. 57–63, 40–42; *Communion et conversion des Églises*, 269–72.

35. Ibid., no. 72 (*Communion et conversion des Églises*, 275–76; *Pour la communion des Églises*, 46).

36. Groupe des Dombes, *Marie dans le dessein de Dieu et la communion des saints*, vol. 1, *Dans l'histoire et l'Écriture*; vol. 2, *Controverse et conversion* [Mary in the plan of God and in the communion of saints, vol. 1, In history and Scripture; vol. 2, Controversy and conversion] (Paris: Bayard éditions/Centurion, 1997 and 1998); reprinted in a single volume in 1999 (we will cite according to this later edition); also reprinted in *Communion et conversion des Églises*, 339–493.

of Jesus"; "one must never say of Mary the slightest thing that would be incompatible with the honor of the Lord, that is, with his identity as an authentic human being and as true God."[37] The text adds to this an exposition on "Mary in Apocryphal Literature"; all the while recognizing that this literature can provide access to some "Christian traditions that go back to the origins of the Church," it draws attention to the danger of some texts that have exalted the figure of Mary without sufficiently respecting her belonging to the human condition and that, indirectly at least, have endangered the equilibrium of Christological dogma—Mary then being "regarded as the mother no longer of God incarnate but of the divinity."[38] Here again, the journey through the early Church contributes to the advancement of the ecumenical dialogue, as shown by the statements on conversion formulated in the last part of the document.

In 2005, a new document on "l'autorité doctrinale dans l'Église" [Doctrinal authority in the Church] gave an even greater scope to the section on the patristic period.[39] In it are tackled in succession: the testimony of Clement of Rome on the exigencies of ecclesial life; the authority of the Church in the confession of the faith and its role in the very constitution of the canon of the Scriptures; the testimony of three Fathers—Irenaeus, Tertullian, and Origen—on the question of doctrinal authority; the great Eastern councils, their own authority, the conflicts that marked them, and their relationships with the popes; expositions on the reflection on doctrinal authority in the West (by Augustine and Vincent of Lerins); lastly, the questions of the primate and the patriarchs (already evoked, as one saw, in the previous document on the ministry of communion in the universal Church). The whole of this journey provides valuable reference points, capable of inspiring ecumenical thought on doctrinal authority and on the manner in which it ought to be exercised today—in keeping with the communal, collegial, and personal dimensions that are essential to the ministry of the Church.

37. Ibid., no. 30 (pp. 30–31; *Communion et conversion des Églises*, 361).

38. Ibid., no. 31–38 (pp. 31–34; *Communion et conversion des Églises*, 361–64).

39. Groupe des Dombes, *"Un seul Maître." L'autorité doctrinale dans l'Église* ["Only one master." Doctrinal authority in the Church] (Paris: Bayard, 2005), nos. 25–95 (pp. 23–57; Communion et conversion des Églises, 512–40).

Lastly, the document of the Groupe des Dombes on the Our Father, published in 2011, highlights the central importance that was recognized in this prayer from the first centuries of the Christian era.[40] It mentions its liturgical and catechetical use, at the same time as its use in personal prayer. It also recalls the specific contribution of two authors: Cyprian, for whom the recitation of the Our Father is in itself an act of unity ("when we pray, it is not for one alone but for the entire people, for our people all together make up only one"); Augustine, who particularly emphasizes the act of faith required by such a prayer and who makes this remark regarding his separated brothers: "like it or not, they are our brothers. They would cease to be our brothers, if they ceased to say: Our Father."[41] The essential place of this prayer has not prevented Christians from being divided (and sometimes even using the words of the *Pater* against one another!), but the witness of patristic literature rather invites looking for ways of ecclesial communion that really honor the vocation of the "children of God," called by Jesus himself to say with one voice: "Our Father...."

The particular example of the Groupe des Dombes, which could be followed with other examples, clearly shows the importance that the study of the first Christian centuries has had from the perspective of the dialogue between Catholics and Protestants—as was also the case, as we saw, for the dialogue with some of the Churches of the East and for the dialogue with Orthodoxy—and it would be necessary to say it also for other dialogues, such as that with the Anglican Communion, which would equally merit being studied from this angle.

This is also full of lessons for the future. For whatever steps may have been taken, the Churches are still on the way toward full communion; and while it is so, the testimony of the Fathers will have to be patiently collected and meditated upon. Of course, ecumenism first requires that the Churches come together to listen to the Word of God in the Scriptures; it also demands a correct awareness of what was historically the cause of division; it above all calls for an attitude of conversion so that the Churches may one day give to the world the

40. Groupe des Dombes, *"Vous donc, priez ainsi" (Mt 6, 9). Le Notre Père, itinéraire pour la conversion des Églises* ["You therefore pray ye." The Our Father, itinerary for the conversion of Churches] (Paris: Bayard, 2011), nos. 29–41 (pp. 35–44).

41. Texts cited ibid., nos. 35 and 41 (pp. 39 and 44).

witness of a perfect unity. But from this same perspective, ecumenism will always benefit by allowing itself to be instructed and nourished by the in-depth study of patristic writings that, in spite of the serious controversies of their time, have known how to open the ways toward the communion of the Churches.

CHAPTER 13

Patristics and the Theology of Religions

If the preceding chapter has shown how profitable patristic literature can be for ecumenical dialogue, it is to be feared that one may have more difficulty in showing the interest that this same literature has for questions arising from the "theology of religions." Of course, in a previous chapter, we observed that attentiveness to the religious situation of our time called for a renewed interest in the patristic era's Christological and Trinitarian reflection and that some real problems could be profoundly enlightened by it. But do not the writings of the Fathers often attest to an anti-Judaism that today causes us difficulty? Did not the famous expression "Outside of the Church no salvation" appear during their era—an expression that, of course, originally referred only to the situation of "schismatic" Christians but that later would serve to describe an "exclusivist" attitude toward non-Christians?

It is, nevertheless, a fact that the patristic renewal of the twentieth century did contribute to the change of attitude that Vatican Council II showed toward "non-Christian religions": this is what it will first be important to recall. Of course, some difficulties have emerged since then, and they account for the "theology of religions" often distancing itself from patristic writings; but we will show that, far from diverting away from work on these writings, they rather invite formulating some conditions and exigencies that today such work must meet. We will lastly point out some major axes where patristic studies can today make a contribution to a reflection on Christianity and other religions.

The Contribution of the Patristic Renewal of the Twentieth Century

Several writings permit showing how, on the question that interests us, the patristic renewal of the twentieth century prepared the change in outlook advocated by Vatican Council II: the text of Yves de Montcheuil on "L'Église et le salut des non-croyants";[1] Jean Daniélou's books *Le mystère du salut des nations* and *Les saints païens de l'Ancien Testament*;[2] Yves Congar's article "*Ecclesia ab Abel*," his study on the adage "Outside of the Church no salvation," and even some pages from his book *Vaste monde, ma paroisse*, etc.[3] We are here choosing to focus rather on Henri de Lubac—not, moreover, because of the three volumes that he devoted to Buddhism (even though one of them develops comparisons between some Buddhist doctrines and patristic themes) but because of several other publications and, in particular, his synthetic study on the theme "Les religions humaines d'après les Pères" [The pagan religions and the Fathers of the Church].

It is worthwhile to recall that in his first work, *Catholicisme*, de Lubac had presented an extensive reflection on Christianity as a "historical" religion, in this way highlighting its originality compared with views of a cyclical universe (such as one notably finds in eastern religions), and that his argumentation precisely relied upon references to patristic literature.[4] A little later, in 1941, de Lubac gave two lectures on

1. Yves de Montcheuil, "L'Église et le salut des non-croyants" [The Church and the salvation of unbelievers], in Yves de Montcheuil, *Aspects de l'Église* [Aspects of the Church] (Paris: Cerf, 1949), 124–38.

2. Jean Daniélou, *Le mystère du salut des nations* [The mystery of the salvation of the nations] (Paris: Seuil, 1946); translated by Nigel Abercrombie as *The Lord of the History. Reflections on the Inner Meaning of History* (London: Longmans, 1958); *Les saints païens de l'Ancien Testament* [The pagan saints of the Old Testament] (Paris: Seuil, 1956).

3. Yves Congar, "*Ecclesia ab Abel*," 79–108; "Hors de l'Église pas de salut" [Outside of the Church no salvation], in *Sainte Église. Études et approches ecclésiologiques* [Holy Church. Ecclesiological studies and approaches] (Paris: Cerf, 1963), 417–32; *Vaste monde, ma paroisse: Vérité et dimensions du salut* [Big world, my parish: Truth and dimensions of salvation] (Paris: éd. du Témoignage chrétien, 1959); republished in Foi vivante 413 (Paris: Cerf, 2000), 37–42 and 108–64.

4. Cf. Henri de Lubac, *Catholicisme. Les aspects sociaux du dogme* (Paris, Cerf, 1938), chap. 5, "Le christianisme et l'histoire" [Christianity and history], 107–32; repr. in *Œuvres complètes du Cardinal de Lubac*, vol. 7 (Paris, Cerf, 2003); translated as *Catholicism. A Study of Dogma in Relation to the Corporate Destiny of Mankind* (London: Burns, Oates & Washbourne, 1949).

"The Theological Foundation of Missions." While justifying these by the very will of Christ (this was his fundamental thesis), he emphasized that Christianity had to glean the religious spirit that, in humanity's diverse traditions, was like the mark of a properly supernatural call:

> Let us thus say, then, borrowing the language of the Bible and the Fathers of the Church, that any soul is naturally Christian, not because it possesses already an equivalent or, as it were, a first stage of Christianity, but because the image of God shines in the depths of this soul; or rather, because it is itself that image, and because, burning to be reunited with its Model, it can be so only through Christ.
>
> If Christianity must be the religion of the world, if it is truly supernatural and transcendent to any human effort, it then follows that it must gather into its midst all the diversity of this effort. This is one of the essential views that preside over the missionary impulse of the Church. The Church knows that she herself, far from representing one small fragment of this effort, has the mission of embracing it wholly, of purifying it, vivifying it, deepening it, and finally of bringing it to a successful conclusion, thanks to the divine revelation of which she has the deposit.[5]

The allusion to the Fathers of the Church—more precisely to Tertullian, for he is the one who had spoken of "the naturally Christian soul"[6]—here supported de Lubac's fundamental vision regarding human beings who had not been able to be reached by the Gospel message. Being themselves created in the image of God, these human beings were already filled with an aspiration or a supernatural spirit (de Lubac thus rejected what one would later call an "exclusivist" interpretation of the adage "Outside of the Church no salvation"). However, it was necessary to bring to humankind the knowledge of Christ: this missionary task rightly fell to the Church, a task that ought not to consist of wiping the slate clean but of gleaning the best of the religious spirit from the history of humanity in order to orient it and to allow it to achieve its true fulfillment. Nothing could a priori be excluded from such a plan, and de Lubac's second lecture concluded with a firm denunciation of the "racist objection"—a highly important denunciation in those years during which Nazi ideology raged.

It is above all necessary to be interested in the study on "Les reli-

5. Henri de Lubac, "Le fondement théologique des missions," 197; *Theology in History*, 405.

6. Cf. Tertullian, *Apologétique*, 17, 6 (Waltzing, 40).

gions humaines d'après les Pères" [The pagan religions and the Fathers of the Church], for, even if this study is slightly after Vatican II, it at best shows how the patristic renewal of the previous decades contributed to the change of attitude advocated by the council.[7] De Lubac assuredly begins by recognizing that the first Fathers "declared very severely against contemporary pagan cults." He, however, adds that they are more favorable toward some philosophical doctrines such as Platonism; and, by immediately referring to the famous theme of the "seeds of the *Logos*" in Justin and Clement of Alexandria, he points out that some passages of Vatican II have precisely repeated such notions, "known collectively, since Eusebius of Caesarea, as the 'evangelical preparation.'"[8] The expositions that follow, on Origen and Augustine, show that these Fathers clearly noted the difference of Christianity from other traditions. Nevertheless, Origen attributes to some of the philosophers' doctrines a "propaedeutic" role, and Augustine admits that the Platonists "have really perceived 'in some manner, though distantly and with strained eyes,' the end of human life, which is the vision of God," even if they have not recognized the "way" that leads toward the "Father"—namely the Word made flesh.[9] In any case, de Lubac, using patristic writings, supports this fundamental idea that the Word of God has always been present to humanity, and he then cites the famous expression of Tertullian on "a naturally Christian soul." Above all, he uses these words to summarize the fundamental contribution of early Christianity:

> What appears from the thinking of the Fathers, taken very broadly as we have just done, is that if one may discover, either in the spontaneous movement of the human spirit or in the theories that it has elaborated, preparations for welcoming the gospel, this can only be because all men are created for salvation; and it is the Gospel that brings the gift and revelation of salvation to them. God's creation, namely, is something coherent. The Fathers of the Church and the great medieval theologians had a more unified, more organic view about it than later theology generally has had. God created man for a divine end. There must therefore be—however one is to explain it—something in man that pre-

7. Henri de Lubac, "The Pagan Religions and the Fathers of the Church," in *The Church*, 68–95.

8. Ibid., 69.

9. Ibid., 70 (with a citation from Augustine, *The City of God*, bk. 8, chap. 11).

pares him for this end and for its revelation.... Deep in human nature (and so in every man) the image of God is imprinted, that is, a quality that constitutes in it—and even without it—a kind of secret appeal to the object of the full and supernatural revelation brought by Christ.[10]

Such is the patristic doctrine, and it is of "vital importance."[11] On this basis, de Lubac specifies the judgment that the Fathers made on the religious phenomenon. He summarizes it in these terms: the Church must, according to the Fathers, "integrate (by converting) all the religious efforts of mankind," which implies, on one hand, an exigency of "purification, the opposition to and the elimination of the error or evil," and, on the other, an exigency "of assumption, assimilation, and finally transfiguration." And de Lubac comments: "Such a way of looking at things, associating unity and truth so intimately, is at once, we should note, very exclusive and very broad, very strict and remarkably all-embracing."[12] On one hand, it is "very exclusive" and "very strict," in the sense that it is expressed "according to the sole Church of Christ." The whole redemptive design found its fulfilment in the Word made flesh; "All the more reason then for not regarding other religions—whatever their merits—as 'salvific,' that is, entering into or remaining in 'concurrence' with faith in Christ."[13] But on the other, the doctrine of the Fathers is "very broad" and "remarkably all-embracing." "The things we commonly say today about the integration of cultures—or 'values'—into the Christian faith were once said by the Fathers, often with considerable audacity, of the very religions themselves. They would have integrated all that might be salvaged from them and not just their 'cultural' elements—if indeed the religious and cultural elements of certain religions are susceptible of adequate distinction at all."[14] This second aspect does not contradict the first since one is not considering non-Christian religions from a "static" point of view but

10. De Lubac, "The Pagan Religions," 71–72, trans. modified.

11. Ibid. De Lubac points out a certain analogy of this doctrine with another patristic doctrine, concerning the connection of mankind to the Word made flesh: on one hand, the Word assumed all human nature, and in this sense every man has "an organic link with Christ"; on the other, there exists a second kind of relationship for those who have received Christ: it is the relationship that unites the members of the "mystical Body" to the One who is the "Head" (ibid., 72–73).

12. Ibid., 74.

13. Ibid., 75.

14. Ibid., 74.

from a "dynamic" point of view, in the cadre of a "theology of history" according to which "all the good in them ... are such elements as may be integrated in Christ."[15] And de Lubac emphasizes that the principle of such a "dynamism" is not "Christianity" but "the very person of Jesus Christ." The "exclusive" adherence to this truth of Christ does not mean that one must ignore the values of other religions; far from it, "once this unicity of the Christ who reveals and saves is established in the heart, we can only regard with the greatest respect and, sometimes, the greatest admiration the discoveries sought after and, to some extent, found in the spiritual history of mankind, outside the revelation of Jesus Christ."[16] And "the more we see ... elements of truth, beauty, and goodness, the more we must feel that a place must be found for them—whatever their parentage—in the Christian synthesis."[17]

De Lubac adds that, on this same question, "the teaching of the Fathers is still vigorous today": he notably shows this by relying upon the thinking of Jules Monchanin, Hans Urs von Balthasar, and Pierre Teilhard de Chardin. He lastly emphasizes, at the end of his study, the "newness" brought by Christ. This emphasis undoubtedly bears the mark of a new preoccupation of the 1960s: the fear that openness to the values of other religions—an openness that de Lubac, as one has seen, himself advocated—might lead to underestimating the newness of the Incarnation and of the Pascal mystery. The theologian, of course, reiterates that, on one hand, one has always recognized an action of Christ outside of the visible Church: "The famous axiom '*extra Ecclesiam nulla salus*' did not bear the same general sense when it was first enunciated by the Fathers as many today appear to think. It applied to certain very concrete situations, to the cases of those responsible for schism, revolt, or betrayal."[18] De Lubac admits that one can even speak of "anonymous Christians"—according to the famous expression of Karl Rahner. He does not, on the contrary, follow him in the use of the expression "anonymous Christianity." Such an expression could indeed lead to believing that the revelation of Jesus Christ is "no more than the surfacing of something that had always existed;"[19]

15. Ibid., 76.
16. Ibid., 78.
17. Ibid., 79–80.
18. Ibid., 87.
19. Ibid., 87–88.

it would not give enough honor to the "Christian Newness" as it was so strongly affirmed by the Fathers of the Church:

> As we have seen, someone like St. Irenaeus insisted at length on the secret action and the illuminations of the Logos all through history, while nevertheless vigorously underlining the newness of Christ: "We would not have been able," he observes, "to know the things of God unless our Master had become human while yet remaining the Logos." He goes further. Christ brought to us, with himself, the principle of newness that the prophets themselves had foretold, a principle "that was to renew and give life to humanity." And once having really "contemplated his face, heard his words, and enjoyed his gifts, a person—or at least a sensible one—will no longer be asking what more he has brought" than those who preceded and announced him. Irenaeus was affirming the indissoluble union between revelation and salvation in Christ.[20]

Whatever may be the debates sparked by the expression "anonymous Christianity," the study of de Lubac clearly shows the important contribution that the patristic renewal, over the course of the twentieth century, brought to the subject of religions.[21] And this renewal was very fecund for the life of the Church—even if, as we will also see, there was a further widening of the distance between the "theology of religions" and the heritage of early Christianity.

Vatican Council II and the Post-Conciliar Years

On this point, as on others, Vatican Council II clearly bears the influence of the return to the Fathers illustrated by de Lubac and other

20. Ibid., 91 (with a reference to Irenaeus, *Against the Heresies*, IV, 34, 1), trans. modified (James R. Dunne translates: "As we have seen, an Irenaeus insists at length on the secret action and the illuminations of the Logos all through history. For all that, he vigorously underlines the novelty of Christ: 'We would have had no way of knowing the things of God had not our master become man while remaining the Logos.' Christ, he says again, brought with him that innovatory principle foretold by the prophets which 'was to renew and revitalize humanity'; and once having really 'contemplated his face, heard his words and enjoyed his gifts, the man of sense will not ask what more have you brought' than did the men who preceded and announced him. This is to affirm the indissoluble union between revelation and salvation in Christ").

21. Henri de Lubac's book *Paradoxe et mystère de l'Église*, which contains the study on "Les religions humaines d'après les Pères," appeared in the same year that A. Luneau also published an important study on the same subject: "Pour aider au dialogue: les Pères et les religions non chrétiennes" [To help to dialogue: the Fathers of the Church and non-christian religions], in *Nouvelle Revue Théologique* 89 (1967): 821–41 and 914–39.

theologians of his generation. This is first of all verified by the attitude shown toward the Jews; indeed, whatever may be the criticisms today expressed against the "anti-Judaism of the Fathers" (we will return to this later), the declaration *Nostra aetate* takes account of the fact that the Church has not rejected the earlier Scriptures, received from "that people with whom God in his inexpressible mercy established the ancient covenant;"[22] this is a major legacy of the patristic era, all the more remarkable since the Fathers of the second and third centuries were confronted by the radical dissent of Marcion and of those who, like him, wanted a complete break with the Old Testament. The renewal also manifests itself in the way in which the council states its fundamental position regarding other religions: the Church "rejects nothing of what is true and holy in these religions" and all the while has "to proclaim without fail, Christ who is the way, the truth, and the life;"[23] and one additionally recalls that in *Ad gentes* the council repeats in an explicit manner the famous theme of the "seeds of the Word."[24]

The fecundity of the patristic renewal also appears in the heritage of this council, and we will here illustrate this with an example: the document *Dialogue and Proclamation*, which was promulgated in 1991 and which includes two paragraphs on the Fathers' position regarding religions.[25] Of course, states this document, one can easily find in their writings "negative judgments on the religious world of their time"; one, nonetheless, detects in them a "remarkable openness":

> A number of Church Fathers take up the sapiential tradition reflected in the New Testament. In particular, writers of the second century and the first part of the third century such as Justin, Irenaeus, and Clement of Alexandria, either explicitly or in an equivalent way, speak about the "seeds" sown by the Word of God in the nations. Thus it can be said that for them, prior to and outside the Christian dispensation, God has already, in an incomplete way, manifested

22. Vatican Council II, *Nostra aetate*, no. 4.

23. Ibid., no. 2.

24. Vatican Council II, *Ad gentes*, nos. 11 and 15; cf. also *Lumen gentium*, no. 17 (with the expression "whatever good is found sown"); and see chap. 2, 26–27.

25. Pontifical Council for Inter-Religious Dialogue, *Dialogue and Proclamation. Reflection and Orientations on Interreligious Dialogue and the Proclamation of the Gospel of Jesus Christ* (1991), http://vatican.va/roman_curia/pontifical_councils/interelg/documents/rc_pc_interelg_doc_19051991_dialogue-and-proclamatio_en.html.

himself. This manifestation of the *Logos* is an adumbration of the full revelation in Jesus Christ to which it points.[26]

The text in a note refers to some passages from authors here mentioned: texts of Justin in which appear the theme of the "seeds"; texts of Irenaeus, for whom the Son of God "is revealed to humans 'from the beginning,'" even though the Incarnation brought a decisive newness; texts of Clement of Alexandria, according to whom "'philosophy' was given to the Greeks by God as a 'covenant,' a 'preparation for the philosophy according to Christ,' a 'pedagogue' who would lead the Greek mind to him."[27] Then, in the following paragraph, the document explains that, in fact, the Fathers of the first centuries present a "theology of history":

> History becomes salvation history, inasmuch as through it God progressively manifests himself and communicates with humankind. This process of divine manifestation and communication reaches its climax in the incarnation of the Son of God in Jesus Christ. For this reason, Irenaeus distinguishes four "covenants" given by God to the human race: in Adam, in Noah, in Moses, and in Jesus Christ. The same patristic current, whose importance is not to be underestimated, may be said to culminate in Augustine who in his later works stressed the universal presence and influence of the mystery of Christ even before the Incarnation. In fulfillment of his plan of salvation, God, in his Son, has reached out to the whole of humankind. Thus, in a certain sense, Christianity already exists "at the beginning of the human race."[28]
>
> It was to this early Christian vision of history that the Second Vatican Council made reference.[29]

The two paragraphs of *Dialogue and Proclamation* that we have cited thus make explicit the patristic foundations of the vision developed by *Nostra aetate*; this confirms the influence of the return to the Fathers on the council itself and, more precisely, on its way of considering other religions.

26. Ibid., no. 24.

27. Ibid., note 7; trans. slightly modified, on the basis of the Italian text published in the *Bulletin du Pontificium Consilium pro Dialogo inter Religiones* 77 (1991).

28. Ibid., no. 25; notes 8 and 9 make a few references to passages from Irenaeus and Augustine.

29. Ibid., no. 26. For a detailed commentary on these paragraphs, we refer to our article "Les Pères de l'Église face aux religions de leur temps d'après le document 'Dialogue et annonce' de 1991" [The Fathers of the Church facing the religions of their time, according to the document "Dialogue and Proclamation" of 1991], *Bulletin du Pontificium Consilium pro Dialogo inter Religiones* 80 (1992): 173–85.

One must, however, recognize that, in past decades, the "theology of religions" has often distanced itself from patristic literature. It is necessary for us to point out the reasons for this phenomenon; and we will above all show that the difficulties that have arisen must not detract from a work on patristic texts, and that they, on the contrary, call for clarifying the conditions and the issues for the present situation.

Even if some "theologies of religions" have, in recent decades, also invoked traditional themes such as that of the "seeds of the Logos,"[30] one above all has the impression of an increasing distance from the problems inherited from the patristic period.[31] This development can be explained by at least three factors. First, a keener awareness of the historical distance between our era and the era of the Fathers (and as a consequence, doubt concerning the possibility that Christian theology could still benefit from patristic approaches, those that appear to be too linked to situations arising in the past). Next, and more radically, a suspicion about the shadows of Christian Antiquity, due to some behaviors affected at that time by the attitude of Christians toward other believers, in particular toward the Jews. Lastly, the developments in contemporary thought on religions, in the cadre of what one has called the theology of religious pluralism: such a theology, above all in its most radical forms, is not satisfied with the "exclusivist" and "inclusivist" positions that it generally associates with patristic literature.

We, nevertheless, think that these difficulties and objections must not dissuade us from being interested in this literature from the perspective of a contemporary reflection on Christianity and other religions.

A Response to the Present Difficulties

In fact, apart from any general consideration on the relationship that theology must necessarily maintain with tradition,[32] we can already

30. See, for example, Jacques Dupuis, *Toward a Christian Theology of Religious Pluralism* (Maryknoll, N.Y.: Orbis Books, 1997), 79.

31. We are reproducing almost word for word, in this section and the following, the reflections that we developed in our article "Relire les Pères de l'Église pour penser le dialogue interreligieux" [Rereading the Fathers of the Church to think about interreligious dialogue], *Chemins de Dialogue* 32 (2008): 205–25. We greatly thank Christian Salenson for having been willing to authorize it.

32. See chap. 6.

recognize a first reason for examining the patristic writings from the angle that we hold here. It is that the Fathers of the Church and, much more broadly, the Christians of the first centuries were directly confronted by the question of religions. Of course, some clarifications must immediately be made. First, the concept of "religion" is to some extent anachronistic. Apart from Judaism, which in the early era actually corresponded to what we today call a religion, Greco-Roman Antiquity attests rather to a great diversity of religious practices and beliefs, and it is in retrospect that one unified them under the common denominator of "Greek religion" and "Roman religion." Moreover, the Christian authors of the first centuries do not know Hinduism and Buddhism (even if some of them, such as Clement of Alexandria, had heard about Hindu Brahmans and the Buddha). Lastly, it is only in the seventh century that Islam was born, and it is thus necessary to await Maximus the Confessor and, especially, John Damascene for this religion to be mentioned in some patristic writings. These clarifications are important: from the outset, they warn that a patristic work cannot claim to relate in a very direct manner the reflections of the Fathers and the reflections that we have to develop today in our own religious situation.

The fact remains that Christians of the first centuries really were confronted by "religions." First, of course, by Judaism. But also by all sorts of religious practices spread throughout the Nations: thus the veneration of objects and statues, divinization, the invocation of celestial and cosmic powers and forces, etc. The Christians of the first centuries were, as well, confronted not only by mythological beliefs inherited from Homer but also by forms of wisdom, philosophies, and spiritualities that asked them questions that were at times radical. How to respond, for example, to the objection according to which Christianity was a quite new religion, compared to the multi-secular traditions that inspired the adherence of numerous believers? How to account for the faith in Jesus Christ Son of God without implying that the divine essence would in some way be divided or without undermining the monotheist faith? How to relate to the mystics who promoted the ideal of a faraway transcendence, radically separated from the world, and for whom the Christian doctrine of the Incarnation seemed to put into question this deep sense of transcendence?

Or even, how to debate with the neo-Platonic philosophies regarding the Christian distinction between the Son and the Father, and more broadly the mystery of the Trinity, which would appear not to respect the mystery of the One supreme beyond all? It is clear that these questions, which were formerly asked with intensity, are no less asked today in other situations—including in the cadre of the dialogue with Islam and with Hinduism, however foreign to the reflection of Christian authors during the first centuries. It would also be necessary to mention the questions that were asked in the Middle East, when Christianity found itself in the presence of Mazdeism and Manicheism (that, as one knows, knew a great expansion in the West). It would be necessary as well to mention the first contact of Nestorian Christianity with the religions of China toward the end of the patristic era. The field is thus immense.

This does not mean to say that the difficulties formulated above must not be understood and that, in some cases, must not be taken into account in the way of relating to patristic texts. It is not necessary to return at length to the first of these difficulties concerning the distance between the period of early Christianity and ours. We have responded to it in the first part of the book, and it suffices to recall here that, far from seeing in the historical distance an objection regarding a theological work on the writings of the Fathers, we must rather glean from it exigencies for the methodological order: those of taking into account the achievements of research undertaken by historians of Antiquity and of knowing, as well as is possible, the contexts in which the early authors expressed themselves—essential conditions so that one may be dedicated to an appropriate hermeneutic of the patristic texts for our time.

The second difficulty concerned more specifically the relationships of Christians with other believers. It is incontestable that, from this point of view, the patristic period experienced true dramas. Thus there were very harsh behaviors toward paganism, at least beginning at the point when Christianity became the official religion of the empire (for in the first centuries, it is rather Christianity that was itself attacked, and sometimes even persecuted). It is undeniable, on one hand, that the statements against the Jews were sometimes highly vehement. One can, of course, point out that, in many of these cases, the Christian authors were attacking less the Jews than "Judaizing" Christians (as Paul had already done in his day), and that their intention was above all to safeguard the radical newness of Christianity. Besides—and this is as valid for the writings against the "pagans" as for the writings against the Jews—it is necessary to take into account the literary genres and usual canons of Antiquity. At that time one was less shocked by the diatribes and *ad hominem* polemics that today cause us difficulties. The fact remains that, henceforth, we must distance ourselves from behaviors and forms of language that appear to us not to be respectful of other believers. But this does not justify, for all that, an overall suspicion that, at the same time, would dissuade us from being interested in early Christianity from the perspective of a reflection on religions. Patristic writings are in fact extremely diverse, and one of the tasks of interpretation is precisely to know how to distinguish what in the literature of early Christianity is legitimately open to criticism and what, on the contrary, must be gleaned as a good from the tradition from which Christian theology today merits being the beneficiary. So in spite of the existence of vehement diatribes against the Jews in some early texts, it is necessary, on the contrary, to commend Origen's statement that, in the third century, defends the Jewish people against the attack of the philosopher Celsus and that takes very seriously the affirmation of Saint Paul in chapter 11 of the Letter to the Romans: "God has not disowned his people whom he foreknew."[33] Or even, the acts of violence carried out against the paganism of the fourth and fifth centuries must not prevent hearing some of the exhortations of Gregory the Great that encouraged the missionaries of Britain to reject the savage destruction of idols and of temples and to respect the local populations in a way that perhaps would one day lead them to embrace the Christian faith.[34]

As for the third difficulty—the criticism of the "exclusivist" and "inclusivist" positions in the name of "religious pluralism"—it can no longer be considered as a decisive objection. On one hand, the judg-

33. Cf. Rom 11:2. See Origen, *Contra Celsum*, IV, 3; Chadwick, 207–8; *Contre Celse*, SC 136, 261–63; Origen, *Commentary on the Epistle to the Romans*, 7, 14; 8, 7; 8, 12; 2:110–11; 155–59; 181–85; see also Origène, *Commentaire sur l'épître aux Romains*, VII, 12; VIII, 6; VIII, 11; SC 543, 371–73; 499–509; 565–75.

34. Cf. Bede, *Ecclesiastical History of the English People*, I, 30 (p. 57). See also Bède le Vénérable, *Histoire ecclésiastique du peuple anglais*, I, 30, SC 489, 247–51.

ment of the Fathers on religions is more complex than it would first seem and does not allow so easily summarizing it with the categories of "exclusivism" and "inclusivism" into which one would like to enclose them. But above all, the difficulty can be reversed: would it not be serious if a theology of religions departed entirely from the approaches of the patristic era, and that, in order quite rightly to want to emphasize the exigency of dialogue with other believers, it no longer retains the fundamental preoccupation that filled the Fathers—that of evaluating religious beliefs and practices in light of their faith in Christ? All things considered, the development of the theology of religions would also have to pay attention to the teachings of Christian Antiquity. Indeed, contemporary reflection has largely been dominated by the question "can one reconcile the affirmation of salvation by Christ the sole Mediator and the affirmation of a plurality of religions leading toward the ultimate Reality?" and it gave divergent responses to this question—from the most negative to the most open, from the "exclusivism" attributed to Karl Barth to the "radical pluralism" of John Hick or Paul Knitter. Yet, even if it is necessary to recognize the interest and the value of the debates occasioned by this problem, the time has undoubtedly come to examine more closely the concrete experience of Christians who, in the course of their lives, encounter other believers and who have to live and understand their faith in this very situation; and such a perspective quite precisely opens another way of accessing the writings from early Christianity: it calls for looking into how Christians in the past were able to live and understand their faith in the religious situations of their own time. We would like to specify how this new access to the patristic writings can rightly be fecund with respect to contemporary theology.

The Fecundity of Patristics for the Theology of Religions

The response that we have given to the third objection itself indicates an essential condition of this fecundity: it is a matter of here undertaking a work of contextual theology, that is, a work that attempts to show how Christian authors of Antiquity were able to think about the Christian faith in what were themselves diverse religious contexts—

and more precisely, how taking these contexts into account led them to deepen the meaning of the Christian faith by its very relationship with other traditions.

Undoubtedly, from this point of view, the contemporary situation invites being especially interested in the period of the second and third centuries—a period when Christianity first presented itself as a "way," perceived by Christians as unique by the very reason of its reference to Jesus Christ who had been revealed as "the way."[35] Our age of pluralism, in one sense, brings us closer to this earlier period than to the period that followed the conversion of Constantine and the recognition of Christianity as a religion of the Empire. However, the second half of the patristic era is equally very instructive for the question that concerns us here. Apart from the fact that Christianity remained in the minority in some countries outside of the Empire and there it encountered oppositions and even persecution (as, for example, in Persia), Christians of the Greek and Latin languages themselves remained confronted, from the fourth to the eighth century, by all kinds of beliefs, practices, wisdom, and spiritualties that other traditions raised—and even their purely internal discussions and controversies (such as those with Arianism, or later, with Nestorianism and Monophysitism) today appear to have a great deal to offer us in view of the debates with these non-Christian traditions.[36] In any case, no matter which period is being considered, patristic literature calls for a recognition that the deepening of the faith was developed around three major axes: those of apologetics, dogmatics, and spirituality. It is important to focus somewhat on these three axes and to show how, *mutatis mutandis*, they can enlighten our contemporary theological reflection.

The first axis is that of apologetics. For the early authors, this was actually two-sided: on one hand a negative or critical side, in the sense that it was necessary to defend against the objections coming from those who did not share the Christian faith; on the other, a positive or constructive side, in the sense that the Christian authors did not

35. Cf. Jn 14:6.

36. On this point, we refer to the second volume of our study *La voie du Christ*, vol. 2, *Développements de la christologie dans le contexte de l'Orient ancien, d'Eusèbe de Césarée à Jean Damascène (IVe–VIIIe siècles)* [The way of Christ, vol. 2, Developments of Christology in the context of the ancient Orient (fourth–eighth centuries)] (Paris: Cerf, 2013).

simply want to be on the defensive but attempted to establish reasons likely to substantiate Christianity among the religions of the world.

By today examining the importance of this apologetic axis, one must assuredly take account of the evolution of the word—itself linked, to a large extent, to the history of the theology of the modern era. We are indeed dependent on what happened in the eighteenth and nineteenth centuries, in the era when the objections of deists and atheists against Christians led them, in reaction, to develop all kinds of arguments in favor of their religion. It is necessary to recognize that, whatever may have been its merits and courage, this apologetics sometimes found itself to be, because of its defensive position, a prisoner of a questionable problem, wanting "to prove" based on natural reason what was primarily the subject of Christian Revelation, being insufficiently attentive to the values of the modern world and, above all, to the way in which every human being could be filled by an aspiration toward the supernatural, by a deep vocation to know God and to love Him. It was just as well necessary to distance oneself from this apologetics, as one sees from the philosophical point of view with Maurice Blondel, then, from the theological point of view, with de Lubac and Henri Bouillard. This was the passage from apologetics to "fundamental theology." This latter discipline actually assumes some of the tasks of traditional apologetics, to the extent that it has to account for the Christian faith, but, henceforth, it does it in a manner that, without claiming to impose the truth of the Christian faith, is rather committed to showing the credibility of Revelation in the world today. We thus have to take account of this development and the fact that, correlatively, the word "apologetics" came to receive a sometimes pejorative connotation.

Nevertheless, already in the 1970s, a theologian such as Johann Baptist Metz took up the term "apology" in order to describe the exigency that is incumbent upon Christians to defend Jesus Christ—that is, in his language, to preserve the "dangerous memory of Jesus Christ" in a world that risked overshadowing or deforming it.[37] And in

37. See Jean-Baptiste Metz, *La foi dans l'histoire et dans la societé. Essai de théologie fondamentale pratique*, trans. Paul Corset and Jean-Louis Schlegel (Paris: Cerf, 1979); translated by J. Matthew Ashley as Johann Baptist Metz, *Faith in History and Society. Toward a Practical Fundamental Theology* (New York: The Crossroad Publishing Company, 2007).

this twenty-first century there is no shortage of reasons for speaking of Christianity as finding itself, in many cases, in situations in which it must justify itself. That is the case in the countries of Western Europe and North America, to the extent that Christianity has lost ground for thirty years and finds itself commanded to respond to the objections formulated by atheism; it is also the case in the countries of other continents where Christianity is not only a minority but also hindered and threatened at times. This itself does not mean to imply any adversity toward other humans—believers or non-believers—with whom Christians can in many circumstances have relationships of great esteem and friendship; but the fortunate advances that the interreligious dialogue has permitted does not prevent being clear about the situations in which Christianity has, even today, to defend and justify itself. Rereading, in this context, the argumentations of Justin, Irenaeus, and Origen (and other later authors) against the theses with which one opposed them in their time is not simply to inquire into some authors from the past. It is to learn from them how we in our turn can account for the Incarnation and the other mysteries of our faith, in a manner that takes into account the objections that are heard but that, nevertheless, helps to overcome them.

However, as we have recalled, the apologetic dimension of the Fathers did not have only a defensive side but a constructive one as well, for it was a matter of contributing to the credibility of Christianity among existing traditions. Yet this goal is, even today, a part of the tasks of fundamental theology in the pluri-religious context. Our way of doing it, assuredly, is different; whereas the Christian authors of earlier times, in the expositions of their convictions, did not back down from some diatribes and polemics against those who did not believe as they, we are intent upon respecting the exigencies of a well-understood interreligious dialogue, which implies the respect of others and attention to what other believers themselves say. But we ought to glean from the Fathers of the Church their concern for saying, even in the debates and confrontations with other beliefs, how the Christian faith can be thought about and how it really is credible for contemporaries. Let us take, as an example, Origen's response to the objection of the philosopher Celsus, who held the following reasoning: if God wanted to deliver the totality of human beings, he ought to have "breathed into many bodies ... and sent them all over the world," rather than being limited to a single place and a single time by being incarnated in Jesus of Nazareth. Origen opposes this with: "though the advent of Jesus was apparently in one corner, it was quite reasonable." He affirms that this advent is justified by the existence of the people of Israel who prepared it, and he adds: "there was no need for many bodies to be in several places and to have many spirits like Jesus, so that the whole world of men might be enlightened by the Word of God." It is that, for Origen, the universality of the gift of God happens in reality by Christ, provided that he, in his turn, be revealed to others in diverse places—and thus he is revealed through all those who become, in their turn, "other christs" on the face of the earth.[38] That is a good example of an effort to understand the Christian faith regarding a question that remains current in our day in other forms (for example in the cadre of the dialogue with Hinduism, that clearly admits a plurality of manifestations of the divine in the world but not a unique incarnation of God in one precise place and time in history).

From this we are directly introduced to the second dimension that we stated above: the properly doctrinal or dogmatic dimension. It would be possible to show at length how the Christian authors' debates with those who did not share their faith have in some way provoked them to deepen their understanding of the Christian mystery. Such are the different forms of "gnosis" in the second century that led Irenaeus to develop, in reaction against them, his admirable theology of history with Christ the "recapitulator" of all things in its center. Such are the diverse forms of Docetism that prompted Tertullian above all to emphasize vigorously the realism of the Incarnation, as well as the subject of Christian hope that is not a simple immortality of the soul but the "resurrection of the flesh." Such are the objections of middle Platonism that pushed Origen to show that faith in Jesus does not place into question the transcendence of God but that Jesus is rather the way to the Father. It is in response to Porphyry that Augustine clarified his own thinking on Christ as the sole Mediator—the "Way" by which believers can have access to the divine "Homeland." One will again notice that this deepening of doctrine, more often than

38. Cf. Origen, *Contre Celsum*, VI, 78–79 (Chadwick, 391–93).

not, came about not through dialogue but in the cadre of controversies with others. It is true, and one can be delighted, that in the spirit of Vatican II and the meeting of Prayer for Peace, October 27, 1986, at Assisi, Italy, we have endeavored to give more honor to the exigencies of true dialogue with the mutual listening and understanding that it implies. But one of the fruits that we must await from this dialogue—at least from the doctrinal and theological dialogue with other believers—is precisely that it helps us to advance in the understanding of our own faith. And it is here that the contribution of patristic literature is very valuable for us because the Fathers have rightly had such a concern. They help us to understand that the debates between Christianity and other traditions have some stakes for Christian thinking itself. From the doctrine of God to eschatology through creation, the Incarnation, and salvation, all the great questions of Christian dogmatics have been tackled and deepened by the Christian authors of Antiquity, and this has occurred—not exclusively, of course, but at least partially—in the very cadre of their debates with the wisdom, philosophies, and religious traditions of their era.

Let us observe in passing that on this point, as in every other area, meditation on the Scriptures held a major place. And among all the subjects to which the Fathers attest to the inspiration thus received from the Bible, one of them is of a particular importance for the question that here concerns us: the way of inseparably taking into account the unicity of the Revelation in Jesus Christ and the universality of the gift of God. The Fathers recognize, on one hand, that Jesus Christ is unique, and they do not fail to emphasize this when they are led to compare Christ with Dionysius or Heracles or when they must specify the irreducible originality of the Incarnation and the Resurrection in relation to some doctrines from the Greek, Roman, and Egyptian traditions with remote resemblances. However, they also maintain not only that the Gospel is offered to all but that God wants the salvation of all—including those who have not been able to be reached by the knowledge of Christ. It is from this perspective that they develop, with Justin and Clement of Alexandria, the theme of the "seeds of the Word"; it is also from this perspective that they reread, with Origen, the famous prophecies of the diviner Balaam in the book of Numbers, showing how God was able to make use of a man who was not an Israelite (but who was adept at a religious practice of divination) in order to predict the coming of Christ and his epiphany among the Nations.[39] Let us not here speak of "inclusivism": the thinking of the Fathers, let us repeat, should not be confined to this type of category; it simply tries to be faithful to what emerges from the Scriptures—namely, the exigency to hold in the same thought the unicity of the gift of God in Jesus Christ and the desire for a salvation for all, which is possible thanks to a theology of the preexistent *Logos* and also thanks to a reflection on the action of the Spirit among the Nations. The same exigency must today reside within Christians who are engaged in dialogue: it cannot be put in parentheses; rather, it really is indispensable because it touches upon an essential element of the Revelation received through Scripture, and it thus contributes to defining the position of Christians in their dialogue with other believers.

But the importance of the doctrinal dimension must not close our eyes to the third dimension that we referred to as spirituality. For the Fathers, the attitude of Christians in their relationships with other believers is indeed measured not only by their capacity to account for their faith and by the quality of their doctrinal reflection but also, and even above all, by the witness of a life filled with the Spirit. As we will see in the following chapter, this witness took shape in very diverse ways in the first centuries of the patristic era, sometimes in a dramatic way in the case of the martyr but most often in the form of an existence fashioned by the Gospel, even in daily life. What we would here like to emphasize is that this spiritual dimension of existence was, to some extent, also affirmed thanks to contact with diverse traditions of the ancient world.

One could first recall the famous writing *To Diognetus*, that we have already mentioned above, and that, around the year 200, gives a famous description of Christians and their presence in the world:

> Christians are not different from other people in terms of their country, language, or customs. Nowhere do they inhabit cities of their own, use a strange dialect, or live life out of the ordinary.... They live in their respective countries, but only as resident aliens.... Every foreign territory is a homeland for them, every homeland foreign territory.... They are found in the flesh but do not live

39. Origène, *Homélies sur les Nombres*, XIII, 7, 4, vol. 2, *XI–XIX*, trans. Louis Doutreleau, SC 442 (Paris: Cerf, 1999), 151. See also Origen, *Homilies on Numbers*.

according to the flesh. They live on earth but participate in the life of heaven.... To put the matter simply, what the soul is in the body, this is what Christians are in the world.[40]

Here, in these lines, a position has already been taken, at least implicitly, toward what could be other forms of life in Antiquity.

But it often happens that, in a more explicit way, Christian authors of the first centuries were led by the religious situation of their time to specify the contours of an existence in the Spirit. In particular, the Fathers of the Church highlight that the veneration of idols is not simply characteristic of some religious practices inherited from previous centuries but that it takes other forms in the very heart of mankind, including some Christians when, by their vices, they interiorly prostrate themselves toward this or that good that they consider as an idol. Thus Origen writes:

Moreover, did not the error of all paganism receive a beginning from the fact that men want those things which they love much to be gods and they ascribe a divine name to each of the human vices and desires? ... Therefore, in this way, we also, since we are so dedicated to some vices that we "love" them "with the whole heart and the whole soul and all strength," we are said to worship idols and "to have gone after foreign gods."[41]

Here there is, if one wishes, a kind of spiritual interiorization of the confrontation with the religious practices marked by idolatry. Of course, one could object that this is not transposable to the current situation of interreligious dialogue; but we also know that idolatry, under other forms, always remains a temptation or a danger of religions, including Christianity, and that theology must reflect upon what there is of it in the religious (and its possible deviations) of the contemporary world.

All things considered, the literature of early Christianity shows that other ways have also allowed developing a true spirituality in the cadre of confrontations with other religious traditions. A very remarkable case is, for example, that of Clement of Alexandria who did not fear applying to the Christian the Stoic or Gnostic ideal of the absence

40. *Epistle to Diognetus*, 5, 1–9 and 6, 1, *Apostolic Fathers*, 2:139–41. See also *À Diognète*, V, 1–9 and VI, 1, SC 33, 63–65.

41. Origen, *Homilies on Judges*, II, 3, Fathers of the Church 119, 57.

of passions (or *apatheia*), in terms that apparently are not far from leading to thinking about the doctrine of the Buddha on the renunciation of desire. There is here the integration, into Christian spirituality, of a type of experience recommended by the sages of Antiquity—up to a certain point at least, for Clement of Alexandria does not fail to say that, in the advanced Christian, such an indifference regarding the passions is itself moved by *agapè*, which is in some way its Christian signature and marks its difference from other spiritualties.[42] Such an example shows how Christianity can be enriched by what it finds in other traditions, all the while with a renewed awareness of what makes up, in regard to the Gospel, the authentic fidelity to the Spirit.

It is necessary to add that the first centuries of Christian history attest to an important development, the one that made possible the birth of monasticism toward the middle of the third century. Persecutions being rarer, one saw the conviction being developed that access to the supernatural passed through men and women who, without being martyrs, realized through their person and way of life a kind of encounter between heaven and earth—or, to say it in another way, they themselves appeared as "other christs." This is what was notably perceived in the figure of Antony, who withdrew in order to look for God in solitude.[43] Of course, the way of life of the "desert Fathers" was very exceptional, but their impression on society was so strong that their ideal later connected with men and women who, themselves, remained "in the world" but tried in their way to respond to the same call to holiness. This was like a "return to the Gospel": the experience of a renewed presence of Christ through those men and women who had accepted being his disciples. Apparently, this had no relationship with other religions. And yet, something is said to us about this very field even through the birth and the development of early monasticism—namely Christianity's original position regarding the super-

42. Cf. Clément d'Alexandrie, *Stromate VI*, 9, 73, 2–6, trans. Patrick Descourtieux, SC 446 (Paris: Cerf, 1999), 205–7; *Stromate VII*, 11, 67, 1–2 and 11, 68, 1–5; trans. Patrick Descourtieux, SC 428 (Paris: Cerf, 1997), 211 and 215–17.

43. In the biographical narrative that he devotes to him, Athanasius writes that others (even those who were not Christian) "came to the church saying: 'We would like to see the man of God'—for so they all called him. Moreover, there also the Lord through him rid many of demons and cured mental cases.... We must not show ourselves skeptical when it is through a man that all these great wonders came to pass"; Athanasius, *The Life of Saint Antony*, 70 and 83; Ancient Christian Writers 10, 79 and 89.

natural, which is fundamentally not to look first at this or that exterior cult but to look for the way of allowing oneself to be shaped by Christ and thus of being as a presence of heaven on earth.[44]

Thus, in spite of the difficulties and objections that have been mentioned above, today it remains very fruitful to read the patristic writings from the perspective of a reflection on Christianity and other religions. One can even have the feeling that the religious situation of our time calls for enlarging the field of work bequeathed by the theology of the twentieth century: what we must take into account regarding the problems raised by religions is not only the themes most often invoked so far—such as those of the "seeds of the Word" and the "evangelical preparation"—but also the debates of the Fathers with the Neoplatonic mystics, their argumentations with the beliefs of reincarnation, the developments of the spiritual experience under the movement of monasticism and their meaning in relation to other forms of spirituality, the problems connected to the presence of ancestral cults and the way of conceiving the announcement of the Gospel in these situations, etc. Patristic literature, of course, will never give a direct response to the specific questions of our era, but—in spite of some forms of language that are at times polemical and that we can no longer make our own—it will continue to bring decisive clarifications to Christian thinking, and most of all, it will help it in thinking about, at the same time, the universal offer of salvation and the unicity of the One who "brought all [possible] novelty, by bringing Himself who had been announced."[45] If the "theology of religions" must go forward and make its way through the new avenues of the situations of our times, it will only be able to do so by means of a right relationship to the heritage of Christian Antiquity. The oceans of our world are vast—vaster than the Mediterranean—but at this time of globalization, Christianity must more than ever immerse itself in the waters that brought it, in order to make known, even in the pluri-religious situation of our time, the response of Simon Peter to the question formerly asked by Jesus "But who do you say that I am?" (Mt 16:15).

44. We will return to this point in chapter 14.

45. Irenaeus, *Against Heresies*, IV, 34, 1; Ante-Nicene Fathers 1, 511.

CHAPTER 14

The Fathers of the Church and Christian Spirituality

One last field remains for us to tackle, that of the contribution of patristics to spiritual theology. In the literature of early Christianity, spirituality actually does not appear simply as one dimension among others. It has a profound effect on the whole of this literature—one could say almost in the same way as the reading of the Scriptures; how, moreover, not to remember that this reading of the Scriptures places essential importance on precisely what is called the "spiritual" meaning? In order to speak about patristic spirituality and its contribution to spiritual theology, it is first necessary to take into account what meditation on the Scriptures represented for the Fathers and their constant concern for not being confined by their literal meaning but to glean from the Scriptures the "spirit"—such an exigency being itself inseparable, according to them, from the progress of the soul in its journey toward God.

Without forgetting this essential point (which we have already developed in our chapter on exegesis),[1] without being able to consider all the other questions that our subject raises, we would like to give at least a general idea of the whole that may show the richness of patristic spirituality and to suggest its importance for our time.[2]

1. See chap. 5.

2. For a more developed presentation, one can refer to Gustave Bardy, *La vie spirituelle d'après les Pères des trois premiers siècles* [The spiritual life according to the Fathers of the first three centuries] (Paris: Bloud & Gay, 1935); Jules Gross, *La divinisation du chrétien d'après les Pères grecs. Contribution historique à la doctrine de la grâce* [The divinization of the Christian according to the Greek Fathers. A historical contribution to the doctrine of grace] (Paris: Gabalda, 1938); Louis Bouyer, *Histoire de la spiritualité chrétienne*, vol. 1, *La spiritualité du Nouveau Testament et des Pères* [History of Christian spirituality, vol. 1, The spiritualilty of the New Testament and the Fathers] (Paris: Aubier-Montaigne, 1960), 209–627.

Prayer, Martyrdom, a Presence in the World: The Spirituality of the First Centuries

From the earliest literature, we have preserved some admirable prayers that are themselves masterpieces of Christian spirituality—thus the prayers connected to the liturgy, such as those of the *Didache*:

Give thanks in the following manner. First, concerning the cup:
We thank you, our Father, for the holy vine of David your servant,
which you have made known to us through Jesus your Servant.
Glory to You forever!
And concerning the broken loaf:
We thank you, our Father, for the life and knowledge
which you have made known to us through Jesus your Servant.
Glory to You forever!
Just as this loaf previously was scattered on the mountains, and when it was gathered together it became a unity,
So may your Church be gathered together from the ends of the earth into your kingdom.
For glory and power are yours forever, through Jesus Christ![3]

Or even the prayers that Clement of Rome inserts into his *Epistle to the Corinthians*:

We beseech thee, Master, to be our helper and defender.
Save those of us in affliction,
have mercy on the humble,
raise up the fallen,
show thyself to those in need,
heal the sick,
turn back those of thy people who have gone astray.
Feed the hungry,
release our imprisoned ones,
receive the weak,
encourage the fainthearted.
Let all the heathen know that thou art God alone, and that Jesus Christ is thy Servant, and that we are thy people and the sheep of thy pasture.[4]

3. *The Didache*, 9, 1–4, trans. Robert A. Kraft, in *The Apostolic Fathers*, vol. 3 (New York: Thomas Nelson & Sons, 1965), 165–66. See also *La Doctrine des douze apôtres (Didachè)*, 9, 1–4; ed. Willy Rordorf and André Tuilier, 2nd ed., SC 248 (Paris: Cerf: 1998), 175–77.

4. *First Clement*, 59, 4, *Apostolic Fathers*, 2:93–94 (with citations from Ps 78:13).

These texts and many more (in the collection of the *Odes of Solomon*, in the stories of martyrdoms, in the letters of Ignatius of Antioch, in *The Pedagogue* of Clement of Alexandria, etc.) express or indeed presuppose a theology that would have be to expounded case by case—but they do it precisely in the form of prayers. This will occur in innumerable writings throughout the patristic era: for the East, let us think of the poems of Gregory of Nazianzus, of Romanos the Melodist, and of Andrew of Crete (without forgetting the simple invocation of the name of Jesus and the "prayer of the heart" in the cadre of the monastic experience). Let us think as well, for the West, of the hymns of Ambrose, of the prayers of Augustine in the *Confessions*, and later of the poems of Venantius Fortunatus.[5] Such texts are very valuable for theology, and this is not only due to their content but also owing to their form itself and, above all, to the spiritual experience to which they are the witnesses.

Yet, for the Fathers, it is the whole of Christian life that must be profoundly influenced by the Spirit of Christ. This exigency is formulated in the earliest writings, as for example the *Didache* (with its teaching on the two ways), *The Shepherd of Hermas* (a witness to the call to penance in the early Church), and some passages of Justin's *Apology*.[6] It also appears, in a very developed way, in some later writings such as *The Pedagogue* of Clement of Alexandria; we have treated it in another chapter,[7] and it is thus not necessary to return to it here, except to emphasize again that the teaching given in this work is not simply "moral" but "spiritual" (it is the Spirit of Christ who, for Clement, must shape and penetrate the totality of human existence). Here, on the contrary, it is necessary to focus on a manifestation—undoubtedly extreme, but highly significant—of the spiritual life in early Christianity: the witness of the martyr.

5. See *Prières des premiers chrétiens* [Prayers of the first Christians], ed. Adalbert-Gautier Hamman (Paris: Arthème Fayard, 1952; Paris: Desclée de Brouwer, 1981), translated by Walter Mitchell as *Early Christian Prayers* (Chicago: Henry Regnery Co., 1961); Jacques Fontaine, *Naissance de la poésie dans l'Occident chrétien. Esquisse d'une histoire de la poésie latine chrétienne, du IIIe au VIe siècle* [The birth of poetry in the Christian West. A sketch of a history of Christian Latin poetry, from the third to the sixth century] (Paris: Institut d'Études Augustiniennes, 1981).

6. See *The Didache*, in *The Apostolic Fathers*, 3:134–60; *The Shepherd of Hermas*, trans. Graydon F. Snyders, in *The Apostolic Fathers*, vol. 6 (1968), 71–72; Justin, *Apology on Behalf of Christians*, 14–16, in *Apologies*, 111–21.

7. See chap. 10, pp. 237–38.

The writings of the first century indeed show the influence of the persecutions inflicted upon Christians and of the meaning that was then recognized in their deaths. These are themselves of a diverse nature: the letters of Ignatius of Antioch, at the moment when he was being taken to Rome in order to be subjected to martyrdom; the letter from the Churches of Vienne and Lyon, reporting the supreme witness of Blandina and other Christians affected by the persecution of the year 177; acts of the martyrs, such as the acts of Saint Justin and his companions; and even the *Exhortations to Martyrdom* composed by Origen and by Cyprian.

But this last expression—"exhortation to martyrdom"—must not lead to misinterpretation. In a general way, martyrdom is not understood by the Fathers as the consequence of a voluntarist attitude nor as the expression of contempt toward the world. It is much rather the way, in extreme situations, in which the imitation of Christ, who was the "witness" or "martyr" par excellence (Rv 1:5), takes shape. This, among other things, is what the famous lines of Ignatius of Antioch show:

> God's wheat I am, and by the teeth of wild beasts I am to be ground that I may prove Christ's pure bread.... Then only shall I be a genuine disciple of Jesus Christ when the world will not see even my body.... Once I have suffered, I shall become a freedman of Jesus Christ, and, united with Him, I shall rise a free man.... May nothing, *seen or unseen*, fascinate me, so that I may happily make my way to Jesus Christ.... *I would rather die* and come to Jesus Christ than be king over the entire earth. Him I seek who died for us; Him I love who rose again because of us. The birth pangs are upon me.... Permit me to be an imitator of my suffering God.... My Love has been crucified, and I am not on fire with the love of earthly things. But there is in me a *Living Water*, which is eloquent and within me says: "Come to the Father."[8]

Thus, as Louis Bouyer correctly writes, "it is not death itself that the martyr is seeking by dying, it is Jesus Christ."[9] Ignatius's words "I am God's wheat," moreover, suggest a link with the Eucharist. Indeed, the

8. Ignatius of Antioch, *To the Romans*, IV, 1–3, V, 3, VI, 1–3, VII, 2, Ancient Christian Writers 1, 82–83. Cf. Col 1:16; 1 Cor 9:15; Jn 4:10. See also Ignace d'Antioche, *Aux Romains*, 131–37) cf. 1 Cor 7:22; Jn 4:10 and 7:38; Jn 14:12.

9. Bouyer, *La spiritualité du Nouveau Testament et des Pères*, 249. Tertullian's writing *Ad martyres* is a slight exception: the exhortation to martyrdom is here matched with very pessimistic considerations on the world, which is compared to a "prison" (see ibid., 259–60).

Eucharist, by giving the food of the risen Christ, allows taking part in his Passion and in the *agapè* that gives meaning to it; and reciprocally, the martyr, by achieving in his own life the perfection of *agapè*, by himself being associated with Christ who gives himself in the Eucharist and on the cross, receives within himself the presence of the Resurrected One and finds himself in some way configured to him.[10] Martyrdom thus expresses, above all, the most intimate relationship with Christ, when the Christian is led to follow him as far as the ordeal of death and, in the same movement, shares in the life of the Resurrected One. This is also what emerges from the *Letter of the Churches of Lyon and Vienne to the Churches of Asia and Phrygia*;[11] this letter reports on the bishop Pothinus: "He was conveyed to the tribunal by the soldiers, escorted by the city authorities and the whole multitude, who gave utterance to all sorts of cries, as if he were Christ Himself."[12] And the same letter writes about Blandina:

> Blandina, suspended on a stake, was exposed as food to wild beasts which were let loose against her. Even to look on her, as she hung cross-wise in earnest prayer, wrought great eagerness in those who were contending, for in their conflict they beheld with their outward eyes in the form of their sister Him who was crucified for them, that He might persuade those who believe in Him that all who suffer for the glory of Christ have unbroken fellowship with the living God.[13]

It is rightly so because martyrdom consummates the union to Christ and fulfills to the very end the exigency of *agapè*; for the catechumens put to death because of their faith, martyrdom was perceived as being the equivalent of a baptism, and for those who had already been baptized, it was understood as a second baptism, more perfect than the first—as Origen and Cyprian explain it.

But every Christian life is called to such a perfection, even outside of the exceptional situation of martyrdom; or more exactly, since the deep meaning of martyrdom is to follow Christ to the very end, every

10. Cf. Bouyer, *La spiritualité du Nouveau Testament et des Pères*, 251–52.

11. See Eusebius of Caesarea, *Ecclesiastical History*, V, 1, 3–63; 2, 2–7; 3, 2–3; Lawlor and Oulton, 140–49.

12. Eusebius of Caesarea, *Ecclesiastical History*, V, 1, 30 (Lawlor and Oulton, 143); see Lk 23:1.

13. Eusebius of Caesarea, *Ecclesiastical History*, V, 1, 41 (Lawlor and Oulton, 145).

Christian is called to such a witness even in the most ordinary conditions of life and of death. This is what Clement of Alexandria wrote in the *Stromata*:

> If the confession of God is a testimony, each soul who has lived purely in the knowledge of God, who has listened to His commandments, is a witness both by its life and its word, in whatever way the soul may have been released from the body, for it shed its faith like blood during its whole life, and particularly at its departure. This is why the Lord says in the Gospel, "Whosoever shall leave his father, his mother, his brothers," and so forth, "for the sake of the Gospel and my name," he is blessed. He is thus not simply designating martyrdom, but gnostic martyrdom, since this man lived according to the rule of the Gospel, because of his love for the Lord.[14]

The "gnostic" martyr, in Clement's language, is no one other than the perfect Christian who, without even having to shed his blood in the ordeal of a persecution, makes his whole life—and even his death—a testimony given to Christ.

That the possibility of martyrdom must not lead Christians to withdraw from the world is strongly said in one of the most beautiful texts of patristic literature, the writing *To Diognetus*, on which we should once again focus:

> Christians are not different from other people in terms of their country, language, or customs. Nowhere do they inhabit cities of their own, use a strange dialect, or live life out of ordinary.... They inhabit both Greek and barbarian cities, according to the lot assigned to each. And they show forth the character of their own citizenship in a marvelous and admittedly paradoxical way by following local customs in what they wear and what they eat and in the rest of their lives. They live in their respective countries, but only as resident aliens; they participate in all things as citizens, and they endure all things as foreigners. Every foreign territory is a homeland for them, every homeland foreign territory....
>
> They are found in the flesh but do not live according to the flesh. They live on earth but participate in the life of heaven.[15]

14. Clément d'Alexandrie, *Stromate IV*, 15, 3–4; SC 463, 81–83. "Gnostic" here does not have the prevailing pejorative meaning in the fight against "the gnosis of the name liar," such as was refuted by Irenaeus in his treatise *Contre les hérésies*.

15. *Epistle to Diognetus*, 5, 1–2, 4–5 and 8–9 (*Apostolic Fathers*, 2:139–41). See also *À Diognète*, V, 1–2, 4–5, 8–9, SC 33, 63–65.

The author also mentions other paradoxes of the Christian existence: Christians "love all humans" and, nevertheless, "all persecute them"; they "lack everything" and "are abundant in all things"; even in the midst of their persecutions they "bless" and "are joyful." Then the text continues:

> To put the matter simply, what the soul is in the body, this is what Christians are in the world. The soul is spread throughout all the limbs of the body; Christians are spread throughout the cities of the world. The soul lives in the body, but it does not belong to the body; Christians live in the world but do not belong to the world. The soul, which is invisible, is put under guard in the visible body; Christians are known to be in the world, but their worship of God remains invisible. The flesh hates the soul and attacks it, even though it has suffered no harm, because it is hindered from indulging in its pleasures. And the world hates the Christians, even though it has suffered no harm, because they are opposed to its pleasures. The soul loves the flesh that hates it, along with its limbs; Christians love those who hate them. The soul is imprisoned in the body, but it sustains [or constrains] the body; Christians are detained the prison of the world, but they sustain [or constrain] the world. The soul, which is immortal, dwells in a mortal tent; Christians temporarily dwell in perishable surroundings but await that which is imperishable in the heavens. The soul grows stronger even when mistreated by what the body eats and drinks; Christians increase daily even when punished. God has appointed them to such a position, and it would not be right for them to abandon it.[16]

The author's statement indeed implies a criticism of the view according to which Christians should constitute a "third people" beside the "Greeks" and the Jewish people.[17] So where is the originality of Christians, if it does not reside in the constitution of a particular people? It is a matter of a "mystery,"[18] which is manifested in an eminently "paradoxical"[19] manner. Christians, at first glance, are not distinguished

16. *Epistle to Diognetus*, 6, 1–10 (*Apostolic Fathers*, 2:141–43); *À Diognète*, SC 3, 65–67.

17. One found this view of a "third people" (*triton genos*) in the *Prédication de Pierre* [The preaching of Peter] and the addressee of the writing *To Diognetus* had in his turn taken it up in another form by speaking of "this new people" (*kainon touto genos*); cf. *Prédication de Pierre*, fragment 5; see *Écrits apocryphes chrétiens*, vol. 1 [Christian apocryphal writings], ed. F. Bovon and P. Geoltrain, Bibliothèque de la Pléiade (Paris: Gallimard, 1997), 17; *Epistle to Diognetus*, 1, 1.

18. *Epistle to Diognetus*, 4, 6 (*Apostolic Fathers*, 2:139): "the mystery of the Christians' own way of worship."

19. *Epistle to Diognetus*, 5, 4 (*Apostolic Fathers*, 2:139–41): "they show forth the character of their own citizenship in a marvelous and admittedly paradoxical way."

from other human beings in any way, but they indeed belong to another "homeland." The author's thesis is, in any case, that the world is not simply useful to Christians but that they must assume a role in it and make their own contribution to it—what is more, that they "sustain the world."[20] The exposition recalls the words of Jesus in John 17:15–16: "I do not pray that thou shouldst take them out of the world, but that thou shouldst keep them from the evil one. They are not of the world, even as I am not of the world." And the idea according to which Christians "preserve the world" itself transposes the teaching of the Sermon on the Mount: "You are the salt of the earth.... You are the light of the world ..." (Mt 5:13–16). Such is the spirituality of *To Diognetus*, and one finds a beautiful echo of it in the meditation that Origen devotes precisely to the Gospel image of the "salt of the earth": "For the men of God are the salt of the world, preserving the permanence of things on earth, and earthly things hold together so long as the salt does not turn bad. For if the salt has lost its savor, it is of no further use either for the earth or for the dunghill, but is cast out and trodden under foot by men."[21]

The Journey of the Soul toward God

Whether it be a matter of prayer, of the supreme witness in the case of persecution, or of ordinary life as it reflects the "paradoxical" situation of Christians—"to be in the world without being of the world"—the themes that we have tackled so far all presuppose an ardent quest of the soul, desirous of being intimately united to Christ and of communing with the very life of God. Of course, such an experience comes up against many obstacles, not only the ordeals coming from the outside but also all forms of evil that threaten the believer and take hold of him: from the beginning, the Fathers are aware of this, as seen in the letter of Clement addressed to the Corinthians plagued by jealousy and envy or with the call of *The Shepherd of Hermas* for the conversion of sinners; and it is for them the occasion to develop a deep reflection on the difficulties of the spiritual life and the battles that it must overcome. But rather than focus on this aspect (that,

20. *Epistle to Diognetus*, 6, 7 (*Apostolic Fathers*, 2:143).
21. Origen, *Contra Celsum*, VIII, 70; Chadwick, 506.

moreover, we will again come upon regarding monastic literature), we would here like to accentuate the most positive side of the experience—that we summarize by the expression "the journey of the soul toward God." The spirituality of the patristic era, considered from this point of view, indeed achieves true heights.

Although present from the beginning (as the words of Ignatius of Antioch already cited recall: "My Love has been crucified, and I am not on fire with the love of earthly things. But there is in me a *Living Water*, which is eloquent and within me says: 'Come to the Father'"),[22] the experience evoked here gives rise to some particularly remarkable expositions in the third and fourth centuries; and we will illustrate them with both Origen and Gregory of Nyssa. Such expositions have undoubtedly benefitted, to some extent, by contacts with the philosophy of Middle Platonism and Neoplatonism, which had raised to great heights the idea of the divine transcendence and which, in some of its writings, gave way to a true mysticism of the "Good" or of the "One." But they are above all indebted to the properly Christian experience: the meditation on the Scriptures, the discovery of the stages by which the Hebrew people formerly made their way in the desert, the openness to the mystery of God as it is revealed in the Old and the New Testaments—a mystery infinitely more grand than one could first suspect. Thus the exodus of Israel is, for Origen, a figure of the Christian journey (a journey that has itself an ecclesial dimension for it happens, when the time comes, by the gift of Baptism):

> For both when someone is led from the darkness of errors to the light of knowledge, and when one is converted from an earthly way of life to a spiritual manner of life, he seems to have made an exodus from Egypt and to have come to a solitude, that is, to that state of life in which, by means of silence and quiet, one becomes practiced in the divine laws and is imbued with heavenly speech. Educated and guided by these things, when he has crossed the Jordan, he hastens to the Promised Land, that is, through the grace of baptism, he arrives at a life according to the gospel.[23]

But it is above all necessary to draw attention to the passage in which Origen comments on the prophesy of Balaam in the book of Numbers:

22. Ignatius of Antioch, *To the Romans*, VII, 2; Ancient Christian Writers 1, 83.
23. Origen, *Hom. Nm.*, XXVI, 4, 1; (Scheck, 164).

"How fair are your tents, O Jacob, your encampments, O Israel!" (Nm 24:5). Those who are seeking God, he explains, are not satisfied with houses, "for they have not reached the end," whereas with tents "they are always on the move and making progress. And the more progress they make, the more the road to be traveled is lengthened for them and extends into the measureless":

> And truly, if someone has made some progress in knowledge and has acquired some experience in such matters, he really knows that when he has come to some idea and recognition of spiritual mysteries, his soul tarries there, as it were, in a kind of tent. But when, on the basis of these things it has discovered, it again fathoms other things and advances to other understandings, it picks up its tent from there, so to speak, and heads for the higher things. And there it establishes a seat for its mind, fixed in the stability of the meanings.
>
> And once again from there, on the basis of these things, it finds other spiritual meanings, which doubtless are logical inferences that have come to light by the previously apprehended meanings. And in this way, always "striving for what is ahead," the soul seems to advance by means of tents, as it were. For there is never a time when the soul that has been set on fire by the spark of knowledge can sink into leisure and take a rest, but it is always summoned from the good to the better, and again from the better to the superior.[24]

The image of the "tents" thus leads to highlighting a major trait of the spiritual experience: the soul is not satisfied by what it has already attained, it is still looking to progress toward new mysteries. And the Christian experience is here very prominent, as the expression "always 'striving for what is ahead'" shows, which repeats the famous saying of Paul in the Letter to the Philippians "forgetting what lies behind and *straining forward* [*epekteinomenos*] to what lies ahead, I press on toward the goal" (Phil 3:13–14). This, moreover, does not mean that the soul's quest should be desperately doomed to never attaining its object. Origen also commented on the Canticle of Canticles, which presents the coming of the Spouse, and it is this coming of the Spouse that is rightly fulfilled with Christ. But the soul's desire is not, for all that, extinguished; even though the Spouse has dwelled among humans, the soul must still seek him so that he may come dwell within it:

24. Ibid., XVII, 4, 3 (Schenk, 106). Translation modified: "tent" replaces "tabernacle."

> God is my witness that I have often perceived the Bridegroom drawing near me and being most intensely present with me; then suddenly He has withdrawn, and I could not find Him, though I sought to do so. I long, therefore, for Him to come again, and sometimes He does so. Then, when He has appeared and I lay hold of Him, He slips away once more; and, when He has so slipped away, my search for Him begins anew. So does He act with me repeatedly, until in truth I hold Him and go up, "leaning on my Beloved's arm."[25]

In the fourth century, Gregory of Nyssa repeats these themes and develops them further. Meditating on the life of Moses, he sees in him the figure of the soul who has never achieved his quest—not only because of the inherent limits of the human condition but also because what is at stake is the very mystery of God:

> the soul rises ever higher and will always make its flight yet higher—by its desire of the heavenly things *straining ahead for what is still to come,* as the Apostle says.... The divine voice granted what was requested in what was denied, showing in a few words an immeasurable depth of thought. The munificence of God assented to the fulfillment of his desire, but did not promise any cessation or satiety of the desire.
>
> He would not have shown himself to his servant if the sight were such as to bring the desire of the beholder to an end, since the true sight of God consists in this, that the one who looks up to God never ceases in that desire. For he says: *You cannot see my face, for man cannot see me and live.*[26]

The text of Paul in Philippians 3 is here evoked as it was in Origen. Gregory gives to it an even greater importance since he develops on its foundation the concept of *epektasis* in order to describe the journey of the soul toward God. However, even if he particularly emphasizes the always unfinished character of the spiritual experience, he, nevertheless, does not say that the soul's quest may not attain its object. Like Origen, he commented upon the Canticle of Canticles, and he sees in Christ the One who was prefigured in the traits of the Spouse coming to dwell among human beings. That is the boundary that separates Christian mysticism from Neoplatonic mysticisms: the soul is not only carried away in a movement from low to high—a movement

25. Origen, *Hom. Song*, I, 7; *The Song of Songs*, 280, translation modified.

26. Gregory of Nyssa, *The Life of Moses*, II, 225, 232 and 233; trans. Abraham J. Malherbe and Elizabeth Ferguson, Classics of Western Spirituality (Mahwah, N.J.: Paulist Press, 1978), 113 and 115; cf. Phil 3:13; Ex 33:20.

that would never attain its end to the extent that the divine Transcendence would be radically inaccessible—it also recognizes how God, by an inverse movement, himself came to our humanity, and it finds in this abasement the very paradoxical revelation of the divine power, as Gregory explains in *The Great Catechism*:

> that the omnipotence of the Divine nature should have had strength to descend to the humiliation of humanity, furnishes a clearer proof of that omnipotence than even the greatness and supernatural character of the miracles. For that something pre-eminently great should be wrought out by Divine power is, in a manner, in accordance with, and consequent upon the Divine nature; nor is it startling to hear it said that the whole of the created world, and all that is understood to be beyond the range of visible things, subsists by the power of God, His will giving it existence according to His good pleasure. But this His descent to the humility of man is a kind of superabundant exercise of power, which thus finds no check even in directions which contravene nature.
>
> ... The way, in fact, in which sublimity, existing in lowliness, is actually seen in lowliness, and yet descends not from its height, and in which Deity, entwined as it is with the nature of man, becomes this, and yet still is that.[27]

Simply said, the fact that the Divinity thus abased himself and that the soul may rest in it does not bring its aspiration to an end. It must rather be identified with rest and with movement,[28] not only because the soul never finishes welcoming Christ and, through him, communing with the divine life, but also because the humility of the Word become man, far from diminishing the transcendence of God, on the contrary, reveals its unsuspected profundity. "It is no small matter, quite worthy of research—writes Gregory—to know how the one who is always present comes."[29]

One would, of course, have to describe the evolutions of this Christian mysticism, both in the East (notably in Dionysius and Maximus the Confessor) and in the West (here, we are particularly thinking about Augustine's debate with Neoplatonism). But the reflections

27. Gregory of Nyssa, *The Great Catechism*, XXIX, in *Select Writings and Letters of Gregory, Bishop of Nyssa*, trans. William Moore and Henry A. Wilson, A Select Library of Nicene and Post-Nicene Fathers of the Christian Church, 2nd ser., 5 (London: Parker, 1893), 494.

28. Gregory of Nyssa, *The Life of Moses*, II, 243 (Classics of Western Spirituality, 117):"This is the most marvelous thing of all: how the same thing is both a standing still and a moving."

29. A homily on "as you did it to one of the least of these my brethren, you did it to me" (Mt 25:40), 2, in *Riches et pauvres dans l'Église ancienne*, 184.

that we have devoted to Origen and Gregory of Nyssa already suffice to speak of the importance of the patristic reflection on the journey of the soul toward God and of the light that it can today bring even in the field of spiritual theology. This journey of the soul toward God takes a particular form in the cadre of the monastic experience, as witnessed to by the writings of the "Fathers of the Desert."

The Spirituality of the Fathers of the Desert

Even if monasticism has a prehistory, it is only beginning in the second half of the third century that it was truly developed in Egypt, Palestine, Syria, and Asia Minor, before also being propagated in the West. It first took shape in "anachoresis": some men withdrew to the desert in order to look for God in solitude; such was notably the case of Antony, the "father of monks," to whom Athanasius would later devote a famous biography. But soon, under the influence of Pachomius, monasticism was organized in the communitarian form: this was the birth of "cenobitism," which in turn was going to experience a very rapid expansion. One could not overly emphasize the importance of this monastic expansion in early Christianity. Some factors undoubtedly contributed to it; it has been argued that, to the extent that the threat of persecutions were lessened and that Christianity became more tolerated and thus risked being more compromised by the surrounding world, Christians felt more deeply the call to a form of life that would allow them to respect seriously the radicalness of the Gospel exigencies. Furthermore, the works of P. Brown have very clearly shown how the very evolution of society and mentalities had created a propitious environment for the emergence of a new figure, that of "friends of God" who, at the point when the traditional forms of ancient religion had lost most of their attraction, seemed by their very person to witness to a real communication between the divine world and the human world.[30] Nonetheless, the considerable expansion of the monastic movement remains an exceptional fact, for which no historical or sociological explanation by itself suffices to account.

30. See Peter Brown, *The Making of Late Antiquity* (Cambridge, Mass.: Harvard University Press, 1978). The last part of the book is titled "From the Heavens to the Desert: Anthony and Pachomius."

What we would like to highlight in these pages is, in any case, that the experience lived by so many monks and consecrated virgins during the patristic era was the occasion of an unprecedented deepening of Christian spirituality and that it, because of its richness, has made a major contribution to the spiritual theology of subsequent eras—including our own. We will use for an example one of the most famous texts, the *Life of Antony* by Athanasius. This writing first gives us a story about a vocation, by telling how Antony heard in all its radicalness Jesus' words to a rich young man: "If thou wilt be perfect, go sell all that you hast, and give it to the poor; and come, follow me and thou shalt have treasure in Heaven."[31] The text then describes the practice of asceticism to which Antony was committed; it also evokes the spiritual combat that he had to go through and of which he came out the winner: the anchorite was freed from temptations by "filling his thoughts with Christ" and by "reflecting upon the nobility of the soul that comes from Him, and its spirituality"; he benefited from the nearness of the Son of God who worked by his side: "the Lord worked with this man—He who for our sakes took on flesh and gave to his body victory over the Devil."[32] Antony afterwards discovers that this nearness of Christ was never missing, not even in the strongest spiritual struggle:

> here again the Lord was not forgetful of Antony's struggle, but came to help him.... The demons suddenly were gone and the pain in his body ceased at once and the building was restored to its former condition. Antony, perceiving that help had come, breathed more freely and felt relieved of his pains. And he asked the vision: "Where were you? Why did you not appear at the beginning to stop my pains?"
>
> And a voice came to him, "I was right here, Antony, but I waited to see you in action. And now, because you held out and did not surrender, I will ever be your helper and I will make you renowned everywhere."[33]

Through the experience that Antony lived, his entire being is transformed—not only his soul, but his soul and his body; such is, in any case, the image that the anchorite himself presents at the time of his appearance after twenty years of solitude:

31. Mt 19:21; cited in Athanasius, *The Life of Saint Antony*, 2; Ancient Christian Writers 10, 19. See also Athanase, *Vie d'Antoine*.

32. Athanasius, *The Life of Saint Antony*, 5 (Ancient Christian Writers 10, 23).

33. Ibid., 10 (Ancient Christian Writers 10, 28–29).

Antony came forth as out of a shrine, as one initiated into sacred mysteries and filled with the spirit of God. It was the first time that he showed himself outside the fort to those who came to him. When they saw him, they were astonished to see that his body had kept his former appearance, that it was neither obese from want of exercise, nor emaciated from his fastings and struggles with the demons: he was the same man they had known before his retirement.

Again, the state of his soul was pure, for it was neither contracted by grief, nor dissipated by pleasure nor pervaded by jollity or dejection. He was not embarrassed when he saw the crowd, nor was he elated at seeing so many there to receive him. No, he had himself completely under control—a man guided by the Word and stable in his character.[34]

Furthermore, although Antony's experience had been influenced by the search for God in total solitude, the story shows that paradoxically, by this very way, the anchorite had been prepared to help others. Thus it is that "through him the Lord healed many of those present who were afflicted with bodily ills," that he "freed others from impure spirits," and that he "gave Antony charm in speaking, and so he comforted many in sorrow, and others who were quarrelling he made friends."[35] It was thus granted to Antony to be able, to the very extent of his union with the Word of God, to speak and to act like Christ! And the text adds: "now monasteries also sprang up in the mountains, and the desert was populated with monks who left their own people and registered themselves for citizenship in Heaven."[36]

Athanasius afterwards tells us that the anchorite escaped martyrdom during a persecution, but on this occasion, he implies that asceticism was itself a form of *marturia*; he indeed writes about Antony:

he also appeared grieved that he did not suffer martyrdom.

But the Lord was guarding him for our own good and for the good of others, that to many he might be a teacher of the ascetic life which he himself had learned from the Scriptures.

... When the persecution finally ceased and Bishop Peter of blessed memo-

34. Ibid., 14 (Ancient Christian Writers 10, 32–33). Robert T. Meyer translates "a man guided by reason"; G. J. M. Bartelink (in the French translation) writes: "someone whom reason governs"; he clarifies in a note: this expression is Stoic, but "one can assume here an underlying allusion to the Christian Logos" (SC 400, 175n1). We prefer to translate: "guided by the Word"; it seems to us that Athanasius wants above all to highlight, here as elsewhere, the presence of the Lord to Antony.

35. Athanasius, *The Life of Saint Antony*, 14 (Ancient Christian Writers 10, 32).

36. Ibid., 14 (Ancient Christian Writers 10, 33).

ry had suffered martyrdom, he left and went back to his solitary cell; and there he was a daily martyr to his conscience, ever fighting the battles of the Faith.[37]

But so many people came to see him, he wanted to withdraw further into the "inner mountain." There he found some palm trees, some water, a corner of earth that he sowed and cultivated; the text also says that he "gently" captured a wild beast so that it would not harm any of his plants.[38] This is an allusion to the Garden of Eden and to the mission that Adam had received to subdue the animals—as if Antony found himself, thanks to his experience, in the condition of the first man before the Fall. Athanasius also mentions other battles against the demons and new healings. He highlights as well the perfect orthodoxy of Antony who was opposed to Arianism (thus showing the deep coherence between the life of the anchorite and his faith in Christ as the eternal Son of God). Other episodes could also be mentioned, but those that we have noted already suffice to show the importance of the spiritual experience here reported. At the end, Athanasius highlights that Antony's life fulfilled the very promises of the Lord:

We must not show ourselves skeptical when it is through a man that all these great wonders came to pass. For it is the promise of the Savior who says: *If you have faith as a grain of mustard seed, you shall say to this mountain, "Remove hence!" and it shall remove; and nothing shall be impossible to you.* And again: *Amen, amen, I say to you, if you ask the Father anything in my name, he will give it to you.... Ask, and you shall receive.* And it is He who says to His disciples and to all who believe in him: *Heal the sick; ... cast out the demons; freely have you received without pay, freely give.*[39]

The *Life of Antony* is thus a remarkable witness to the spiritual experience that was developed at the beginnings of monastic life. And this experience has itself given rise to numerous other writings between the fourth century and the end of the patristic era. Among them, it is first necessary to mention the *Apophtegmata* of the Fathers, that admirable collection of maxims and advice given by some anchorites, gathering the fruits of the monastic experience concerning asceticism and

37. Ibid., 46 and 47 (Ancient Christian Writers 10, 59 and 60).

38. Ibid., 49–50 (Ancient Christian Writers 10, 61–63).

39. Ibid., 83 (Ancient Christian Writers 10, 89); cf. Mt 17:20; Jn 16:23–24; Mt 10:8. Athanasius adds that it is a witness not only for the "other brothers" but also for the "pagans" themselves.

spiritual combat faced with diverse temptations. It is also necessary to mention the name of Evagrius, some of whose doctrines have assuredly been condemned because of Origenism but who was, nevertheless, a remarkable theoretician of the spiritual life through his statements on prayer and contemplation, his analysis of the virtues and vices, and even his understanding of the discernment of spirits. Evagrius himself had for his master Macarius the Egyptian (Macarius of Scetes), to whom have been attributed fifty homilies as well as a text known under the name of *Great Letter*; one notably finds in it some teachings on prayer as the principle activity of the monk, on the purity of the heart, on the state of quietude (*hèsychia*) that thus ought to be sought, and even on the progressive character of the spiritual life.[40] And many other writings, from quite different literary genres, could be mentioned: the *Rules* (such as those of Basil in the East and, later, of Benedict in the West); the lives of monks (such as the *Lausiac History*); the *Conferences* of Cassian and his *Institutes of the Coenobia*; the correspondence (such as that of Barsanuphius and John of Gaza); the spiritual writings of Diadochos of Photiki, John Moschos, John Climacus, and still others.[41] An immense literature that not only reveals the history of monasticism in the centuries of Antiquity but also makes us aware of the treasures of the experience and the wisdom formerly acquired thanks to anachoresis and cenobitism and that also remains today as a fundamental source of inspiration for spiritual theology.

The Experience of Augustine

We cannot end our journey without evoking the great figure who dominates Latin patristics and whose work gives such a great place to the spiritual experience and to the reflection inspired by it.[42] It

40. The teaching of Macarius is sometimes close to that of Gregory of Nyssa. This is the occasion to point out that the Cappadocians were themselves very influenced by the monastic ideal: two of them, Basil of Caesarea and Gregory of Nazianzus, had themselves embraced this way of life for a period of time; and the third, Gregory of Nyssa, wrote several treatises that develop some of the major themes of monastic spirituality.

41. This obviously does not exclude some limits here and there: beside Origenism to which we have alluded, some monastic milieus were affected by the error of Messalianism that, in its way of giving the greatest importance to prayer, came to devalue work and even the struggle of asceticism.

42. See notably the book of Isabelle Bochet, *Saint Augustin et le désir de Dieu* [Saint Augustine and the desire for God] (Paris: Institut d'Études Augustiniennes, 1982).

would be necessary to focus at length on the story of the *Confessions*, a testimony to the itinerary that led Augustine to the major event of his conversion in the year 386. This event, although sudden, had at least been prepared for by some episodes, encounters, reflections, and readings (notably that of the *Life of Antony*). Several moments can thus be distinguished:[43] the discovery (thanks to the first sermons of Ambrose) of spiritual exegesis, that which was used to expose the falseness of the accusations made by Manicheism against the Scriptures; then, after a phase of Skepticism (tempered, nevertheless, by the decision to remain a catechumen in the Catholic Church), the discovery of the grandeur that characterizes the Christian faith and of its profoundly spiritual value, even if the soul still remains subject to interior anxieties and the need for carnal pleasures; from there—still under the influence of Ambrose's preaching—an increasing sympathy for the Church and progress in what is properly called belief, although it may not be the full certitude of faith; then comes the reading of the Platonic books that provide the intellectual resources for understanding this faith, and even for some of the most difficult questions such as that of the question of evil. This point being attained, there would, of course, be the risk of either being satisfied with a religion that is both speculative and mystical (such as that of Plotinus) or of being satisfied with a connection to the Absolute that would not entail belonging to a Church; but it is at this point that Augustine makes the discovery of Christ as "Mediator," as the One who is the "way" toward the "Homeland." And he experiences his actual presence in the Church thanks to the testimonies given by Simplicianus and Ponticianus, then above all in his personal life through the famous scene in the garden:

> And, behold, I heard from a nearby house the voice of someone—whether boy or girl I know not—chanting, as it were, and repeating over and over: "Take it, read it! Take it, read it!" And immediately, with a transformed countenance, I started to think with greatest concentration whether it was the usual thing for children to chant words such as this in any kind of game, and it did not occur to me that I had ever heard anything like it. Having stemmed the flow of my tears, I got up, taking it to mean that nothing else was divinely commanded me than I should open a book and read the first passage that I should find. For I

43. We are here following Aimé Solignac in his introduction to Augustin, *Les Confessions*, 161–63.

had heard about Antony that he had been admonished from a reading of the Gospel on which he had come by chance, as if what was being read was said for him: "Go, and sell what thou hast, and give to the poor, and thou shall have treasure in heaven; and come, follow me," and by such a revelation he was at once converted to Thee.[44]

Augustine then returns to the bench where his friend Alypius was seated and, taking up the "Book of the Apostle," read the first chapter on which his eyes fell. It was the passage from the Letter of the Romans: "not in reveling and drunkenness, not in debauchery and licentiousness, not in quarreling and jealousy. But put on the Lord Jesus Christ, and make no provision for the flesh, to gratify its desires" (Rom 13:13–14). The story of the *Confessions* then adds: "No further did I desire to read, nor was there need. Indeed, immediately with the termination of this sentence, all the darknesses of doubt were dispersed, as if by a light of peace flooding into my heart."[45] This is the decisive moment, the one where the will and the habits inscribed in the flesh find themselves actually converted by Christ the Mediator. And this outcome is also a new beginning: the conversion will be deepened thanks to the reflections at Cassiciacum, the meditations recorded in the *Soliloquies*, the teachings of the baptismal catechesis, and the studies at the monastery of Thagaste. And throughout his life, Augustine will not cease to scrutinize the Scriptures in order to conform his life more to them: as Aimé Solignac writes of him, "he will never cease to be converted."[46]

By his very way of thus retracing the diverse phases of his journey, Augustine transmits a teaching that touches upon more than his own experience and that is of exceptional importance for all reflection on the access to faith. Moreover, it is not the only, but much to the contrary, aspect by which the *Confessions* are of such a great richness for spiritual theology. It may suffice to recall here the famous vision of Ostia—the experience of Augustine and his mother, Monica, who, leaning on the sill of a window that opened to the garden, came to the contemplation of uncreated Wisdom:

44. Augustine, *Confessions*, VIII, 29 (Fathers of the Church 21, 224–25); cf. Mt 19:21.
45. Ibid., 225.
46. Solignac, introduction to Augustin, *Les Confessions*, 163.

then, lifting ourselves up in the yet greater ardor of our feeling toward the Selfsame, we advanced step by step through all bodily things up to the sky itself, from which the sun, moon, and stars shine out over the earth, and we ascended still farther in our interior cogitation, conversation, and admiration of Thy works and came to our own minds.

Then, we transcended them, so that we might touch that realm of unfailing abundance in which Thou feedest Israel eternally on the food of truth. There, life is wisdom, through which all these things come into being, both those which have been and those which will be. Yet, it is not made, but is as it was, and thus it will be forever. Or, rather, to have been in the past, or to be in the future, do not pertain to it, but simply *to be*, for it is eternal. To be in the past, or to be in the future, is not to be eternal.

And, while we are so speaking and panting for it, we did touch it a little, with an all-out thrust of our hearts. We sighed and left behind "the first fruits of the spirit" which were bound there, and we came back to the clattering of our mouths, where the spoken word has its beginning and end. How is it like Thy Word, our Lord, "remaining ageless in Itself and renewing all things"?[47]

A summit of the spiritual experience is here being evoked, the one whereby the soul, in the fervor of its prayers, finds itself penetrated by the divine wisdom to the point of "touching" this—a sudden illumination without duration, but the effects of which really remain beyond the vision itself. The experience thus reported must be incontestably described as "authentically mystical."[48]

It is not simply the *Confessions* but all the other writings of Augustine that would need to be presented from the point of view of their spiritual importance. Of course, the reflection of the bishop of Hippo on the journey of the soul will show some change within the framework of the Pelagian controversy: his mysticism will appear more and more clearly "as that of simply being aware of grace, of its sovereignty in our salvation, an awareness that takes place to the very extent that we surrender to this grace that calls upon us."[49] However, a unilateral insistence on this point would not grant enough to the extraordinary richness of the spirituality that Augustine, furthermore, develops in the entirety of his work. Thus the *Enarrationes in Psalmos* contain remarkable expositions on the relationship between the Church as the

47. Augustine, *Confessions*, IX, 24 (Fathers of the Church 21, 251–52).
48. Solignac, introduction to Augustin, *Les Confessions*, 197.
49. Bouyer, *La spiritualité du Nouveau Testament et des Pères*, 572.

body of Christ and Christ as the Head of this body, and also between the Church-Bride and Christ-Bridegroom:

"Like as the hart desireth the water-brooks, so longeth my soul after Thee, O God." Who is it then that saith this? It is ourselves, if we be but willing! And why ask, who it is other than thyself, when it is in thy power to be the thing which thou art asking about? It is not however one individual, but it is "One Body;" but "Christ's Body is the Church."[50]

For the Bride is the Church, the Bridegroom is Christ.... For we who believe, may this Bridegroom always appears in his Beauty. He is beautiful like God, like the Word with God; he is beautiful in the Virgin's womb, where he clothed himself in human nature without divesting himself of his divine nature.[51]

So also that great work, the *City of God*, develops a spiritual reading of history by applying to humanity itself the fight that Augustine had experienced in his personal life:

What we see, then, is that two societies have issued from two kinds of love. Worldly society has flowered from a selfish love which dared to despise even God, whereas the communion of saints is rooted in a love of God that is ready to trample on self. In a word, this latter relies on the Lord, whereas the other boasts that it can get along by itself. The city of man seeks the praise of men, whereas the height of glory for the other is to hear God in the witness of conscience. The one lifts up its head in its own boasting; the other says to God: "Thou art my glory, thou liftest up my head."

In the city of the world both the rulers themselves and the people they dominate are dominated by the lust for domination; whereas in the City of God all citizens serve one another in charity, whether they serve by the responsibilities of office or by the duties of obedience. The one city loves its leaders as symbols of its own strength; the other says to its God: "I love thee, O Lord, my strength."[52]

Augustine then draws upon the first chapter of the Letter to the Romans in order to describe the contrast of the two Cities:

Hence, even the wise men in the city of man live according to man, and their only goal has been the goods of their bodies or of the mind or of both; though some of them have reached a knowledge of God, "they did not glorify him as

50. Augustine, on Ps 42, in *Expositions on the Book of Psalms* (Grand Rapids, Mich.: Wm. B. Eerdmans Publishing Company, 1956), 132.

51. Augustine, on Ps 45 in *Expositions on the Book of Psalms*, 146.

52. Augustine, *The City of God*, XIV, 28 (Fathers of the Church 14, 410–11).

God or give thanks but became vain in their reasonings, and their senseless minds have been darkened. For while professing to be wise" (that is to say, while glorying in their own wisdom, under the domination of pride) "they have become fools, and they have changed the glory of the incorruptible God for an image made like to corruptible man and to birds and four-footed beasts and creeping things" (meaning that they either led their people, or imitated them, in adoring idols shaped like these things), "and they worshipped and served the creature rather than the Creator who is blessed forever." In the City of God, on the contrary, there is no merely human wisdom, but there is a piety which worships the true God as He should be worshiped and has as its goal that reward of all holiness whether in the society of saints on earth or in that of angels of heaven, which is "that God may be all in all."[53]

To pride is opposed humility and then charity—as Augustine notably highlights in his *Commentary on the First Letter of John*: "for love alone extinguishes offenses. Pride extinguished love; therefore, humility strengthens love, love extinguishes offenses."[54] And the *Commentary* devotes many beautiful pages to this charity that is a participation in the very life of God:

"We are of God." Let us see why. See if for any other reason than for love....

Love could not have been more commended to you than that it be said to be God....

The more joyfully I speak of love, the less I wish this epistle to reach its end. No epistle is more abundant in commending love. Nothing sweeter is preached to you, nothing healthier is drunk—but would that by living well you strengthen in yourselves the gift of God....

I do not know whether love could be commended to us more magnificently than in the words "God is pure love." Brief praise and great praise! Brief in word and great in meaning. How quickly one says it: "God is love." And this is brief: if you were to count it, it is one thing; if you were to weight it, how substantial it is! "God is love. And he who abides in love," [John] says, "abides in God and God in him." Let God be your house, and be the house of God. Abide in God, and let God abide in you. God abides in you that he may hold you; you abide in God that you may not fall. For so the Apostle says about love itself: "Love never falls." How does he whom God holds fall?[55]

53. Ibid., XIV, 28 (Fathers of the Church, 14, 411); cf. Ps 3:4 and 17:2; Rom 1:21–24; 1 Cor 15:28.

54. Augustine, *Tractates on the First Epistle of John*, I, 6; trans. John W. Rettig, The Fathers of the Church 92 (Washington, D.C.: The Catholic University of America Press, 1995), 129.

55. Ibid., VII 4; VIII, 14; IX, 1 (Fathers of the Church 92, 219, 244, 245, and 247); cf. 1 Jn 4:6 and 4:16; 1 Cor 13:8.

By all these themes, and by many more, Augustine's reflection remains of immense importance for Christian spirituality. Of course, one must never forget what was the starting point of such a reflection: the personal journey to which the *Confessions* attest. Such a journey, and the very manner in which Augustine speaks of it—in a story that has no precedent in the literature of Antiquity—largely contributes to explaining how the figure of this convert has had such a great influence on each era and why it continues to do so in our day. But Augustine does not just attest to his own conversion, and his genius is precisely to have known how, with all the resources of his literary and philosophical knowledge and, above all, thanks to his unceasing meditation on the Scriptures, to develop with such profundity the most fundamental themes of the spiritual experience.

As we stated, here we have given only a simple glimpse of the spirituality of the patristic era, or rather of *the* spiritualities of this era, for, as one will have noted, they were very diverse according to the movements and the authors—even if they all participated in the same fundamental inspiration: to allow oneself to be formed to Christ by his Spirit, to endure ordeals that arise on this way and to learn to overcome them, to gather the fruits of the experience thus lived, bringing out from them the profound laws and communicating them to others so that they might in their turn make progress in their journey toward God. Many other points could be tackled as well—thus, from the Greek East, the emphasis of John Chrysostom on the call of every Christian to perfection, the deepening of mystical theology in Dionysius the Areopagite and Maximus the Confessor, the expositions of John Damascene on the veneration of images; and also, from the Latin West, the spiritual themes that nourished the sermons of Pope Leo, Caesarius of Arles, and Gregory the Great, etc. The choices that we have made here suffice, however, to show the major importance that patristic literature gives to the spiritual life. They especially suffice to make clear the richness of this literature for our own era. The writings of the Fathers convey to us, as far as spirituality is concerned, treasures of wisdom, experience, and reflection. They must be, in this domain more than in any other, valuable nourishment for those who are fortunate enough to discover them and, at the same time, a source of inspiration for the present tasks of theology.

Epilogue
The Future of the Fathers

Today, patristic literature is giving rise to numerous studies that allow us to know the texts better, to shed light on them from the historical situations in which they were born, to understand their meaning in a more exact way, to clarify their importance within the whole of the writings that the ancient world has bequeathed to us. One can only rejoice in such a fact, which numerous studies from previous centuries have already provided but that have been considerably expanded in the past several decades. This first calls for gratitude, which, it is true, can also be mixed with some fear for the future: since ancient languages are increasingly less well-known, will there be enough researchers for pursuing, completing, and also deepening our knowledge of the patristic texts? Vigilance is called for, but trust must prevail—as improbable as it may seem since our societies are not preserving the minimal conditions for research on the writings of Christian Antiquity, the knowledge of which (as that of Antiquity in general) is essential for the full awareness of their own identity.

Nevertheless, it does not suffice for the texts of early Christianity to be better edited and known. It is also necessary that, as was the case for past generations, the studies on the Fathers continue to make a contribution to the specific tasks of Christian theology. To highlight such an exigency is clearly not to idealize the patristic era (as if it did not have its shadows and its dramas); nor is it is to misunderstand that some texts, very much influenced by the language and the views of their time, no longer have for us the same importance as for their former addressees; nor is it to ignore that some early authors were able to be mistaken on this or that point or at least to appeal to some views or schemas of thought that today can be disputed. To highlight such an exigency is, on the contrary, to respect the very intention of the Fathers who were intent upon accounting for the Christian faith. Besides their sometimes outmoded or questionable aspects, their works bequeath to us immense resources for taking into account in our turn this faith—even if we must do it in situations that are necessarily different. To emphasize such an exigency is also to grant an essential request of theology that, as history has taught us, can move forward only by means of the memory of its past. The return to the Fathers that marked the 1930s–50s cannot be considered as a stage henceforth outdated. More broadly, the link between the return to the patristic sources and the renaissances that have regularly marked the history of Christian thought is not accidental but rather very much constitutive, for the theology of each generation must have an active contact with the Fathers. Of course, each time it can only tackle them within a new context and with new concerns. But in this very situation it is essential and vital for it to allow itself to be inspired by those who, in Christian Antiquity, have contributed so much to the understanding of the faith among the Nations.

In the first part of the book, we have attempted to expound the essential reasons that, even today, establish the importance of patristic studies for theological reflection. Then, in the second part, we have presented the more specific motifs of a work on the Fathers in the different fields of Christian theology. But, undoubtedly, it is necessary at the end to invoke an ultimate justification, which is from an order other than the preceding ones and that is undoubtedly more decisive than any other: *the very fact* that, in spite of or through the centuries that separate us from the era of the Fathers, some of their writings continue to connect with us, that they also speak to us, that they enlighten and nourish our understanding of the faith. This is like a miracle, and this miracle is sufficient so that, even independent of any other consideration, we may continue to read the Fathers and to learn with them to make progress in the understanding of the faith.

Such an experience must never cease to astonish us—and even, to fill us with wonder. Some patristic texts today appear quite as new as they were in their time. Whether it is a matter of the letters of Ignatius of Antioch burning "to imagine the passion of [his] God," of the admirable description of the Christian existence in the writing *To Diognetus*, of rich expositions by Irenaeus on the history of salvation, of Origen's commentaries that fervently scrutinize the mysteries of the Canticle of Canticles and the Gospel of John, of Athanasius's profound meditations, or of Basil on the eternal generation of the Word, of that masterpiece of mystical theology that Gregory of Nyssa has left us with in his *Life of Moses*, of the ardent sermons of John Chrysostom on the love for the poor, the experiential treasures bequeathed to us by monastic literature and the incomparable story of Augustine in his *Confessions*, all these texts—and many more—continue to speak to us as they have done so for so many readers in the past. And even where these texts are more difficult to access (being more influenced by words and concepts that are not immediately familiar to us) the experience teaches us that, if we have consented at all to study them patiently, they too can, one day or another, become accessible to us to the point that, even miraculously, they in some way become for us contemporaries, penetrating into our world, connecting with us in spite of the difference in times. Then the memory of the Fathers dwells in us to the point of no longer being experienced as a memory of a past but as the reality of multiple voices that, bursting forth from this past, convey to us today the very mysteries of the faith, give us access to their meaning, and thus contribute to making them present to us.

But it is *we* who thus allow ourselves to be connected to the writings of the Fathers, in a time that is ours and no longer theirs. From then on, far from our being able to repeat on every point what they have said, we are led—*and this by the very contact with their works*—to find words, images, concepts, and ways of thinking that allow us to take into account in our turn, as we are able, major affirmations of the Christian faith and their impacts in the diverse fields of theology, in a way that may be, as much as possible, pertinent and credible in the new situations of our times. This is why the in-depth reading of the Fathers, to the extent that it is deepened, implies also a form of detachment. In the very act by which we welcome their writings—at the point that the memory of them becomes a true presence in us—in this very act we experience that we will be faithful to their goal only by accepting to distance ourselves from them and by expressing ourselves in a different way, in the situations that are henceforth ours. But it is precisely the reading of the Fathers that produces this. In the response to the miracle of this reading, capable of connecting to us in our time, there is thus another miracle, that of the echo heard in the words and writing of the theologian who finds in the in-depth reading of patristic writings a way for today elaborating his own language. The memory of the Fathers, from the moment that it becomes present, is by this very fact an inspiration for the future. It thus sparks new languages on the faith, according to the newness of places and times. The more the theologian will have read the Fathers and will have allowed himself to be imbued with their writings, the more he will experience the interior necessity of speaking on his own account and in his own language—not from infidelity toward them but, on the contrary, because the very contact with their writings will have brought to him an unexpected light capable of sparking and making fruitful his own work of understanding the faith. A necessary detachment, sensitive to the wound that it leaves in the spirit and the heart—that of not being able to associate with the Fathers without also being invited, when the time comes, to be detached from their writings in order to speak and to write in his turn. But this brings infinite joy. Because the in-depth reading of the Fathers, today as yesterday, will have contributed to engendering the understanding of the faith. Because the work thus accomplished will not dispense with continuing to read and reread the writings from early Christianity. Because, even tomorrow, the Church will be able to harvest its fruit. Because the Fathers have a future, and this is essential for the very future of theology.

Bibliography

In addition to the books and articles already mentioned in the French edition (2013), we will mention here some books that have been published since this edition, as well as many works in English.

Texts and Translations

Texts

Migne

Let us first point out the two great collections of Greek and Latin texts edited in the nineteenth century by Abbé Migne.

Patrologiae Cursus completus. Series graeca (Patrologia Graeca).
Patrologiae Cursus completus. Series latina (Patrologia Latina).

French Collections

The French-speaking reader can above all refer to following collections:

Textes et documents pour l'étude historique du christianisme [Texts and documents for the historical study of Christianity]. Directed by Hippolyte Hemmer and Paul Lejay. 18 vols. Paris: Picard, 1904–.

The collection Sources Chrétiennes, 600 vols. (Paris: Cerf, 1942–). This collection is published under the direction of the Institut des Sources Chrétiennes in Lyon. It publishes the Greek, Latin, and Eastern texts. See *Lire les Pères de l'Église dans la collection Sources Chrétiennes*, new recast and enlarged ed., ed. Claude Mondésert and Jean-Noël Guinot. (Paris: Cerf, 2010).

The collection Bibliothèque augustinienne, 59 vols. (Paris: Institut d'Études Augustiniennes, 1933–), for the works of Saint Augustine.

Other Collections

Die Griechischen christlichen Schriftsteller der ersten drei Jahrhunderten. Berlin: Akademie Verlag. This collection is known as the Corpus de Berlin, and publishes only Greek texts.

Corpus Scriptorum Ecclesiasticorum Latinorum. Vienna: Verlag der österreichischen Akademie der Wissenschaften. This collection is known as the Corpus de Vienne, and it publishes only Latin texts.

Corpus Christianorum (series latina and series graeca). Turnhout, Belgium: Brepols. This collection is progressively replacing the Patrologies of Migne, which remain, however, useful for many patristic writings. Corpus Christianorum also includes a specific series for the apocryphal texts (Series Apocryphorum).

Eastern Patrology

Lastly, for Eastern patrology, two collections must be mentioned

Patrologia Orientalis. Turnhout, Belgium: Brepols.

Corpus Scriptorum Christianorum Orientalium. Leuven: Peeters.

These two collections give both the original text and a translation in a modern language. Additionally, as said above, the collection Sources Chrétiennes also publishes eastern texts.

Translations

Texts in English

English-speaking readers can refer to these collections

The Complete Ante-Nicene & Nicene and Post-Nicene Church Fathers Collection.

The Fathers of the Church series. Washington, D.C.: The Catholic University of America Press.

The Ancient Christian Writers series. Mahwah, N.J.: Paulist Press.

Oxford Early Christian Texts. Oxford: Oxford University Press, 1971–2009.

Ancient Christian Texts. Westmont, Ill.: InterVarsity Press, Academic.

The Classics of Western Spirituality series. Mahwah, N.J.: Paulist Press.

The Oxford Apostolic Fathers series. Oxford: Oxford University Press.

The Apostolic Fathers, vols. 1–6. London: Thomas Nelson & Sons.

Main Collections in the French Language:

Textes et documents pour l'étude historique du christianisme.

Sources Chrétiennes. Paris: Cerf.

Bibliothèque Augustinienne. Paris: Institut d'Études Augustiniennes (for the works of Saint Augustine, see above).

Les Pères dans la foi. 104 vols. Paris: Desclée de Brouwer, 1977–. This collection only provides the French translation, whereas the two preceding ones also give the original text (except for most of the writings in Eastern languages. One will as well find some translations in the collection Lettres Chrétiennes (Paris: Grasset/Centurion, 1957–), as well as in the collection of the Universités de France (Paris: Les Belles Lettres).

Patrologia Orientalis and Corpus Scriptorum Christianorum Orientalium (for the Eastern texts, see above).

Other Collections

One will also find French translations (without the original text) in several other collections.

Foi Vivante. Paris: Cerf.

Sagesses–Points. Paris: Seuil.

Spiritualité Orientale. Bégrolles-en-Mauges: Abbaye of Bellefontaine.

See also:

Premiers écrits chrétiens. Edited by Bernard Pouderon, Jean-Marie. Salamito, and Victor Zarini. Paris: Gallimard, 2016.

Philo of Alexandria; Apocryphal Literature; Gnostic Literature

Œuvres de Philon d'Alexandrie [Writings of Philo of Alexandria]. Greek text and French translation. Edited by Roger Arnaldez, Jean Pouilloux, and Claude Mondésert. Paris: Cerf, 1961–.

Corpus Christianorum, Series Apocryphorum. Leuven: Peeters.

Écrits apocryphes chrétiens [Christian apocryphal writings]. 2 vols. Edited by F. Bovon and P. Geoltrain. Bibliothèque de la Pléiade. Paris: Gallimard, 1997 and 2005.

Also see the translations assembled in the collection Apocryphes. Turnhout, Belgium: Brepols.

Écrits gnostiques. La bibliothèque de Nag Hammadi [Gnostic writings. The library of Nag Hammadi]. Edited by Jean-Pierre Mahé and Paul-Hubert Poirier. Bibliothèque de la Pléiade. Paris: Gallimard, 2007.

Dictionaries, Catalogues, Bibliographies

Dictionaries of Greek and Latin Patristics

Blaise Albert, and Henri Chirat. *Dictionnaire latin-français des auteurs chrétiens*. "Le latin chrétien." Strasbourg, 1954.

Lampe, Geoffrey William Hugo. *A Patristic Greek Lexicon*. Oxford: Oxford Clarendon Press, 1961.

Also see the dictionaries relating to various authors (such as the *Lexicon-Gregorianum*, or the *Augustinus-Lexikon*).

Dictionaries of the Fathers of the Church

Berardino, Angelo di, ed. *Dictionnaire Encyclopédique du Christianisme Ancien*. Under the direction of A. di Berardino. French adaptation under the direction of F. Vial. 2 vols. Paris: Cerf, 1990.

Berardino, Angelo di, ed. *Encyclopedia of Ancient Christianity*. 3 vols. Produced by the Institutum Pontificium Augustinianum. Translated from Italian. Downers Groved, Ill.: InterVarsity Press Academic, 2014.

Bercot, David W., ed. *A Dictionary of Early Christian Beliefs. A Reference Guide to More Than 700 Topics Discussed by the Early Church Fathers*. Peabody, Mass.: Hendrickson Publishers, 1998.

Buchwald, Wolfgang, Armin Hohllweg, and Otto Prinz, eds. *Dictionnaire des auteurs grecs et latins de l'Antiquité et du Moyen Âge*. Translated from the German. Turnhout, Belgium: Brepols, 1991.

Cross, Frank Leslie, and Elizabeth A. Livingston, eds. *The Oxford Dictionary of the Christian Church*. 2nd ed., reprint with corrections and revisions. Oxford: Oxford University Press, 1984 (this dictionary is not limited to the patristic period).

Hamman, Adalbert-Gautier. *Dictionnaire des Pères de l'Église*. Les Pères dans la foi, new edition. Paris: Desclée de Brouwer, 1977. Abridged edition of A. Hamman, *Guide pratique des Pères de l'Église* (Desclée de Brouwer, Paris, 1967).

Hazaël-Massieux, Marie-Christine. *Dictionnaire contemporain des Pères de l'Église. Leurs mots, leurs textes, leur langage*. Montrouge: Bayard, 2011.

One can also refer to the dictionaries of theology that include numerous articles on patristic authors and themes. See in particular:

Catholicisme. Paris: Letouzey & Ané.

Dictionnaire de Spiritualité. Paris: Beauchesne.

Dictionnaire critique de théologie. Paris: Presses Universitaires de France.

Catalogues

These volumes give the list of Greek and Latin texts to which it is possible to have access, indicating, if needed, the different editions.

Dekkers, Eligius. *Clavis Patrum Latinorum*. Bruges: Beyaert, 1961.

Geerard, Maurice, et al. *Clavis Patrum Graecorum*. Turnhout, Belgium: Brepols, 1983–98.

Ortiz de Urbina, Iñigo. *Patrologia syriaca (altera editio)*. Rome: Institut d'études orientales, 1965.

Bibliographies

L'Année philologique. Bibliographie critique et analytique de l'Antiquité gréco-latine (founded by J. Marouzeau, and continued by J. Ernst). Now published by Société Internationale de Bibliographie Classique.

Bibliographia Patristica.

Bulletin de Théologie ancienne et médiévale.

Bulletin d'information et de liaison de l'Association Internationale d'Études Patristiques. Turnhout, Belgium: Brepols.

Sieben, Hermann-Josef. *Voces. Eine Bibliographie zu Wörtern und Begriffen aus der Patristik.* Berlin: Walter de Gruyter, 1980.

Wolinski, Joseph. "Bibliographie patristique." In *Introduction à l'étude de la théologie* ("Manuel de theologie," no. 3), edited by Joseph Doré, 199–347. Paris: Desclée, 1992.

Special Bibliographies on Origen, Gregory of Nyssa, and Augustine

Altenburger, Matthias, und Friedhelm Mann. *Bibliographie zu Gregor von Nyssa.* Leiden: Brill, 1988.

Andresen, Carl. *Bibliographia augustiniana.* 2nd ed. Darmstadt: Wissenschaftliche Buchgesellshaft, 1973.

Crouzel, Henri. *Bibliographie critique d'Origène.* La Haye: Nijhoff, 1971. Supplément I, La Haye: Nijhoff, 1982. Supplément II, Brepols, Turnhout, Belgium, 1996.

Collections and Reviews

See the dictionaries of theology mentioned above, and the works and reviews containing articles and reviews of books:

- collections or reviews specializing in patristics: *Studia Patristica*; *Revue d'Études Augustiniennes et Patristiques*; *Augustinianum*; *Vigiliae Christianae*; *Adamantius*; *Connaissance des Pères de l'Église*, etc.
- other reviews such as the *Recherches de Science Religieuse*, the *Revue des Sciences Philosophiques et Théologiques*, the *Bulletin de Littérature Ecclésiastique*, *Gregorianum*, the *Nouvelle Revue Théologique*, etc.

Patrologies

Altaner, Berthold. *Patrology.* Translated from German. New York: Herder & Herder, 1960. Translated as *Précis de patrologie*, adapted from the German (Mulhouse: Salvator, 1961). Also see the more recent German edition: B. Altaner and A. Stuiber, *Patrologie. Leben, Schriften und Lehre der Kirchenväter* (Freiburg: Herder, 1978).

Berardino, Angelo di, ed. *Patrologia. I Padri latini (secoli V–VIII).* Institutum Patristicum Augustinianum. Genova: Marietti, 1996. Translated as *Patrology,* vol. 4 (Westminster, Mass.: The Newman Press, 1986). Translated as *Initiation aux Pères de l'Église*, vol. 4 (Paris: Cerf, 1986).

Berardino, Angelo di, ed. *Patrologia. I Padri orientali (secoli V–VIII)*. Institutum Patristicum Augustinianum. Genova: Marietti, 2000. Translated as *Patrology. The Eastern Fathers from the Council of Chalcedon (451) to John of Damascus († 750)* (Cambridge: James Clarke, 2006).

Campenhausen, Henri von. *Les Pères de l'Église*. Vol. 1, *Les Pères grecs*. Vol. 2, *Les Pères latins*. Translated from the German. Paris: éd. de l'Orante, 1963–1967.

Cayré, Fulbert. *Patrologie et histoire de la théologie*. 2nd ed. 2 vols. Paris: Desclée & Co., 1927–30.

Drobner, Hubertus R. *Les Pères de l'Église. Sept siècles de littérature chrétienne*. Translated from the German, revised and adapted for the French edition. Paris: Desclée, 1999.

Guillaumont Antoine, ed. *Christianismes orientaux. Introduction à l'étude des langues et des littératures*. Paris: Cerf, 1993.

Hamman, Adalbert-Gautier. *Guide pratique des Pères de l'Église*. Paris: Desclée de Brouwer, 1967.

———. *Les Pères de l'Église*. Les Pères dans la foi. Paris: Jean-Paul Migne, 2000.

Laporte, Jean. *Les Pères de l'Église*. Vol. 1, *Les Pères latins*. Vol. 2, *Les Pères grecs*. Paris: Cerf, 2001.

Liébaert, Jacques, and Michel Spanneut. *Les Pères de l'Église*. Vol. 1, *Du Ier au IVe siècle*. Paris: Desclée, 1986.

Peters, Gabriel Sr. *Lire les Pères de l'Église. Cours de patrologie*. Paris: Desclée de Brouwer, 1981.

Quasten, Johannes. *Patrology*. Vol. 1, Utrecht: Spectrum, 1950. Vol. 2, Utrecht: Spectrum, 1953. Vol. 3, Utrecht: Spectrum, Westminster: The Newman Press, 1960. Translated as *Initiation aux Pères de l'Église* (Paris: Cerf, 1959–63).

Spanneut, Michel. *Les Pères de l'Église*. Vol. 2, *Du IVe au VIIIe siècle*. Paris: Desclée, 1990.

Tardieu, Michel, and Jean-Daniel Dubois. *Introduction à la littérature gnostique* [Introduction to Gnostic literature]. Paris: Cerf, 1986.

Patristic Writings

Athanase. *Vie d'Antoine*. Translated by G. J. M. Bartelink. SC 400. Paris: Cerf, 1994.

Athanasius. *The Life of Saint Antony*. Translated by Robert T. Meyer. Ancient Christian Writers 10. Westminster, Mass.: The Newman Press, 1950.

Augustine. *Letter* 54. PL 33, 200–204.

———. *Questions sur l'Heptateuque*. Translated into French. In *Œuvres complètes de saint Augustin*, 7:579–80. Paris: Vivès, 1870.

———. *The City of God*. Translated by Gerald G. Walsh and Grace Monahan. The Fathers of the Church 8, 14, and 24. Washington, D.C.: The Catholic University of America Press, 2010, 1952, and 1954.

———. *La Cité de Dieu*. Translated by G. Combès. 5 vols. Bibliothèque augustinienne 33–37. Paris: Desclée de Brouwer, 1959–60.

———. *Confessions*. Translated by Vernon J. Bourke. The Fathers of the Church 21. Washington, D.C.: The Catholic University of America Press, 1953.

———. *Les Confessions*. Translated by E. Tréhorel and G. Bouissou. 2 vols. Bibliothèque augustinienne 13 and 14. Paris: Institut d'Études Augustiniennes, 1992.

———. *Expositions on the Book of Psalms*. Grand Rapids, Mich.: Wm. B. Eerdmans Publishing Company, 1956.

———. *Sancti Aurelii Augustini opera, epistulae ex duobus codicibus nuper in lucem prolatae*. Edited by Johannes Divjak. CSEL 88. Vienna: Hoelder-Pichler-Tempsky, 1981.

———. *Tractates on the First Epistle of John*. Translated by John W. Rettig, The Fathers of the Church 92. Washington, D.C.: The Catholic University of America Press, 1995.

———. *Teaching Christianity. De Doctrina Christiana*. Translated by Edmund Hill. Hyde Park, N.Y.: New City Press, 1996.

———. *La doctrine chrétienne*. Edited by Madeleine Moreau and Isabelle Bochet. Bibliothèque augustinienne 11/2. Paris: Desclée de Brouwer, 1997.

———. *Vingt-six sermons au peuple d'Afrique* [Twenty-six sermons to the people of Africa]. Edited by François Dolbeau. Paris: Institut d'Études Augustiniennes, 1996.

Basil of Caesarea. *Epistula* 104. PG 32, 509–12.

Basile de Césarée. *Homélies sur la richesse*, édition critique and exégétique [Homilies on wealth. A critical and exegetical edition]. Edited by Yves Courtonne. Paris: Firmin-Didot, 1935.

———. *Homélies sur l'Hexaéméron*. Translated by Stanislas Giet. 2nd. ed. SC 26. Paris: Cerf, 1968.

———. *Traité du Saint-Esprit*. In *Sur le Saint-Esprit*. 2nd. ed. Translated by B. Pruche. SC 17. Paris: Cerf, 1968.

———. *Homélie 6*. In *Riches et pauvres dans l'Église ancienne* [Rich and poor in the ancient Church], edited by Adalbert-Gautier Hamman, 76–77. Paris: Desclée de Brouwer, 1982. New, revised and enlarged ed. Paris: J.-P. Migne, 2011.

Bede. *The Ecclesiastical History of the English People*. Edited by Judith McClure and Roger Collins. Oxford: Oxford University Press, 1994.

Bède le Vénérable. *Histoire ecclésiastique du peuple anglais*. Vol. 1. Translated by Pierre Monat and Philippe Robin. SC 489. Paris: Cerf, 2005.

Clément d'Alexandrie. *Stromate* I. Translated by Marcel Caster. SC 30. Paris: Cerf, 1951.

———. *Le Pédagogue, Livre I*. Translated by Marguerite Harl. SC 70. Paris: Cerf, 1960.

Clement of Alexandria. *Stromateis*, Books 1–3. Translated by John Ferguson. The Fathers of the Church 85. Washington, D.C.: The Catholic University of America Press, 1991.

———. *The Instructor* (*Paedagogus*). In *Fathers of the Second Century: Hermes, Tatian, Athenagoras, Theophilus, and Clement of Alexandria*, edited by Alexander Roberts and James Donaldson, revised by A. Cleveland Coxe. The Ante-Nicene Fathers 2. Edinburgh: T & T Clark. Reprinted, Grand Rapids, Mich.: Eerdmans, 1994.

———. *The Stromata, or Miscellanies*. In Ante-Nicene Fathers 2. Grand Rapids, Mich.: Eerdmans, 1994.

———. *Stromate* VII. Translated by Alain Le Boulluec. SC 428. Paris: Cerf, 1997.

———. *Stromate* VI. Translated by Patrick Descourtieux. SC 446. Paris: Cerf, 1999.

———. *Stromate* IV. Translated by Claude Mondésert. SC 463. Paris: Cerf, 2001.

———. *Quel riche sera sauvé?* Translated by Patrick Descourtieux. SC 537. Paris: Cerf, 2011.

Clement of Rome. *First Clement*. In *The Apostolic Fathers*, vol. 2. Translated by Robert M. Grant and Holt H. Graham. New York: Thomas Nelson & Sons, 1965.

Clément de Rome. *Lettre aux Corinthiens*. In *Épître aux Corinthiens*. Translated by Annie Jaubert. SC 167. Paris: Cerf, 2000.

Pseudo-Denys. *Les noms divins*. Translated by Maurice de Gandillac. In *Œuvres complètes du Pseudo-Denys l'Aréopagite*. Paris: Aubier-Montaigne, 1943.

Pseudo-Dionysius. *The Complete Works*. Translated by Colm Luibheid. The Classics of Western Spirituality. Mahwah, N.J.: Paulist Press, 1987.

Pseudo-Denys l'Aréopagite. *Les noms divins*. Translated by Ysabel de Andia. SC 578 and 579. Paris: Cerf, 2016.

The Didache. Translated by Robert A. Kraft. *The Apostolic Fathers*, vol. 3. New York: Thomas Nelson & Sons, 1965.

À Diognète. Translated by Henri-Irénée Marrou. 2nd. ed. SC 33. Paris: Cerf: 1965.

To Diognetus, Epistle. In *The Apostolic Fathers*, vol. 2. Edited and translated by Bart D. Ehrman. The Loeb Classical Library 25. Cambridge, Mass.: Harvard University Press, 2003.

La Doctrine des douze apôtres (Didachè). Edited by Willy Rordorf and André Tuilier. 2nd ed. SC 248. Paris: Cerf: 1998.

Eusebius of Caesarea. *Contra Marcellum*. PG 24, 707–826.

———. *The Ecclesiastical History*. In *A Select Library of Nicene and Post-Nicene Fathers of the Christian Church*, vol. 1. Oxford: Parker and Company, 1890.

———. *The Ecclesiastical History*. Translated by Hugh Jackson Lawlor and John Ernest Leonard Oulton. London: Society for Promoting Christian Knowledge, 1927.

Eusèbe de Césarée. *Histoire ecclésiastique*. Translated into French by Gustave Bardy, SC 31, 41 and 55. Paris: Cerf, 1952–58.

———. *Louanges de Constantin*. In *La théologie politique de l'empire chrétien* [The political theology of the Christian empire]. Translated by Pierre Maraval. Paris: Cerf, 2001.

Évagre. *Traité pratique*. Vol. 1. Translated by Antoine and Claire Guillaumont. SC 171. Paris: Cerf, 1971.

Grégoire de Nazianze. *Discours 32–37*. Translated into French by Paul Gallay. SC 318. Paris: Cerf, 1985.

Gregory of Nyssa. *The Great Catechism*. In *Select Writings and Letters of Gregory, Bishop of Nyssa*. Translated by William Moore and Henry A. Wilson. A Select Library of Nicene and Post-Nicene Fathers of the Christian Church, 2nd ser., 5. London: Parker, 1893.

———. *The Life of Moses*. Translated by Abraham J. Malherbe and Elizabeth

Ferguson. The Classics of Western Spirituality. Mahwah, N.J.: Paulist Press, 1978.

Grégoire de Nysse. *Homélies sur l'Ecclésiaste*. Translated by Françoise Vinel. SC 416. Paris: Cerf, 1996.

———. *L'âme et la résurrection* [The soul and resurrection]. Translated by Christian Bouchet. Les Pères dans la foi 73. Paris: Migne, 1998.

Gregory the Great. *Registri epistolarum*. PL 77, 496–98.

Gregoire le Grand. *Homélies sur Ezéchiel*. Translated by Charles Morel. SC 327 and 360. Paris: Cerf, 1986–90.

Hilary of Poitiers. *On the Trinity*. In *Hilary of Poitiers, John of Damascus*, translated by E. W. Watson, L. Pullan and others, 40–233. A Select Library of Nicene and Post-Nicene Fathers of the Christian Church, 2nd ser., 9. Edinburgh: T & T Clark. Reprinted, Grand Rapids, Mich.: Eerdmans, 1997.

———. *The Trinity*. Translated by Stephen McKenna. The Fathers of the Church 25. Washington, D.C.: The Catholic University of America Press, 1954.

Ignatius of Antioch. *To the Romans*. In *The Epistles of St. Clement of Rome and St. Ignatius of Antioch*. Translated by James A. Kleist. Ancient Christian Writers 1. Westminster, Mass.: The Newman Bookshop, 1946.

Ignace d'Antioche. *Aux Romains*. Translated by Pierre Thomas Camelot. 2nd. ed. SC 10. Paris: Cerf, 1998.

Irenaeus. *Against Heresies*. In *Apostolic Fathers, Justin Martyr, Irenaeus*, edited by Alexander Roberts, James Donaldson, and A. Cleveland Coxe, 315–567. *The Ante-Nicene Fathers* 1. 1885. Reprinted, Grand Rapids, Mich.: Eerdmans, 1996.

Irénée. *Contre les hérésies*. Translated by Adelin Rousseau. Paris: Cerf, 1984.

Irenaeus. *Against the Heresies*, Book 1. Translated by Dominic J. Unger, with further revisions by J. Dillon. Ancient Christian Writers 55. New York, N.Y.: Paulist Press, 1992.

———. *Against the Heresies*, Book 2. Ancient Christian Writers 65. New York: Paulist Press, 2012.

———. *Against the Heresies*, Book 3. Translated by Dominic J. Unger. Ancient Christian Writers 64. New York: Paulist Press, 2012.

Jean Cassien. *Conférences*. Vol. 1. Translated by E. Pichery. SC 42. Paris: Cerf, 1955.

———. *Institutions cénobitiques*. Translated by Jean-Claude Guy. SC 109. Paris: Cerf, 1965.

John Cassian. *The Conferences*. Translated by Boniface Ramsey. Ancient Christian Writers 57. New York: Newman Press, 1997.

———. *The Institutes*. Translated by Boniface Ramsey. Ancient Christian Writers 58. New York: Newman Press, 2000.

Jean Chrysostome. *Homélie 48 in Mt*. PG 58, 487–94.

———. *Homélie 50 in Mt*. PG 58, 503–10.

———. *Homélie 20 in Acts*. PG 60, 157–64.

Jean Damascène. *Écrits sur l'islam*. Translated by Raymond Le Coz. SC 383. Paris: Cerf, 1992.

———. *La Foi orthodoxe*. Translated by P. Ledrux. SC 535. Paris: Cerf, 2010.

Jerome. *Lives of Illustrious Men*. Translated by Ernest Cushing Richardson. The Nicene and Post-Nicene Fathers, 2nd ser., 3, 359–84. 1892. Reprint, Edinburgh: T&T Clark, 1996.

———. *Les hommes illustres*. Translated by D. Viellard. Les Pères dans la foi 100. Paris: Migne, 2009.

Justin. *Apologie pour les chrétiens*. Translated by Charles Munier. SC 507. Paris: Cerf, 2006.

———. *Apologies*. Edited by Denis Minns and Paul Parvis. Oxford Early Christian Texts. Oxford: Oxford University Press, 2009.

———. *Dialogue avec le juif Tryphon*. 2 vols. Translated by Georges Archambault. Paris: Picard, 1909.

———. *The Dialogue with Trypho*. Translated by A. Lukyn Williams. London: Society for Promoting Christian Knowledge, 1930.

Martyrdom of Polycarp. In *The Apostolic Fathers*, vol. 5, translated by William R. Schoedel. London: Thomas Nelson & Sons, 1967.

Martyrdom of Polycarp. Translated by Paul Hartog. Oxford: Oxford Apostolic Fathers, 2013.

Maximus the Confessor. *Epistula 12*. PG 91, 460–509.

———. *Epistula 13*. PG 91, 509–33.

Maxime le Confesseur. *Opuscules théologiques et polémiques*. Translated by Emmanuel Ponsoye. Les Pères dans la foi 64. Paris: Cerf, 1996.

Origen. *Contra Celsum*. Translated by Henry Chadwick. Cambridge: Cambridge University Press, 1953.

———. *The Song of Songs, Commentary and Homilies*. Translated by R. P. Lawson. Ancient Christian Writers 26. Mahwah, N.J.: Paulist Press, 1957.

Origène. *Contre Celse*. Translated by Marcel Borret. SC 132, 136, 147, and 150. Paris: Cerf, 1967–69.

———. *Commentaire sur Matthieu*. Translated by Robert Girod. SC 162 (Paris: Cerf, 1970).

———. *Homélies sur Jerémie*. Vol. 1 Translated by Pierre Nautin and Pierre Husson. SC 232. Paris: Cerf, 1976.

Origen. *On First Principles*. Translated by Rowan A. Greer. The Classics of Western Spirituality 10. Mahwah, N.J.: Paulist Press, 1979. Other translations: *On First Principles*, translated by G. W. Butterworth (New York: Harper & Row, 1966); *On First Principles*, 2 vols, translated by John Behr, Oxford Early Christian Texts (Oxford: Oxford University Press, 2017).

Origène. *Traité des principes*. 3 vols. Translated by Henri Crouzel and M. Simonetti. SC 252, 253, and 268. Paris: Cerf, 1978–80.

———. *Homélies sur le Lévitique*. 2 vols. Translated by Marcel Borret. SC 286 and 287. Paris: Cerf, 1981.

Origen. *Commentary on the Gospel According to John, Books 1–10*. Translated by Ronald E. Heine. The Fathers of the Church 80. Washington, D.C.: The Catholic University of America Press, 1989.

———. *Homilies on Leviticus*. Translated by Gary Wayne Barkley. The Fathers of the Church 83. Washington, D.C.: The Catholic University of America Press, 1990.

Origène. *Fragm. sur le Cantique* [Fragm. in Song]. In *Commentaire sur le Cantique*. Translated by Luc Brésard, Henri Crouzel, and Marcel Borret. SC 376. Paris: Cerf, 1992.

Origen. *Homilies on Luke*. Translated by Joseph T. Lienhard. The Fathers of the Church 94, Washington, D.C.: The Catholic University of America Press, 1996.

———. *Homilies on Jeremiah*. Translated by John Clark Smith. The Fathers of the Church 97. Washington, D.C.: The Catholic University of America Press, 1998.

Origène. *Homélies sur les Nombres*. Vol. 2, *XI–XIX*. Translated by Louis Doutreleau. SC 442. Paris: Cerf, 1999.

Origen. *Commentary on the Epistle to the Romans*. 2 vols. Translated by Thomas P. Scheck. The Fathers of the Church 103 and 104. Washington, D.C.: The Catholic University of America Press, 2001 and 2002.

———. *Homilies on Judges*. Translated by Elizabeth Ann Dively Lauro. The Fathers of the Church 119. Washington, D.C.: The Catholic University of America Press 2002.

———. *Homilies on Numbers*. Translated by Thomas P. Scheck. Ancient Christian Texts. Westmont, Ill.: InterVarsity Press Academic, 2009.

———. *Homilies 1–14 on Ezechiel*. Translated by Thomas P. Scheck, Ancient Christian Writers 62. New York: The Newman Press, 2010.

———. *Homilies on Genesis*. Translated by Ronald E. Heine. The Fathers of the Church 71. Washington, D.C.: The Catholic University of America Press, 2010.

Origène. *Commentaire sur l'épître aux Romains (Livres VI–VIII)*. Translated by Luc Brésard and Michel Fédou. SC 543. Paris: Cerf, 2011.

Philosophoumena ou Réfutation de toutes les hérésies. Translated by Auguste Siouville. Paris: Rieder, 1928.

Prédication de Pierre [The preaching of Peter]. In *Écrits apocryphes chrétiens* [Christian apocryphal writings], 1:11–22. Edited by F. Bovon and P. Geoltrain. Bibliothèque de la Pléiade. Paris: Gallimard, 1997.

The Shepherd of Hermas. Translated by Graydon F. Snyders. In *The Apostolic Fathers*, vol. 6. London: Thomas Nelson & Sons, 1968.

Le Pasteur d'Hermas. Translated by Robert Joly. 2nd. ed. SC 53. Paris: Cerf, 1968.

Sulpice Sévère. *Vie de saint Martin*. Translated by Jacques Fontaine. SC 133. Paris: Cerf, 1967.

Tertullien. *Traité de la prescription contre les hérétiques*. Translated by Pierre de Labriolle. SC 46. Paris: Cerf, 1957.

———. *Apologétique*. Translated by Jean-Pierre Waltzing. Paris: Les Belles Lettres, 1929.

———. *De anima*. In *Opera II*, 781–869. Corpus Christianorum, Series Latina 2. 1954. Reprint Turnhout, Belgium: Brepols, 1996.

———. *Adversus Praxean*. In *Opera II*, 1159–1205. Corpus Christianorum, Series Latina 2.

Vincent of Lérins. *The Commonitories*. Translated by Rudolph E. Morris. The Fathers of the Church 7. 1949. Reprint Washington, D.C.: The Catholic University of America Press, 1970.

———. *Tradition et progrès* [Tradition and progress]. Edited by Adalbert-Gautier Hamman. Paris: Desclée de Brouwer, 1978.

Other Sources from Antiquity or the Modern Period

Antiquity

Thucydides. *History of the Peloponnesian War*. Vol. 1. London: William Heinemann, 1928.

Modern Period

Daillé, Jean. *Traicté de l'employ des saincts Pères pour le jugement des differends, qui sont aujourd'huy en la Religion*. Geneva: Pierre Aubert, 1632. Translated by Thomas Smith as *A Treatise on the Right Use of the Fathers in the Decision of Controversies Existing at This Day in Religion* (London: W. White, 1841).

Des Gallars, Nicolas. Preface to *Irénée*. Geneva: Jean Le Preux and Jean Petit, 1570.

Harnack, Adolf von. *History of Dogma*. 7 vols. London: Williams & Norgate, 1894–1899.

———. *Grundriss der Dogmengeschichte*. Tübingen: J. C. B. Mohr, 1889. Translated by Eugène Choisy as *Histoire des dogmes* (Paris: Cerf, 1993).

———. *Mission et expansion du christianisme aux trois premiers siècles*. Translated by Joseph Hoffmann. Paris: Cerf, 2004. Translated by James Moffatt as *The Expansion of Christianity in the First Three Centuries*, 2 vols (New York: Putnam's Sons, 1904–5).

Loyola, Ignatius of. *The Spiritual Exercises and Selected Works*. Edited by George E. Ganss. Classics of Western Spirituality. Mahwah, N.J.: Paulist Press, 1991.

Loyola, Ignace de. *Écrits* [Writings]. Edited by Maurice Giuliani. Paris: Desclée de Brouwer, 1991.

Möhler, Johann Adam. *L'Unité de l'Église ou le principe du Catholicisme d'après l'esprit des Pères des trois premiers siècles de l'Église*. Translated by Joseph Hoffmann. Paris: Cerf, 1938. Translated by Peter C. Erb as *Unity in the Church or the Principle of Catholicism: Presented in the Spirit of the Church Fathers of the First Three Centuries* (Washington, D.C.: The Catholic University of America Press, 1996).

Newman, John Henry. *Historical Sketches*. London: Longmans, Green, and Co., 1906–9.

———. *Apologia pro vita sua*. London: Penguin Books, 1994.

———. *An Essay on the Development of Christian Doctrine*. 6th ed. Notre Dame, Ind.: University of Notre Dame Press, 1989.

History, Literature, Exegesis

History of Later Antiquity

Baslez, Marie-Françoise. *Comment notre monde est devenu chrétien* [How our world became Christian]. Tours: CLD éditions, 2008.

Bernardi, Jean. *Les premiers siècles de l'Église* [The first centuries of the Church]. Paris: Cerf, 1987.

Brown, Peter. *The Making of Late Antiquity.* Cambridge, Mass.: Harvard University Press, 1978. Translated by Aline Rousselle as *Genèse de l'Antiquité tardive* (Paris: Gallimard, 1983).

———. *The Rise of Western Christendom: Triumph and Diversity, A.D. 200–1000,* 2nd ed. Malden: Blackwell Publishers, 2003.

Daniélou, Jean, and Henri-Irénée Marrou. *Nouvelle Histoire de l'Église,* vol. 1, *Des origines à saint Grégoire le Grand.* Paris: Seuil, 1963 [A new history of the Church, vol. 1, From the origins to Saint Gregory the Great]. Also published in the collection Points-Histoire, 2 vols., 1985.

Dumeige, Gervais. *Synopsis scriptorum Ecclesiae antiquae ab A.D. 60 ad A.D. 460.* [Synopsis of writers of the ancient Church from 60 A.D. to 460 A.D.]. Uccle: W. Rousseau, 1953.

Fouilloux, Étienne. *La collection "Sources Chrétiennes," Éditer les Pères de l'Église au XXe siècle* [The Sources Chrétiennes collection. Publishing the Fathers in the twentieth century]. Paris: Cerf, 1995. New revised and enlarged ed., 2011.

Hamman, Adalbert-Gautier. *La vie quotidienne en Afrique du Nord au temps de saint Augustin* [Daily life in North Africa in the days of Saint Augustine]. Paris: Hachette, 1971.

———. *La vie quotidienne des premiers chrétiens (95/197)* [Daily life of the first Christians (95/197)]. 3rd ed., revised and corrected. Reprint, Paris: Hachette, 1979.

Labriolle, Pierre de. *La Réaction païenne. Étude sur la polémique antichrétienne du Ier au VIe siècle* [The pagan reaction. Study on the anti-Christian polemic from the first to the sixth century]. Paris: L'Artisan du Livre, 1950.

Lepelley, Claude. *L'empire romain et le christianisme* [The Roman Empire and Christianity]. Paris: Flammarion, 1969.

Lietzmann, Hans. *A History of the Early Church.* Foreword and bibliography by W. H. C. Frend. 2 vols. Cambridge: James Clarke & Co, 1993.

Maraval, Pierre. *Le christianisme de Constantin à la conquête arabe* [Christianity from Constantine to the Arab conquest]. Paris: PUF, 2005.

Mattei, Paul. *Le christianisme antique de Jésus à Constantin* [Ancient Christianity from Jesus to Constantine]. Paris: Armand Colin, 2008.

Mayeur, Jean-Marie, Charles and Luce Pietri, André Vauchez and Marc Venard, eds. *Histoire du Christianisme* [History of Christianity]. 2 vols. Paris: Desclée, 1995–2000.

Mimouni, Simon Claude, and Pierre Maraval. *Le christianisme des origines à Constantin* [Christianity from the origins to Constantine]. Paris: PUF, 2006.

Simon, Marcel. *Les premiers chrétiens* [The first Christians]. Paris: PUF, 1952. 3rd ed., 1963.

Simon, Marcel, and André Benoît. *Le Judaïsme et le Christianisme antique, d'Antiochus Epiphane à Constantin* [Judaism and ancient Christianity, from Antiochus Epiphanes to Constantine]. 2nd ed., updated. Paris: PUF, 1985.

Tardieu, Michel. *Le manichéisme* [Manicheism]. Paris: PUF, 1981.

Vallin, Pierre. "Du second siècle à la conquête islamique" [From the second century to the Islamic conquest]. In *Les chrétiens et leur histoire* [The Christians and their history], "Manuel de théologie," edited by Joseph Doré, 75–160. Paris: Desclée, 1985.

Van der Meer, Frédéric, and Christine Mohrmann. *Atlas de l'Antiquité chrétienne* [Atlas of Christian antiquity]. Paris-Bruxelles: ed. Séquoia, 1960.

History of Early Christian Literature

Fontaine, Jacques. *La littérature latine chrétienne* [Latin Christian literature]. Paris, 1970.

———. *Naissance de la poésie dans l'Occident chrétien. Esquisse d'une histoire de la poésie latine chrétienne, du IIIe au VIe siècle* [The birth of poetry in the Christian West. A sketch of a history of Christian Latin poetry, from the third to the sixth century]. Paris: Institut d'Études Augustiniennes, 1981.

Labriolle, Pierre de. *Histoire de la littérature latine chrétienne* [History of Latin Christian literature]. 3rd ed., revised by Gustave Bardy. Paris: Les Belles Lettres, 1947.

Malingrey, Anne-Marie. *La littérature grecque chrétienne* [Greek Christian literature]. Paris: Cerf, 1968.

Moreschini, Claude, and Norelli Enrico. *Histoire de la littérature chrétienne ancienne grecque et latine* [History of Ancient Greek and Latin Literature]. Translated from the Italian. Geneva: Labor et Fides, 2000.

Norelli, Enrico, and Bernard Pouderon, eds. *Histoire de la littérature grecque chrétienne des origines à 451* [History of Christian Greek literature]. Vol. 1, *Introduction*. Vol. 2, *De Paul apôtre à Irénée de Lyon* [From Paul the Apostle to Irenaeus of Lyons]. Paris: Cerf, 2008–2013.

Pouderon, Bernard, ed. *Histoire de la littérature grecque chrétienne des origines à 451*. Vol. 3, *De Clément d'Alexandrie à Eusèbe de Césarée* [History of Christian Greek literature from the origins to 451. 3. From Clement of Alexandria to Eusebius of Caesarea]. Paris: Les Belles Lettres, 2017.

Puech, Aimé. *Histoire de la littérature grecque chrétienne.* [History of Christian Greek literature]. 3 vols. Paris: Les Belles Lettres, 1928–30.

Tardieu, Michel, and Jean-Daniel Dubois. *Introduction à la littérature gnostique* [Introduction to Gnostic literature]. Paris: Cerf, 1986.

Patristic Exegesis

One may here refer to the three first volumes of the collection Bible de tous les temps (Paris: Beauchesne):

Le monde grec ancien et la Bible. Paris: Beauchesne, 1984.
Le monde latin antique et la Bible. Paris: Beauchesne, 1985.
Saint Augustin et la Bible. Paris: Beauchesne, 1986.

One knows that the Fathers of the first centuries normally were referring to the Greek Bible and not at all to the Hebrew Bible. A translation of the Septuagint was undertaken under the direction of Marguerite Harl; see *La Bible d'Alexandrie* (Paris: Cerf, 1986–). There are, moreover, valuable tools of the trade:

Biblia patristica. Index des citations et allusions bibliques dans la littérature patristique [Index of biblical citations and allusions in patristic literature]. Vol. 1, *Des origines à Clément d'Alexandrie and Tertullien.* Vol. 2, *IIIe siècle (Origène excepté).* Vol. 3, *Origène (Supplément: Philon d'Alexandrie).* Vol. 4, *Eusèbe de Césarée. Cyrille de Jérusalem. Epiphane de Salamine.* Vol. 5, *Basile de Césarée. Grégoire de Nazianze. Grégoire de Nysse. Amphiloque d'Iconium.* Vol. 6, *Hilaire de Poitiers. Ambroise de Milan. Amrosiaster.* Vol. 7, *Didyme d'Alexandrie.* Paris: CNRS, 1975–2000.

These biblical references, and many other references, are available on the site Biblindex (Lyon: Institut des Sources Chrétiennes).

See also Kannengiesser, Charles. *Handbook of Patristic Exegesis. The Bible in Ancient Christianity.* 2 vols. Leiden: Brill, 2004.

Some other books on patristic exegesis (such as those of Isabelle Bochet, Jean Daniélou, and Henri de Lubac) are mentioned in the following section.

History of Doctrines and Christian Theology

Albanel, Véronique. *Amour du monde. Christianisme et politique chez Hannah Arendt* [Love of the world. Christianity and politics by Hannah Arendt]. Paris: Cerf, 2010.

Alexandre, Jérôme. *Le Christ de Tertullien* [The Christ of Tertullian]. Paris: Desclée, 2003.

Amman, Émile. "Pères de l'Église." In *Dictionnaire de théologie catholique* [Dictionary of Catholic theology], 12, pt. 1, col. 1192–1215. Paris: Letouzey & Ané, 1933.

Badilita, Cristian, and Charles Kannengiesser, eds. *Les Pères de l'Église dans le monde d'aujourd'hui* [The Fathers of the Church in today's world]. Paris: Beauchesne, 2006.

Badilita, Cristian, ed. *Patristique et œcuménisme. Thèmes, contextes, personnages* [Patristics and ecumenism. Themes, contexts, people]. Paris: Beauchesne, 2010.

Balthasar, Hans Urs von. "Le *mystèrion* d'Origène." *Recherches de Science Religieuse* 26 (1936): 513–62; and *Recherches de Science Religieuse* 27 (1937), 38–64. Republished under the title *Parole et mystère chez Origène* [Word and mystery by Origen] (Paris: Cerf, 1957).

———. *Origenes. Geist und Feuer.* Ein Aufbau aus seinen Schriften. Salzburg: Otto Müller, 1938. Translated by Robert J. Daly as *Origen, Spirit and Fire: An Anthology of His Writings* (Washington, D.C.: The *Catholic University of America Press*, 1984).

———. *Der versiegelte Quell. Auslegung des Hohen Liedes, in Kürzung übertragen und eingeleitet* [The sealed source. Interpretation of the Song of Songs, shortened and introduced]. Zurich: Otto Müller, 1939.

———. *Présence et Pensée. Essai sur la philosophie religieuse de Grégoire de Nysse.* Paris: Beauchesne, 1942. Translated by Mark Sebanc as *Presence and Thought: An Essay on the Religious Philosophy of Gregory of Nyssa* (San Francisco: Ignatius Press, 1988).

———. *Liturgie cosmique, Maxime le Confesseur.* Paris: Aubier, 1947. Translated by Brian E. Daley as *Cosmic Liturgy: the Universe according to Maximus the Confessor* (San Francisco: Ignatius Press, 2003).

———. *La Gloire et la Croix. Les aspects esthétiques de la Révélation*, vol. 2, *Styles. 1. D'Irénée à Dante*, 27–192. Paris: Aubier-Montaigne, 1968. Translated by Andrew Louth, Francis McDonagh, and Brian McNeil as *The Glory of the Lord: A Theological Aesthetics*, vol. 2, *Studies in Theological Style: Clerical Styles* (Edinburgh: T & T Clark, 1984), 31–210.

———. *De l'intégration. Aspects d'une théologie de l'Histoire* [On integration. Aspects of a theology of history]. Translated from German into French. Paris: Desclée de Brouwer, 1970.

———. *Theo-Drama: Theological Dramatic Theory.* 5 vols. San Francisco: Ignatius Press, 1988–98.

———. *Mysterium Paschale. The Mystery of Easter.* London: T & T Clark, 1990.

———. *L'Amour seul est digne de foi.* Translated from German into French. Saint-Maur: Parole et Silence, 1999. Translated by Alexander Dru as *Love Alone, the Way of Revelation: A Theological Perspective* (London: Burns & Oates, 1968).

Bardy, Gustave. *En lisant les Pères* [By reading the Fathers]. New ed. Paris: Bloud et Gay, 1933.

———. *La vie spirituelle d'après les Pères des trois premiers siècles* [The spiritual life according to the Fathers of the first three centuries]. Paris: Bloud & Gay, 1935.

———. "La voix des Pères" [The voice of the Fathers]. In Chaillet, *L'Église est une*, 61–81.

———. *La théologie de l'Église*, vol. 1, *De saint Clément de Rome à saint Irénée* [The theology of the Church, vol. 1, From Saint Clement of Rome to Saint Irenaeus]. Paris: Cerf, 1945.

———. *La théologie de l'Église*, vol. 2, *De saint Irénée au concile de Nicée* [The theology of the Church, vol. 2, From Saint Irenaeus to the Council of Nicaea]. Paris: Cerf, 1947.

Bauer, Walter. *Rechtgläubigkeit und Ketzerei im ältesten Christentum* [Orthodoxy and heresy at the beginning of Christianity]. Tübingen: Mohr, 1934. Translated by Philippe Vuagnat as *Orthodoxie et hérésie aux débuts du christianisme* (Paris: Cerf, 2009).

Beauchamp, Paul. *L'un et l'autre Testament*, vol. 1, *Essai de lecture* [The one and the other Testament, vol. 1, An attempt at a reading]. Paris: Seuil, 1976.

———. *L'un et l'autre Testament*, vol. 2, *Accomplir les Écritures* [The one and the other Testament, vol. 2, Fulfilling the Scriptures]. Paris: Seuil, 1990.

Beaude, Pierre-Marie. *L'accomplissement des Écritures. Pour une histoire critique des systèmes de représentation du sens chrétien* [The fulfillment of the Scriptures. Towards a critical history of the systems of representation of Christian meaning]. Paris: Cerf, 1980.

Benoît, André. *L'actualité des Pères de l'Église* [The current relevance of the Fathers of the Church]. Cahiers Théologiques 47. Neuchâtel: Delachaux et Niestlé, 1961.

Benoît XVI. *Les Pères de l'Église, de Clément de Rome à Maxime le Confesseur* [The Fathers of the Church, from Clement of Rome to Maxim the Confessor]. Paris: Bayard, 2008.

Berardino, Angelo di. "Orientations actuelles des recherches patristiques" [Current directions of patristic research]. In Sources Chrétiennes, *Les Pères de l'Église au XXe siècle*, 386–89.

Berndt, Rainer, and Michel Fédou, eds. *Les réceptions des Pères de l'Église au Moyen Âge. Le devenir de la tradition ecclésiale* [The receptions of the Fathers of the Church in the Middle Ages. The process of the ecclesial tradition]. Münster: Aschendorff, 2013.

Bertrand, Dominique. "Les Pères de l'Église et la rencontre des cultures" [The Fathers of the Church and the encounter of cultures]. In *Penser la foi. Recherches en théologie aujourd'hui, Mélanges offerts à Joseph Moingt* [Thinking the faith. Essays in honor of Joseph Moingt], edited by Joseph Doré and Christoph Theobald, 473–86. Paris: Cerf–Assas Éditions, 1993.

———. "Poids théologique de la collection des Sources Chrétiennes" [Theological significance of the Sources Chrétiennes collection]. *Esprit & Vie*, no. 168 (2007): 1–11.

———. Ed. *Dieu Trinité d'hier à demain avec Hilaire de Poitiers (actes du congrès-colloque du Futuroscope de Poitiers, 15 au 17 November 2002)* [God Trinity from yesterday to tomorrow with Hilary of Poitiers. Proceedings of the congress-colloquium of Poitiers's Futuroscope]. Paris: Cerf, 2010.

Bitton-Ashkelony, Brouria, Théodore de Bruyn, and Carol Harrison, eds. *Patristic Studies in the Twenty-First Century*. Proceedings of an International Conference to Mark the 50th Anniversary of the International Association of Patristic Sutdies. Brepols: Turnhout, Belgium, 2015.

Blanchard, Yves-Marie. "Les Pères de l'Église ont-ils quelque chose à dire à l'exégèse biblique d'aujourd'hui?" [Do the Fathers have anything to say to today's exegesis?]. *Recherches de Science Religieuse* 99 (2011): 235–47.

Bochet, Isabelle. *Saint Augustin et le désir de Dieu* [Saint Augustine and the desire of God]. Paris: Institut d'Études Augustiniennes, 1982.

———. *Augustin dans la pensée de Paul Ricoeur* [Augustine in Paul Ricoeur's thought]. Paris: Éditions Facultés jésuites, 2003.

———. *"Le firmament de l'Écriture." L'herméneutique augustinienne* ["The firmament of Scripture." Augustinian hermeneutics]. Paris: Institut d'Études Augustiniennes, 2004.

Bori, Pier Cesare. *L'interprétation infinie. L'herméneutique chrétienne ancienne et ses transformations* [The infinite interpretation. Ancient Christian hermeneutics and its transformations]. Translated from Italian into French. Paris: Cerf, 1991.

Bouwen, Frans. "Ravenne 2007. Xe Session plénière de la Commission mixte internationale pour le dialogue théologique entre l'Église catholique et l'Église orthodoxe" [Ravenna 2007. Tenth plenary meeting of the International Joint Commission for Dialogue between the Catholic Church and the Orthodox Church]. *Proche-Orient Chrétien* 58 (2008): 59–78.

Bouyer, Louis. *Histoire de la spiritualité chrétienne*, vol. 1, *La spiritualité du Nouveau Testament et des Pères* [History of Christian spirituality, vol. 1, The spirituality of the New Testament and the Fathers]. Paris: Aubier-Montaigne, 1960. New revised and enlarged ed., Paris: Aubier, 1966.

———. *L'Église de Dieu. Corps du Christ et Temple de l'Esprit* [The Church of God. Body of Christ and temple of the Spirit]. Paris: Cerf, 1970.

Boyarin, Daniel. *Border Lines: The Partition of Judaeo-Christianity.* Philadelphia: University of Pennsylvania Press, 2004. Translated by Jacqueline Rastoin as *La partition du judaïsme et du christianisme*, with the collaboration of Cécile and Marc Rastoin (Paris: Cerf, 2011).

Broc-Schmezer, Catherine. *Les figures féminines du Nouveau Testament dans l'œuvre de Jean Chrysostome* [The female figures of the New Testament in the work of John Chrysostom]. Paris: Institut d'Études Augustiniennes, 2010.

Brown, Peter. *The Making of Late Antiquity*. Cambridge, Mass.: Harvard University Press, 1978

———. *Through the Eye of a Needle: Wealth, the Fall of Rome, and the Making of Christianity in the West, 350–550 A.D.* Oxford: Oxford University Press, 2012. Translated by Béatrice Bonne as *À travers un trou d'aiguille. La richesse, la chute de Rome et la formation du christianisme* (Paris: Les Belles Lettres, 2016).

Brox, Norbert. "Patrologie" [Patrology]. In *Dictionnaire de Théologie*, edited by Peter Eicher, 514–19. Paris: Cerf, 1988.

Bury, Emmanuel, and Bernard Meunier, eds. *Les Pères de l'Église au XVIIe siècle* [The Fathers of the Church in the seventeenth century]. Paris: Cerf, 1993.

Camelot, Pierre-Thomas. *Éphèse et Chalcédoine* [Ephesus and Chalcedon]. Paris, Orante, 1962.

Certeau, Michel de. "Un maître: le père Henri de Lubac" [A master: Father Henri de Lubac]. *Ecclesia*, no. 187 (1964): 83–90.

———. "La rupture instauratrice, ou le christianisme dans la culture contemporaine" [The innovative rupture or Christianity in contemporary culture]. *Esprit* (June 1971): 1177–1214.

Chaillet, Pierre, ed. *L'Église est une. Hommage à Moehler* [The Church is one. Tribute to Moehler]. Paris: Bloud & Gay, 1939.

Chang Ch'un-shen, Aloysius B. *Dann sind Himmel und Mensch in Einheit. Bausteine chinesischer Theologie* [Then heaven and man are in unity. Building blocks of Chinese theology]. Freiburg: Herder, 1984.

Chantraine, Georges. *Henri de Lubac*, vol. 2, *Les années de formation (1919–1929)* [Henri de Lubac, vol. 2, The years of training (1919–1929)]. Paris: Cerf, 2009.

Chauvin, Charles. *L'Abbé Migne et ses collaborateurs (1800–1875)* [Abbé Migne and his collaborators]. Paris: Desclée de Brouwer, 2010.

Chrétien, Jean-Louis. *Saint Augustin et les actes de parole* [Saint Augustine and the acts of speech]. Paris: PUF, 2002.

Congar, Yves. "*Ecclesia ab Abel*" [Ecclesia from Abel]. In *Abhandlungen über The-*

ologie und Kirche. Festgabe für K. Adam [Treatises on theology and Church. Commemorative volume in honor of K. Adam], edited by Marcel Reding, 79–108. Düsseldorf: Patmos, 1952.

———. *Vaste monde, ma paroisse. Vérité et dimensions du salut* [Big world, my parish. Truth and dimensions of salvation]. Paris: éd. du Témoignage chrétien, 1959. Republished in Foi vivante 413 (Paris: Cerf, 2000).

———. "Hors de l'Église pas de salut" [Outside of the Church no salvation]. In *Sainte Église. Études et approches ecclésiologiques* [Holy Church. Ecclesiological studies and approaches], 417–32. Paris: Cerf, 1963.

———. *La Tradition et les traditions.* 2 vols. 1960–1963. New ed., Paris: Cerf, 2010. Translated by Michael Naseby and Thomas Rainborough as *Tradition and Traditions: An Historical and a Theological Essay* (London: Burns and Oates, 1966).

———. *Diversité et communion. Dossier historique et conclusion théologique* [Diversity and communion. Historical record and theological conclusion]. Paris: Cerf, 1982.

Conticello, Carmelo Giuseppe. *La théologie byzantine et sa tradition I/1 (VIe–VIIe s.)* [Byzantine theology and its tradition (sixth–seventh centuries)]. Turnhout: Brepols, 2015.

Corbin, Michel. *La Trinité ou l'Excès de Dieu* [The Trinity or the excess of God]. Paris: Cerf, 1997.

Courtonne, Yves. *Un témoin du IVe siècle oriental. Saint Basile et son temps d'après sa correspondance* [A witness of the Eastern fourth century. Saint Basil and his time according to his correspondence]. Paris: Les Belles Lettres, 1973.

Crouzel, Henri. *Origène et la "connaissance mystique"* [Origen and "mystical knowledge"]. Paris: Museum Lessianum, 1961.

———. "Patrologie et renouveau patristique" [Patrology and patristic renewal]. In *Bilan de la théologie du XXe siècle* [Review of twentieth century theology], 2:661–83. Tournai-Paris: Casterman, 1970.

———. *Origène.* Paris: Lethielleux, 1985.

Dahan, Gilbert. "Les Pères dans l'exégèse médiévale de la Bible" [The Fathers in the medieval exegesis of the Bible]. *Revue des Sciences Philosophiques et Théologiques* 91 (2007): 109–27.

Daley, Brian E. *The Hope of the Early Church: A Handbook of Patristic Eschatology.* Cambridge: Cambridge University Press, 1991.

Daniélou, Jean. *Platonisme et théologie mystique. Essai sur la doctrine spirituelle de saint Grégoire de Nysse* [Platonism and mystical theology. Essay on the spiritual doctrine of Gregory of Nyssa]. 2nd ed. 1944; Paris: Aubier-Montaigne, 1954.

———. "Le symbolisme des rites baptismaux" [Symbolism of baptismal rites]. *Dieu vivant* 1 (1945): 15–43.

———. *Le mystère du salut des nations* [The mystery of the salvation of the nations]. Paris: Seuil, 1946. Translated by Nigel Abercrombie as *The Lord of the History. Reflections on the inner Meaning of History* (London: Longmans, 1958).

———. "Les orientations présentes de la pensée religieuse" [Current directions of religious thought]. *Études* 79, no. 249 (1946): 5–21.

———. "Traversée de la mer Rouge et baptême aux premiers siècles" [Crossing the Red Sea and Baptism in the first centuries], *Recherches de Science Religieuse* 33 (1946): 402–30.

———. *Origène*. Paris: La Table ronde, 1948; Paris: Cerf, 2012. Translated by Walter Mitchell as *Origen* (London: Sheed and Ward, 1955).

———. *Sacramentum futuri. Études sur les origines de la typologie biblique* [Sacramentum futuri. Studies on the origins of biblical typology]. Paris: Beauchesne, 1950.

———. *Les Anges et leur mission*. Paris: Chevetogne, 1952. Translated by David Heimann as *The Angels and Their Mission according to the Fathers and the Church* (Westminster, Md.: Christian Classics Inc., 1982).

———. *Les saints païens de l'Ancien Testament* [The pagan saints of the Old Testament]. Paris: Seuil, 1956.

———. *Les manuscrits de la mer Morte et les origines du christianisme*. Paris: Orante, 1957. Translated by Salvator Attanasio as *The Dead Sea Scrolls and Primitive Christianity* (Baltimore, Md.: Helicon Press, 1958).

———. *Philon of Alexandrie*. Paris: Fayard, 1958. Translated by J. G. Colbert as *Philo of Alexandria* (Eugene, Ore.: Cascade Books, 2014).

———. *Théologie du judéo-christianisme*. Vol. 1 of *Histoire des doctrines chrétiennes avant Nicée*. Paris-Tournai: Desclée, 1958. 2nd ed., with a text established by Marie-Odile Boulnois from the Italian edition of 1974, reviewed and corrected by Joseph Paramelle and Marie-Josèphe Rondeau (Paris: Desclée, 1992). Translated by John A. Baker as *The Theology of Jewish Christianity: A History of Early Christian Doctrine before the Council of Nicaea* (London: Darton, Longman and Todd, 1964).

———. *Message évangélique et culture hellénistique aux IIe et IIIe siècles*. Vol. 2 of *Histoire des doctrines chrétiennes avant Nicée*. 1961. Reprint Paris: Desclée, 1990. Translated by John A. Baker as *Gospel Message and Hellenistic Culture*, vol. 2 of *A History of Early Christian Doctrine before the Council of Nicaea (*London: Darton, Longman and Todd, 1973).

———. *Bible et liturgie. La théologie biblique des sacrements et des fêtes d'après les Pères de l'Église*. 2nd ed. 1967; Paris: Cerf, 1982. Translated as *The Bible and the Liturgy* (London: Darton, Longman and Todd, 1960).

———. *Études d'exégèse judéo-chrétienne (les Testimonia), "Théologie historique"* [Studies of Jewish Christian exegesis (the testimonies)]. Paris: Beauchesne, 1966.

———. *Les origines du christianisme latin. Vol. 3 of Histoire des doctrines chrétiennes avant Nicée*. Paris: Cerf, 1978. Translated by David Smith and John Austin Baker as *The Origins of Latin Christianity*, vol. 3 of *A History of Early Christian Doctrine before the Council of Nicaea* (London: Darton, Longman and Todd, 1977).

Deneken, Michel. *Johann Adam Möhler*. Paris: Cerf, 2007.

Descourtieux, Patrick. "Théologie patristique et byzantine" [Patristic and Byzantine theology]. In Lacoste, *Histoire de la théologie*, 51–152. Paris: Seuil, 2009.

Dorival, Gilles. "Sens de l'Écriture–Pères grecs" [Senses of Scriptures–Greek Fathers]. In *Supplément au Dictionnaire de la Bible* [Supplement to the Bible dictionary], vol. 12, col. 426–42. Paris: Letouzé & Ané, 1996.

Dosse, François. *Michel de Certeau. Le marcheur blessé* [Michel de Certeau. The wounded walker]. Paris: La Découverte, 2002.

Dujarier, Michel. *Église–Fraternité. L'ecclésiologie du Christ-Frère aux huit premiers siècles* [Church–brotherhood. The Ecclesiology of the Christ-Brother in the first eight centuries]. Vol. 1, *L'Église s'appelle "Fraternité" (Ier–IIIe siècle)* [The Church is called brotherhood (first–third centrury)]. Vol. 2, *L'Église est "Fraternité en Christ" (IVe–Ve siècle)* [The Church is "brotherhood in Christ" (fourth–fifth century)]. Paris, Cerf, 2013 and 2016.

Dumeige, Gervais. *Nicée II* [Nicaea II]. Paris: Orante, 1978.

Duperray, Édouard, and Jacques Gadille, eds. *Théologie et spiritualité missionnaires* [Missionary theology and spirituality]. Paris: Beauchesne, 1985.

Dupuis, Jacques. *Toward a Christian Theology of Religious Pluralism*. Maryknoll, N.Y.: Orbis Books, 1997.

Faivre, Alexandre. "La question des ministères à l'époque paléochrétienne. Problématique et enjeux d'une périodisation" [The issue of ministries in the Paleochristian era. Problematic and stakes of a periodization]. In Alexandre Faivre, *Chrétiens et Églises. Des identités en construction. Acteurs, structures, frontières du champ religieux chrétien* [Christians and churches. Identities under construction. Actors, structures, boundaries of the Christian religious field], 115–50. Paris: Cerf, 2011.

Falque, Emmanuel. *Dieu, la chair et l'autre. D'Irénée à Duns Scot* [God, the flesh, and the other. From Irenaeus to Duns Scot]. Paris: PUF, 2008.

Fédou, Michel. "Les Pères de l'Église face aux religions de leur temps d'après le document 'Dialogue et annonce' de 1991" [The Fathers of the Church facing the religions of their time, according to the document "Dialogue and Proclamation" of 1991]. *Bulletin du Pontificium Consilium pro Dialogo inter Religiones* 80 (1992): 173–85.

———. "Patristique et théologie" [Patristics and theology]. In *Penser la foi. Recherches en théologie aujourd'hui, Mélanges offerts à Joseph Moingt*, edited by Joseph Doré and Christoph Theobald, 487–95. Paris: Cerf–Assas Editions, 1993.

———. "Liturgie cosmique. Lecture de Maxime le Confesseur par Hans Urs von Balthasar" [Cosmic liturgy. A reading of Maximus the Confessor by Hans Urs von Balthasar]. In *Avec les Pères de l'Église, penser l'homme devant Dieu*, vol. 1, *L'homme image de Dieu* [With the Fathers of the Church, thinking the man before God, I. Man, image of God], 141–54. Paris: Médiasèvres, 2001.

———. "Diversité ecclésiale et communion dans la foi: le témoignage de la littérature patristique" [Ecclesial diversity and communion in faith: The testimony of patristic literature]. In *L'Église catholique dans le monde: entre unité et diversité* [The Catholic Church in the world: Between unity and diversity], edited by M. Fédou, 77–104. Paris: Médiasèvres, 2002.

———. "La passion de l'humanité. Enjeux de l'anthropologie patristique pour la théologie contemporaine" [The passion of humanity. The stakes of patristic anthropology for contemporary theology]. In *Avec les Pères de l'Église, penser l'homme devant Dieu*, vol. 2, *Figures d'hier, questions d'aujourd'hui* [With the Fathers of the Church, thinking of man before God, vol. 2, Figures of yesterday, questions of today], edited by Isabelle Bochet and Michel Fédou, 133–57. Paris: Médiasèvres, 2002.

———. "'Boire à son propre puits'. Des mystiques chrétiennes de l'action sociale hier et aujourd'hui" ["We drink from our own wells." Mystics of social action yesterday and today]. In *Aux sources de la charité. Les spiritualités* [To the sources of charity], edited by Paul Huot-Pleuroux, 61–80. Paris: Cerf, 2003.

———. "Karl Rahner et Hans Urs von Balthasar lecteurs et interprètes des Pères" [Karl Rahner and Hans Urs von Balthasar, readers and interpreters of the Fathers]. In *Balthasar, Rahner. Deux pensées en contraste* [Balthasar, Rahner. Two thoughts in contrast], edited by Henri-Jérôme Gagey and Vincent Holzer, 141–59. Paris: Bayard, 2005.

———. *La voie du Christ. Genèses de la christologie dans le contexte religieux de l'Antiquité, du IIe siècle au début du IVe siècle* [The Way of Christ. Genesis of Christology in the religious context of antiquity, from the second century to the beginning of the fourth century]. Paris: Cerf, 2006.

———. "Des Pères de l'Église à l'Église des Pères" [From the Fathers of the Church to the Church of the Fathers]. In Michel Fédou, *L'Église des Pères Initiation à la théologie patristique* [Introduction to patristic theology]. Paris: Médiasèvres, 2007.

———. "La redécouverte des anténicéens et ses enjeux pour la théologie trinitaire." In *Les sources du renouveau de la théologie trinitaire au XXe siècle* [The sources of the renewal of Trinitarian theology in the twentieth century], edited by Emmanuel Durand and Vincent Holzer, 59–73. Paris: Cerf, 2008.

———. "Relire les Pères de l'Église pour penser le dialogue interreligieux" [Rereading the Fathers of the Church to think about interreligious dialogue]. *Chemins de Dialogue* 32 (2008): 205–25.

———. "La théologie anténicéenne: quelles ressources pour la christologie?" [Ante-Nicene theology: What resources for Christology?]. In *De Jésus à Jésus-Christ*, vol. 2, *Christ dans l'histoire* [From Jesus to Jesus Christ, vol. 2, Christ in history], edited by Joseph Doré, 189–207. Paris: Mame-Desclée, 2011.

———. "Les débats sur le 'sens spirituel' dans les *Recherches de Science Religieuse* (années 1940–1950)" [Debates on the "spiritual sense" in *Recherches de Science Religieuse* (years 1940–1950)]. *Recherches de Science Religieuse* 99 (2011): 195–205.

———. "Sources Chrétiennes. Patristique et renaissance de la théologie" [Christian sources. Patristics and the rebirth of theology]. *Gregorianum* 92 (2011): 781–96.

———. *La voie du Christ.* Vol. 2, *Développements de la christologie dans le contexte de l'Orient ancien, d'Eusèbe de Césarée à Jean Damascène (IVe–VIIIe siècles)* [The way of Christ. Vol. 2, Developments of Christology in the context of the ancient orient (fourth–eighth centuries)]. Paris: Cerf, 2013.

———. *La voie du Christ.* Vol. 3, *Évolutions de la christologie dans l'Occident latin d'Hilaire de Poitiers à Isidore de Séville (IVe–VIIe siècles)* [The way of Christ. Vol. 3, Developments of Christology in the Latin West from Hilary of Poitiers to Isidor of Seville (fourth–seventh centuries)]. Paris: Cerf, 2016.

Fiedrowicz, Michael. *Theologie der Kirchenväter. Grundlagen frühchristlicher Glaubensreflexion* [Theology of the Church Fathers. Foundations of early Christian faith reflection]. Freiburg-in-Breisgau: Herder, 2007.

Fontaine, Jacques, ed. *Actualité de Jean Daniélou* [Current relevance of Jean Daniélou]. Paris: Cerf, 2006.

Fouilloux, Étienne. *Une Église en quête de liberté. La pensée catholique française entre modernisme et Vatican II. 1914–1962* [A Church in search of freedom. French Catholic thought between Modernism and Vatican II]. Paris: Desclée de Brouwer, 1998.

———. *La collection Sources Chrétiennes. Éditer les Pères de l'Église au XXᵉ siècle* [The Sources Chrétiennes collection. Publishing the Fathers in the twentieth century]. Paris: Cerf, 1995. New revised and enlarged ed., 2011.

Gagey, Henri-Jérôme. "La théologie entre urgence phénoménologique et endurance herméneutique" [Theology between phenomenological urgency and hermeneutical endurance]. *Recherches de Science Religieuse* 98 (2010): 31–57.

Geffré, Claude. *Le christianisme au risque de l'interprétation* [Christianity at the risk of interpretation]. Paris: Cerf, 1983.

Gibert, Pierre. *L'invention critique de la Bible. XVᵉ–XVIIIᵉ siècle* [The critical invention of the Bible. Fifteenth–eighteenth centuries]. Paris: Gallimard, 2010.

Giet, Stanislas. *Les Idées et l'Action sociales de saint Basile* [The social ideas and action of Saint Basil]. Paris: Gabalda, 1941.

Gilson, Étienne. *Introduction à l'étude de Saint Augustin* [Introduction to the study of Saint Augustine]. Paris: Vrin, 1929. New ed., 1987.

Godin, André. *Érasme lecteur d'Origène* [Erasmus, reader of Origen]. Geneva: Droz, 1982.

Gonnet, Dominique, and Michel Stavrou, eds. *Les Pères de l'Église aux sources de l'Europe* [The Fathers of the Church at the source of Europe]. Introduction by Jean-Dominique Durand. Paris: Cerf, 2014.

Grillmeier, Aloys. *Le Christ dans la tradition chrétienne* [Christ in Christian tradition]. Translated from German. For the most recent volumes, with the collaboration of Th. Hainthaler. Paris: Cerf, 1973–96.

———. *Le Christ dans la tradition chrétienne*, vol. 1, *De l'âge apostolique au concile de Chalcédoine (451)*. Paris: Cerf, 1973, and new ed. in 2003. Translated by John Bowden as *Christ in Christian Tradition*, vol. 1, *From the Apostolic Age to Chalcedon (451)* (London: Mowbrays, 1975).

———. *Le Christ dans la tradition chrétienne*. Vol. 2/1, *Le concile de Chalcédoine (451). Réception et opposition (451–513)* [The Council of Chalcedon (451). Reception and contradiction (451–513)]. Paris: Cerf, 1990.

———. *Le Christ dans la tradition chrétienne*. Vol. 2/2, *L'Église de Constantinople au VIᵉ siècle* [The Church in Constantinople in the sixth century]. Paris: Cerf, 1993.

———. *Le Christ dans la tradition chrétienne*. Vol. 2/4, *L'Église d'Alexandrie, la Nubie et l'Ethiopie après 451* [The Church of Alexandria with Nubia and Ethiopia after 451]. Paris: Cerf, 1996.

———. "De Jésus de Nazareth 'dans l'ombre du Fils de Dieu' au Christ, image de Dieu" [From Jesus of Nazareth "in the shadow of the Son of God" to Christ, Image of God]. In *Comment être chrétien? La réponse de Hans Küng* [How to be a Christian? Hans Küng's answer], edited by Jean-Robert Armogathe, 99–130. Paris: Desclée de Brouwer, 1979.

Grillmeier, Aloys, and Heinrich Bacht, eds. *Das Konzil von Chalkedon, Geschichte und Gegenwart* [The Council of Chalcedon. History and Current Relevance]. 3 vols. Würzburg: Echter Verlag, 1951–54.

Gross, Jules. *La divinisation du chrétien d'après les Pères grecs. Contribution historique à la doctrine de la grâce* [The divinization of the Christian according to the Greek Fathers. A historical contribution to the doctrine of grace]. Paris: Gabalda, 1938.

Guerriero, Elio. *Hans Urs von Balthasar*. Translated by Frances Georges-Catroux, 43–80. Paris: Desclée, 1993.

Guggenheim, Antoine. "La théologie de l'accomplissement" [The theology of fulfillment]. In Fontaine, *Actualité de Jean Daniélou*, 165–87.

Guillet, Jacques. "Les exégèses d'Alexandrie et d'Antioche. Conflit ou malentendu?" [The exegeses of Alexandria and Antioch. Conflict or misunderstanding?]. *Recherches de Science Religieuse* 34 (1947): 257–302.

Guinot, Jean-Noël. "Rétablir l'unité après la déchirure: Cyrille d'Alexandrie et Théodoret de Cyr, des modèles pour le dialogue entre les Églises?" [Restoring unity after tearing: Cyril of Alexandria and Theodoret of Cyrus, models for the dialog between the Churches]. In *Les Pères de l'Église dans le monde d'aujourd'hui* [The Fathers of the Church in todays's world], 183–208. Paris: Beauchesne, 2006. Reprinted in Jean-Noël Guinot, *Théodoret de Cyr exégète et théologien*, vol. 2, *Un théologien engagé dans le conflit nestorien (431–451)* [Theodoret of Cyrus exegete and theologian] (Paris: Cerf, 2012), 373–97.

Gutiérrez, Gustavo. *Dieu ou l'or des Indes occidentales, 1492–1992*. Paris Cerf: 1992.

Hadot, Pierre. "Patristique." In *Encyclopædia Universalis*, 17:638–43. Paris: Encyclopaedia Universalis France, 1996.

———. *Exercices spirituels et philosophie antique* [Spiritual exercises and ancient philosophy]. Paris: Institut d'Études Augustiniennes, 1981. New ed., Paris: Albin Michel, 2002.

———. *Études de patristique et d'histoire des concepts* [Studies in patristics and the history of concepts]. Paris: Les Belles Lettres, 2010.

Halleux, André de. *Patrologie et œcuménisme. Recueil d'études* [Patrology and ecumenism. A collection of studies]. Leuven: Leuven University Press, 1990.

Hamman, Adalbert-Gautier, ed. *Prières des premiers chrétiens* [Prayers of the first Christians]. Paris: Arthème Fayard, 1952; new revised ed., Paris: Desclée de Brouwer, 1981. Translated by Walter Mitchell as *Early Christian Prayers* (Chicago: Henry Regnery Co., 1961).

———, ed. *Riches et pauvres dans l'Église ancienne* [Rich and poor in the ancient Church]. Edited by Adalbert-Gautier Hamman, with introduction by Pierre Bigo. Paris: DDB, 1982. New, revised and enlarged ed., Paris: J.-P. Migne, 2011.

———. *L'homme, image de Dieu. Essai d'une anthropologie chrétienne dans l'Église des premiers siècles* [Man, image of God. Essay of a Christian anthropology in the Church of the first centuries]. Paris: Desclée, 1987.

Henry, Michel. *Incarnation. Une philosophie de la chair* [Incarnation. A philosophy of the flesh]. Paris: Seuil, 2000.

Jaeger, Werner. *Early Christianity and Greek Paideia*. Cambridge, Mass.: The Belknap Press of Harvard University Press, Cambridge, 1961.

Jungmann, Josef Andreas. *La liturgie des premiers siècles jusqu'à l'époque de Grégoire le Grand* [Liturgy of the Christian early period up to Gregory the Great]. Paris: Cerf, 1962.

Kabasélé, François. "L'au-delà des modèles" [Beyond the models]. In *Chemins de la christologie africaine* [Ways of African Christology], edited by François Kabasélé, Joseph Doré, and René Luneau, rev. ed., 245–67. Paris: Desclée, 2001.

Kalaïtzidis, Pantelis. "Du 'Retour aux Pères' à la nécessité d'une théologie orthodoxe moderne" [From "return to Fathers" to the need for a modern Orthodox theology]. *Istina* 56 (2011): 227–51.

Kannengiesser, Charles. "Avenir des traditions fondatrices. La christologie comme tâche au champ des études patristiques" [Future of founding traditions. Christology as a task in the field of patristic studies]. In *Visages du Christ* [Faces of Christ], *Recherches de Science Religieuse*, 65 (1977): 85–168.

Kelly, John Norman Davidson. *Early Christian Doctrines*. Londres: Continuum, 1958. Translated as *Initiation à la doctrine des Pères de l'Église* (Paris: Cerf, 1968).

Lacoste, Jean-Yves, ed. *Histoire de la théologie* [History of theology]. Paris: Seuil, 2009.

Ladaria, Luis. *Mystère de Dieu et mystère de l'homme*. Vol. 1, *Théologie trinitaire* [Mystery of God and mystery of man. Vol. 1, Trinitarian theology]. Translated by Philippe Curbelié. Paris: Parole et Silence, 2011.

Larchet, Jean-Claude. *Pour une éthique de la procréation. Éléments d'anthropologie patristique* [For an ethics of procreation. Elements of patristic anthropology]. Paris: Cerf, 1998.

———. *Une fin de vie paisible ... sans douleur sans honte* [A peaceful end of life ... without pain or shame]. Paris: Cerf, 2010.

———. *Personne et nature. La Trinité–Le Christ–L'homme* [Person and nature. The Trinity–Christ–man]. Paris: Cerf, 2011.

Le Boulluec, Alain. *La notion d'hérésie dans la littérature grecque. IIe–IIIe siècles* [The notion of heresy in the Greek literature. Second–third centuries]. Paris: Institut d'Études Augustiniennes, 1985.

Lebreton, Jules. *Histoire du dogme de la Trinité des origines au concile de Nicée*. Vol. 2, *de saint Clément à saint Irénée* [History of the dogma of the Trinity from the origins to the Council of Nicaea]. 3rd ed. Paris: Beauchesne, 1928.

Lenoir, Frédéric. *Comment Jesus est devenu Dieu* [How Jesus has become God]. Paris: Fayard, 2010.

Libera, Alain de. *La philosophie médiévale* [Medieval philosophy]. Paris: PUF, 1993.

Liébaert, Jacques. *L'Incarnation. I. Des origines au Concile de Chalcédoine* [The Incarnation. I. From the origins to the Council of Chalcedon]. Paris: Cerf, 1966.

———. "Patrologie" [Patrology]. *Catholicisme* 10 (1985): col. 829–58.

Lods, Marc. *Protestantisme et tradition de l'Église* [Protestantism and Church tradition]. Edited by Jacques-Noël Pérès and Jean-Daniel Dubois. Paris: Cerf, 1988.

Lossky, Vladimir. *Essai sur la théologie mystique de l'Église d'Orient*. Paris: Aubier-

Montaigne, 1944. New ed., Paris: Cerf, 2005. Translated by members of the Fellowship of St. Alban and St. Sergius as *The Mystical Theology of the Eastern Church* (Cambridge: James Clarke, 1973; Crestwood, N.Y.: SVS Press, 1997).

Lubac, Henri de. *Catholicisme. Les aspects sociaux du dogme.* Paris, Cerf, 1938. Reprinted in *Œuvres complètes du Cardinal de Lubac*, vol. 7 (Paris, Cerf, 2003). Translated as *Catholicism. A Study of Dogma in Relation to the Corporate Destiny of Mankind* (London: Burns, Oates & Washbourne, 1949). Translated by Lancelot Shepard and Elizabeth Englund, OCD, as *Catholicism: Christ and the Common Destiny of Man* (San Francisco: Ignatius Press, 1988).

———. "Le fondement théologique des missions" [The theological foundation of the missions]. 1941 and 1946. Reprinted in *Théologie dans l'histoire*, vol. 2, *Questions disputées et résistance au nazisme* (Paris: Desclée de Brouwer, 1990), 159–219. Translated by Ann Englund Nash as *Theology in History* (San Francisco: Ignatius Press, 1996), 367–427.

[———]. "La théologie et ses sources. Réponse" [Theology and its sources. An answer]. *Recherches de Science Religieuse* (1946): 385–401. Anonymous article, but probably written by de Lubac.

———. "'Typologie' et 'allégorisme'" ["Typology" and "allegorism"]. *Recherches de Science Religieuse* 34 (1947): 180–226.

———. "Sur un vieux distique. La doctrine du 'quadruple sens'" [About an old couplet. The doctrine of the "quadruple sense"]. In *Mélanges offerts au R. P. Cavallera*, 347–66. Toulouse: Bibliothèque de l'Institut Catholique, 1948).

———. "Sens spirituel" [Spiritual sense]. *Recherches de Science Religieuse* 36 (1949): 542–76.

———. *Histoire et Esprit. L'intelligence de l'Écriture d'après Origène.* Paris: Aubier-Montaigne, 1950. Reprinted in *Œuvres complètes du Cardinal de Lubac*, vol. 16 (Paris: Cerf, 2002). Translated by Anne Englund Nashas *History and Spirit: The Understanding of Scripture according to Origen* (San Francisco: Ignatius Press, 2007).

———. *Aspects du bouddhisme* (Paris: Seuil, 1951). Reprinted in *Œuvres complètes du Cardinal de Lubac*, vol. 21 (Paris: Cerf, 2012), 13–164. Translated by George Lamb as *Aspects of Buddhism* (London: Sheed and Ward, 1953).

———. *Méditation sur l'Église*, 3rd rev. ed. Paris: Aubier-Montaigne, 1954. Reprinted in *Œuvres complètes du Cardinal Henri de Lubac*, vol. 8 (Paris: Cerf, 2003). Translated by Michael Mason as *The Splendor of the Church* (London: Sheed and Ward, 1956).

———. "À propos de l'allégorie chrétienne" [About the Christian allegory], *Recherches de Science Religieuse* 47 (1959): 5–43.

———. *Exégèse médiévale. Les quatre sens de l'Écriture*, 4 vols. Paris: Aubier-Montaigne, 1959–64. Translated by Mark Sebanc and E. M. Macierowski as *Medieval Exegesis: The Four Senses of Scripture*, 3 vols. (Grand Rapids, Mich.: Eerdmans, 2009).

———. *Le Mystère du Surnaturel.* Paris: Aubier-Montaigne, 1965. Reprinted in *Œuvres complètes du Cardinal Henri de Lubac*, vol. 12 (Paris: Cerf, 2000). Translated by Rosemary Sheed as *The Mystery of the Supernatural* (London: G. Chapmans, 1967).

———. *L'Écriture dans la Tradition* [Scripture in tradition]. Paris: Aubier, 1966.

———. *Images de l'abbé Monchanin* [Images of Father Monchanin]. Paris: Aubier-Montaigne, 1967.

———. "La constitution 'Lumen gentium' et les Pères de l'Église" [The constitution "Lumen Gentium" and the Fathers of the Church]. In de Lubac, *Paradoxe et mystère de l'Église*, 59–119.

———. *Paradoxe et mystère de l'Église*. Paris: Aubier-Montaigne, 1967. Reprinted in *Œuvres complètes du Cardinal de Lubac*, vol. 9 (Paris: Cerf, 2010). Translated by James R. Dunne as *The Church: Paradox and Mystery* (Shannon, Ireland: Ecclesia Press, 1969).

———. "Les religions humaines d'après les Pères" [The pagan religions and the Fathers of the Church]. In de Lubac, *Paradoxe et mystère de l'Église*, 120–67. Translated by James R. Dunne in *The Church: Paradox and Mystery*, 68–95.

———. Preface to F. Quéré-Jaulmes and A. Hamman, *Les Chemins vers Dieu* [The paths to God]. Paris: Centurion, 1967.

———. "Un témoin du Christ dans l'Église: Hans Urs von Balthasar" [A Witness of Christ in the Church: Hans Urs von Balthasar]. In *Paradoxe et mystère de l'Église*, 180–212.

———. *Pic de la Mirandole. Études et discussions* [Pico della Mirandola, studies and discussions]. Paris: Aubier-Montaigne, 1974.

———. *La postérité spirituelle de Joachim de Flore. II. De Saint Simon à nos jours* [The spiritual posterity of Joachim of Flore. II. From Saint Simon to the present day]. Paris: Lethielleux, 1981.

———. *Mémoire sur l'occasion de mes écrits*, 2nd ed. Namur: Culture et vérité, 1989. Reprinted in *Œuvres complètes du Cardinal de Lubac*, vol. 33. (Paris: Cerf, 2006). Translated by Anne Elizabeth Englund as *At the Service of the Church: Henri de Lubac Reflects on the Circumstances that Occasioned His Writings* (San Francisco: Ignatius Press, 1993).

———. "Hommage à Hans Urs von Balthasar" [Tribute to Hans Urs von Balthasar]. In *Œuvres complètes du Cardinal de Lubac*, vol. 9, *Paradoxe et mystère de l'Eglise suivi de L'Eglise dans la crise actuelle*, 363–66. Paris, Cerf, 2010.

Luneau, Auguste. "Pour aider au dialogue: les Pères et les religions non chrétiennes" [To help to dialogue: The Fathers of the Church and non-Christian religions]. *Nouvelle Revue Théologique* 89 (1967): 821–41 and 914–39.

Mahn-Lot, Marianne. *Bartolomé de Las Casas. L'Évangile et la force* [Bartolomeo de Las Casas. The Gospel and the force]. 3rd rev. ed. Paris: Cerf, 1991.

Malingrey, Anne-Marie. *"Philosophia." Étude d'un groupe de mots dans la littérature grecque, des présocratiques au IVᵉ siècle après J.-C.* ["Philosophia." Study of a group of words in Greek literature from the Presocratics to the fourth century A.D.]. Paris: Klincksieck, 1961.

Marion, Jean-Luc. *Au lieu de soi. L'approche de Saint Augustin* [In the place of oneself. The approach of Saint Augustine]. Paris: PUF, 2008.

Marrou, Henri-Irénée. *A History of Education in Antiquity*. Translated by George Lamb. Mentor Books. New York: The New American Library of World Literature, 1956. Translated from *Histoire de l'éducation dans l'Antiquité*, 2nd revised and expanded ed. (Paris: Seuil, 1950).

Massie, Alban. *Peuple prophétique et nation témoin. Le peuple juif dans le* Contra Faustum manichaeum *de saint Augustin* [Prophetic people and witness nation. The Jewish people in Augustine's *Contra Faustum*]. Paris: Institut d'Études Augustiniennes, 2011.

Mersch, Émile. *Le corps mystique du Christ. Études de théologie historique* [The mystical body of Christ. Studies of historical theology], vol. 1. Louvain: Museum Lessianum, 1933. Translated by John R. Kelly as *The Whole Christ: The Historical Development of the Doctrine of the Mystical Body in Scripture and Tradition* (London: Dennis Dobson LTD, 1938).

Meslin, Michel. "Jean Daniélou et les religions non chrétiennes" [Jean Daniélou and non-Christian religions]. In Fontaine, *Actualité de Jean Daniélou*, 155–64.

Metz, Jean-Baptiste. *La foi dans l'histoire et dans la societé. Essai de théologie fondamentale pratique*. Translated by Paul Corset and Jean-Louis Schlegel. Paris: Cerf, 1979. Translated by J. Matthew Ashley as *Faith in History and Society: Toward a Practical Fundamental Theology* (New York: The Crossroad Publishing Company, 2007).

———. "Une liberté solidaire. Crise et mission de l'esprit européen" [A freedom in solidarity. Crisis and mission of the European spirit]. *Concilium* 240 (1992): 121–28.

Meunier, Bernard, ed. *La personne et le christianisme ancien* [The person and ancient Christianity]. Paris: Cerf, 2006.

Meyendorff, John. *Le Christ dans la théologie byzantine*. 1969. Reprint, Paris: Cerf, 2010. Translated as *Christ in Eastern Christian Thought* (Crestwood, N.Y.: St. Vladimir's Seminary Press, 1975).

Mimouni, Simon Claude. *Le Judéo-christianisme ancien. Essais historiques* [Ancient Jewish Christianity]. Paris: Cerf, 1998.

Moingt, Joseph. *Théologie trinitaire de Tertullien* [Trinitarian theology of Tertullian]. 4 vols. Paris: Aubier-Montaigne, 1966–69.

———. *L'homme qui venait de Dieu* [The man who came from God]. Paris: Cerf, 1993.

Monchanin, Jules. *Écrits spirituels* [Spiritual writings]. Introduction by Édouard Duperray. Paris: Centurion, 1964.

———. *Mystique de l'Inde, mystère chrétien. Écrits et inédits* [Mysticism of India, Christian mystery. Writings and unpublished works]. Introduced by S. Siauve. Paris: Fayard, 1974.

Mondésert, Claude. *Clément d'Alexandrie. Introduction à l'étude de sa pensée religieuse à partir de l'Écriture* [Clement of Alexandria. Introduction to the study of his religious thought from Scripture]. Paris: Aubier-Montaigne, 1944.

Montcheuil, Yves de. "L'Église et le salut des non-croyants" [The Church and the salvation of unbelievers]. In Yves de Montcheuil, *Aspects de l'Église* [Aspects of the Church], 124–38. Paris: Cerf, 1949.

Mueller, Joseph Gerard. *L'Ancien Testament et l'ecclésiologie des Pères. Une lecture des Constitutions apostoliques* [The Old Testament and the ecclesiology of the Fathers. A reading of the apostolic constitutions]. Turnhout, Belgium: Brepols, 2004.

Munier, Charles. "La sollicitude pastorale de l'Église ancienne en matière de divorce et de remariage" [The Church's pastoral concern for divorce and remarriage]. *Laval théologique et philosophique* 44 (1988): 19–30. Reprinted in Charles Munier, *Autorité épiscopale et sollicitude pastorale. IIe–VIe siècles* [Episcopal authority and pastoral concern. Second–sixth centuries], *"Variorum"* (Aldershot: Gower House, 1990).

Murphy, Francis Xavier, and Polycarp Sherwood. *Constantinople II et Constantinople III*. Paris: Orante, 1974.

O'Leary, Joseph Stephen. *Christianisme et philosophie chez Origène* [Christianity and philosophy by Origen]. Paris: Cerf, 2011.

Orbe, Antonio. "La patristica y el progreso de la teologia" [Patristics and the progress of theology]. *Gregorianum*, 50 (1969): 543–70.

———. *Introduction à la théologie des IIe et IIIe siècles* [Introduction to the theology of second and third centuries]. Translated from Spanish. 2 vols. Paris: Cerf, 2012.

Ortiz de Urbina, Iñigo. *Nicée et Constantinople* [Nicaea and Constantinople]. Paris: Orante, 1963.

Pelikan, Jaroslav. *The Christian Tradition: A History of the Development of Doctrine*. 5 vols. Chicago: University of Chicago Press, 1971–89. Translated as *La tradition chrétienne. Histoire du développement de la doctrine*, 5 vols. (Paris: PUF, 1994).

Pelland, Gilles. "Que faut-il attendre de l'histoire de l'exégèse ancienne?" [What is to be expected from the history of ancient exegesis?]. *Gregorianum* 69 (1988): 617–28.

Pelletier, Anne-Marie. *Lectures du Cantique des cantiques. De l'énigme du sens aux figures du lecteur* [Readings of the Song of Songs. From the enigma of the meaning to the figures of the reader]. Rome: Pontificio Istituto Biblico, 1989.

Pépin, Jean. *Mythe et allégorie. Les origines grecques et les contestations judéo-chrétiennes* [Myth and allegory. The Greek origins and the Jewish-Christian protests]. Paris: Aubier: 1958.

Pieris, Aloysius. "Western Models of Inculturation: Applicable in Asia?" In *An Asian Theology of Liberation*, 51–58. Edinburgh: T & T Clark, 1988. Translated by Joseph Feisthauer as *Une théologie asiatique de la liberation* (Paris: Centurion, 1990), 95–108.

———. *Love Meets Wisdom: A Christian Experience of Buddhism*. Maryknoll, N.Y.: Orbis Books, 1988.

Pottier, Bernard. "Le Grégoire de Nysse de Jean Daniélou. Réflexions autour de 'platonisme et théologie mystique'" [The Gregory of Nyssa of Jean Daniélou. Reflections on "platonism and mystical theology"]. In Fontaine, *Actualité de Jean Daniélou*, 79–96.

Prestige, George Leonard. *God in Patristic Thought*. London: Heinemann, 1936. Translated by D. M. as *Dieu dans la pensée patristique* (Paris: Aubier, 1955).

Quantin, Jean-Louis. *Le catholicisme classique et les Pères de l'Église. Un retour aux sources (1669–1713)* [Classical Catholicism and the Fathers of the Church. A return to the sources]. Paris: Institut d'Études Augustiniennes, 1999.

Rahner, Hugo. *Mythes grecs et mystère chrétien*. Translated by Henri Voirin. Paris:

Payot, 1954. Translated by Brian Battershaw as *Greek Myth and Christian Mystery* (New York: Harper and Row, 1963).

———. *L'Église et l'État dans le christianisme primitif.* Translated by G. Georges Zinck. Paris: Cerf, 1964, 2010. Translated by Leo Donald Davis, SJ, as *Church and the State in Early Christianity* (San Francisco: Ignatius Press, 1992).

Rahner, Karl. "Le début d'une doctrine des cinq sens spirituels chez Origène" [The beginning of a doctrine of the five spiritual senses by Origen]. *Revue d'Ascétique et de Mystique* 13 (1932): 113–45. Reprinted in *Schriften zur Theologie*, vol. 12, *Theologie aus Erfahrung des Geistes* (Zürich: Benziger, 1975), 111–36. Translated by David Morland as "The 'Spiritual Senses' according to Origen," in *Theological Investigations*, vol. 16, *Experience of the Spirit: Source of Theology* (London: Darton, Longman & Todd, 1979), 81–103.

———. "'Cœur de Jésus' chez Origène?" ["Heart of Jesus" by Origen?]. *Revue d'Ascétique et de Mystique* 15 (1934): 171–74.

———. *E latere Christi. Der Ursprung der Kirche als zweiter Eva aus der Seite Christi des zweiten Adam. Eine Untersuchung über den typologischen Sinn von Jo 19,34* [*E latere Christi.* L'origine de l'Église comme seconde Ève surgie du côté du Christ, deuxième Adam] [*E latere Christi.* The origin of the Church as second Eve emerged from the side of Christ, the second Adam. An investigation into the typological meaning of Jn 19:34.]. 1936. In Karl Rahner, *Sämtliche Werke*, vol. 3, *Theologie der Kirchenväter* [Complete works, vol. 3, Theology of the Fathers of the Church], 1–84. Zürich: Benzinger, 1999.

———. "La doctrine d'Origène sur la pénitence" [Origen's doctrine of penance]. *Recherches de Science Religieuse* 37 (1950): 47–97, 252–86, and 422–56. Translated by Lionel Swain as "The Penitential Teaching of Origen," in Karl Rahner, *Theological Investigations*, vol. 15, *Penance in the Early Church* (London: Darton, Longman & Todd, 1983), 246–328.

———. "Dieu dans le Nouveau Testament. La signification du mot 'Theos.'" Translated from German. *Écrits théologiques*, 1:11–111. Paris: Desclée de Brouwer, 1959. Translated by Cornelius Ernst as "Theos in the New Testament," in Rahner, *Theological Investigations* (London: Darton, Longman and Todd, 1961), 79–148.

———. "Problèmes actuels de christologie." In *Écrits théologiques*, 1:113–81. Translated by Cornelius Ernst as "Current Problems in Christology," in Karl Rahner, *Theological Investigations* (London: Darton, Longman and Todd, 1961), 1:149–213.

———. "Essai d'une esquisse de dogmatique." In *Écrits théologiques*, vol. 4, 7–50. Paris: Desclée de Brouwer,1966. Translated by Cornelius Ernst as "The Prospects for Dogmatic Theology," in *Theological Investigations* (London: Darton, Longman and Todd, 1961), 1:1–18.

———. "Pour la théologie du symbole." In *Écrits théologiques*, 9:9–47. Paris: Desclée de Brouwer, 1968. Translated by Kevin Smyth as "The Theology of the Symbol." In *Theological Investigations*, vol. 4, *More Recent Writings* (Baltimore: Helicon Press, 1966), 221–52.

———. *Schriften zur Theologie*, vol. 11, Frühe Bußgeschichten in Einzeluntersuchungen. Zurich: Benzinger Verlag, 1973. Translated by Lionel Swain as *Theo-*

logical Investigations, vol. 15, *Penance in the Early Church* (London: Darton, Longman & Todd, 1983).

Ratzinger, Joseph. "Die Bedeutung der Väter für die gegenwärtige Theologie" [The meaning of the Fathers for today's theology]. *Theologische Quartalschrift*, 148 (1968): 257–82.

Régnon, Théodore de. *Études de théologie positive sur la Sainte Trinité, Première série, exposé du dogme* [Studies of positive theology on the Holy Trinity, first series, presentation of the dogma]. Paris: Victor Retaux, 1892.

Ricoeur, Paul. "Entre décrire et prescrire: raconter" [Between describing and prescribing: Telling]. In *Soi-même comme un autre* [Self as an other], 180–93. Paris: Seuil, 1990.

Ringenbach, R., ed. *Mysterium salutis. Dogmatique de l'histoire du salut*. Translated into French. 15 vols. Paris: Cerf, 1969–75.

Rondeau, Marie-Josèphe. "Jean Daniélou, Henri-Irénée Marrou et le renouveau des études patristiques" [Jean Daniélou, Henri-Irénée Marrou and the renewal of patristic studies]. In *Les Pères de l'Église au XXe siècle*, 351–78.

———. "Jean Daniélou théologien" [Jean Daniélou, theologian]. In Fontaine, *Actualité de Jean Daniélou*, 127–54.

Sachot, Michel. "L'ère patristique" [The patristic era]. In *Les chrétiens et leurs doctrines* [The Christians and their doctrines]. Vol. 3 of "Manuel de théologie," edited by J. Doré, 48–97. Paris: Desclée, 1987.

Santedi Kinkupu, Léonard. *Les défis de l'evangélisation dans l'Afrique contemporaine* [The challenges of evangelization in contemporary Africa]. Paris: Karthala, 2005.

Schillebeeckx, Edward. *Church: The Human Story of God*. Translated by John Bowden. New York: The Crossroad Publishing Company, 1992.

Schmaus, Michael, Alois Grillmeier, Leo Scheffczyk, and Michael Seybold. *Handbuch der Dogmengeschichte* [Textbook on the history of dogmas]. Freiburg: Herder, 1971–87.

Sesboüé, Bernard. "Le procès contemporain de Chalcédoine: bilan et perspectives" [The contemporary trial of Chalcedon. Assessment and outlook]. *Recherches de Science Religieuse* 65 (1977): 45–80. Reprinted in Sesboüé, *Les "trente glorieuses" de la christologie (1968–2000)* [The "glorious thirty" of Christology] (Brussels: Lessius, 2012), 21–51.

———. *Jésus-Christ l'unique Médiateur* [Jesus Christ the unique mediator]. Vol. 1, *Problématique et relecture doctrinale* [Problematic and doctrinal review]. Paris: Desclée, 1988. Re-published, 2003. Vol. 2, *Les récits du salut* [The stories of salvation]. Paris: Desclée, 1991.

———. *Pour une théologie œcuménique. Église et sacrements. Eucharistie et ministères. La Vierge Marie* [Towards an ecumenical theology. Church and sacraments. Eucharist and ministries. The Virgin Mary]. Paris: Cerf, 1990.

———. *Histoire des dogmes* [History of dogmas]. Edited by B. Sesboüé. 4 vols. *Le Dieu du salut* [The God of salvation]; *L'Homme et son salut* [Man and his salvation]; *Les Signes du salut* [The signs of salvation]; *La Parole du salut* [The Word of salvation]. Paris: Desclée, 1994–96.

———. *Saint Basile et la Trinité. Un acte théologique au IVe siècle. Le rôle de Basile dans l'élaboration de la doctrine et du langage trinitaires* [Saint Basil and the Trinity. A theological act in the fourth century. The role of Basil in the development of Trinitarian doctrine]. Paris: Desclée, 1998.

———. *Jésus-Christ dans la tradition de l'Église. Pour une actualisation de la christologie de Chalcédoine* [Jesus Christ in the tradition of the Church. Toward an update of Chalcedon's Christology]. Revised, corrected, and updated ed. Paris: Desclée, 2000.

———. *Tout récapituler en Christ. Christologie et sotériologie d'Irénée de Lyon* [Recapitulating everything in Christ. Christology and soteriology of Irenaeus of Lyons]. Paris: Desclée, 2000.

———. *Christ, Seigneur et Fils de Dieu. Libre réponse à Frédéric Lenoir* [Christ, Lord and Son of God. Free answer to Frédéric Lenoir]. Paris: Lethielleux, Groupe DDB, 2010.

———. *Les "trente glorieuses" de la christologie (1968–2000)* [The "glorious thirty" of Christology (1968–2000)]. Brussels: Lessius, 2012.

Sesboüé, Bernard, and Joseph Wolinski. *Histoire des dogmes*. Vol. 1, *Le Dieu du salut* [The God of salvation]. Edited by Bernard Sesboüé. Paris: Desclée, 1994.

Simoens, Yves. *Selon Jean*. Vol. 1, *Une traduction*. Vol. 2, *Une interprétation* [According to John. Vol. 1, A translation. Vol. 2, An interpretation]. Brussels: Éditions de l'Institut d'Études Théologiques, 1997).

———. *Le Cantique des cantiques, Livre de la plénitude. Une lecture anthropologique et théologique* [The Song of Songs, book of the fullness. An anthropological and theological reading]. Brussels: Lumen vitae, 2004. New revised edition, Paris: Médiasèvres, 2012.

———. *Apocalypse de Jean, Apocalypse de Jésus-Christ* [Revelation of John, revelation of Jesus Christ]. Paris: Éditions Facultés jésuites, 2008.

———. *Croire pour aimer. Les trois lettres de Jean* [Believe to love. The three letters of John]. Paris: Éditions Facultés jésuites, 2011.

Simoens, Yves, François Cassingena-Trévedy, and Michel Fédou, eds. *Au service de Saint Jean. Lectures du corpus johannique* [In the service of Saint John. Readings of the Johannine corpus]. Paris: Médiasèvres, 2012.

Solignac, Aimé. "Péchés capitaux" [Deadly sins]. In *Dictionnaire de spiritualité*, vol. 12/1, col. 853–62. Paris: Beauchesne, 1984.

———. Introduction to Augustine, *Les Confessions*. Translated by E. Tréhorel and G. Bouissou, 7–270. Bibliothèque augustinienne 13. Paris: Institut d'Études Augustiniennes, 1992.

Sources Chrétiennes, ed. *Les Pères de l'Église au XXe siècle. Histoire–Littérature–Théologie, "L'aventure des Sources Chrétiennes"* [The Fathers of the Church in the twentieth century. History–literature–theology. "The adventure of the Sources Chrétiennes"]. Paris: Cerf, 1997.

Spanneut, Michel. *Le stoïcisme des Pères de l'Église, de Clément de Rome à Clément d'Alexandrie* [The Stoicism of the Fathers of the Church, from Clement of Rome to Clement of Alexandria]. Paris: Seuil, 1957.

Studer, Basil. *Dieu sauveur. La rédemption dans la foi de l'Église ancienne* [God the Savior. Redemption in the faith of the ancient Church]. Translated by Joseph Hoffmann. Paris: Cerf, 1989.

Theobald, Christoph. "Lire les Écritures dans un contexte de mutation ecclésiale. À propos du chapitre VI de *Dei Verbum*" [Reading the Scriptures in a context of ecclesial change. About chapter 6 of *Dei Verbum*]. In *La Bible sans avoir peur* [The Bible without fear], edited by J.-F. Bouthors, 263–91. Paris: Lethielleux, 2005. Reprinted in the work *"Dans les traces . . ." de la constitution "Dei Verbum" du concile Vatican II. Bible, théologie et pratiques de lectures* ["In the footsteps . . ." of the constitution "Dei Verbum" of the Second Vatican Council. Bible, theology and reading practices] (Paris: Cerf, 2009), 163–86.

———. "Vers une nouvelle théorie des sens?" [Toward a new theory of senses]. *Recherches de Science Religieuse* 99 (2011): 249–58.

Tilliette, Xavier. "Jean Daniélou et la culture" [Jean Daniélou and culture]. In Fontaine, *Actualité de Jean Daniélou*, 99–103.

Todorov, Tzvetan. *Symbolisme et interpretation* [Symbolism and interpretation]. Paris: Seuil, 1978.

Turchetti, Mario. "Jean Daillé et son *Traicté de l'employ des saincts Pères (1632)*. Aperçu sur les changements des critères d'appréciation des Pères de l'Église entre le XVIe et le XVIIe siècles" [John Daillé and his treaty of the use of the Holy Fathers (1632). Overview of the changes in the criteria for assessing the Church Fathers between the seventeenth and the eighteenth centuries]. In *Les Pères de l'Église au XVIIe siècle* [The Fathers of the Church in the seventeenth century], edited by Emmanuel Bury and Bernard Meunier, 69–85. Paris: IRHT–Cerf, Paris, 1993).

Turmel, Joseph. *Histoire des dogmes* [History of dogmas]. 6 vols. Paris: Rieder, 1931–36.

Vilanova, Evangelista. *Histoire des théologies chrétiennes*. [History of Christian theologies]. 3 vols. Translated from Spanish. Paris: Cerf, 1997.

Viller, Maurice. *La spiritualité des premiers siècles chrétiens* [The spirituality of the early Christian centuries]. Paris: Bloud et Gay, 1930.

Viller, Maurice, and Karl Rahner. *Aszese und Mystik in der Väterzeit* [Ascesis and mysticism in the era of the Fathers]. Freiburg im Breisgau: Herder, 1939. Re-published in vol. 3 of Rahner, *Sämtliche Werke* (Zürich: Benzinger, 1999), 123–390.

Vogüé, Adalbert de. *Histoire littéraire du mouvement monastique dans l'Antiquité* [Literary History of Monastic Movement in Antiquity]. *Première partie. Le monachisme latin* [First part. Latin monasticism], 12 vols. Paris: Cerf, 1991–2008. *Deuxième partie. Le monachisme grec* [Second part. Greek monasticism], 3 vols. Rome: Pontficio Ateneo Sant'Anselmo, 2015.

Wolinski, Joseph. "Jean Daniélou et la théologie du Logos avant Nicée (325)." In Fontaine, *Actualité de Jean Daniélou*, 57–78.

Church Documents, Ecumenical Agreements

Church Documents

Pius XII. *Divino afflante Spiritu*. Encyclical letter. September 30, 1943.

———. *Humani Generis*. Encyclical letter. August 15, 1950.

Paul VI. Address to Patriarch Athenagoras. July 25, 1967. *La Documentation catholique* 1499 (1967): col. 1380–83.

John Paul II. *Fides et ratio*. Encyclical letter. September 14, 1998. http://w2.vatican.va./content/john-paul-ii/en/encyclicals/documents/hf_jp-ii_enc_14091998_fides-et-ratio.html.

Benedict XVI. *Verbum Domini*. Apostolic exhortation. September 30, 2010.

Decrees of the Ecumenical Councils. Vol. 1. Edited by Norman P. Tanner. London: Sheed and Ward, 1990.

Vatican II. L'integrale. Revised bilingual ed. Paris: Bayard, 2002.

Vatican Council II. *Sacrosanctum concilium* (Constitution on the Sacred Liturgy). December 4, 1963.

———. *Lumen gentium* (Dogmatic Constitution on the Church). November 21, 1964.

———. *Unitatis redintegratio* (Decree on Ecumenism). November 21, 1964.

———. *Nostra aetate* (Declaration on the Relation of the Church to Non-Christian Religions). October 28, 1965.

———. *Optatam totius* (Decree on Priestly Training). October 28, 1965.

———. *Dei Verbum* (Dogmatic Constitution on Divine Revelation). November 18, 1965.

———. *Ad gentes* (Decree on the Mission Activity of the Church). December 7, 1965.

———. *Dignitatis humanae* (Declaration on Religious Freedom). December 7, 1965.

———. *Gaudium et spes* (Pastoral Constitution on the Church in the Modern World). December 7, 1965.

———. *Presbyterorum ordinis* (Decree on the Ministry and Life of Priests). December 7, 1965.

Pontifical Council for Inter-Religious Dialogue. *Dialogue and Proclamation. Reflection and Orientations on Interreligious Dialogue and the Proclamation of the Gospel of Jesus Christ*. May 19, 1991. http://vatican.va/roman_curia/pontifical_councils/interelg/documents/rc_pc_interelg_doc_19051991_dialogue-and-proclamatio_en.html. Also in *Bulletin du Pontificium Consilium pro Dialogo inter Religiones* 77 (1991).

Pontifical Biblical Commission. *The Interpretation of the Bible in the Church*. April 15, 1993. http://Catholic-resources.org/ChurchDocs/PBC_Interp-FullText.htm.

Pontifical Council for Promoting Christian Unity. "The Greek and Latin Traditions about the Procession of the Holy Spirit: Clarification." September 8, 1995. http://ewtn.com/library/CURIA/PCCUFILQ.HTM.

Ecumenical Agreements

"Common Declaration of Pope Paul VI and the Pope of Alexandria Shenouda III." May 10, 1973. http://vatican.va/roman_curia/pontifical_councils/chrstuni/anc-orient-ch-docs/rc_pc_christuni_doc_19730510_copti_en.html.

"Common Declaration of Pope John Paul II and His Holiness Mar Ignatius Zakka I Iwas." June 23, 1984. http://vatican.va/roman_curia/pontifical_councils/

chrstuni/anc-orient-ch-docs/rc_pc_christuni_doc_19840623_jp-ii-zakka-i_en.html.

John Paul II and Mar Denkha IV. "The Common Christological Declaration between the Catholic Church and the Assyrian Church of the East." November 11, 1994. http://vatican.va/roman_curia/pontifical_councils/chrstuni/documents/rc_pc_chrstuni_doc_11111994_assyrian-church_en.html.

"Common Declaration of John Paul II and Catholicos Karekin I." December 13, 1996. http://vatican.va/roman_curia/pontifical_councils/chrstuni/anc-orient-ch-docs/rc_pc_christuni_doc_19961213_jp-ii-karekin-i_en.html.

Joint International Commission for the Theological Dialogue between the Roman Catholic Church and the Orthodox Church. "Ecclesiological and Canonical Consequences of the Sacramental Nature of the Church: Ecclesial Communion, Conciliarity and Authority." October 13, 2007. http://vatican.va/roman_curia/pontifical_councils/chrstuni/ch_orthodox_docs/rc_pc_chrstuni_doc_20071013_documento-ravenna_en.html.

Groupe des Dombes. *Le ministère épiscopal. Réflexions et propositions sur le ministère de vigilance et d'unité dans l'Église particulière* [The episcopal ministry. Reflections and proposals on the ministry of vigilance and unity in the particular Church]. Taizé: Les Presses de Taizé, 1976. Reprinted in Groupe des Dombes, *Communion et conversion des Églises. Édition intégrale des documents publiés de 1956 à 2005* [Communion and Conversion of the Churches. Full edition of documents published fron 1956 to 2005]. Montrouge: Bayard, 2014, 93–126.

———. *L'Esprit-Saint, l'Église et les sacrements* [The Holy Spirit, the Church and the sacraments]. Taizé: Les Presses de Taizé, 1979. Reprinted in *Communion et conversion des Églises*, 127–66.

———. *Le ministère de communion dans l'Église universelle* [The ministry of communion in the universal Church]. 1985. Paris: Centurion, 1986. Reprinted in *Communion et conversion des Églises*, 167–232.

———. *Pour la conversion des Églises. Identité et changement dans la dynamique de communion* [For the conversion of the Church. Identity and change in the dynamics of communion]. 1990. Paris: Centurion, 1991. Reprinted in *Communion et conversion des Églises*, 233–338.

———. *Marie dans le dessein de Dieu et la communion des saints* [Mary in the plan of God and in the communion of saints]. Vol. 1, *Dans l'histoire et l'Écriture* [In history and Scripture]. Vol. 2, *Controverse et conversion* [Controversy and conversion]. Paris: Bayard éditions/Centurion, 1997–1998. Reprinted in *Communion et conversion des Églises*, 339–493.

———. *"Un seul Maître." L'autorité doctrinale dans l'Église* ["Only one master." The doctrinal authority in the Church]. Paris: Bayard, 2005. Reprinted in *Communion et conversion des Églises*, 497–685.

———. *"Vous donc, priez ainsi" (Mt 6, 9). Le Notre Père, itinéraire pour la conversion des Églises* ["You therefore pray ye." The Our Father, itinerary for the conversion of Churches]. Montrouge: Bayard, 2011.

Index

Antiquity

The Middle Ages

The 16th to 19th Centuries

The Contemporary Period

The Fathers of the Church in Christian Theology was designed in Frutiger Serif and Quadraat Sans display type and composed by Kachergis Book Design of Pittsboro, North Carolina. It was printed on 55-pound Natural Hi Bulk and bound by Data Reproductions of Auburn Hills, Michigan.